CROSSING THE LINE

A JOURNEY OF PURPOSE AND SELF BELIEF

DAWN BATES

© 2018 Dawn Bates

Published by Dawn Bates
www.dawnbates.com

Cataloguing-in-Publication entry is available from the British Library.

ISBN: 978-0-9957322-4-7 (paperback)
978-0-9957322-5-4 (ebook)

Other titles by Dawn Bates:
Friday Bridge (2013)
Walaahi (2017)

Book cover design – Jerry Lampson
Publishing Consultant – Linda Diggle

CONTENTS

FOREWORD

When you think of a single mother, what do you think of? What is the first image that comes to mind? Visualise her – how old is she, what is she wearing, how does she speak, what does she do for a living, how does she move, what are her children like? What do you think of her?

My name is Libby Liburd. I'm an actor and writer. And I am a single mother.

In late 2016, I wrote and presented a video for *The Guardian* titled, 'What is Our Problem with Single Mothers?' The video was released on 4th January 2017 and quickly hit viral proportions, with over a million views on Facebook within just three days. It was clear from reading the comments section beneath the video that this was a subject that needed to be spoken about. I experienced many people reaching out to me to thank or congratulate me. It was also clear that it's still a thorny issue – the backlash was something I never expected. There's a saying 'never read the comments' and I now have first-hand experience as to why you shouldn't! I received trolling comments and cruel messages. It affected me, it got to me, I questioned what on earth I had done. If you've watched the video, you will see it's about two minutes of me talking about the social and political stigmatising of single mothers. The piece is heavily researched, and features direct quotes from politicians. There's a tiny mention of my personal circumstances, but nothing other than I used to be married and now I'm not.

Do I regret the video? No. Not at all. I had hundreds of wonderful comments, I received emails from all over the country, all over the world, offering support and kindness and thanking me for speaking out. It's how I met Dawn, who wrote this book; we connected via Twitter and found out that we had so much more in common than just our 'single mother' status!

The response to the video generally made me realise that this is something that we as a society do need to speak about, we can't sweep this under the rug anymore.

My journey into single motherhood began nearly a decade ago. I was married to my son's father, and sadly the marriage ended. I didn't choose to be a single parent, and honestly and unreservedly had bought into the idea of the two-parent nuclear family. As a result, I was woefully under-prepared for life as a single parent. I have always been independent and the sort of person that gets things done, but there I was, gobby go-getter me, suddenly in a situation that left me feeling vulnerable and out of control. If I'm totally honest, I can barely remember those first few months of being a single parent. There are a few key pivotal moments that stand out for me – the time that I was very nearly late to collect my son from his after-school club and I cried all the way there in a panic, the sudden realisation of being the only available parent. The time I went to court to dispute an illegal eviction order from our rental home and the judge sneered at me and upheld the order on the basis that I was a 'single mother' and would therefore get a council house. The fallout of the eviction – sitting in the housing office on my own begging for help, being told that if I agreed to stop working it'd be easier to re-house me. The pain of having to ring government agencies and explain that I was now a lone parent and hear the person at the other end of the line react with either disdain or pity. The panic of trying to organise childcare for acting jobs that required me on set at 4am. Overwhelmingly, my experience was that of trauma. And, of course, in amongst this tornado of my own emotions I was also supporting my child in coming to terms with the entire experience.

I HATED the label 'single mother', I hated it, I hated this new, unfamiliar situation, I hated the sudden unexpected stigma. I was negotiating a new world where declaring yourself a single parent elicits a range of responses: pity being one of them, and I wasn't used to being pitied. I felt shame and embarrassment when strangers conversationally asked, as if they had a right to know, why my child's father wasn't around. I felt shame and embarrassment when I was described as 'brave'. I felt shame and embarrassment when I had to turn down acting work because I couldn't get childcare. So, I did what I had to do to survive. I ignored it. I didn't call people out on their questions or opinions, I distanced myself from the term 'single mother'. To my own shame, I even tried to tell myself that I was not like other single mothers, I was different, they weren't my people, my tribe. I tried to ignore the prejudice. I buried my pain. I got on with my life. I tried very hard to continue with my acting career.

I got more and more tired. I felt worn down with having to do everything alone. When I asked for help I felt I had to explain my circumstances and just saying those words again and again wore me down too so I simply stopped asking. I became tired with dealing with a system that wanted me to fight constantly. I took some time away from acting.

I took up boxing – a part of me felt that if I was having to fight figuratively I may as well fight literally as well. I had three fights. I learned a lot about myself, my own strength and my capacity for resourcefulness. I learned to keep moving forward.

Life went on, my child grew. I decided, on the spur of the moment, to make the very thing that I found painful into a show. I interviewed other single mothers and I made a theatre show based on mine and their experiences. The show was called *Muvvahood* and it started with just 20 minutes of me telling the stories those mothers had told me.

Through interviewing those mothers I felt a sense of comradeship that I'd never felt before. I was like other single mothers, I wasn't different, they were my people, they were my tribe. We spoke about things I'd never allowed myself to even think before, let alone speak out loud. I felt the old pain resurface. I questioned doing what I was doing. I had a choice. Did I bury it again, or was this my time to stand and fight?

In September 2015, I stood on a stage on my own in a small theatre in Camden and presented my 20 minutes of *Muvvahood*. It was the first time I had ever stood up in front of anyone and actually said the way I felt. The first time I publicly and unashamedly owned the title of 'single mother', the first time I spoke the universal truths that we as single mothers have. It felt like it was exactly what theatre should be and exactly what I should be doing.

After that, I was asked to develop the show into an hour-long performance. I began working with an incredible director and friend, Julie Addy. And that is where it got political.

I'd started with the women's stories, to me, that was everything. Speaking aloud our truths, our pains, our joys, was everything. But there were things that the mothers had spoken about which I understood, but I didn't know if a wider audience would. And there followed an extensive research period. Julie and I delved into government policy, into stereotypes, into the world of political propaganda, the current 'war on the poor' and 'age of austerity'. Suddenly the trauma my family had endured didn't seem so isolated, suddenly I made the connection that we'd been a victim of an endemic issue, with its foundations built on government policy.

When I presented the hour-long version of *Muvvahood* including the statistics, the facts, the policies, the response was phenomenal. Audience members gasped, shouted out, openly sobbed, got angry. People had no idea about these policies. How would they know? I hadn't known about them and I was living with the effects of them! People had no idea that the accepted societal norm of the two-parent family was used as a stick to beat single mothers with.

The single mother can't win – if she doesn't work, she is a drain on society, a sponger and a scrounger. If she does work, she doesn't parent properly, she should be at home more. Her actual mothering may be called into question and when it is, the prejudice runs deep and the effects can be devastating.

We, as a society, have somehow wholeheartedly bought into the stereotype. We laugh at Vicky Pollard (a bloke dressed up as a tracksuit-clad single mum with a football team of children that clearly have different fathers), we accept the stereotype of the young fag-smoking council-housed teenage single mum, we moan openly about we the tax payer 'having to pay for other people's children', we mock mothers that don't stand up to our unforgiving scrutiny, we label them 'scummy mummies'. We write newspaper headlines denouncing single mothers, we make and watch TV shows, both fictionalised and real, that perpetuate the stereotype. We use social media to judge, vilify and tear down the single mother further.

The current statistics are that in the UK one in four families are single parent families, that around 90% of single parents are mothers, about half had their children within marriage, that the average age of a single mum is 38, that just two percent are teenagers, that the vast majority of single parents are in work. Yet, even if working, single parent families are twice as likely to be in poverty than couple parent families.

However, the media and politicians delight in propagating the myths. Single parent families are frequently reminded that we are the wrong kind of family – we are broken. During the riots of 2011, the Tory rhetoric centred on broken Britain, broken homes, broken families. Britain was broken, Britain was rioting and the main reason for that was, apparently, the broken family, families with 'no fathers at home'. And in the eyes of many, we're not even a family. Some of the comments in response to my Guardian video exemplify this opinion. One troll emailed me directly (several times to be sure that I got the message) to let me know that, I was 'just a single woman with a kid' that should stop making 'stupid videos'.

In *Muvvahood*, I delve into the government policies that directly attack and disempower single mothers and their children. I explore the stereotypes, the myths and the facts and I question how we have got to a place where as a society we just seem to accept that single mothers are somehow lesser mothers, that the title 'single mother' is synonymous for 'bad mother'.

As a result of *Muvvahood*, I was asked to write a few pieces for various blogs and magazines and then the piece for The Guardian. In less than a year and a half, my life has changed dramatically. I feel not only peace with the title 'single mother' but also now an overwhelming sense of pride.

The family unit is ever evolving and yet the role of a parent, any parent, remains a difficult, challenging and joyous one. Parents are without any formal training, any manuals, any real guidance and yet every day it seems we have to make the most momentous decisions. Making those decisions as a single parent family can be even more challenging, even more daunting, even more consuming, yes, but we still have the right to make those decisions without fear of judgement or interference simply on the basis that our family is considered 'broken'.

So, let me ask you again, when you think of a single mother, what do you think of?

Nowadays, when I think of a single mother, I think of myself. I see myself. And I am proud.

Libby Liburd
Tweet me: @LibbyLiburd
#Muvvahood
www.LibbyLiburd.co.uk
Agent: www.denmarkstreet.net

PREFACE

Remember when we used to play out until dark? Without mobile phones, internet cafes and no change in our pockets to use the telephone boxes? When you did not dare to do a reverse charge call to your parents for being 'late' home because that would be worse than actually being late home?

Remember when your mum would tell you your dinner would be ready when you got back, but no time was agreed? You just got back, as if by magic, when the food was being dished up.

Do you remember when being a child meant playing in rivers and streams, climbing trees, playing ball in the road, having water fights with both water bombs and water pistols.

Do you remember when a broken arm was a rite of passage, and the popularity it gave you from everyone, I mean come on! Everyone wanted all their friends and random people to sign their cast! And some of us wanted it to be our arm that got broken next!

Remember how, when playing outside, for hours without your parents, exploring your neighbourhood, was encouraged? Instead of seeing signs, 'Please keep off the grass!' and 'No ball games allowed'.

Remember when you didn't have to wear silly cycle helmets because you would be 'off roading' through all the little back passages and between the allotments and fields, going through the woodlands and dirt tracks?

Do you remember when, if you got up to anything whilst out and about up the village, in the town or the neighbourhood, your parents would know every step of your night out before you had even got home? Because people knew back then, that is takes a community to raise children.

Do you remember those times when parents were able to teach a child cause and effect, self-discipline and self-control, without the fear of some do-gooder sticking their nose in to the last two seconds of a half hour conversation, and chastising you for speaking with your child firmly?

Remember the days when children were allowed to do paper rounds, wash the pots in restaurants, wash the neighbour's cars, fill the washing machines in laundrettes and work in chip shops, being mentored and given the trust by a member of the community, someone to mentor them, help the family to build the child's confidence and competence?

Remember when parents and schools worked together for the well-being of the child, keeping them back after school to catch up, or making them stay in at lunchtime if they had been disruptive? Instead of the schools now dictating what the parents can and cannot do with their own child?

Do you remember when the '10 second rule' didn't bother anyone, and if you dropped your food on the floor and picked it up again, or you ate your sandwiches with dirty hands and no one battered an eyelid?

Do you remember when children weren't overloaded with homework and actually had a childhood or exploring, which meant exploring their own boundaries, their own limits and they learnt to trust themselves and grow in confidence and ability, rather than arrogance and expectance?

Remember when you would make a mistake, and allowed to apologise for it and make amends, being seen as someone who is morally and socially responsible, rather than weak and ineffective?

Remember when you used to get back from school before your parents got home and you sneaked a biscuit before sitting down to watch your favourite television programme before doing your homework?

Do you remember being on holiday and just going off exploring, all the family together?

Do you remember sitting around the meal table every night, or at least every Sunday, for a Sunday roast, having to eat everything on your plate because of the starving children in Africa?

Remember when you had to do your own chores, just to earn your pocket money, and the value of money?

Remember when a clip around the ear wasn't child abuse, it was simple a reminder that you stepped out of line?

Do you remember when you feared your parents, just because they were your parents, and you did as you were told? And *that* look, or the use of your full name, meant you were for the high jump?

Do you remember when you did something wrong, you were grounded? Like proper grounded, sent to your room without any dinner and made to stay there until the morning to think about your actions?

Remember when all the seats at the front of the bus that were reserved for the elderly and the disabled, were actually left empty, and no one sat in them unless they were elderly and disabled?

Remember when you used to tell yourself, "I'm never going to do that when I am a parent!" and years down the line you do it, because you know it was the tough love every child needs from their parents? You know the boundaries of respect and self-control, manners and values?

Do you remember all these things? The stuff of childhood memories… the things that have all but been wiped out? The very things that actually made our societies better because people were allowed to grow up, allowed to make mistakes. When we as parents were allowed to trust the local butcher to give our sons the little Saturday job, to teach them about food, life and a valuable life skill. When we as parents were actually allowed to make choices about how our children learnt new subjects and life skills, without it always having to be in the classroom? Without us being made into criminals because we choose to live our lives differently, to live unconventional lives; and because we choose to think for ourselves, instead of following the crowd in thoughts, fashion and celebrity status?

I've raised my boys that environment is everything, that is why they have been in eight different schools in their short lives; which is why we left Egypt when Sisi took over. I teach them it is better to have one really great friend than lots of 'okay' friends. It is also why I tell them to choose and make friends wisely, and which is why my boys are strong within themselves and know that when other kids in schools are messing about, those children are actually stealing their education, as well as their own, and why they should be removed from the classroom.

I have also raised my boys to know that 'smart people do not follow stupid rules', to question everything, because the more you question, the more you understand.

The way I have raised my boys, into the educated, well spoken, articulate and polite young men they are may not be to everyone's liking, but my boys are centred in themselves. They are confident boys, happy, loving and incredibly funny. I personally don't like the over protective 'anti bac brigade' who wrap their kids up in bubble wrap, the ones who 'over praise and over reward' their children, and I find it shameful when I see a parent 'begging and bribing' their kids to do the basics. I want my boys to be prepared for life and everything it throws at them. I want them to be strong, resilient and competent; and I know they already are.

I am proud of my boys, immensely so.

I acknowledge my boys, every day.

I am so incredibly proud of who they are, who they are showing up to be in this world already.

They are incredible boys.

And they will have the childhood of adventures, grazed knees, playing out until dark, and earning their own money through chores and either getting a job or creating a business. I will allow them to climb trees, eat food they have dropped on the floor (within reason!) and eat it with dirty hands because it strengthens their immune system.

I will teach them responsibility for their actions, and respect for others, as well as themselves.

They already know I am their mother and not their maid, and they will continue to know that when I give *that* look that I mean business, and its game on time!

My mum and dad raised me well upon these very same principles. My mum and dad are awesome parents. I am who I am today because my mum and dad taught me to be responsible, to be respectful and to do my best. They taught me life is hard, that I can't have everything my own way, to say please and thank you, to hold doors open for mothers with push chairs, people in wheelchairs and to always give up my seat, never sitting at the front of the bus, and it is these things I have, and will continue to pass onto my children.

I gave birth to my boys, no one else.

I have given my all into becoming the best mother I can, before they were even conceived and since the moment they were born.

I invest everything I have into my boys, my energy, my cash, my love, my thoughts and my hugs.

My boys are my world, and they are the adults of the future. I want a bright future for everyone, and it is my responsibility as a parent to enable them to think, to make informed choices, to make risk assessments based on what they know and have experienced.

Our children are the future… are you children ready for it? Are you confident in the 'Millennials' to lead our country, our world and the children that follow them? Are you confident in the system? Are you confident in the so-called leadership we have in place around the world at the moment?

Read on. Then answer these last few questions.

PROLOGUE

Writing this book was never in my plan, but then life throws something in your direction and you just have to deal with it in the best way you know how.

What you are about to read is my own personal journey over the last four years. The healing I went through after my shock divorce to my husband of 18 years, and the grieving process; because it is a grieving process, but one where the loved one didn't die, they are still there for you to see, hear and communicate with for the sake of the children. It is a nasty grief, full of mind games, and not the ones the other person plays (although in some cases, spiteful mind games are very much present and the sole intention of one or both parties).

I am going to talk about how I threw myself into fitness and my business, and was doing really well, up until the police in Scotland decided to throw me into a cell for two-and-a-half days, without questioning, without charging me, taking my children off me and all for something that they have no evidence for, because what I was eventually charged with, and convicted of, didn't happen and would never happen.

I have spent the last two years researching the law, fighting the law and now I want you to all have the knowledge that I have to help prevent you from falling foul of the law.

I know what I am about to write will have the trolls out in their thousands. I know that those among you that wrap your kids up in bubble wrap, with your helicopter parenting and different style of parenting to me, will be some of my harshest critics.

I also know that the majority of parents will read what I have to say and identify with the majority of what I am about to share with you, you will have been doing what I did on a weekly basis, sometimes a daily basis.

I also know that the police, the media and the government dictatorial nanny state that we now live in, around the world, not just in the UK, have all done such a great job of making us all police each other, and be our own worst enemies.

We as parents have lost our confidence, been burdened with guilt for not doing this or that in the 'correct' way. We live in fear that people are either going to report us for disciplining our children, for teaching them cause and effect. We live in fear that any mistake that we make is no longer an opportunity to learn from it, but an opportunity for someone else to condemn us, cause trouble and in my case end up with a conviction which has already caused me problems and will continue to do so for another 11 years, unless sense is seen and it is removed.

I am not writing this book as a 'poor me, look at what they did to me'. I am writing it to highlight the problems we as parents are facing here in the UK today, and in other countries around the world. I have been strong enough to deal with what has happened, but others are not as strong, and others are in a much more vulnerable situation than me, which is scary. Very scary; because if what I am about to share with you could happen to me, then I dread to think what it must be like for those in a less fortunate situation.

I know I am a brilliant mother. I know I am a strong, educated and independent woman. I know I inspire others to be better parents, better citizens, better employers/employees and better in so many other ways. I know I know what I am talking about. I know that this went against me in many ways. For me to remain quiet about what happened to me and my boys would be an injustice to so many who have lost their voice. It would be an injustice to those who do not have the courage to speak up for themselves. It would be an injustice to know that this is happening daily, and for me to stay quiet. It would be an injustice to single mums, single dads, parents in general who are doing their absolute best to raise well rounded, competent, confident and happy children; ones that think, are responsible for themselves and their actions, ones that innovate and go on to create amazing results in their lives, for themselves and others.

As you read this book, I invite you to walk in my shoes with me, imagine yourself in my space, imagine the pain and the fear I have experienced. I invite you to think about what you can do to help make this world a better place. What story can you share that has a positive and powerful impact on your community, your country and around the world.

I invite you to stand up to injustice, to corruption, to bullying, to a broken system, and I invite you to step up and make your voice heard. You have the right to make choices, to make your own risk assessments. You have the right to mistakes without the fear of being considered weak or vulnerable. You have the right to learn from mistakes because success comes from failing. Consider yourself a baby learning to crawl, learning to walk. You didn't just fall out of your mother's womb and start running did you? No. You had a go, you fell down, you got back up again, and you repeated this pattern many times. This is exactly the same with every area of your life, especially parenting.

As we all know, parenting doesn't come with a rule book that you can buy from all good book shops, helping you, guiding you; there are a variety of experts that have written various different ways to parent. Many successful people have shared their lives growing up so we can learn from them too. As parents we are told by the various governing bodies that we have no rights over our children, that we are not to do this or that, but only AFTER we have done this or that. What I have discovered over the last two years is that parenting does come with a rule book, it is called the law. A book that is so hidden and complex, that it doesn't matter if you are the best parent on the planet, it will still go against you, because it can be manipulated. Evidence can be fabricated. Evidence will be fabricated. Evidence will be withheld and when you fight back, they will do whatever they can to silence you. As parents you have rights to parent in ways that you choose to enable your children to be happy, confident and competent; to be thinkers, to succeed, and you have the right to do so without being made into a criminal.

You have the right to live a life you love without fear of persecution or prosecution.

So, own who you are. Know your rights. Know that you don't have to be burdened with guilt and fear. Know that whatever it is you are going through, you have a voice, so speak up! Be your own voice, be the voice of many, be a hero to many, and as my friend Jenee Michelle says, "Be you own damn hero."

ONE

RE-INTEGRATION INTO THE UK

Arriving back in the UK was an interesting experience to say the least. Re-integration is very different to integration. To begin with you already know a lot of the customs, the people, the mindset and attitudes, so you are in a space of knowing but not connecting because things have changed, and boy had things changed in the UK! Returning home where people and things has changed so much makes the process of re-integration much harder. Integrating into a new country is easier by far because you have no prior knowledge, no reference points and no existing friendship groups. The biggest challenge comes from others in a lot of ways because people think you are returning home so it just like returning home after a long holiday, slipping back into your life and just carrying on, when this isn't the case. You change when you live abroad and integrate. I'm not so sure how easy re-integration is for the ex-pats who do not integrate into the country they reside in for short periods of time, but for me, being submerged into the Egyptian culture, and living through the Uprising, was a massive challenge. I wasn't the same woman I was went we left, and neither were my boys the same. Our lives in the UK would never be the same, something I had overlooked whilst making the plans to live abroad.

Adjusting to the way English people spoke English, rather than the

US and Egyptian ways of using English, not only gave me a few giggles but also quite a few frustrations. Forgetting how to speak your own language gives you an idea of just how deeply you integrated into the new country. Forgetting what simple things such as a minced beef are called, when you can't even recall what it is in Arabic provided many moments of amusement and searching through the soup in my brain at the time. I've always been quite fluid when speaking, so to stumble on simple everyday words sometimes made it hard to converse with others, especially the ones who didn't understand what it is like to speak another language.

I would also confuse people during our conversations as I would flip between Arabic and English and not realise I was doing it. Some would find it amusing, and some ... not so amusing. My style of expression had also changed. Talking with my hands became more common, and the 'kissing of teeth' was causing a few problems. You see in Egypt, when you 'kiss your teeth' you do it when you are saying no. In the UK, it's akin to tutting at someone, something that is deemed quite offensive. I had mentioned before whilst back in Egypt, to my dear friend Amira, "This is going to get me into trouble when I go back." To which we both laughed and carried on looking at how different people expressed themselves through body language as well as spoken language. A subject we both found fascinating.

The first challenge was decoding the accent back home in Friday Bridge, an accent I grew up with, but struggled to understand, and in some cases did my best not to giggle as words heard filled my mind with happy memories and getting up to mischief. Memories long forgotten, and yet so wonderful to remember. It was as if I was being embraced again by my home country, a welcome that was very much needed. Being surrounded by the people of Friday Bridge, knowing my book *Friday Bridge* had just been published was a bit surreal. For the first time since writing it, I actually had a moment of how real it all was. I had put Friday Bridge on the map... and in some instances not in a good light. Having spent less than 48 hours back in Friday Bridge, the closed mindset, scarcity mentality had started to show themselves, and yet I wasn't actually bothered this time. I was back home at my mum and dads, surrounded by fields and there was not one army tank, soldier with Kalashnikov or AK-47 in sight.

The one thing that did set me off though was the bird scarer. The first time I heard it, I froze and had flashbacks to the protests and the relentless gunfire that had kept me awake through the first year of being in Cairo. Mum noticed and shouted, "Oi! You're not there anymore," came over and gave me a long tight hug, and I burst into tears. She hadn't hugged me like this since I was a little girl. With both of us stood in the kitchen crying in each other's arms, it was a magical moment. I felt safe, safer than I had in a very long time. I was in my Mummy's arms and the world seemed as it should do.

Then I heard my dad say, "The troops are here."

Thinking the army had arrived, I had a moment of panic, but quickly realised he meant my nieces and nephew. Mum and I quickly dried our eyes and turned to look at the door. What I saw next set me off crying again. My three nieces Naomi, Karlie and Sophie were walking in the door, and there was Leon my nephew I had never met, in my sister's arms. I was crying like a baby. Such emotional overwhelm. I left when the girls were little. Sophie adored Dora the Explorer, and here she was wearing a One Direction t-shirt and nearly the same age as Naomi had been when we left. Naomi was now a teenager... and boy did it suit her. They were beautiful girls anyway, but they had blossomed. Karlie, my middle niece (and the best birthday present I have ever had) was transformed. And Leon... just walking and my dad's shadow, and already turning into a cheeky little dude. I couldn't stop staring at them all.

It is always children that make you realise just how much time has passed.

They grow so fast, their ideas of the world change and their sense of identity transform. I was so proud to see the young ladies my nieces had become, and excited to see how 'my little bruiser' would evolve (If I had anything to do with it, I'd nurture that cheeky little rascal in him!) He already had the charm, like Nassir, it came naturally to both of them; but Leon... there was something very magical about having a nephew. That glint in his eye. Yeah. We were going to get on just fine.

My boys and the girls headed off to the park for a bit, whilst last minute wedding plans were discussed. My sister got married three days after we landed and ramO, the boys and I had nothing to wear. Cash was limited and so we went through our suitcases to see what we had and then Mum took us shopping. It was all a bit too much for one day, sensory overload from the massive cultural differences. Everyone was white, many were grossly obese and the amount of pubs was a lot to take in. Welcome back to England. I started to feel anxious and all I wanted to do was go home and sit in my mum and dad's back garden and just allow my face to soak up the sun. You'd think I would have had enough sun back in Egypt, but the sun in my mum and dad's back garden always felt different. With the cool breeze coming off the fields and the smell of fresh soil, cup of tea in hand, in my china cup, sat on the garden bench… my favourite spot. The place I would go to first thing in the morning when I got up. Regardless of how warm or cold it was, and sometimes wearing my dad's slippers and hoodie, I would sit out on the bench and listen to the birds singing. Blissful.

The day of the wedding, I was faced with having to see my estranged brother and my cousin Michael. Two people I didn't really want to see, but it's a family occasion so you just suck it up, smile politely and be civil. The day was not about any of us. It was about my sister. Mum told me to, "Behave myself, keep my mouth shut and not make any trouble."

"Mum, seriously? You know me better than that, and don't you think I have just lived through enough without making a scene, especially today?"

"I know, I just don't want any trouble," she said as she gave me another big hug.

I don't think I had had as many hugs off my mum as I had in the first few days of being back. It was nice. It was more than nice. The wedding was over in a blur for me, I don't remember much about anything really other than how beautiful my sister and nieces looked, and how dapper Leon looked in his little suit. Still wandering around in a daze, just watching, almost staring. People spoke to me, and most of them I had no idea who they were. Most didn't know I was Ellen's sister, until mum told them, and then I'd get, "Oh, you're Dawn?"… Whatever that was supposed to mean. I had no idea, I was still in culture shock mode.

Bear in mind, since being back in the UK, there was so much hair and flesh on show. In the streets I was faced with tattoos covering people's arms and legs entirely, piercings all over faces, big holes were in people's ears and there were more openly gay people than I remember there being. Mix a handful of these people with relatives that now looked much older, being told 'x, y and z' had died and 'so and so' were now married, and when a neighbour Emily spoke to me, I just couldn't believe she'd a baby... she was still about 11 in my head, the age she was when I last saw her.

I was doing my best, especially as I was wearing heels and a knee length shift dress, something very alien to me after wearing linen trousers and my Birkenstocks. I laughed and smiled in all the right places, but went and sat back down next to my boys and ramO. All of us in a state of overwhelm, it was all too much. We wanted to stay, but just had to leave. We said goodbye, and walked home. On the way home we met up with a friend Fuzzi Lu and it was so lovely to see her. She came back to my mum's for a cup of tea and then headed off. We needed to sleep. It had been an exhausting day. Information overload. How on earth could things have changed so much? Or was it just my view of the world that had changed dramatically? Yes the visual changes such as the amount of body mutilation, or enhancement (depending on the way you saw it) had shocked me, but it was the amount of international fast food chains that were everywhere too. Things such as Coffee Nation had disappeared from the service stations and had been replaced by Costa Express; 'luxury apartments' were springing up everywhere – carbon copies of each other and lacking in character or soul; empty fields now had housing developments on them, or a new retail park. Being home in Friday Bridge without all of this commercial materialism felt safer. Egypt may have lost its mind, but the UK had lost its soul. I told mum I needed to go to the beach, and asked her when we could go. Was there a bus to Hunstanton? Or Cromer? I needed the sea. I needed energising. So we went a couple of days after Ellen's wedding and that... that was just what I needed! The smell of the ocean. The salty spray of the waves on my face. The crash of the waves and the endless horizon. I felt centred. I felt at peace, even more so than when I was being hugged by mum a few days before. This was my safe zone, my anchor point. This is where I needed to be for my soul to rest, by the ocean, on it would be better.

This is when I had another flashback. Of growing up on the beach whilst dad was beach fishing. Sitting in my deckchair, moon boots on, windproof coat, mittens and ear muffs, holding a cup of tea from the flask, the night sky lit up with stars, mum and dad with their rods in the water, and me looking out to sea, seeing the odd liner and the gas platforms. That is where I wanted to be. I felt like my soul was being pulled from my chest, pulling me out to sea every time I was by the sea. I knew that is where I would spend most of my adult life once the boys were grown up… I just didn't know how it would happen. ramO didn't like being by the sea and hated getting sand in his shoes or clothes. He wasn't a great swimmer either, so being in the water wasn't even his thing. I just knew it was mine, and I would have my own boat one day, go off to sea and write my books. There was also another dimension to these visions I had. I would be on the top of cliffs walking my dogs back to a little cottage, waves crashing below, wind blowing strongly and I would return to my little cottage, fire roaring away and enjoy a cup of tea and a good book in my armchair. I never saw anyone else in this vision, just me and my dogs. Still to this day I don't know why I am alone, but I the older I get, the more I enjoy my own company. I don't know whether I am alone because I am single, widowed or simply if there is someone special in my life that just isn't there, but I have never seen anyone in this vision. Just me and my dogs, on a cliff top cottage, waves crashing below; and I feel at peace. And after life in Egypt… peace is all I needed.

Whilst looking for a home to live in back up in Sheffield, I told the estate agent I wanted somewhere really quiet, surrounded by fields if possible, and the boys and I struck lucky. There was a beautiful Cotswold cottage in the village of Dore, just on the outskirts of Sheffield. A short bus ride away from the city centre and it was one road away from the edge of the Peak District. Both the boys and I were incredibly happy. I couldn't have asked for a better location, and the house was really old and quirky, had history oozing out of it; just our kind of thing! And just as well really, especially as three months of moving in, ramO walked out on the three of us. The boys didn't see him for the best part of nine months and so it was just the three of us and Kelt. Although this was the most painful time in my life, losing my best friend and coming to terms with the betrayal, just being able to go for long walks through the countryside to clear my head, sitting in the middle of the field and crying to release the pain, watching Kelt run around smelling all the new smells and running free was just what I needed. Having a garden was also great, especially as I had bought a barbeque, and that meant I could teach the boys how to barbeque and make fires safely. The barbeque also acted as a healing tool, as I had several fires burning 18 years of mementos that I had saved from our travels around the world, tickets to events or places and of course the wedding cards I had kept. I burnt the lot. I didn't want to be reminded of our time together, of his countless betrayals, his deceit and lies. I burnt all these whilst the boys were at school as I did not want them to see me in so much pain. They could see I was really sad, and yes sometimes I cried in front of them, but to not cry would be inhuman, and for them to not see me cry would tell them our family meant nothing, which was the exact opposite. Our family meant everything. I had given up so much of who I was to be with him, invested half my life into our marriage and I was broken. Not what I needed after his mother sold the family home from underneath us, Baaba dying and having lived through the Uprising. I needed him more than ever, and so did the boys, but he went, to be with his fiancé in America just two weeks after telling me he wanted a divorce, leaving us to just get on with it.

And get on with it we did.

TWO
GROWING STRONGER

Knowing that I was now on my own gave me a steely determination to succeed more than I had ever done before. A fire that already raged within me, felt as though it had just had petrol poured over it. I had two boys to take care of, to provide for and I had to figure out a way of how to do this all on my own.

It had been seven months since I had been back in the UK and so many of the friends I had had before I went seemed to have disappeared. A handful had moved to another country, and others were just too busy with their own lives. I was feeling incredibly lonely. I had a couple of girlfriends who I'd known for 20 years come and see me, which I really appreciated, but it was obvious to me that we were just not the same people anymore. Our lives and outlook on life was so vastly different I felt lonelier in their company, than I did when I was by myself. I needed to talk, I needed to share, but they made it all about them and wanted to get wasted. I was not in that space. I was now a single mum and I couldn't take my eye off the ball for a second. I felt the pressure to make sure I was alert at all times, just in case my boys were taken ill, or woke up early. I couldn't be lying in bed nursing a hangover or a come down, I was a mother. A single mother, and that meant I had the responsibility of both parents on my shoulders. I had to keep my wits about me. I had to keep my mind sharp and my body agile.

I had no family nearby, the closest was my mum and dad, and they were three hours away. Most friends lived at least two hours away, apart from Jools, Debbie, Ali and Khaadiija, but they were busy. Jools had more grandchildren and was enjoying the role of being Grandma, Ali now had four boys, Debbie was doing a lot more hours at work and more community work, as well as looking after her mum, and Khaadiija… well what wasn't she up to! A local activist for disability awareness and of course shaking up people's molecules in many ways! They didn't have time to visit, and I found that if I wanted to see friends across the country, then I would be the one that did all the travelling. It was great to see people, but the travelling really put a drain on my finances.

I also started to realise that if I didn't make the effort to go and see people, then they wouldn't come and see us. I began to see a lot of friendships were heavily one sided, and now my priorities had changed. My boys and I getting through this stage, relied on me and me alone. If friends wanted to see us, then they would have to make the effort. I had to focus all my efforts and energies on them, as I had always done, but now things were different, and my main priority was finding an income stream to put food on the table, keep a roof over our heads and not fuel in the car.

Don't get me wrong, ramO did support us and continues to do so. He paid six month's rent up front, and a monthly maintenance, but it wasn't enough. I was balancing keeping them in our martial arts lessons, something I believed to be highly valuable for us all as it enabled us to challenge any emotional pain and mental barriers. It gave us a focus, a family environment, it provided us with friendships, a support group and we met Sensei Joel; someone who would play a very large part in our recovery process.

Finding work was an interesting process. Every job I knew I could do, and applied for, that enabled me to be home for my boys after school, I was refused, for a variety of different reasons. I was either too over qualified or too experienced. The employers were also only looking for people to work set hours of 9:00am-5:30pm. Had the working world still not moved on? Were the managers and business owners still so archaic in their understanding of how employee engagement and productivity wasn't being sat at a desk, being micro managed and unaware of the fact that it didn't matter if someone was over qualified, or had lots of experience. They would be valuable assets to the business at a fraction of the cost, and could actually help accelerate the business (but then I guess that is the whole crux of why they don't, they don't want to out done, out shone or up-level). I had been running my own businesses and working on community regeneration projects for the last 15 years, but all I wanted at this point was to put food on the table, gain independence and be there for my boys. It made me realise just how restrictive the job market is for those of us with children; I mean you'd think with the amount of single parents in the UK, employers would respond in a more innovative way to the growing trend? Sadly this wasn't, and isn't the case.

The job market operates in a way where you either show up at 9am and work until 5:30, or you don't get the job. It would be so much more productive to enable members of your team to work from home, or get into the office after school drop off, and leaving before school pick up, without taking a lunch break if they so wished. Allowing your team to take work home, maybe even working from home, would enable so many more families. It would also reduce the amount of traffic on the roads at certain times and help with employee engagement, but sadly no; too many employers are not willing to work in this way, and with single parent families on the increase, employees are favouring those who don't have children, or are men that have a wife/partner that can do the school runs. Companies refusing to adapt to new ways of working, refusing to take on single parents due to childcare commitments, gives politicians (and other bigots) the evidence they need to say that single parent families are a burden on society due to the amount of us who are forced into a position to claim benefits. The spending on the public purse could easily be reduced, not to mention the negative effects and the damage it does to the mental and emotional state to those of us who have a very strong work ethic. I updated my CV, I tailored it, played down my experiences, I did everything I could to get a job in the early days, but just kept getting rejected. This only added to the rejection I felt following the breakdown of my marriage and the friendships that broke down. I was at a really low point, and yet, I knew that I was being guided to do other things, to look at other options and create something else.

The only work that was suitable for me was in London, which would mean we had to relocate again, which was not an option. There was no way I was removing the boys from another school, relocating again, and living in another capital city. We were happy to be back in Sheffield, and getting to know mums and friends in the school again was a lifeline we all needed. I could have taken job with huge salaries, but when would I get to be a mother? I wouldn't. So it didn't matter to me whether the salaries were some of the largest I had been offered, being a mother was, and still is, the most important role I have, and nothing was going to take me away from my boys after everything we had been through. They were my children, my responsibility and I wanted to be with them.

Being in Sheffield and seeing Mr Leighton at the school, along with Laura and Kirstin, two of the most wonderful mums I have ever met and have become really dear friends with, gave me courage each and every day. I put a smile on my face and did the school run. My social life was predominantly the ten minutes at the beginning and at the end of the school day. The rest of the day was spent planning my future. So that's what I did, stopped when the boys were home, so we could do their homework, cook and eat together, play board games, go to the rec (the local park) and then when they were in bed, I cleaned the house. I would fall into bed around midnight, after taking Kelt for his midnight walk, only to wake up again at 6am to walk him again and get a little head start on breakfast, so when the boys came downstairs in their uniforms, we could sit together at the table and enjoy our time together. I had always believed that breakfast and dinner should be eaten together as a family; it anchors the family together, gives everyone a chance to share their thoughts, ideas and opinions, as well as their plans for the day and the things achieved. It also helps with social skills and prevents me from worrying about how my boys would behave in a restaurant, which is something I hadn't worried about for years. My boys have always done themselves, and me, proud with their table manners and conversational skills. We also go over the things that are making us happy, and what/who we are grateful for. Something we have done ever since they could string a sentence together. It gives us perspective on how blessed we are to have a roof over our head, clothes on our backs and food in the cupboard, but also to have each other. The things my boys would say would melt my heart, and made me feel so proud of them.

The boys and I would do a family clean at the weekends which meant I could enable them to improve on their household skills, because what if I became ill and couldn't get out of bed? How were they going to eat, have clean clothes or live in a clean home? I also didn't want them to grow up to be incompetent husbands and fathers. I wanted them to be able to support their future wife, 100% from each of them (none of this 50% from each – why would you only invest 50% of yourself into a relationship? Never made sense to me that one!). I wanted them to be able take care of their homes and set a great example to their children. Add to this the thought of going to visit them before they had their own family and turning up to a home where the washing up isn't done, the toilet seat is covered in urine and not being confident on where to sit in case I sat in goodness knows what! No! My boys were going to be house proud. They were going to know what it was like to take care of a home, and they were going to make sure our home would be so clean and tidy that they would be happy to pay to stay in it. I was their mother, not their maid and they were going to learn this on a whole new level now it was just the three of us. Family is the best team, and together we were going to achieve a lot more.

Before ramO walked out, I had enquired at the St John's University in York to do a Masters in Leading Innovation and Change. Sadly, not enough people signed up to do the course, so I asked the lead lecturer Sarah if I could have the reading list so I could purchase the books and 'do the course' by myself. She gladly provided me with the reading list and told me if I needed anything else, to just let her know. She also gave me a breakdown of everything they would be covering in the different subjects over the period of study. I purchased the books, studied the subject objectives and made a list of all the gaps in the curriculum. I then went about creating more lists on all the stuff I was great at, good at and not so good at; followed by more lists of what I enjoyed, loved doing, as well as the things I didn't enjoy and the things I hated.

Next up came the list of hobbies I had and of course a list of current outgoings, followed by the 'needed outgoings' and right up to the dream list of outgoings. I invested in a coaching course with The Coaching Academy because I knew I needed support on this journey and coaching others was something I knew I was great at. I purchased other materials that would help me on my journey to financial freedom and put aside the remaining amount of money that was for my Masters in a savings account. This was going to be my back up.

The next task was making sure I had adequate life insurance, because what happened if something did happen to me? I couldn't just ask friends to take on my boys at a cost to themselves. I needed to make sure there was a financial input for them, so my boys weren't a burden to them; as well as a way for any lost income to be covered.

This is how I met two wonderful guys called Rob and Chris Downham. They had a business which promoted Vitality Life and Health Insurance. To me it was a no brainer – getting rewarded for keeping fit, with cinema tickets and coffee as rewards, along with half price gym membership and money off toiletries and a whole host of other goodies… the only problem was, how was I going to afford it? I had walked into the meeting feeling powerful and positive, but when Rob asked me about who was to be included on the policy and the work I had, I crumbled. Here I was sat in front of a guy I didn't know and I just cried my eyes out. I felt like a complete failure. I had a husband who had walked out on me, no steady income, living in fear that if my ex didn't pay, then the boys and I would be homeless. I had nothing but me. I was struggling to see my own value, although I knew I had loads of experience, knowledge and knowing I was a great mum, what I was starting to experience made me feel like a burden to everyone. Rob took it all in his stride, told me to just sit where I was, take a moment and went to make me a cup of tea. He then called his twin brother in and after about ten minutes, I was ready to carry on. They told me to send them my CV, come back into the office in a couple of days and they would see what they could do to help. Both of them gave me a big hug and told me everything would be okay; and I believed them.

Going back to see them on the Friday was nerve wracking. I had no idea what they had in mind, what they would come up with, and how what I ultimately wanted to achieve would fit into it all; but it did, and the value add, the energy of these two and being part of a team was just what I needed. With a reference from another friend Martin Manning, who I'd known through business for almost 15 years, and who Rob and Chris both knew, I became a Vitality Insurance Consultant, and it was a perfect fit in my life. I could continue my study with The Coaching Academy, study my text books recommended by the lecturers at St John's and work around my boys. I could be a full-time Mummy, study and earn my own money. I felt like I was on top of the world! I didn't have much, but what I did have I was working for.

There were others who needed the benefits more than I did, I was a strong and capable woman. I didn't want to be a 'benefits mum', 'a scrounger'. I had worked since the age of 11, doing paper rounds, working on the farm my dad worked at pulling fruit and vegetables, so paying my own way, being independent, this was my style, not sat around wasting my life watching mindless TV and eating junk food – the image I had created in my mind of what it meant to be on benefits. An image I was not going to be associated with; but here I was a mum being supported by benefits to make up the shortfall of income from the sales I was making and the child maintenance. I was a single mum on benefits, and I struggled with that. Until I realised that I had fallen into the trap of propaganda brainwashing.

Meeting Rob and Chris was such a blessing, being introduced to Nikki, Rob's wife, was also a blessing. She was, and still is, such a wonderful woman, always with a smile on her face and such a friendly genuine person. I had found three new friends, through work, something very new to me as most of the people I met through work were peers, colleagues, clients or suppliers. Very few of the people I worked with I connected with on a friendship level, so it was nice to be able to have someone to wave to as they drove by in the car, or chat to at work. Plus they knew my situation and were incredibly supportive. With Rob, Chris, Nikki and Martin's help I started to see a much brighter light at the end of what felt like a very dark tunnel. The last four years had been incredibly dark, and now I truly felt I was turning a corner. Everything was going to be alright, more than alright... and nothing and no one was going to stop me.

For the next few weeks I sat there making sense of all the lists I had created, drawing on the experiences and passions I had. What did my future look like? What was it I was building? I knew I would have my own coaching business yet wasn't quite sure how they would look, what exactly I was going to be doing or how it would work. I know what I wanted to do, but with limited funds and no official qualifications in Coaching yet, or being registered with the ILM (Institute of Leadership and Management) or the ICF (International Coaching Federation), would people really buy from me? I knew I had the skills and the talent for it, I had been doing it for years as a volunteer with the Sheffield Business School, Business Links, Yorkshire Forward and The Institute of Business Advisors. I was a walking example of how coaching and mentoring enabled people. I also had years of experience coaching, mentoring and training my own employees and those inspiring individuals that I had met along the way. I met quite a few coaches who had gone through a coaching programme funded by their employers, or had previously been counsellors, but I had real experience of running a business, of creating results by identifying what I wanted, funding it myself and go after it. This was going to be my unique selling point, plus I had a whole lot of life experience that was so very unique and worth using. Not having the qualifications had been something that had stumped me in the past, but the benefit of it was this: it filtered out those who are only interested in qualifications had enabled me to work with a group of people that were hungry, driven and able to see beyond the qualifications.

At this stage of my life though, I knew I wanted to have all my knowledge and experience recognised with an official qualification. I had my eye on doing a PhD, but I wanted it to be a practical one, not one that was research for the sake of research. I wanted to do a PhD that actually impacted the lives of millions around the world; one that added a real, living, breathing dimension to daily life; and it had to have social impact immediately. Was I going to do it around the field of equality, especially as I had just seen so much inequality in Egypt between the social classes and the harassment I had experienced in Egypt? Or was I going to do a political one addressing something completely different? I added these thoughts and all the accreditations to the list of things that I would need to help grow my business.

I sat there looking at the lists and mind maps I had just created and then hung them up on the walls in the dining room. What were they telling me? What was shouting out at me? Who were going to be my clients? Where did they come from? What kind of things did they want to achieve in life? I knew I didn't want excuse makers. I knew I didn't want people who got into stress jealousy or went into victim mode. I had no time for time wasters either. I knew I didn't want to work with people who were not decisive, or people who had to get permission from their spouse or partner. I was passionate about succeeding in all areas of life, I was passionate about always doing my best, and I wanted to work with people who had the same kind of thinking, they just needed someone to believe in them, support them and help them accelerate their results. People who wanted to do their best, at all times. People who wanted to perform to the very best of their ability, constantly growing, constantly up-levelling. The people who I would work with were the kind of people that understood that you rest when you are dead. Live is for living, it is an adventure and you just have to go after your dreams. Then I laughed... my mum popped into my head with, "All you can do is your best, so long as you do your best, then no one can ask anything more from you."

Then I cried. I loved my mum so much. Her strong work ethic, her strong core and her 'no messing' attitude really had rubbed off on me even more than I had realised. Then I cried a bit more because of the woman my mother was. She had raised my brother, sister and I on her own, worked three jobs to keep a roof over our heads and she had gone without many times just to make sure the three of us got what we needed. It may not have been what we wanted, but we always got what we needed; and I drew upon that strength. I wanted to be a mum just like my mum. I wanted to do whatever it took to be the best mum I could ever be. My boys were my world, and they had been through so much. I was not prepared to put them through any more turmoil. I was going to enable them to be courageous, interdependent and responsible adults. I was going to make them proud of me, proud of themselves and we were going to be the best team ever, because the best team is family and it didn't matter that ramO was no longer in our home, we would always be the Aysha family.

I had told the boys that, days after ramO told me he wanted a divorce, but now it resonated through me like shockwaves through the earth after an earthquake. It didn't matter what ramO had done, or not done. It didn't matter how hurt or betrayed I felt, I had to let it go. Ego was ugly, holding onto pain, upset and anger was going to be toxic for all of us. I had to channel all my positive energy into creating something positive and powerful for the three of us, with ramO joining us for birthday parties, school events and the odd Sunday lunch. It was time to step up. Right there in that moment. This was not about me or ramO, this was about the boys. Their happiness, their future relationships, their inner peace, because for me, so long as my boys are happy and growing into confidence, intelligent and successful young men with a zest for life, a sense of adventure and of course all of it being underpinned by a sense of honour, truth and justice then what more could I want for them as a mother?

I was still stood in the dining room, with Kelt in my arms just hugging him and talking to him about the plans and the tweaks I was making to the lists and mind maps when the boys came home from the rec. They giggled when they heard me discussing my plans with Kelt. When Kelt saw them both though, he jumped out of my arms and jumped up at the boys. We all had hugs and then went into the kitchen to make dinner together. Tonight we were making homemade gluten free chicken kievs and nanny chips. Processed food was not welcome in our stomachs… unless it was the odd treat of ice-cream or chocolate, which was a monthly thing... something Khaalid was starting to understand. So much so one day when we were in the kitchen washing up together he just turned to me and asked, "Mummy do most women only eat chocolate once a month?" with a cheeky grin on his face.

I responded, "Many women eat chocolate all the time Khaalid, but not me."

He looked deep in thought for a moment and then came back with, "You mean like the 'emergency chocolate' we saw in Sainsbury's that time?"

I giggled, gave him a big hug, held him tight and kissed the top of his head and replyed, "Yes prince, just like emergency chocolate."

As he pulled away he just looked up into my face and said, "Mummy, everything is going to be okay you know."

With tears in my eyes I said, "I know Baaba, I know it is; so long as we've got each other, we'll be fine."

Naasir came into the kitchen and threw his arms around us both and cheered, "Family hug!" something that the three of us had always done, because you could never have too many family hugs, they were the best kind of hugs, and we were a huggy, snuggly bunch.

Arriving at Castle Martial Arts the following night was great. I was so excited to share my vision with Sensei, as this was the word of the month. Everyone was working on vision. When I walked in, he knew I was in a much better space. He too was a huggy bear and I loved the way he acknowledged each and every one of the children, but also how he hugged my boys, especially Khaalid. It was just what they needed, and he knew it. "'Ello you tiger! Been a good day then?" he said as he smiled his beaming smile giving me a big hug too.

"Oh yes!" I giggled. "Great! Now let's get to work!" We hit the mats and from that point on it was only onwards and upwards. I had got my fight back, quite literally! The punching and kicking drills that night were awesome. How I was going to move the next day was beyond me, but activity recovery was the only way I knew, even if I did walk like John Wayne for the next three days.

One of the things I had written down on my list was complete my next two books. I needed to have income streams that just kept flowing in. Plus I needed to get the book about Egypt written. I also wanted to get the book about Besma written; a book I had already written the synopsis to in Egypt; a book I had already done loads of research for. Looking at the lists of things I wanted to achieve on my mind maps and lists, I had an 'aha!' moment. I would include my knowledge of cultural diversity in the book, as well as my coaching and mentoring into it. It would then be a great marketing tool for my business, showcasing my knowledge and calling in my clients. Both books would be the entry level product to what I do for all those that didn't think they could afford a coach or a mentor. I knew that if I wrote about cultural diversity, coaching and mentoring as a text book, it would probably almost likely be a bit dry, and it would limit my market. However if I included it in my first work of fiction, then that would be 'two birds, one stone'.

I sat in the Curators tea rooms with my notebooks, laptop and cup of coffee most days writing both of them in tandem. I was finding both of them challenging. *Walaahi* was challenging because it was bringing back memories of Egypt, and *The Wife* was too close to home what with ramO having walked out on us months before. I knew I had to do more healing before I could sit down and write them properly, so I just made notes, writing the ideas that came to me, and organising them into the different chapter ideas I had. My brain enjoyed this creative process, especially as the Vitality training was intense. All those technical terms, the figures, health issues people had, but I loved the thought that I was able to help people protect their families, as well as get rewarded for being healthy, and motivated to become healthier.

Since becoming a single mum, my own health had taken on a whole new level of importance. I had to keep my health in top condition. I had to make sure I was not ill, my boys needed me more now to be fitter and stronger than ever before. Mental and physically strong in my mind equalled emotionally strong, they all fed into each other. Plus I wanted to set a great example to my boys. I had become grossly overweight whilst I was in Egypt. Being back in Egypt and without ramO being in the house, I was in charge of all the foods that were brought in to the home, and being an 'old school' mother, I used every meal time as a lesson in how to cook, to teach about food groups, to talk about nutrition. We made everything from scratch, built the sauces up using herbs, spices and stock. I got the boys to choose recipes from the books and then we would get the remaining ingredients and cook our dinner. Weight started to drop off me, especially as it was combined with the martial arts.

I also had some personal training sessions with Steve Whittle, a Personal Trainer at Esporta, or rather Virgin Active. He was amazing, still is! He taught me about managing the food groups and taught me to look at food in a whole new way than before, and he pushed me hard, harder than I had been pushed before. I loved it.

The combination of Steve's PT sessions, the Martial Arts with Sensei Joel and eating the way I wanted to meant I started to look good and feel great. I had a new sense of energy, a more focused and happier energy, and I loved it! I felt like me again. I felt like I had when I was first with ramO. I had missed this feeling. Getting pregnant, nearly dying with Naasir and the growing businesses had left me no time to invest in myself properly; which deep down I knew to be a lie. I knew how to make time, I knew how to master time, I had just forgotten to love myself properly, but now that was coming back. I really had forgotten what being fit and energised felt like. I loved it. The boys loved it and we were all so much happier.

There were a few external things that were causing me a headache, such as problems with the landlord, sorting out the utilities and the general day to day admin. I began to realise just how important it was to keep my head clear, my energy levels up, because doing the jobs of two parents was exhausting on many levels. There was no one to hand the baton to when I felt tired; No one else to back me up when tweaks in behaviour were needed when it came to the boys; No one else to give me a hug when I had dealt with the upset the boys had when ramO hadn't called, or they were reminded by other kids at school that we were a 'broken' family. There was no one to cuddle up to in bed and just hold me when the tears came due to all the challenges that kept showing up. There was no one to share my mini victories with, other than my boys, and I couldn't share a lot of the victories with them because they were either not old enough or the victories were too complex. We did share a lot of our victories together at 'news time' at the dinner table, when we'd do the happiness and gratitude flood.

One of the things I was really grateful for was my early morning and late night walks with Kelt. Seeing the sun rise, hearing the birds sing and the dew on the leaves and grass in the morning, and then the abundance of stars in the sky with the moon lighting my way at night was such a beautiful experience. This alone time would be where I would work on my mindset, work on absorbing all the healing elements of nature. I would rejoice in the silence of the world. I may have been alone, but in this setting I didn't feel lonely. Although getting up early and going to bed late to make sure all the jobs were done, I began to really get present to the fact that there was no one else but me to do all this. When I had agreed to have children with ramO, it had been under the agreement that we would parent together, raise the boys together and that we would be married for life. Getting married was a big deal to me, and not something I took lightly. It was on these walks that I began to realise just how much single parents had to deal with, whether they were single parents through choice, partner or spouse working away, a relationship breakdown or by death. There are so many variables as to why parents are single handedly raising children alone, but the support from others is, in my experience, limited. Many of my friends wanted to help, but being in different cities or on different continents the only help they could give was a message of encouragement on social media, which was really my only connection with others my own age, on a social level. There were friends who lived locally but they were either busy running their own businesses or dealing with their own family. I felt alone. I felt isolated. I was exhausted, and yet I still kept pushing forward, with a smile on my face and a spring in my step. Thank goodness I was investing in my fitness because if I wasn't as fit as I was, there would be no way I would have been able to keep going.

It was during one of these walks in the morning that I realised I wanted to tackle the various issues I was facing. I wanted to highlight the various problems and challenges I had had since returning to the UK with attitudes, finding work and the isolation. I wanted to tackle the attitude I had faced when I first returned and visited the job centre to find out about and sort out the various support that was available to me. I had only ever been in a job centre when I was 19 and looking for work when I first moved to Banbury. I hadn't liked the environment then so chose to use recruitment agencies instead, but during an 'interview' with the woman in this job centre I had got flustered with my words and got English and Arabic mixed up. When she shouted at me, in slow sentences, as if I was stupid and didn't understand English, what I had done for work before, I told her I had just written a book and had previously had my own businesses, she just looked at me as if she didn't believe me and then said, "Well, I hope you write better than you speak because your English isn't very good."

I just thought to myself, *If this is how you are treating me as a white, English woman who has only lived out of the country for three-and-a-half years, how on earth do you treat others that have only just arrived in this country? The ones escaping civil wars and goodness knows what else and just need support and guidance.* I didn't like this woman and thankfully my 'interview' with her was over very quickly; she passed me along the conveyor belt of others in the job centre to sort out my 'employment status' so I could get the relevant paperwork sorted.

I also wanted to work on transforming organisations and coaching the business owners on how they engaged their teams. I wanted to deal with gender equality, how women, especially mothers were dealt with in the workplace, including single mums. I wanted to mentor women, creating more female entrepreneurs to give them the financial freedom, the support and confidence they deserved and needed to enable them to be a full-time Mummy, as well as be able to provide for themselves. I was seeing first hand just how single mums were the best project managers on the planet. We juggled so many balls when it came to the children, the home and work (and the crap that came from others in the community) that when put in charge of projects, there would be nothing that stopped us from succeeding. We didn't just do things for our own sense of success, or for our own mental stimulation, we were doing it to provide for our children, and like the saying goes 'Hell hath no fury like a mother scorned'. Come between a mother and her children, and you had better be ready for the fire that raged within her. They were part of her. She grew them inside of her, risking her life to do so. She nurtured them, gave everything she had to provide them with a safe and stable home, and nothing and no one was going to stop them.

These were the women I wanted to elevate.

These were the women I wanted to work with.

These were the women that inspired me and I wanted to inspire, support and enable them to live a life they truly loved.

Not become beholden to anyone.

Not afraid to go after what they wanted.

I wanted to work with women that not only wanted to invest in themselves and their family, but also in others.

My thinking was simple: The more we receive, the more we give; and the more the world became a better place to raise our children. I wanted to positively impact the world, and this was just one of the ways in which I was going to do it. And although I write this in a past tense remembering these moments, this is still the work that I wish to do, and I am doing. These are still the women I wish to work with, still the intentions I have, because I know the more women I impact, the more empowered we become and the more our children grow in confidence, in ability and in happiness; creating a never-ending snowball effect. The world will only become a much better place when we empower each other instead of tearing each other apart, criticising each other, comparing ourselves to each other and not loving ourselves and the incredible power that we have. I mean come on, how many men do you know that can grow a baby inside of them, push out a child, and more importantly, how many other species do you know that bleed for a whole week every month and continue to live? Hmm not many! Women are powerful, if only we would let go of the negativity and the patriarchal toxicity that rules this world, making us feel inadequate and not good enough.

I experienced a lot of spitefulness from one particular woman. A woman I had welcomed into the school community; a woman who I encouraged to follow her dreams, a woman who I acknowledged; a woman who couldn't stop herself from being nasty when I started to turn a corner.

I remember one particular day when the school was having some building work done, one of the builders Paul fell in love with Kelt, reminding him of his dog. We had got chatting and were laughing away with each other, nothing more, nothing less. Just strangers connecting over a shared love of dogs. Walking on into the school grounds, this particular woman looked me up and down and with so much venom in her voice said, "I suppose you think now you look like that all the men fancy you."

I was shocked, it hadn't even crossed my mind. I didn't see myself in that way. I was just Dawn, a woman who was getting fit and healthy to be around as long as possible for my boys, to regain my energy to keep up with them, a woman who was gaining confidence in herself after having had it ripped out of her. A woman who had lost her best friend, her lover, her soul mate and the man she had wanted to spend the rest of her life with, feeling the worst kind of rejection and betrayal, I wasn't even thinking about being with another man. I wasn't even thinking about a relationship. The only men in my life were my two boys, my dog and of course my dad. The only men outside of those who I turned to were my two chosen brothers Rob and Alan. They were the only men I wanted and needed. I had help from other guys in a variety of ways such as Mr Leighton, Sensei, Rob and Chris, Martin, my friends Jay, Si, DJ and a few others – but romantic interest – no. Thinking all men fancied me, certainly not.

I couldn't believe she could be so spiteful, but it was something I would have to start getting used to because once you start to look good, and people know you are single, you become the scarlet woman. You get to see who the insecure women are as if they have a huge neon sign above their heads. They stand between you and their partners, husband or not. They watch every move you make when you are speaking to their friend's husbands; they let you know almost immediately that the man you are talking to is married or with so and so. You don't get invited out to coffee anymore, but when you do it is for them to start fishing.

One of the saddest things I experienced was bumping into a mum in the park, I knew her husband through martial arts. We would compare bruises and injuries, talk about our training and our children and whenever I asked him how his wife was, I was blown away by the love this man had for his wife. His whole face lit up, his eyes came alive and he would just gush about her. This man was so in love with his wife it flowed from every part of him. I would stand there and wonder if I would ever find a man that would love me in the way this man so obviously loved his wife. His wife invited me to join her for a coffee whilst our kids played, and as I never really got to speak with her, I said I'd love to. It soon became very obvious from the conversation that certain people, who had seen me talking with her husband, had decided to gossip, and had put doubts in this woman's head. Here before me was a beautiful woman, who had a family who adored her, allowing toxic people to get into her head. She didn't come right out and ask me, she didn't have to. I knew where the conversation was going and diverted it immediately with how lucky she was to have a man who was so in love with her, and how I had someone who was helping me to heal. Her shoulders dropped and a breath escaped her body. The look she gave me was one of relief, but I couldn't help feeling sad for her. Sad that she had allowed these toxic gossips to give her doubt, or feed the doubt. I felt sad for these gossiping women who had nothing better to do than be spiteful and hate on others because they didn't love themselves enough, or have enough going on in their own lives that they had to talk about others in such a vile way.

I didn't realise it at the time, but it was just another barrier going up for me when it came to other women. I didn't want to be around them. Knowing how many women had chosen to sleep with married men, knowing how many women had been spiteful towards their ex-husbands through the research I had done for my book *The Wife*, and having experienced the back-handed compliments from one or two of my female friends on how good I was looking, I was moving further away from women, and isolating myself more and more. I didn't want to be around these kinds of women. I didn't want to be around toxic people, so I kept myself to myself, only talking to my lovely Jools, Debbie, Tina, Michey and Jane. They knew the pain of divorce and where I was at, being single mums themselves for various reasons. Getting to know Nicky, Rob's wife, and some of the mums down at the dojo[3], was difficult for me. I had always been shy, and although I can walk into a networking meeting or business event and 'do the business', when it came to a personal basis, I found it hard, especially now.

ramO had really done a number on my level of confidence, and so I sat down and coached myself. What would I tell a friend who was in my situation? What would I do if this was a business situation? I had to get a grip. I had to work through my rejection issues and social and personal life the way I had worked through my business and education life. It was affecting my sales – being told 'no' – people wasting your time gathering quotes, with no intention of going ahead. Rejection was painful, and cut like a knife. So out came the flip charts and white board markers, my journal and pens and I started writing. What kind of man did I want when the time came? What kind of women did I want to surround myself with? What kind of environment did I want to be in? I asked myself so many questions, deep and confronting questions and I journaled late into the night. I couldn't stop. I was creating my future. I was stepping into the next level of my life. I had to, because if I didn't then how on earth could I teach the boys how to move on?

How could I teach them to have a healthy relationship with other people?

How could I show them how to love themselves, love another after heartbreak, if I was blocking all areas in my life relating to it?

The hardest thing to tackle was how was I going to deal with ramO?

I didn't want to play mind games like so many of the women I interviewed for *The Wife*. I didn't want to keep receiving nasty emails from him and his new fiancé. I didn't want any animosity between any of us. I wanted peace between ramO and I because we were parents together, which made us a family. So I wrote to him. I asked him the questions I wanted answering and although they were tough questions, I had to have them answered. The responses were painful. They were hurtful and yet they were just what I needed to move on, because he killed any remaining love and respect I had left for him. Now he was just the boys' father. A man I would parent with, and a man that I thought I had known so well, when in fact I didn't know him at all. After 18 years I didn't know him. I could never be a character witness for this man because I didn't know him. How could that be?

How could you spend 18 years with someone and feel like this?

How could you share so much but know nothing about them?

I cried. I had normally such a great sixth sense about people, had used it time and time again in business to avoid doing business with people whose energy felt 'off', the only three clients in 12 years of business that ended up owing us money were the three that I told ramO to get rid of after me only spending moments in their company. But they were his clients, and so he kept them, costing us over £20,000. So why if I had been so right about these guys, had I not picked up on it with my own husband?

I remember crying, head in my hands, shaking my head. I was grieving. I had lost the love of my life without even knowing it. Yes, I was grieving. Grieving for the man I had lost. Grieving for the loss of a loved one, no different to the loss of someone through death, except this loved one keeps resurfacing and it plays with your heart and mind in so many ways, that it can be harder to move forward than if the person dies. I was grieving for my broken heart, and yet to so many others out in the street I was just another single mum who was out to move in on another woman's husband; something I would never do; something that makes me feel sick to the stomach. Marriage is sacred. Other people's relationships are sacred. You don't mess with them. You stay the fuck away from them. And if you are the cheater, then you are a coward. You are selfish. Don't get married or be in a relationship if you are going to mess around behind someone's back. I have always believed this, but now, it is stronger than ever. So I knew these had to go into my journaling. I didn't want to be around liars, cheats and backstabbers. I wanted to be around people who are loyal, honest, empowering and inspiring. I wanted to be around people who built each other up, like Chris, Rob and Nicky, like Alan and Rob my chosen brothers, like Jools, Debbie, Tina and Michey.

It was time to choose wisely. It was time to step the next steps forward. It was time for a holiday.

––––––––––––––

[3] Dojo – a space where martial arts is practiced.

THREE
TRAVELLING TRIO AND ONE DOG

Choosing to go on holiday when you are saving like a mad woman 'just in case' anything happens was a challenge. I knew once I had my business up and running things would be fine, but it was the first year that was going to test me. I had always said I would make a million by my 40th birthday, and that was fast approaching. I had three years to do it, so I had better get my head down and get focused. Creating the Dr Merhi Ayche Foundation to support and invest in those who were from disadvantaged, marginalised backgrounds would need serious capital behind it, as well as a plethora of mentors, coaches and trainers who were willing to give up their time, as well as donate into this global fund. Baaba dying had left a huge void in my life, and I was going to honour him in the best way I knew possible. He was an inspiration. He gave to others so generously, so selflessly and I wanted my boys to know the great man he was by continuing his work of paying it forward and helping those less fortunate. It also meant I needed to invest in myself, get a coach and surround myself with the right people that would enable me to get to where I wanted.

I knew I didn't have much money, everything I had was going into making sure the boys had everything they needed, keeping some kind of normality for us all by going to martial arts and the gym. A luxury to many, but being surrounded by friends, strong male role models and exercising, to me, they were not luxuries, they were essentials.

I knew the holiday had to be here in the UK, which is what I wanted to be honest. I wanted to reacquaint myself with the UK, and show them the beautiful countryside that we have here. I knew I had camping equipment, and with a few extra items from Decathlon, we would have everything we needed. I loved camping when I was little. Waking up to the fresh air, the dew freshness and hearing the birds right outside the tent in the trees. The adventure of it all! Watching mum cooking on the camping stove, and the dad cooking on the barbeque was great. Giggling with my brother and sister whilst trying to get to sleep because the airbeds made funny farting noises; the smell of campfire, and being surrounded by nature, I loved it! I knew I would be a little more adventurous than my parents, and with zero to little money, I told the boys we were going on a road trip. They had no idea what a road trip was but I made sure they were excited about just driving to the coast, parking up and having a sleepover in the car, and then when we found a good place to camp, we would camp there. Khaalid described it a bit like the Famous Five, but instead he named us the Travelling Trio and One Dog. We all wanted to go to the beach and there were many friends that we wanted to see on the way. So we headed to Manchester to see a friend for the night before making our way over towards Wales to see another friend called Sorrel in Powys. Khaalid was navigating – using his map reading skills for the first time. There was going to be no technology on this holiday, other than my phone to take photos and make phone calls. We were going old school!

We travelled through small villages and towns, played 'I spy with my little eye' and with so many more things to see, the guessing and the giggles were flowing big time! Me being me, I had to discuss the benefits of driving through the smaller villages; obviously in a guessing game kind of way. It's the teacher in me, what can I say? The boys kept coming up with some fantastic answers, ones I hadn't even thought of! There's me thinking saving fuel because we have to drive slower than on the motorway, getting to see the local areas and support local businesses, and the boys were coming up with how each town looks different in each part of the country, how some villages look cosy, and they would laugh that a village can't be a village if it only has one house. There were some villages we drive through that just had a sign and the moment we had read the sign we were leaving the village. Naasir thought this was hilarious, not to mention how funny some of the names were! They were saying how much nicer the food was in the smaller cafes rather than the service stations and we were able to just stop at a park, or the toilets rather than waiting for a layby or the services. Yep! My boys were converted to travelling on the A roads. They also loved looking for the local signage to help us follow the route that Khaalid had planned out for us. Khaalid described it as one big treasure hunt, which then set Naasir off on his magical story telling of treasure hunts! Being on the road with the boys was such a great laugh. We would sing the songs on the radio, play the quiz games and discuss how much we missed Dixie and Emma on Heart FM. They had to be our absolute favourites! We spent the night in Powys with Sorrel and her family, and it was so lovely to catch up with her after so many years. We walked along the tow path and the boys played with Sorrel's three children. Her eldest was now a teenager and I had last seen her as a baby! I was so happy for Sorrel as she now had her own business making handcrafted silver jewellery and it was beautiful! She told us to head towards Barmouth in Wales, and so we did. Khaalid got the map out and started plotting the route. Naasir helped and we said our goodbyes and off we went.

Arriving in Barmouth was a relief as it was getting dusk and we were wanting to eat and find somewhere to stop for the night. We drove around for a while, unable to find somewhere. I saw a taxi driver and said, "He'll know!" So we approached the taxi driver and he gave us directions to a little camp site just on the outside of the town, on the way in. It was £5 per night and included hot running showers, a communal campfire, a barbeque at each spot and access to a private beach; and they had space for us! It was fantastic! There was a field behind us with horses in it, the owners were great and dogs were also very welcome, something that I would soon realise would become a rarity.

We spent five days in Barmouth playing in the sea, hiking in the local woodlands, cycling along the Mawdacch trail, which for my boys was a huge feat. I'd only taught them to ride their bikes some six months earlier, something I had always imagined doing with their dad, so for them to do the full 18 miles along the Mawdacch Trial was so impressive. We stopped off after nine miles to get ice cream and have a little rest, before heading back towards Barmouth. Kelt was also doing incredibly well, but after about 12 miles he was happier to be in the basket on the front of my bike, which gave lots of the passers-by a real delight. We may have been a 'broken' family, but the travelling trio and one dog were having the best times. I had promised the boys they could choose dinner that night as a reward for completing the trail on their bikes, so off we went for pizza and salad at the local gluten free café right on the sea front. It was gorgeous. The sun was still out, the weather was warm and the salad was amazing! I was tempted to have a glass of wine, but again, I hesitated. I am not a big drinker, and could tell you exactly how many drinks I've had in the last 20 years, so knowing I had to drive the car back to the campsite, some two miles up the road, and be alert for the boys, just in case was weighing on my mind. Then the boys asked if we could go and play on the beach after dinner. I agreed, and then in a moment chose to have a small glass of wine, of which I thoroughly enjoyed. I was on holiday, I was incredibly responsible, and I wouldn't be getting back into the car for at least two hours, by which time, the boys and I had devoured a huge triple waffle fruit sundae between us. As I looked out over the bay, the little fishing boats and the dogs on the beach playing, I knew that this is the kind of life I wanted; woodlands, the beach, the ocean and my dogs. The natural life. Simple, humble and natural, enjoying the simplicity of life. I just had to learn to sail and travel by the sea, much more environmentally friendly, more relaxing and no airports full of stressed out people; families, business travellers and security everywhere. I was done with security forces. I had seen enough police and military officers walking around with machine guns and AK-47s to last me a lifetime. If I never saw an armed police officer in my life again, it would be too soon.

Sitting on the beach watching the boys run around with Kelt, I realised I was crying. I had not seen them this happy since before we went to Egypt. They were running around free as angels, laughing and playing, chasing Kelt, then they would build a sand castle, which Kelt would then wee all over before they chased him away, giggling and calling out after him. It was a magical moment, one that still brings tears of joy to my eyes every time I think about it.

As we were walking back up the beach, a couple and their Lurcher dog were just coming onto the beach. The dog came bounding up to us and made firm friends with Kelt. The next thing we knew, both dogs were running around and playing. Kelt attempting to chase his new friend, and literally having no chance! The Lurcher was faster, taller and his legs were longer than Kelt's whole body! The owners of the Lurcher and I stood watching, crying with laughter at the sight before us: two dogs, two boys, all chasing across the beach.

The man turned to me and said, "This is what life is about, this is the magic of childhood."

"Yep! Indeed it is," I replied.

The three of us stood and chatted for a while whilst the dogs and the boys wore themselves out. They lived locally and asked if I was on holiday with the boys or if we lived in the area. When I told them we were on a road trip, both of them said what I was doing was a great thing for my boys, giving them the tools for later in life, connecting them with nature rather than the fake, materialism of the world. Stuff of days gone by, proper childhood memories. Home before dark, back before dinner is ready or the dog gets it, even though you didn't have a watch, a mobile phone or knew when dinner would be ready, you were always home in time for dinner. Climbing trees rather than plastic fantastic climbing frames or the metal ones, climbing out onto a branch you weren't sure was sturdy enough, making you assess risk properly, strengthening your core muscles as the branches moved, and if you fell and broke an arm, you soon learnt to be better at judging the next branch. The praise these two heaped on me that evening for what I was doing for my boys, and how more parents should be doing it with their kids was overwhelming. Then when they asked me if we were waiting for the boys' dad, and I told them it was just me, the boys and Kelt, they were shocked and really impressed.

"Most couples wouldn't do a road trip like yours, so for you to be doing it by yourself, doing all the driving, all the parenting, kudos to you."

At which point, the overwhelm was too much, tears sprang from my eyes. Here I was with little-to-no income, in the process of building a business idea, five months into the life as a single mum and adjusting to the intensity of that, still in a lot of pain and healing with a friend who was also going through something similar, figuring out what to do for the best for my boys, and these two strangers acknowledging me in such a way that I had started to cry, yet again. They asked me how I was coping and I just found myself opening up to these two random strangers. The friendship they offered me that night on the beach had been more than any of my friends had offered me since I had arrived back. We laughed together as they ask me about life in Egypt and what that was like for me, they wanted to hear about my business idea, they wanted to know how I had coped, and then they told me that I was putting too much pressure on myself – especially when I told them about the dilemma I had faced earlier with being so indecisive about having a glass of wine. A glass of wine was nothing to worry about, it was when I started drinking bottles of it that I should worry. It was great to get some perspective from these two random strangers, who as it happened both worked in social care. They worked with kids from troubled backgrounds, kids who had things difficult, so the compliments these two strangers had given me earlier about how I was raising my boys suddenly took on a whole new level of acknowledgement. I had been worrying about the litigious culture that the UK had now turned into. The fact that parents were becoming the biggest enemies of other parents, that so much bubble wrap parenting had become so widespread, leaving children 'dis-abled' in the areas of confidence and basic life skills – because mummy and daddy would do everything for them, because mummy and daddy no longer had the confidence to discipline their children – just in case someone else thought they were a bad parent, or were being too harsh and reported them, something that I had noticed since I had come back to the UK. Or was it just that having been absorbed into the Egyptian culture, the differences were so much more obvious to me now?

I have a very no nonsense approach to parenting, and have five key rules which my boys have to adhere to:

1)Remember to use your manners
2)Respect yourself, others and the environment
3)Keep yourself safe and stick together
4)Love yourself

5)Be smart, but be wise with it

Oh, and have fun! Because my thinking is, when they fulfil those five rules, then everything else falls into place. I tell my boys to trust their instincts and their own judgement, whilst helping them understand what this means at the different stages of life. I know that the earlier I teach them these skills, the more proficient at them they will become. The more they learn to trust in their own instincts, the more confident they become in their own abilities. The more resourceful I gave them the space to be, the more innovative and responsible they would become as they got older. These are skills that I have always believed kids benefit from, something backed up by the likes of Dr Tanya Byron, Michael Gurian, Steve Biddulph, Edward de Bono, Dr William Sears, and something that the boys were learning in Birkdale, a private boys school in Sheffield. Those who pioneered the Outward Bound projects across the globe, worked with forest schools and of course the famous Duke of Edinburgh's Award all encouraged giving children the space to learn by themselves in the open air, in sports such as hiking, abseiling, canoeing, sailing and other sports such as archery, shooting and martial arts.

I had been studying for years the lives of top entrepreneurs such as Richard Branson, whose mother dropped him off a few miles from home and told him to make his own way home at the age of four, developing independence and problem-solving skills. Reading Duncan Bannatyne's book and how he grew up spending most of his life outside, before going on to create opportunities with his paper round just to get a bike. I read Robert Kiyosaki's *Rich Dad, Poor Dad*, learning a lot about perception of money, and what it truly meant to be wealthy. I wanted to nurture the interests of my boys, very much like the parents of Bill Gates and Steve Jobs. I wanted my boys to know that anything they truly wanted was theirs, if they worked smart and hard enough for it. Enabling them to step out of their comfort zones was essential, but so was letting them know I trusted them by giving them different responsibilities, whether that was walking Kelt by themselves, allowing them to go to the park with each other without me. Yes it was only a five minute walk away, but with Naasir being seven and Khaalid being 11, I was trusting Naasir to listen to his older brother and Khaalid to take responsibility not only for himself but Naasir as well.

In short, I wanted my boys to have a similar upbringing to the one I had. One where we were free to explore the village, walk to school by ourselves, play out until dark; trusting in the wider community. We've become so paranoid these days that everyone and anyone is either going to murder, rape or sexually assault us or kidnap our children that we have wrapped ourselves up in invisible prison. I don't believe that people are bad. I don't believe that everyone is out to get me or my children. I believe that 99% of the people in this world are wonderfully kind and helpful, and this has been proven time and time again to me over the years, regardless of which country I have been in. These two random strangers were a case in point. Their kindness and generosity of spirit was what I experienced from people on a regular basis.

As the night was drawing in, we said our goodbyes, and the boys, Kelt and I went back to the campsite. The other campers, Sarah Owen and her family were already back and had got the campfire going. They invited us to join them and my new 'boyfriend' Zeik, aged four, came and sat next to me. He was absolutely adorable, and became my shadow for the few days we were there. Sarah was so lovely, is so lovely, and supported me so much over the few days we were in Wales. We connected on Facebook before I left, and my new boyfriend asked me for my phone number and said he would call me. I'm still waiting Zeik! ;) Bless him!

Once we left Wales, we headed towards Telford to see another friend Tracey, who I had not seen for years. It was great to finally meet her new fella Greg, who had a shared interest in martial arts. Our boys all connected and for 48 hours I felt as though I didn't have children. Not only were they hunting for bugs and bouncing on the trampoline, Greg occupied them with 'boy stuff' and the PlayStation, whilst Tracey and I caught up over a bottle of Baileys. Oh how I loved Baileys, especially in coffee, so smooth and creamy. I remember DJ and I sharing a bottle when I got to his, he'd never really got into Baileys, but he was liking the new buzz it gave him. The amount of people I have introduced Baileys to, I should be given a lifetime supply of it! Problem with that though would be I'd make brownies, ice cream and goodness knows what else with it, and gift it to people... maybe they should just send me a bottle a month?

After Telford we headed back up the country to get back in time for Khaalid's senior school intake day, I did a load of washing and then we headed to Alton Towers with my beautiful Tina, DJ and my friend Bex. The boys hadn't been to Alton Towers since before we left the UK and had stayed at the Splash Landings hotel. Now they were older and able to ride the much bigger and faster rides – something they were both looking forward to. Being able to go one of the biggest roller coasters with Khaalid, due to his height, was amazing! I LOVED rollercoasters and to be able to share this love with him was awesome! To hear him scream with joy and exhilaration made me giggle so much. Naasir loved the Sonic the Hedgehog ride and was gutted he couldn't go on Rita or the Oblivion. When he saw Air he was so excited and even started to negotiate with the ride attendant to let him on. We were all in fits of giggles, this boy could charm the pants off anyone. Unfortunately this time, due to his height, there was no way he was getting his own way. He would have to grow at least another five centimetres. On the way to Leicester, the next destination for camping, Naasir came up with some hilarious ways of growing taller, everything from a stretching rack, to eating more veg to walking taller. This boy was determined. They both were, and they really were growing up to be smart, creative and adventurous, whilst developing much larger comfort zones than most kids their ages, bigger than some adults even. They had seen a lot in Egypt, and been through a lot since we had been back in the UK. They had done a lot of growing up.

This road trip had connected us in such a magical way, helped us all grow in so many others. Putting up tents together is akin to the Ikea flatpack relationship challenge! We spent so many hours just the three of us together in a car, in a tent on the rainy days, and I enjoyed teaching them so many different skills. It reminded us all of the days when I homeschooled them in Egypt, bringing back wonderful memories, and a whole lot of painful ones too. The longest trip that we did was heading on down to Exeter, then Torquay before venturing further down to Plymouth. We visited friends, slept in the car in our sleeping bags, parked up on coastal roads, falling asleep and waking up to the sounds of the sea. It really was the stuff childhood memories are made of. How do I know this? Because the boys are already recalling the memories of the nights we would be giggling and messing about, recalling the location and the holiday in which it happened.

Having a VW Sharan seven-seater, with only four seats in it and blacked out windows, we had the perfect road trip car. We had so much space and so much privacy, that even if someone came up to the car windows and looked in, they wouldn't be able to see in. It was our home on wheels for the entire seven weeks of the school holidays. We would clear the car out weekly, go in to the garage and have a water fight at the jet wash and just have great fun, no matter what we were doing.

After spending time catching up with Sarah and Irfan in Exeter, and Jay and Emma in Torquay, we spent another five days on the road before heading back up the country to visit my beautiful Poots, aka my lovely Tina. It was a flying visit as we were heading on up to Leicester to spend some time with DJ and his daughters. We had helped each other heal in so many ways, giving each other different perspectives, hugs and a lot of laughter. We would talk for hours, and became close in a lot of ways.

Arriving in Leicester at Watery Gates with DJ and his girls, we set up the tents whilst he started to get the fishing rods together. He had agreed to teach my boys how to fish. Just as the second tent went up, DJ had caught his first fish. Dinner was on him – and in the spirit of fishing, we had fish and chips from the nearby chip shop. Both my boys enjoyed learning to fish, and DJ was a great teacher. He had the patience of a saint with all three of the kids, getting the lines caught up in knots and calling his name. I don't think he got much chance to fish himself, until they all decided that they were going to go off and explore, climb trees, and of course when it came to lunch time and they were eating!

My boys and his daughter became good friends, and I became close to his youngest daughter. I even did a 'kidnapping' where I took her on a girlie road trip so he could have some time to just chill out and relax. She was so excited to be 'kidnapped' by me. Now for those who do not understand what this is, a 'kidnapping' is something that my friends and I have done with each other for over 20 years. It's almost like an intervention, but in the best possible sense of the word. I've done birthday kidnappings, clubbing kidnappings and respite care kidnappings, as this one was… and it was a whole lot of fun! We danced in car parks by the beach at night, we danced in the sea, we made up stories and we ate chocolate Lindt bunnies – after we had made up a play with the bunnies as the main characters! She really opened up to me about a lot of things; a very special girl with a heart so big.

The boys and I spent a wonderful few days in Leicester before heading over to my mum and dad's in the Fens, where we spent the final week of the holidays just chilling in the back garden, going to Hunstanton, Holkham beach (my favourite beach in the whole of the UK!) visiting my friend Jane on the way at her gorgeous little traditional sweet shop Mable's in Burnham Market (If you have never been, then you must! She has a ceramic painting studio above the sweet shop, with much more interesting ceramics than your 'average Joe' painting studio; and her milkshakes! Oh my days! Gorgeous! Mum and dad were really pleased with the toffee bon bons, coconut mushrooms and the fudge that I gave them when we got back. Dad did remind me that he had diabetes, but that didn't stop him from popping a bit of fudge in his mouth!

During this week, my and I were sitting outside in the garden in the gorgeous sunshine, when she told me that she was really proud of me for what I had done during the summer holidays and the way in which I was just getting on with things. We spoke about what it was like for her when she chose to leave my father, and the struggles she had, how she had gained her strength, and some of the cost cutting techniques she had used. My mum and I had never really talked about these things before, and I started to realise that living in Egypt during the Uprising, and getting divorced from ramO had bought me and my mum so much closer than we had ever been. I went to sleep that night with contentment in my heart, knowing my mum was proud of me, remembering all the things the boys and I had done, places we had visited and how excited they were to go on another road trip, I felt proud of myself and what I had created for the boys and I over the holidays. Felt grateful that I had found money off coupons for days out like Alton Towers, been frugal with my spending and resourceful with the items I already had in our home, and the friends around the country. I had managed to not dip into the money I had saved over the last five months, something I was also proud of myself for. That was for the business, the boys school trips, school uniforms and clothing. I fell asleep with a big smile on my face and woke up refreshed. Gratitude really is a beautiful thing to fall asleep with in your heart.

By the time lunch time had come around, the boys had already decided on the next road trip. We were off to Scotland for our summer road trip in 2015, and then Ireland the year after. In 2017 we were going to do a river boat trip and the year after that, a Mexican road trip for Khaalid's 16th. They had it all planned out. And who was I to argue!? When your children have this much passion and excitement about doing something, and have thought it through this much, you make it happen, rather than creating all the reasons why it shouldn't.

We were off to see Uncle John in Scotland, and we were going to go surfing and cycling, something that had already been discussed with ramO, but had been postponed due to the divorce. John was still up for hosting us, so the boys and I locked it in. The travelling trio and one dog were off to Scotland for a summer road trip – and boy, were we excited! I hadn't seen John in 18 years, and only then met him briefly. I knew his older brothers Alan and Dave. Alan more so, as he had made me feel really welcome when I first moved in with ramO. I would often stop by his home after work for a cup of tea. He was a very special guy, and just had such a warm heart. I felt protected when I was with him, and it was nice to be able to hang out with him and his friends, some of which I knew from raving, after work, instead of just going home and cooking dinner waiting for ramO to arrive home. Alan also gave great hugs, and being a huggy bear myself, that was all good with me.

Giving and receiving hugs was a big raver thing. We were a loving bunch and gave hugs freely. It had nothing to do with any sexual attraction, or intentions of 'getting it on' with someone, it was just an expression of love and friendship, something most townies who hang out in pubs never really truly understand; a raver friendship is something very special. Some of the best, and longest friendships I have to this day are from my raving days; and it would be a chosen few of these friendships that would get me through the next few years with their love and support, in more ways than I could ever have imagined.

FOUR

A JOURNEY OF SELF-DISCOVERY

After the holiday I felt energised. Having fun on the road with my boys, exploring the UK, growing stronger each day – the boys were in a much better place, mentally and emotionally.

Khaalid was excited to start at Birkdale, but sad to leave Mr Leighton, his favourite teacher at the prep school. Calming, loving and generous, Mr Leighton was the kind of teacher you could only dream of having for your children, and as a friend. The support that Mr Leighton, and many of the teachers at the prep school gave me and the boys during this transition period was overwhelming. For the boys to have such a supportive environment to be in during the day – an environment of some of the kindest people I have ever met – was a huge weight off my mind. I knew the boys were happy in school. They looked forward to going to school every day. Mr Leighton, Mr Oakey and Mr Kirkham had been incredibly supportive to Khaalid during his re-integration into the school environment. Helped me to help Khaalid understand and deal with the fact that the friendships he had with a few of the boys he'd left behind, were not the same. Khaalid had grown so much, seen so much and had a much deeper, emotionally intelligent view of the world than the other boys in his class. His questions were more mature, more insightful, and the tough times that he had experienced in Egypt had made him less materialistic and more grounded in himself, less needy of fitting in. He had become very just, more sensitive to others needs and incredibly aware of social issues; so much so I hadn't even noticed his growth, until I saw the behaviours and mindsets of the boys his own age. It was witnessing this, and the behaviours of some of the boys towards their parents, that created a distance between us and the other families. There were more 'chavs with cash' with a shallow and materialistic view of the world than there used to be. Many of the parents I had known prior to leaving for Egypt had already left, those I had seen whilst out and about told me, "I give you two years Dawn". At the time I hadn't known what they meant, but knowing them in the way I did, and their beautiful souls, as well as witnessing the behaviours I was seeing from both parents and children in the playground, it wasn't hard to put two and two together to come up with four.

Both my boys had developed my sense of speaking out when they saw something they didn't like, so much so that one day when Naasir saw one of the boys in his class throw his bag at his mother's feet and demand a snack, Naasir's eyebrows raised so much, they nearly hit the sky. He looked at me with a look of shock. When this young boy asked Naasir to go and play with him, Naasir turned to him and said, "I don't want to play with you. You're mean to your Mummy and I don't want to be friends with you. If you can treat your Mummy like that, then you can treat me like that." Seven years old. My heart exploded with pride. Both the boy and his mother looked shocked, the mother hurt and embarrassed. A few other mothers heard Naasir's comment and winked at me. I didn't say anything about the incident, I didn't have to. Naasir had said more than enough. I had always raised my boys to say what they thought and felt, and if this is what he felt, then that is what he felt. We needed to get to the gym for Naasir's swimming lessons, so we made our goodbyes and left.

Once in the car, I told Naasir I was proud of him for what he had said. His reply was simple, "Thank you Mummy; but why does his Mummy allow him to speak with her that way?"

"I don't know sweetheart, I don't know." But I had my ideas. I believed there were a multitude of reasons, mainly being she didn't value herself enough, and she didn't want to make a scene in front of the other mothers. Whatever her reasons, they were her own. I just know that I would never, and have never allowed my boys to be so disrespectful to me; and neither would any of my friends allow it.

After a couple of months, I noticed Khaalid was going inside himself a lot more. He wasn't sleeping, was becoming withdrawn and angry. I spoke with him about this and asked him if everything was okay. I spoke with our family support worker, Tariq El Habaashi, who had been referred to us by the MAST[1] and CAMHS[2] team here in Sheffield. A recommendation made to me by Mr Leighton to help us deal with the re-integration, recent death of my father-in-law and my divorce from ramO. We both spoke with Khaalid and Tariq went into the school to see Khaalid's Head of Year and it turned out that he was acting out in the classrooms, due to the bullying by a select few boys. The bullying that Khaalid was being subjected to was vile. Being called a terrorist, a jihadi, a member of ISIS and tormented not just on a daily basis, but an hourly basis. I was furious! *How come I had not been notified of this? And why, were children as young as this, so vulgar inside?*

For several weeks, back and forth I went to the school, and in the end it was agreed by the school, Tariq and I that for Khaalid's own safety I should remove him from the school. The bullies were allowed to continue to stay in the school, and for me that was just not acceptable. They were a cancer in the school, but due to the prestige of the families, nothing was done about their behaviour. Khaalid didn't have bruises, and it was him that reacted... but like I said to the head Dr Owen, "For every action, there is a reaction."

I also asked him when he was going to start taking emotional, mental and social bullying seriously. When he found a young boy hanging from the ceiling in the cloakrooms? He was not interested in dealing with the situation. And it was at this point I knew that Naasir would not step foot inside Birkdale Senior school, especially if Dr Owen was still in the headmaster position. The school really had changed. It used to mean something to be a Birkdale boy. The boys used to be polite, supportive and respectful; inclusive and welcoming, but now it only seemed to matter who your parents were, how big your home was and how much cash you had; a direct opposite to the philosophy that had been present in the school years before, and the one I had taught my boys: It doesn't matter how big your home or your wallet is, it is the size of your heart that matters. Birkdale Senior wasn't the right environment for us anymore, but due to teachers such as Mr Leighton, Mr Oakey, Ms Black and the lovely Mrs Roper, Mrs Riley and Matron at the Prep school, I chose to keep Naasir there for another year, which would give me a year to get Khaalid settled and then start going through the application process for Naasir to get into the school over the road.

I homeschooled Khaalid for a few months whilst the local education authority sorted out his new school placement at Forge Valley, which he was due to start in September 2015. He helped me around the house, studied a lot, dived deep into Stephen Covey's *The 7 Habits of Highly Effective Teenagers*, read Dale Carnegie's *How to Win Friends and Influence People*. I knew all the objectives that he needed to attain before starting school in the September, so if there were any tasks that needed to be done with the planning and preparation of my business, or material I was studying for The Coaching Academy, we would work on them together, creating a portfolio of work for him. I built him up again, and gave him lots of healing space. Then one Bank Holiday Monday the boys and I were in the local park with Kelt enjoying the sunshine, when I felt Khaalid's energy change. I looked over in the direction of where he was looking and saw the bullies from Birkdale. All in a gang of about 20 boys, and girls from the local girl's high. They were mocking us all, me included. Staring over in our direction, making vile comments that I just couldn't believe I was hearing.

Parents and adults who were also in the park looked horrified and when the group of bullies started to close in on us, several dad's formed a barrier around us and advised the bullies to go away. Several mothers offered to be witnesses for us and highly recommended we went to the police. Which we did, but the police were not interested. They went to the school, and the feedback I got was, "These boys come from good families, and are not the bullies you say they are. There is nothing we can do." I was disgusted. Once again, money and prestige had spoken; the bullies had gotten away with it, only to act as a green light for them to continue doing it throughout their schooling, their working career and their family life.

It wasn't just about what had happened to Khaalid, but what message the school and the police were giving these boys, and their parents. They believed they were untouchable. Weeks later I was approached by a mother in Sainsbury's who told me that although she was so upset to hear about what had happened to Khaalid, she was grateful that the bullying towards her son had stopped. I asked her how she knew about the bullying and she told me that he son regularly went home upset about what had been happening in class to Khaalid. Did she approach the school and tell them? Nope. She was only interested in protecting her own son, which I can understand to a certain point, but I have always believed that there are no bystanders in bullying. If you know it is happening and you do nothing, then you are as guilty as the perpetrators. I've always told my boys that if they see someone being bullied, they should speak up; hence why Naasir spoke up to the little boy who was incredibly rude to his mother.

During Khaalid's time off school we were planning the next road trip, this time to Scotland. He had great fun looking at the different places we could stop off at along the way. My friend John had told us he had organised some surfing and a few other activities for when we arrived with him. There was also the Tiree Music Festival, but we wouldn't make it in time. Ferry tickets over to Tiree were booked and a plan was forming. We were all really looking forward to heading up to Scotland, me especially as I was returning 'home' in a way, as my Grandfather on my mother's side was Scottish. I had never met him, but I had always wanted to explore Scotland, and now I was going to be doing it with my boys.

Money was still tight, but I had made a few sales for Vitality and had started putting the coaching into practice. I had saved enough money, and negotiated a deal with The Coaching Academy to enable me to pay off my course. I knew that for me to be able to make money to provide for the boys and I, I had to invest in myself and the business. I had attended four of the six accelerator days and had been studying well. Everything was on track and I was due to complete my qualification with them by the end of the year. Life was working out well, and I was healing from the pain caused by Babaa's death (my father-in-law, whom I was incredibly close to) and the pain caused by ramO walking out. I knew though, no matter how much pain had been caused, I was not going to let any ego or spitefulness get in the way of the four of us remaining a family. It wouldn't be healthy for the boys, or their future relationships. We were the adults, and we had to set a good example. We had to forgive each other for whatever had gone before and just get along with each other. This is why I had continued to send him photos of the boys on our road trip to Wales the year before, why I sent him photos of the boys that I took as the days went by; why I sent him the cinema tickets I got as rewards from Vitality for keeping fit and active. He was still their dad. We had had 18 great years together in my mind, so why throw all that away? The boys had asked if we could all have Sunday lunch together, and so I invited him for lunch. I had such a sick feeling in my stomach, and felt as though there was a hand around my throat, but I asked him, and he said he'd think about it. I had done all I could, and now it was up to him to sort his own stuff out.

I had done lots of healing through the study I had been doing, both for The Coaching Academy and the leadership books I had been studying. To be effective as individuals, organisations and global communities we had to lead, rather than manage. Too much these days was process led, people being expected to follow rules, which half of us knew nothing about, and many of which were redundant. I had seen so much redundant red tape whilst living in Egypt, and within the system here in the UK since I had been back. I had even mentioned to one of the ladies at the tax credits office that the system was encouraging people to lie, to withhold information and was creating more problems than it caused. I was told by the tax credits office that if I didn't work more than so many hours, I would be able to apply for this, this and that.

I replied, "Why would I say that, when it's not true?" The more people lie about what they are doing, or rather not doing, the more money gets paid out, the less there is available for those that really need it.

I had noticed what I call the 'credit card culture' growing at an incessant pace since I had been back. Whether it was the diet pills people were throwing down their throats instead of eating properly and exercising; or those God-awful ready meals with more preservatives and ingredients I can't even read – let alone know what they are – wrapped in far too much packaging. Like apple slices – I mean, who buys apples slices in a plastic bag? Just buy an apple and eat it! Or chopped onions in a plastic bag? Just buy and onion and chop it! It takes less than a couple of minutes. One of the things that shocked me the most was dried mash potato. Who on earth decided that that was a good idea? We're not in outer space, and even if we were... dried mash potato? No thank you! There's nothing better than proper old school mash potatoes, and using the starch water to make onion gravy with; and what about releasing any frustrations of the day out on the potatoes with a masher?

But then I understand the game. Make all the rubbish, processed food cheap, so the lower socio economic members of community can afford to buy it. It is full of unrecognisable ingredients which do goodness knows what to your body, with zero health benefits to it, increases all your sugar content because of the preservatives and extra sugar in the food, making so many people lazy due to lethargy, which increases diabetes and obesity, and then we end up with people distracted by their own health and constantly sick. And don't even get me started on the media circus that meant news channels were 24/7 and the quality of journalism was leading to the now popular phrase 'fake news', or these awful reality TV shows where everyone wanted to be famous so quickly that they were prepared to do, say or wear anything that would catapult them into 'celebrity stardom'. If TV shows weren't an overnight success then they were pulled. Imagine if *Only Fools and Horses* had been created today in these times? We'd have no more Uncle Albert and "In the war..." with a back and forth of his head and certainly no Del Boy falling through the gap in the bar. It would have never got past the pilot series and we wouldn't have the iconic series of classic comedy we have now.

I felt at odds with a lot of things, because here I was taking time to reflect on everything that had happened over the last decade starting off with me nearly dying during the pregnancy with Naasir, life out in Egypt during the Uprising, and now life as a single mum; and everyone else was wanting to bury their heads in the sand. I wanted to make some kind of sense of everything.

Why were the people I was coming across in the utility companies, the lettings agency or the Tax credits office such 'jobs worth'? Why were they not thinking? Why were organisations so controlling and not allowing people to use their own initiative? Why were companies still using an out-dated method of 9-5:30pm, without flexible working hours?

And why were the so-called leaders of our nations focusing the faults of others, rather than showcasing what they were really good at, and incorporating the good ideas of the other parties when it came to them winning the elections?

All I could see was a lot of people wanting to put out another light to make their own shine brighter, or pushing their heads so far up their own backsides, it came out at the shoulders to sit where it had originally started from. I knew why, because the less people thought for themselves, the more control the government had. The more fear that was stirred up by the media, the more people were divided. The more people stayed inside the less active they were, the more health problems and anxiety they got, so the more pharmaceutical drugs they had to take, which would result in them taking more drugs to compensate the side effects and so on, and so on.

We were being treated like a massive experiment, pawns in a chess game between the governments, pharmaceutical companies and that's before the Health & Safety Executives get involved with the insurance companies! People are becoming so conditioned to be gratified instantly, or becoming fearful, insecure and numb from all the toxins in their daily lives, and they are not taking time out to just be. To think about what they truly feel, what they truly want in life. We've got adults stressed out at work, hating their job, moaning about their colleagues, going home and presenting this image to their kids, and we wonder why the younger generations don't want to work?

It saddened me on a huge level, so much so I chose to add Career Coach to my list of coaching types that I would focus on. I would work with people stressed out from their jobs (which on average people only spend two months of the year at work if you minus sleeping, holidays, traveling, eating times from the total number of days) and work with schools, enabling future generations to really tap into who they are, what they love doing and create either their own company or choose a career they love, rather than have 'just a job'. This also meant that I would need to work with employers, so I added Business Coach & Mentor to my list of target markets. The 'jobs worth' had to go. So many processes had to go. As employers we needed to take a leaf out of Google's book and start engaging our teams more, and in some cases, start developing teams. We had to change the way we worked, how we impacted clients – regardless of whether they were from the public or private sector. There was a lot of work to do, and I was up for it.

Due to what I was seeing in the media and in society, I told the boys I didn't want to have the TV channels anymore. We had a family meeting about it and discussed the pros and cons. I explained I couldn't stand the level of toxicity that was being pumped through it, plus we were never there to watch it as we were out training most nights at the dojo or the gym. At the weekends when we were not training, we would be at the park, or at home playing a board game or sat reading. We are pretty old school in a lot of ways. The boys had an Xbox one which they used the TV screen for, and we had a selection of movies that we liked to watch, but when the weather was good enough to go out, which was only when there wasn't a downpour, we'd hit the road and go to the beach or to my mum and dads.

The boys put their views forward and they were pretty much the same as mine and so it was decided we would get rid of the TV – and, as Naasir put it – more money for ice creams on holiday! So the TV subscription went, and that meant another £40 in my pocket each month just from the TV license fee (although the TV licensing agency wouldn't accept it and kept hassling me and even got to the point of threatening me with court action and sending an official round to my home! I don't think so! I called them up and told them that if I received any more threats from them, I would be taking them to court for harassment. The letters soon stopped). Cancelling the BT TV subscription was also another saving; and with all the investments in coaching and mentoring I would be making to accelerate my results in all areas of life, and the up and coming school trips for the boys, making as many savings as I could was going to be essential; not to mention the clothes and shoes the boys needed due to their non-stop growth spurts.

Knowing I was the only income earner in the household was a pressure that I had never had before, and I didn't want to rely on any money that was, or was not coming from ramO. I had to make sure I was financially free and non-dependent on him. I needed a clean break. I wanted to be free from any control that he would have over me. Being reliant on him for money was holding me back in ways I didn't like. It was like a noose around my neck each month, wondering whether he would pay his contribution. He always did, and like I said before, I couldn't fault him on providing for the boys. He'd always been a great dad to the boys and I was glad he hadn't become like many of the absent fathers that I had researched and heard about for my book *The Wife*; a book I had written the synopsis for whilst out in Egypt. Whilst discussing the content of this book with someone they laughed and said, "You do realise you wrote yourself a self-help guide to divorce." Something I had never considered, but looking back now, even though I had never seen the divorce happening, and it was a total shock to me, maybe subconsciously I had known it was going to happen. I still loved the ramO that I knew, but with all the betrayal and the lies, the man I had known had died. I was still grieving, but had moved on in so many ways. I had even made a list of all the qualities in a man that I would be looking for. It was such a long list of qualities that my closest friend and chosen brother Rob, joked that I had priced myself out of the market.

Even my friend Zoe laughed at my list, but also told me not to negotiate on any of it. "If that is what you want, then you stick to it." Zoe had become a very dear friend. We had a lot of mutual friends and people couldn't believe we were not already friends. When she found out I had found a lump in my right breast, she drove up from Leicester to be with me at the hospital for my appointment to have it removed. The irony of the whole situation was the date. My wedding anniversary to ramO.

The day of the operation was really intense, and not just because I was about to have a lump removed. Lying on the operating table, tears started to roll down my face. Yes I was scared, but it wasn't about that. It was the lights, the smell and the green cloth. It was triggering memories of Naasir's birth that I had not previously had access to. My mind had blocked the memories due to the trauma of the events surrounding it. Slowly but surely though, I had a memory dump of Naasir's birth. Being in the hospital, the four lots of syntocinon I had, just to make me go into labour; the endless flood of consultants that were trying to get me to have a caesarean, which I was against having; and then the most magical memory of all, having Naasir handed to me – a memory so precious, so magical that it transformed my whole view of the situation surrounding his birth. I had always felt as though I had been butchered. That I had never 'given birth', that he was 'taken' from me. Having these memories download in my mind was so overwhelming, especially given the fact that I should have been sharing these with ramO, but I wasn't. I was alone. In a cold and lifeless operating theatre. Another reminder that I was alone.

Having found this lump, which thankfully was a cyst filled with toxins, had turned out to be a blessing. I could now piece together the memories friends had of Naasir's birth and my own newfound memories. I could now put them all together in a timeline of events.

Lying in bed the night of the operation, with my mum and dad in the guest room and thinking about how Zoe had travelled up to be with me, I knew I wasn't alone, but I was lonely. I missed having someone to cuddle up to. I missed sharing exciting, as well as fearful times with. I missed having the kind conversations that involved creating a life together, planning holidays together, planning adventures. I missed the intimacy that only a relationship can give you. Yes there is the intimacy you have with yourself, yes you can make plans with friends for holidays, but the companionship of a relationship was something completely different. I knew I was strong enough to be by myself. I knew I loved the single life, being free to make my own choices with regards to every area of my life. I realised I enjoyed setting a goal by myself and just going for it. I loved being able to do what I liked in the evening when ramO had the boys, whether that was watch a chick flick, or read a book and not have to talk with someone. I loved laying in the bath for hours, either singing away to my music or reading a book. I enjoyed the freedom I had of just going away from the weekend when ramO had the boys. I loved so many elements of being single, but I knew I was ready to move on. I didn't want to be alone. I want to share my life with someone special. I wanted to give and receive hugs and cuddles from someone other than my boys. I wanted adult hugs. I wanted kisses. Passionate kisses. I wanted to make love with someone. I wanted to share my dreams with someone. I wanted to share my success with someone. I wanted to hear about someone else's day, someone else's dreams, ideas, opinions and adventures. I want to fall asleep in someone's arms and wake up and watch them sleeping. 18 years with someone, and then with no one, had left an empty void. One I had filled with working hard and lots of exercise. But now I wanted more.

Surprisingly for me, I had had loads of offers. Something I had not expected. Some of ramO's last words resonated with me, that I would find it hard to find someone to love me; and I got it. He wasn't being nasty, at least I didn't see it that way at the time, but I knew lots of people liked the idea of me, but not the reality.

I am full on. An over achiever. I am a powerball of energy. I love to talk, debate and discover new knowledge. I am intense and relentless like the techno music that I loved so much (although these days it was only on nights out to my friend Jay's club TLI in Manchester that I got to lose myself on the dance floor to the music that had fuelled my soul for the last 18 years). I am also very loving, something that most men don't like (it's being needy apparently!). I like things done quickly, no messing about, no need to over complicate things, just getting things done. Having said that, I think a lot. I am a deep person and I like to have deep and meaningful conversations. I love learning, and sharing knowledge. I also want to be the best version of myself always. I giggle a lot. I am silly, I love being silly. I never sit still for five minutes, unless I'm writing a book... like at this moment... but even then I have been for three long walks, danced around my lounge, played with my dogs and done loads of ironing. I am always up-levelling. Pushing myself further and further. I also love a seriously random selection of music, food and books. I read lots. I love discussing politics. I love working out. I speak my mind. I take no prisoners and I will call you on your victim story. I love the ocean, I am a hippie with a back bone of steel and a heart of mush. I also say what I think, no holds barred, especially when pre-menstrual.

After spending 18 years with ramO travelling, I had a hunger for travel and adventure. I wanted someone who was going to be committed to a long-term relationship. I didn't do one night stands, or short term. I am old school in more ways than just my music. I wasn't bothered whether he had money or not, I could always make my own money, and one of us was always going to bring in more money than the other, so I just wanted someone who loved his job, and had a passion for the sea. He had to love the sea. I wanted someone who could and would cook, and had his shit together. Someone who would put me as a high priority in his life, someone who would be there for me when I really needed them; someone who was willing to put 100% into the relationship. I didn't want someone who expected me to be the 'little housewife', nor did I want someone who wasn't prepared to grow with me. I also wanted someone who liked cuddles. Lots of cuddles. I was a huggy monster. The list went on and on, especially in the areas of patience, and a calm nature. I wanted someone who challenged me and who also knew how to take care of their own health and fitness. I wanted someone who would be there for me, and show me he would be there for me. I wanted to be a priority, not fourth or fifth.

I got why Rob had told me I had priced myself out of the market. But I didn't care. I wanted a strong guy, would have to be willing to take me on. I didn't want a push over. I also didn't want someone who had any ink. That was a big no no. I wanted a man who was into adventure, knew how to do manual work, as well as being smart and a deep thinker. I wanted someone as silly as me, someone I could cook with, someone that valued loyalty and honesty. I wanted someone who would support and encourage, be there to hold me tight when the going got tough, and ultimately someone who loved me, valued me and would never cheat. Loyalty and honesty were big for me. So was patience and calmness.

The list I created cover four sides of A4 paper, and it still wasn't done. I knew what I wanted and I was going to focus on it to attract my new partner. I didn't care how long it would take. I wanted the right guy, and if that took two years or 20 years, then so be it. I was too busy focusing on my boys and building my business to have a man in my life anyway; but it was a good practice to do, to know what I wanted. No more lower priority, no more second best. No more cheating. No more lying. I was guarded, not just because I was scared about getting hurt again, but because I didn't want to allow someone to get close to the boys, and vice versa, before they, or I walked away. It was always going to be a forever and always, or nothing.

Just like my business in some ways, you either went for it 100% or you didn't… and if you didn't want to invest in yourself (or your business) then don't have a conversation about 'possibly wanting' coaching. You either want it or you don't'. You are either fully in, or not at all. No excuses. No victim story, no stress jealousy; just pushing on through every barrier that you faced, because that is where the growth came. I had only ever done business with people who I liked in my IT Software Development & Media Marketing company. If I didn't like someone's energy, then I didn't do business with them. As I wrote this phrase, I broke down. If I couldn't tell my ex-husband was cheating and lying to me and everyone we knew, not just others, then how on earth was I supposed to know if anyone else was lying to me. I had a meltdown. I realised I didn't trust anyone. And I mean anyone.

The boys had just reached that age, where they were testing the boundaries, and looking shifty when I walked in the room. I'd ask "What are you two up to?"

And as with all kids that age (I remember it well myself!) they'd say, "Nothing," looking even more shiftier than they did when I first walked in the room!

I'd smile at them and say, "Hmmm, I see."

They would also wind each other up, trying to get each other into trouble, again something really normal for siblings. The thing was though when one of them said what had happened and the other denied it, it activated me. I couldn't stand the lying. I'd get cross with them and one day I even said to them, "Your dad's lies destroyed our family, are you really going to follow in his footsteps?" The moment it came out of my mouth, I knew it was a step too far, and I took myself to my room and cried into my pillow. Like proper cried. How could I have just laid that at their feet when they were doing what normal kids do?

I started making myself wrong and I just kept crying, when there was a knock at my bedroom door. The boys stood there with a cup of tea, and a flower they had got from the garden. They stood there asking if they could come in, and when I said yes, Khaalid put the tea on my bedside unit and we all had a HUGE family hug. I apologised to them for what I had said to them, and reassured them that it was perfectly normal what they had done, and then I shared some of the things my brother and sister got up to when we were their age. It was lovely being able to share those memories with them, especially when the next time we went to my mums they had both remembered the stories and asked my mum all about them… solving some missing pieces in my mum's brain and I knew I was in for it when they both went to bed. 37 years old and knowing your mum is going to tell you off for something you did when you were 12 … feeling like you were 12 all over again. I laugh now, but boy was that an uncomfortable feeling!

One of the things I would discuss with the boys regularly, or at least when it was appropriate or relevant, were the happy times with ramO, and there were loads of them! I'd share memories of places we'd been to if they came up in conversation, or if we drove past somewhere. Or if a song came on that ramO would sing and play air guitar to; I wanted them to know all the happy times, and what a great man their dad was, how smart he was and how he was a great writer. There were so many great things about ramO, and the boys had a right to know how cool their dad was. Yeah, he'd done what he'd done with regards to our marriage, but as time went on, I began to realise how much courage he had shown by walking away, and I wanted the boys to know that. It couldn't have been easy at all. I thought about the courage it had shown, and then got 'My list' out. I started adding more qualities of the kind of guy I wanted, and why I wanted those qualities. The list was getting longer, and if Rob had thought I'd priced myself out of the market before, he was going to laugh his head off at the ever growing list that it had now become!

I giggled to myself thinking about all the things I loved about Rob and Alan. I had been friends with them for the best part of 20 years and they were my brothers from other mothers. What was it about them that I loved so much? Those qualities went on the list too. Then I REALLY laughed, a proper full on belly laugh, declaring myself priceless! That thought stayed with me for days. It was the first time I had felt so comfortable in my own skin and understanding my own self-worth. I was 37. It had taken me bloody long enough!

I walked around with a smile on my face for days. I felt so energised I knew I was ready to move on. I just had to find this impossible guy that was on my list. I knew he'd be out there, and if I had to wait years and years for him, then I would. It would give me the time my boys and I needed to do the stuff we wanted to do as the travelling trio and one dog, as well as give me time to build my business. I had a million to make in the next couple of years and I wanted no distractions. I knew I could do it. I had my books to write and sell. I had my coaching and mentoring. I had my public speaking gigs to do. It was just figuring out how to do it all whilst being a full-time single mum. But I would. The universe would deliver, I just had to be open to the endless possibilities and opportunities she sent my way.

And I was ready. I was in a good place; a great place. The happiest I had ever been; more confident than ever before. The divorce had been great for me in so many ways. Everything in my life was coming together, and for that I was truly grateful.

---

[1] MAST – Multi Agency Support Team
[2] CAMHS – Child and Adolescent Mental Health Service

FIVE
SCOTLAND, HERE WE COME!

As the end of term was drawing ever closer, Khaalid and I went through all the plans to make sure we had everything. We checked over the camping equipment, packed all the clothes needed, and then I spoke with John who wanted to know which ferry we were arriving on. I told him I hadn't booked them yet, and he laughed and said, "Well you'll need to, this is a tiny island Dawn, ferries to Tiree don't have much car space and they don't travel hourly. You'll have two a day and not every day of the week."

I quickly sorted out the tickets and confirmed when we would be arriving, sadly there were no ferries that would get us up to Tiree in time for the music festival, but that was cool. We were going surfing – at which point I remembered my wetsuit – the one I had used for my first ever open water swim in Lake Windemere, in the Lake District. I had set my target on the two mile circuit and was hoping to raise £500. I didn't quite get the £500 but I did complete the swim, and I was so pleased with myself. I had set myself a target and I had gone for it, and achieved it. Not that I doubted it for a moment, I knew once I set my mind to something I would do it. It was just the way I was. I was also training for a 10km run in Worcester with Rob, something that our other raving friend Lee would be joining us for. Lee was intimidating though. I'd nicknamed him 'Mr 10km in the blink of an eye' because he would do a 10km run every weekend. He was incredible! He had raised so much money for charity over the years with his Coast to Coast cycle ride, endless charity runs, cycle rides and he was someone with such a big heart. I'd even added some of Lee's qualities to my 'list'. Whoever this man was, he was going to be amazing, and I would call that in by being so focused on what I wanted.

We collected Naasir from school at lunchtime on the last day of term and gone home to put his uniform in the wash. I had made sure all the laundry was done and with the car packed up and ready to go, school uniforms washed and ironed for when we got back at the end of the summer. There was nothing left to do other than head on up to Scotland. First stop was Blackpool. We had been there for the weekend months before and the boys had wanted to go in the Pleasure Beach. This time they were going to get to go in, with Kelt and I watching... when it wasn't my turn to go on the bigger faster rides. I knew that we all wanted to go on the rollercoaster together so I would just tie Kelt up as we do when we go to the fairs or on the rides on the piers across the country.

We pulled up in the car park behind the cinema in Lytham St Annes, a place we had stayed on our previous visit. The beach was empty and so Kelt had the run of the beach to himself, as did the boys. We walked right out to the water's edge, which was so far out it took us the best part of 30 minutes to get to it. Kelt didn't care. He was having a whale of a time. He loved the beach, wasn't so keen on the sea though, but the beach. The reminded me of the time we were in Barmouth the year before and how Kelt had chased the Lurcher around the beach, which then created a cascade of wonderful memories of that holiday, and all the weekend road trips we had had together since. Naasir made up a song about the travelling trio and one dog, and started strutting his stuff. Back at the car park Naasir climbed on the wall and started balancing across it, and got me to film him as he went. His narration was hilarious! Seriously this boy... makes me giggle until my sides ache. I just love him. He is so confident and outgoing, a proper little charmer. Full of adventure and up for pretty much anything. I am so proud of the way both my boys own who they are and how they continually make the best of everything, and their gratitude... so grateful for everything.

We slept in the car that night, after having washed and cleaned our teeth in the public toilets in the cinema. Naasir was out for the count but Khaalid and I stayed up for ages chatting and giggling. These were the moments that I enjoyed the most, having random non-stop conversations with the boys. Their minds were big, understanding greater than many adults. They continually impress me with their thoughts, ideas and opinions. Ask anyone who knows my boys and they will tell you the same thing, teachers, neighbours, family members and friends.

The boys had such a great day on Blackpool Pleasure Beach. I unfortunately didn't get to go in with them as I had Kelt. Dogs weren't allowed inside the funfair area, and I wasn't going to leave him in the car during the heat of summer. The security guards were great! They worked with me to make sure my boys got to go inside, and were safe. I did struggle with leaving them alone in the theme park; it had been the first time I had done anything like this. But how would I know I could trust them, if I didn't trust them? I was reminded again at this point about how much easier it would be if there were two parents, together; but there wasn't, it was just me.

Then it occurred to me, leaving my boys under the watchful eye of the security team was no different to me leaving the boys under the watchful eye of the lifeguard by the pool at the gym, whilst I was upstairs lifting weights. What was I so worried about. Get a grip Dawn! The lead security guard on the door could tell I was apprehensive, so took a photo of my boys with me and made sure that the photo was shown to all the other security guards in the park. The boys knew exactly which rides they wanted to ride and so the head security guard radioed the ride operatives and sent a security guard with the boys to that area. I was so impressed with the way in which the security handled the situation, enabling my boys to ride the rides, for me to honour my promise and the way they helped me show the boys that people can be trusted, my boys included. I knew they were responsible, I knew they were well behaved and I trusted in the security guards. It takes a community to raise children after all. I had always believed this and now I was trusting in it.

I went for a walk on the beach with Kelt, went back to the car and got my book, and then went back to the café by the entrance of the Pleasure Beach. I went up to the gates and made sure the guards knew where I was and we had a great chat about how kids these days were so wrapped up in cotton wool, and not given the chance to show themselves as capable and responsible. How can kids accelerate and grow in confidence and responsibility if they are never given it by the adults that surround them?

Whilst we were chatting, the guard radioed his colleagues and all the security were reporting back that the boys were great, and how it was a pleasure to speak with such smart kids. They all knew which ride the boys were on and asked if I was ready for them to leave. I told them the boys were more than welcome to stay until the rides shut if they wanted to, as I was going to read my book and have a cup of tea. Before I went to sit down, the head of security thanked me for trusting them. He also said it had been a privilege to take care of such great kids, working together as a team to make sure the boys had had a great time, something they had thoroughly enjoyed. I was so grateful to hear this and thanked the head of security for what he had said, and told him that I believed that people were generally really great, helpful and trustworthy, it is just the media and the governments that tell us otherwise. At the end of the day my boys were 12 and 8 years old, and more than mature enough to go to the park on their bikes by themselves, walk the dog by themselves around the block or to the park. They had to be, I was a single mum who could be ill at any time; they needed to know how to take care of each other and themselves. They were also responsible enough to cook a meal by themselves and they knew that there is safety in numbers. The boys being in the Pleasure Beach, under the watchful eye of the security with me in the café outside was no different to them being in the park play area with me sat outside the park café.

Several chapters and a vanilla milkshake later, I heard the boys call out to me. I looked up and saw HUGE smiles across their faces, with the head of security with an arm around each of them; all of them smiling. As Kelt and I walked over, Kelt's tail wagging as though it was about to fly off, the security guard once again praised me on raising two very well behaved and polite boys. He'd heard nothing but great things about them from his team. He congratulated the boys on their behaviour and told them they were great kids. Gave them a voucher for an ice cream and told us all to enjoy our holiday. The boys shook the head of security's hand and wanted to go and get their ice-creams, so that's what we did.

On the way back to the car, we were planning on whether to stay another night in Blackpool or head on up to Scotland. The boys were so excited about the next phase we headed on up to a place called The Green Welly, in CrianLarich just North of the Trossachs, which we were going to stop at on the way back. We were making good time, and should be there for a late dinner. When we arrived, we had just missed the café, so I got some mince beef from the shop, got the pesto out of the camping box, and made burgers whilst Khaalid and Naasir got the fire pit ready for a barbeque. Their fire making skills were really coming along nicely, both paying attention to safety and wind direction. As they had got the fire going, Khaalid asked for a hot drink, so I sent him to the Green Welly shop for two hot chocolates and a cup of tea for me. The hugs they gave me for the hot chocolate! Khaalid's map reading skills and Naasir's eagle eye for the road signs along the way meant we hadn't taken one wrong turning. I think a hot chocolate was a well-earned treat.

We sat by the fire eating our burgers and salad when I asked the boys how they were getting on with their books they had bought along on the trip. Khaalid told me he had already read three of them and Naasir was close behind on two books. We'd only been on the road a few days! The following morning it was time for a shower, so we took advantage of the shower facilities at The Green Welly. Whilst I was in the shower the boys stayed by the car with Kelt getting their breakfast before putting the breakfast things away. I got back expecting to put away the fire pit and the ashes, but they had both done it already; and done a fantastic job too! Everything was in the car ready to go, so the boys went and had their showers, one after the other and I sat on the picnic table outside the shop smiling to myself. This was already a great holiday.

When we arrived in Oban we needed to get some gas for the camping stove, and whilst we were there, one of the guys pointed us in the direction of a loch just past the Connell Bridge that had several parking spots and told us about a space large enough for a tent and a car. It was just by a farmhouse, so off we went and boy was it a nice spot! We camped there for a good three days, just the travelling trio and one dog. Paddling in the loch, playing with Kelt, leaving the tent whilst we went into Oban to look at the ferries coming in and out, knowing we would soon be on one of them heading over to Tiree. We cooked so many different meals, and the boys were getting more and more adventurous. They were loving all the tress to climb and exploring alongside the loch. Khaalid was charged with building the campfire every night and so they both spent the day collecting wood for the fire.

On the final night by this loch the weather had turned, and the wind had got up. Naasir had been asleep for a good hour by the time Khaalid and I turned in, Khaalid out like a light. I lay there and started to listen to the wind. Almost drifting off I noticed the tent was being blown quite hard. I was getting nervous. This wind was getting stronger and stronger. If we didn't get the tent down we would be in the loch! I jumped out of bed and woke Khaalid up. I told him to wake his brother up, I was going to move the car so it acted as a barrier to the wind. No chance! That tent had to come down now! So Khaalid and I flew into action and that tent was down so fast with everything thrown into the back of the car – apart from the camping kitchen and stove. They were protected by the car, they would be fine. We all got in the car and just started laughing, well apart from Naasir, he was fast asleep again! But Khaalid and I were in fits of giggles. We were laughing so hard we were both crying. It was certainly a story to tell!

We decided to move to another spot just outside of the town and this time it was a freshwater loch, with loads more trees! The boys were so happy! But just as we were halfway through putting the tent up the rain came down... and not just a little bit of rain either, torrential rain! I told the boys to stay in the car I would finish putting the tent up; but I couldn't see anything due to the rain running down my face. I could have stopped, but I was nearly finished and being a stubborn little madam, as my mum called me, I pushed on. I cursed ramO, not that he would have ever come camping in the first place. I cursed the rain. I cried my eyes out. I was tired, cold and wet. What had I been thinking doing all this by myself? I went into full-on victim mode and then started laughing at the absurdity of doing so. I managed to finish putting up the tent, with sleeping bags and air mattresses in as the rain stopped... just as I was finishing with the tent. We all snuggled up inside and we were nearly asleep when I felt a rain drop on my forehead. What? That can't be right.

So I ignored it. And then came another, and another. There was something wrong with the tent, so waking the boys up again, we ran back to the car with our sleeping bags and slept in the car that night.

Waking up Khaalid and I looked at each other and all he said to me was, "Drip, drip drip… the winds getting up!" and we both started giggling, waking Naasir up in the process. He wanted to know what we were laughing at but the more we tried to explain it, the more we laughed, the more we couldn't get our words out, the more our sides ached from laughing. Naasir wasn't happy he wasn't part of the joke but he was really happy that the sun was shining and there wasn't a cloud in the sky.

The boys and I went into the town to get some breakfast, leaving the tent behind for when we got back. We needed fuel for our bodies before we could even think about sorting out the tent. When we got back it was a case of just adjusting some of the pegs and the guide ropes. Nothing major, and so we set about making camp in this gorgeous spot. We spent another three days in the area. Oban was a cool little town, and we loved the Cuan Mor Restaurant on George street, not only because they allowed us to take Kelt in with us, but also because the food and service was amazing! They were also welcoming of us, even though we had only been able to wash our bodies and hair by boiling the kettle and using a bowl by the tent and using baby wipes all over. We didn't smell, and our clothes were clean, but a lovely hot shower would have been nice… a hot bath would have been even better! Roll on arriving at John's!

John and I had kept in touch with messages and I had pre-warned him that we all needed a shower. He told me there was one on the ferry, except there wasn't as we were on a different ferry, the smaller one. A quick wash down in the disabled toilets it was then! Arriving at the ferry terminal on Tiree I couldn't help think what a beautiful island it was. The boys were looking out for Uncle John and then we spotted him. I pulled the car over, jumped out and ran to him, giving him a big hug. I hadn't seen him in 18 years, other than by Facebook photos. It was so good to see him! He climbed in the car and said hi to the boys, who bombarded him with questions, which he never really got chance to answer because we were back at his home in less than two minutes! I knew he said he lived close to the ferry terminal but this made me giggle!

Walking into his home felt like home. It was spotless, tidy, organised and clean. So much nicer than most other guys places, and much more comfortable than the tent had been! It would be nice to sleep in a proper bed tonight.

John showed us to our room and made a cup of tea. We were all a bit hyper and excited so we went for a walk down to the shops to get some food for the next few days. I liked John's choice of ingredients and was looking forward to cooking with him in a kitchen, rather than cooking on a campfire. On the way to the shops we messed about on the rocks. I wasn't really dressed for rock climbing as I had a tight jersey dress on with my Adidas Gazelles. Still I was game for anything, and made sure I was still as ladylike and modest as I could be. The boys were loving it, so was Kelt! He was back on a beach again. We all were. I had spent most of the ferry crossing up on deck, after having got washed and changed, a place I loved to be. After about an hour of messing about we headed back to John's and the boys had proper showers whilst John and I cooked. It was like synergy cooking with him. We just flowed together. We talked non-stop and it was so natural to be in his company. It was like putting on a pair of your favourite slippers, they just fitted you perfectly. We talked about everything and anything. We concentrated on prepping the veg for the dinner. We had comfortable silences. It was nice to have this space between us after all these years. This to me was a sign of a good friendship we had built over the years, simply based on me knowing his older brothers, and watching his journey at sea. I had only allocated three days to be with him as I thought that would be enough, just in case we didn't gel as well as friends in real life, as we did virtually. But I needn't have worried. He was so interesting and funny. His energy was so calming, just like his beautiful photos of the sea, the sunsets, my favourite foods, all caught from the boats he fished from. Here was a guy who not only could dive for my favourite foods, but also knew how to cook it. Bonus! We were going to eat well over the next few days! And we did! We enjoyed delicious food cooked in his kitchen, but I still wanted to cook on a campfire and barbeque on the beach and in his back garden. We had sunny days, why would we not?

The day we went surfing was fantastic! Khaalid had a lesson from the guys at Blackhouse Watersports and John and I took it in turns to help

Naasir, as he didn't want a lesson. He soon got bored of the sea and went to play on the beach, leaving John and I doing our best to ride the waves. Naasir was on the beach pretending to surf and then fall over every time we fell off the board, but then he got bored and started to play by himself in his own little world. Khaalid was doing amazingly well in his lesson, and was loving it! He was a natural surfer, and was getting so confident, that it did scare me a little; but then I hadn't just had a lesson and he had. There was a moment when he went a little too far out, in which I panicked, but another guy in the ocean swam over to Khaalid to bring him in a little closer to the shore line. Khaalid was buzzing and so excited about being able to ride a wave… consistently, time and time again. He was also pretty good at knocking me off my board and laughing. Seeing him this happy after the trauma he'd been through over the last 18 months was so heart-warming I thought my heart was actually melting!

The four of us joined Marty and the other surfers for a barbeque on the beach that night and it was such a great night. I however was not impressed when I realised I had lost my blue mirrored Ray-Bans. I loved those Ray-Bans! But it was my fault and I have no one else to blame. If I want my boys to take responsibility for their things, then I have to as well.

The time with John was magical. I knew there was a strong connection between us and to be honest, I didn't want to leave. I could have stayed with him on the island for a lot longer, but we were expected at friends in Durham and Middlesborough before heading on to my mum and dads in Friday Bridge. As I hadn't known how John and I would get on, I had four extra days in the plan to go and camp somewhere else, but we stayed with John, and I made some bread. Now when I say bread, it wasn't really bread, more like a dead weight that could be used to anchor a small rowing boat! It was so hard and heavy that when we dropped it on the floor to see just how heavy it was it landed with a thud and didn't actually break. None of us could stop laughing, how had I got it so wrong? It did, however, make it a bit weaker so when we tried to break a bit off, the corner actually snapped off. Do we dare leave it outside for it to soften and let the birds and gulls eat it? I set myself a new challenge, to make really nice light and fluffy bread. The next day's bread wasn't much better either… and one of John's friends who came over asked, "Who's made cake?" whilst trying to break a corner off… again too hard and not edible in the slightest. Now I really was on a mission to make the best bread I could!

I started to look at the amount of days left and told John the boys and I would be leaving the next day. I really didn't want to go, but the boys and I had a schedule. John said he would come with us and take us to Loch Coille-Bharr in Lochgilphead, where the beavers had been introduced. We were also going to go over to Tayviallich so I could visit his brother's graves. I'd not had the chance to visit and say my goodbyes before, so really wanted to go and say goodbye at their graveside. We also went onto the Kilmartin Museum and watching John with the boys through all of these was making my attraction to him stronger. His knowledge of nature, the local area, the way he was so patient and calming with them. I had never seen Khaalid be so open and at peace with someone before. All the time in my head, repeating: *No, I do not want this. It is not the right time. It is too soon.* But the moment he'd look in my direction and smile, I knew that I wanted a relationship with him. Just not right now. I was building a business. The boys and I were happy by ourselves. Things were fine just as they were, but I knew what I felt; and I knew he felt it too. Grrr! This is not what I came on holiday for! This was a road trip for the travelling trio and one dog, not Mummy has a holiday romance! But I knew it was more than that for me, and I hoped it would be for him too. I was scared out of my brains though. I had spent 18 years with ramO and that had only ended 16 months earlier. It was too soon.

SIX

ARE YOU DAWN?

The boys and I were headed towards Glasgow when John asked if he could carry on the journey with us to Glasgow. The butterflies that this sent through me! So, of course – I said yes! He said he wanted to show me a proper princess castle, one that he had taken his daughter to many times before. The one where they had filmed the *Downton Abbey* Christmas Special. Did I want to see it? Too right I did! To know ITV and Maggie Smith (and the cast of Downton) had filmed one of my favourite shows there was all I needed to know before agreeing. I didn't let on that I like Downton just yet, but I knew Michey would be so excited to see the photos.

We arrived in Inveraray around lunch time and walked around the local shops. There was a shortbread shop, a traditional tartan shop called The Wollen Mill, The Loch Fyne Whiskies shop, all the quaint little shops you were expect in the vicinity of a castle such as this one. Having travelled the world over the last 20 years from as far as the USA, Australia, Europe, the Middle East and the Gulf, I naturally do a risk assessment of the area, more so since the boys and I had been wild camping, and me travelling alone as a single mum. I do it without even registering I'm doing it. It has become second nature to me, not only because of my travelling but also because of the work I have done over the last 20 years. Working on regional and community regeneration, I have been highlighted for many community projects as a leader and a volunteer, working with projects with such as one I did in Sheffield, where children are sent out to sell themselves or drugs for their parents, you learn a lot. You pick up clues such as is there any graffiti? Is there any litter? Were there any foreigners in the area, and how were they treated? What jobs did they have, or were they on the streets & destitute? How many shops were boarded up? Was it a ghost town? Were the locals friendly to outsiders? What was the street lighting like? Was the town in need of regional regeneration? What were the younger members of the community like? Were there any suspicious looking individuals 'hanging around' the streets? How many pubs were in the area? If so, what were they like? We hadn't known whether we were going to stay in the car for the night or stay in one of the two hotels. But when we had parked up, I knew we wanted to sleep in the car and set the alarms to watch the sun come up over the loch. It was going to be so beautiful, and I was content with what I had gathered from the local area that it was a safe area to sleep in the car, and if the boys wanted to they could play on the grass areas by the loch. There were a couple of little funfair rides for toddlers and small children on the grass area, so I reminded them to be careful.

As we were parking the car on Front Street East, John noticed one of the boats moored up along the pier. He started telling us about the 'wee boat' call the *Vital Spark* which was featured in the 1950s BBC TV show *Para Handy*; all about the life at sea of a lovable rouge. There was another ship that was moored up and it needed a lot of love and attention given to it. I started a cost analysis in my head of what I could see it needed, with John joining in, before I went on to come up with ideas of how to make money on a ship like this and how amazing it would be to be able to implement all of these elements.

I knew in that moment that all the dreams I had had as a little girl, were about to become a reality. I would have my own ship. I would sail around the world, learning about different cultures, having a mad adventure, just taking life as each wave took me. I wanted to go for it; looking at John, I knew that he would be the one to do it with. But then I got scared again. Yes, we'd been friends for years, and we'd got on really well over the last few days, but how could I be so sure of this? I just knew it. I felt it. It was just my head space that was getting in the way. My fears of rejection, but I knew that this was the guy I wanted to sail away with.

John and I took the boys and Kelt up to the castle, and we were disappointed that it wasn't open. As it was passed five o'clock we just assumed it was closed for the day, so we just looked at the architecture and the cannons. Again, John was impressive with his knowledge, and his willingness to share it with the boys was so endearing. I was in my own little world pretending I was walking around with the dowager and Mary, listening to the sarcasm that flowed so easily from their minds and off their tongues. I started giggling and got all excited! This really was a princess castle and I felt like a princess! We would come back tomorrow after breakfast and have a proper look inside and a walk around the gardens. I couldn't wait to show Michey the photos!

We were all getting hungry so we headed to The George Hotel, just a couple of minutes' walk away. We were really pleased that the hotel allowed us to take Kelt in with us for dinner, I didn't think there would be a problem, especially with the look, feel and vibe of the place, and I was right. We took our time over dinner just enjoying the food, the roaring fire and the excellent service from the team there. One of the things I have studied and spoken about on radio and at events is cultural diversity. I even wrote about it in my first book *Friday Bridge*. The team in the hotel comprised of a young lady who had lived in Inveraray for almost ten years. She was from Bulgaria, just outside of Sophia, a place I had been to, so we chatted for a good ten minutes about how beautiful her country was and some of the issues facing it; some of the reasons being why she was here in the UK. She really liked the local people and the area. The barmaid was from Barcelona and she also reported that it was such a great area. Everyone was really friendly, welcoming and it was really safe. I could tell this when we initially drove into the area. There were the obvious signs such as the quality of the shops, the prices of the items in the shops, the well-kept grass area by the memorial, the lack of litter, and the way in which people responded to me and the boys. My boys are obviously from an Arabic decent from the way they look, Khaalid more so than Naasir; and with me flipping between English and Arabic all the time, only just becoming aware I'm doing it, when you go to some places, the locals don't like it. The looks you get, the standoffish 'you're not welcome here' vibe. But you get used to it, and you know it says more about them than it does about you. It is their ignorance, fears and insecurities, in part created by the media and the government.

The boys asked if they could go back to the car, and feed Kelt whilst I finished my coffee and John finished his own drink. We were no longer than 15 mins, as we'd stopped at McColls to obtain a bottle of pinot grigio. I knew I couldn't have more than a glass at most, as I'd already had a couple of glasses with my meal, and would be driving the next morning. As John and I arrived at the car, both Khaalid and Naasir had fed and watered Kelt, and were happily playing by the car. John then proceeded to play with the boys, spinning them around and chasing them. I was getting the sleeping bags out of the boot of the car and playing with Kelt, when he jumped out of the car and ran off. The boys and John went around one side of the building and I was about to go around the front when Kelt was brought back to me by three very polite and kind young girls, aged 15-18. I thanked the girls we had a long conversation about the local area. What it was like growing up in the area? What kind of opportunities were available to them? What was the relationship like between the castle residents and the locals? I also wanted to know more about the ship that was docked along the small pier, which I had found out was for sale at £89,000. I spent around 45-50 minutes talking with these young ladies, who told me about the Inveraray Jail House Museum and recommended that I should take the boys the following day before we left for Durham.

I carried on unpacking the sleeping bags and blanket from the bags they were in, watching John and the boys play together, whilst Kelt was sat beside me as I worked out the schedule for the next day and the budget that was remaining. I noticed the time was about 11:05pm and called to the boys that it was time to get ready for bed, especially as we wanted to watch the sunrise in the morning. They got the baby wipes out and wiped their faces with the wet wipes and cleaned their teeth. The boys took about 15 minutes to do this and get into the car ready to sleep. Whilst the boys were getting ready for bed, I asked John if he had checked, and if he had, could he remember how much the castle was to visit and if he remembered the opening times. I knew I had forgotten to check the kiosk. He said he hadn't. I suggested that we put the boys into

CROSSING THE LINE   75

the car, and then walk to the castle which was no more than 800 metres away, feeling the area was incredibly safe, and posed no risk to my children, simply to check the opening times and prices. I also wanted to see if the castle was lit up at night like a lot of other castles I have visited across Europe, Belgium coming to mind straight away. Both John and I made sure the boys knew we were going to walk to the castle, left my mobile with them, showed them where the toilets were next to the car. I joked with them to either make sure they either held it in or tied a knot in 'it' and to call me to let me know they were going to the toilet, so I knew not to worry when we got to the car in about 15 minutes. To prevent the alarm going off, I left the key in the ignition, reminded them the rules were the same as when they cleaned the car at home. I knew they could be trusted as they often cleaned the car at home with the keys in the ignition, again to prevent the alarm going off, but to also prevent them locking the keys in the car, having left them on the seat, as Naasir had done before. Oh how the AA man had had that kind of call out before! Leaving the key in the ignition was the best way to prevent it he said, so that's what we did! I had always wanted the boys to understand how to make and save money, and if they wanted to earn their pocket money, then cleaning the car, and learning how to be responsible around cars was essential. Allowing the boys to clean the car, was also a great team building exercise between them, each one agreeing which job they were going to do and which music they would be listening to… and singing along to! Khaalid has a great voice and Naasir has got the moves… and the hair!

As John and I are both very physically fit due to his work out at sea diving and sailing; and my mixed martial arts, long distance swimming, hiking and gym workouts, we knew we would be no longer than 15 minutes. John had bought the bottle of wine with us, because I'd reminded him that drinking in the street in the UK is not allowed. We crossed the property line of the castle, started walking up to the kiosk and checked the cost and opening times. As we turned to head back down the path, I noticed some big black things moving in the field. I also noticed that the castle was not lit up with spotlights, which was very disappointing as this would be a great addition to such an intricate and beautiful building. Both John and I sat down by the field to identify the big black things moving around, which we identified as large bulls with horns. I then laid down for a couple of minutes to look at the stars as there was little to no light pollution obstructing the night sky.

I told John about a time when I had been in the Berber Atlas Mountains in Morocco, where my friend Teema and I were on our way back from our mutual friend's wedding, when I told her cousin to stop the car. He pulled over in the layby and I got out and lay down on the floor, just looking at the stars in the sky. Teema thought I was crazy, but I just told her that when I looked at the stars in the sky, they made me realise just how incredible our universe is. These massive stars appeared to be so tiny, and it really does put things into perspective. Stars keep you humble if you look at them from a non egocentric way, and they certainly put me in my place when they sparkle in the sky like they do when there is no light pollution! We got up straight away and I said to John, "Come on, we said we'd only be 15 minutes, it's getting close to that now."

He'd opened the wine and I'd had a little bit, but the rest was for him. I was still very much in the frame of mind that I needed to be in control all the time. Not just because I was driving, but also because… what if something happened to the boys, or Kelt? I needed to keep my mind sharp and my wits about me. We started to walk back to the car, talking and laughing. When we got to the bottom of the drive and was about to cross the road back to the car, we noticed what we thought was a policeman. I didn't think anything of it to be honest; I knew we hadn't done anything wrong, so knew he wouldn't be looking for us. Maybe there had been an accident or something.

And a something it was, and still continues to be.

Upon approaching the car the man called out, "Are you Dawn?" (I asked him to repeat this as I didn't understand him the first time, due to his heavy accent, to which I tuned into very quickly as I have worked as an English Second Language tutor for adults and children, from many countries ranging from the Arab World, Vietnam and South Asia).

I replied, "Yes, I am, what's the matter?"

His response, in an aggressive tone was, "You've abandoned them."

I was shocked. Beyond belief. Why was he talking about the boys? What had happened? My stomach flipped and I ran the next few metres to the car. I opened the back left door, where I found Naasir crying in his seat. I asked him "Idah Baaba? Li kidda? Ma3'lesh! Ma3'lesh!" (What is the matter Baaba? Why this? Why are you crying? It's okay! It's okay!)

Before Naasir had time to answer me, the male arresting police officer, who had made his way to the car, started raising his voice in an aggressive manner telling me repeatedly, "Stop being aggressive to your son."

I tried to inform him I wasn't being aggressive, I was asking him why he was crying and telling him it was going to be okay, but he kept on talking over me and shouting me down. I wanted to speak with Naasir to find out what was wrong.

The police officer kept repeating the accusation of, "You've abandoned your kids, you've neglected them and abandoned them."

I mean, who says that in front of children to their mother? I continued to try and tell the officer I had done nothing of the sort and wanted to calm my child. The police officer then started to demand repeatedly I give him my full name, date of birth. Again there was no space given to me to answer the questions. I again stated I wanted to calm my child as he was becoming more agitated with the aggression directed at me by the police officer. I turned to the police officer and informed him that I was not going to be intimidated by his police uniform, high visibility jacket and his bullying tactics. I returned my attention to Naasir, where upon John stepped in and gently told me to speak with the police officer whilst he saw to Naasir.

I was then moved away from my car by the police officer, where he continued to fire question after question at me, without giving me a chance to answer any of his questions. I asked him to slow down and told him I could not answer his questions whilst he continued to fire question after question at me. I had managed to state my name, date of birth and address, but after many attempts. After approximately 10 minutes of this aggressive attitude from the male officer, another police car turned up with two female officers in. One of the female police officers, came striding over to where I was with the male officer, with an aggressive look on her face. Her whole demeanour suggested she was looking for a fight rather than seeking to understand the situation that was unfolding before her. She stood to the right hand side of me, whilst the male officer was to the front left of me.

The male officer continued to fire question after question at me, but was still not giving me the space to answer his questions, so I turned to the female officer and asked her, "Are you going to encourage your colleague to listen to my answers or are you just going to stand there and allow him to speak with me in this way?"

The next thing I knew I was being strong armed into handcuffs, with my wrists behind my back and bundled into the back of the police car, informing me I was breaching the peace. I asked, "How was this breaching the peace? Please tell me how being asked to be heard is breaching the peace?"

At this point I became really scared, incredibly frustrated and disappointed in the policing that I was experiencing. I was in the back of the police car for quite some time, as they were running their various polices at passed midnight on a Monday evening, in the middle of the school holidays. Whilst I waited in the back of the police car, I tried to explain my current situation as a single mother, about our road trips, who I was, the kind of work that I did, just so that the arresting police officers would hopefully see sense and stop this ugly mess before it went any further. Eventually, in the early hours of the morning, after having waited a long time to hear back from Social Services about what would happen to my children, I left my car, my dog and my banking details with John to take care of. The boys were both put into the back of the police car with me, whilst the other female police officer, who I later learned was called Nicki, woke Khaalid up and bundled him into the back of a police with me and Naasir. As Khaalid was coming round he saw Nassir upset, but no longer crying, next to me in a pair of handcuffs. Not the kind of thing you want your child to wake up and, and what an image to have seared into my sons mind. I was confused. How was me going to check the castle times neglect and abandonment? It was no difference to me going camping and going to the shower block and leaving the boys in the tent whilst I had a shower. I mean they couldn't come in the shower block with me, they are grown boys. The only thing was the car wasn't closed with zips, and was a lot more secure. I spoke with the boys and did my best to answer their questions about what was happening. I had no idea what was happening, so I explained that this was a big misunderstanding and this is why we should always learn to listen to people, reminding

Khaalid of the Steven Covey habit 'seek first to understand' because when we don't, a lot of time, energy and resources are wasted, and a lot of upset and fear caused. I told them we were going to be okay, and that I'd sort everything out when we got to the police station.

Once we arrived at the police station, I was taken away from my boys. I was told to leave them in a police car for other police officers to take care of them. I was extremely unhappy and devastated about this as I was not able to give either of my children a hug or a kiss. Where were they taking me? What was going to happen to my boys? What was going on? Why was I being taken away from them? Why were the police being so heavy-handed? I just kept thinking: *This is just crazy!*

All that needed to be done was for the police officer to have a conversation, gather some understanding and then tell me, "Look this time, your kids are okay, just don't do it again," or something similar, like they did years ago when I was growing up. There would be common sense prevailing; a mutual respect between the police and the community. I didn't know when I would see them again, would it be after I had been questioned? How long would that take? But no. I would not be seeing them again for another two-and-a-half days.

I was taken into a room with two male officers, and the two female officers that arrived on the scene. After I had given the desk sergeant all my basic details (name, date of birth, address ...), they asked if I was on any medication. I said yes I was, intermittently. I was still taking pain killers on days when the pain in my right breast would shoot pains through my breast and into the area of my body behind it. I was told this may happen, and although it wasn't a deep throbbing pain anymore, it was a sharp shooting pain, nerves reconnecting or at least starting to. When I told the desk sergeant this, the energy of the female officer, the one gunning for a fight back in the car park, shifted. And I mean shifted. It felt like a vacuum. After I was checked in, I was then put into a police cell, where I stayed for a further two-and-a-half days without questioning. I still had no idea what I was in the cell for. I still had no idea what was going on. Or what was happening with my boys, Kelt or John.

The cell was small. I could only do three lunges across it in both directions. The cell had a toilet, without flush, a tiny window and a concrete plinth for me to sleep on. There was also a plastic mattress, not dissimilar to my dad's landing mat for his carp fishing. It wasn't very comfortable, but I guess that is the idea. I hadn't been in the cell long when there was a banging on the door and I was asked if I was awake. I answered yes, I mean how was I going to be asleep with what had just happened? In came a guy who was grossly overweight and had a really dark and slimy energy. I really didn't like this man on first sight. I don't know why, I normally get on really well with lots of people, most people in fact. But this man's energy was dark. Really dark. He told me he was from social services and he needed to ask me some questions. He asked me who was available to collect my boys, and I said we are on a road trip, anyone that could collect them wouldn't be arriving for six hours minimum. He said I was being difficult and if I continued to be difficult, then they would take my boys off me. I told him I wasn't being difficult. I would give him the info he needed, but I would need my phone back. He again told me I was being difficult and I said, "I'm not. I could drive you there, I can tell you how to get there, but I can't give you full address and phone numbers."

He then got up and said, "You're being incredibly difficult. We're taking your kids off you." With this he walked out of the cell and my blood ran cold.

I fell to my knees. What on earth was going on? How is this possible? All I did was leave the boys in the car to go to a castle kiosk to check the opening times and the cost of a family ticket. It wasn't as if I'd 'done a McCann' and gone off out to dinner, leaving three children under the age of four alone in a hotel room, night after night. I hadn't parked up in a downtown area with gun crime and drug dens. We were parked up in a tiny car park overlooking the loch, which was just across the road from the driveway to the castle. I mean what did the police want to say about the people of Inveraray? Was this area, which was so pretty and tranquil, a place for paedophile gangs? Mass murderers, maybe? I'm pretty sure the production team would have done their research on the area before taking the cast and crew up to Inveraray and filming for Downton Abbey. The amount of time I was gone, was no longer than 15 minutes, 20 maximum. No longer than it takes for me to pull over in a service station late at night, fill up with fuel and then go through the process of going to the toilet, grabbing a Costa Coffee and then going to pay, before walking back out to the car. Or do we parents have to wake up our children and take them into the services with us to pee every time we are travelling by ourselves? Khaalid was 12; Nassir was 8. Kelt was in the car and the boys had my phone with John's number in it. I trusted that they would be okay. I hadn't bought into the media and government paranoia that everyone was a murderer, a paedophile or a rapist. I also knew from all the travelling, community projects I worked on and the daily interactions I had with people, to know this.

The tears rolled down my face. I kept thinking about the boys. Where were they? How were they feeling? What must they be thinking? I knew I had wanted them to have an adventure, but this wasn't part of the plan. Just like Egypt, that adventure hadn't panned out the way I had envisaged either!

I was left alone in the cell for ages. I did some squats, some planks, press ups and stretching. I lay down on the concrete plinth and just cried. I was woken up by Nikki, the police officer who was playing good cop, when she walked into the cell with another woman (I would learn just how wrong and deceitful this good cop could be months later). This young woman was from social services who asked me to sign over my children to social services as they were not allowed to stay in the police station. I was really confused by this time. Why couldn't I see my boys? Why were they detaining me? What were they detaining me for? When would I be questioned and released? I felt sick to my stomach. Had leaving the boys alone for that long been a crime? At their ages? Didn't the parenting guidelines state that it was down to the parent to use their own judgements? I knew there was no legal age limit to when you could and could not leave a child alone. I also knew that there were some 18 year olds I wouldn't leave alone, whereas some of the children I had got to know over the years, would be more than capable to be left alone at this age, child carers in particular. I had come across some incredible youngsters over the years, ones that made many adults look incompetent (which isn't that hard these days with the amount of spoilt, expectant millennials, who have been wrapped up in bubble wrap their whole lives).

I remember crying from a pain and a feeling of fear I've never experienced before; by far the worst moment of my life. I was given a document to sign and I couldn't read a word of it. Tears were streaming down my face. It didn't matter how much I wiped my eyes, I still couldn't see. Nicki sat down to the right of me and put her arm around me and reassured me I had to do this, otherwise things would become much worse. I had never been in a situation like this before. Why couldn't they just question me, see it was all a massive misunderstanding, that the course of action taken thus far was too heavy-handed and not at all appropriate. I had the woman from the social services being nice and gentle in an almost patronising way. The kind of way that people ask you how your children are in the same way they ask you how your new dishwasher is working. There was no depth. No real understanding of what it was to have someone stand in front of you, hand you a pen and tell you to sign over the two most important people in your life to people you didn't know. I really felt sick and I looked at the document again. I still couldn't see the words on the page for the tears in my eyes. I had the pen in my hand and I looked at Nicki. She showed me where to sign, and as I blinked I saw the signature line. I hesitated. What was I about to do? What was I signing? I couldn't even read the document, let alone sign it! I was told that if I didn't sign the boys over, they would be taken off me anyway. The end result would be they would be taking the boys into care, regardless of whether I signed the paper or not, so it would be best if I co-operated. So I signed. I didn't want to make this ugly situation any worse than it already was.

After they left, I sat on the floor, knees tucked up tight to my chest and I just rocked, and cried. And I mean cried. I have never felt such pain in my life. I felt as if my whole soul had been ripped out of me. I felt empty. Hollow. My two boys, who I had so badly wanted and had cared for all their lives; studying to understand the best way of developing their thinking, their resilience, their confidence, their happiness. I had studied parenting the way most people study to become a doctor. My thinking was: *These lives were in my care, I have been gifted by God, the Universe, Mother Nature to raise these beautiful souls. These boys had grown inside of me. I knew them better than anyone else. Who were these nobodies to come in and tell me my way of parenting wasn't adequate? What do they know about us, our lives, and what had led us to this point.*

I eventually fell asleep on the concrete plinth, covered in the thin itchy blanket. There was a lady at the door, an older lady, and she asked if I wanted a cup of tea. Yes please! A drink would be lovely. I also told her that I wanted to wash my face and clean my teeth. And that I was hungry. She said she would see what she could do.

As I waited for my cup of tea, I recalled the events of the hours before. I knew that is was early in the morning, but thought, now it is the start of the day, I would be taken somewhere else and questioned now. But time came and went. No one came to question me; no one could tell me anything about my boys. No one could tell me about whether John had been in touch. Where was he? And Kelt? What was going on? I really needed to wee at this point and I remember looking for the flush on the toilet. There was a button. So I pressed it. Maggie came back to the door and asked me what the matter was. I said, "Oh I thought it was the flush, but it doesn't seem to work."

She responded, "Oh that's because we have to flush the toilet from the outside."

Seriously? So, I and any others that ever got put in a police cell here, would be left with our own urine and faeces in the toilet, whilst waiting for someone to be free to come and flush it. Nice.

Now I got to do a lot of thinking. I understood that people make choices that others don't deem inappropriate all the time. One person's comfort zone is very different to another. I mean there were not many parents that would spar with their two children in a dojo. There were not many parents that would move to a different city in the same country, let alone go and live in another country, on a different continent. There were many parents that would allow their children to use the knives and the oven in the kitchen. I couldn't work out why what I had done, seemed to be a big deal to the police. Why had I still not been questioned? I needed to move so I started walking around the tiny cell and did my lunges as I did so. I did more press ups, more planks. I worked my shoulders and triceps by bench pressing against the concrete plinth. I did knee ups, star jumps, and then lots of stretching. The more pain I felt at this whole situation, the more I pushed through to the next rep. Feel the burn. I knew when they questioned me, they would realise that Khaalid was at that age in which he was stepping up. He was incredibly mature for his age. We'd been camping and sleeping in the car and the tent, on our road trips for a year now. I just knew once I was questioned this would all be sorted.

For the next two-and-a-half days I was kept in the cell and only allowed out when I begged them to let me wash myself, as I was in the same clothes I had arrived at the police station in. I still had not been questioned, unless you count the time one of the officers had asked me what I was doing here in Scotland. I told him we were on a wild camping holiday and road trip. It was the only kind of holiday I could afford and it was a way of getting the boys ready for life and the Duke of Edinburgh's Award. He told me the holiday sounded idyllic and the stuff of proper child hood memories. I urged me, quite strongly in fact, to speak with my lawyer. At this point I realised I hadn't even seen my lawyer since the first night I had been put into the cell, and that was a blur at best. I remember being brought fruit and a bowl of porridge, and the lovely lady called Maggie who managed to find me a 'prison' toothbrush and some less caustic soap. Due to the lack of light and time measurement within the cell, I could not tell what the time was. I just knew this was the third breakfast I had had in the police cell. I had slept a little, but this time I was told I needed to wake up, as I was going into court. Before I was taken out of the cell in handcuffs, Nicki told me I was going to be formally charged with one count of Disturbance of the Peace and two counts of Wilful Neglect and Abandonment, Under the Child Protection Act, Section 12. What did that mean? Sorry, I missed that memo that came in the Bounty Pack I had been given whilst being a new mum. My pack only came with a pot of Sudocrem, leaflets about Tommee Tippee products, breast pads and a free sample nappy. How on earth had they got to these charges – especially as they hadn't even questioned me yet! They were going on what evidence? How do they know I had *wilfully* done anything!? How is that provable? They can't see my intentions! They cannot tell me what I *wilfully* did or did not do.

I was taken to this small narrow room where another police officer read the charges that were being made against me. They took my photo, which wasn't the best representation of me. Here I was, having left John's the four days before, in need of a shower, having not slept the last three nights, and when I had slept it was restless sleep. I also had a cold sore which had appeared during the last few days. Great! Talk about setting me up to look like I don't even take care of myself, let alone my children. Nicki took a swab out of a packet and took my DNA, she then fingerprinted me. After this I was taken back to the cell in handcuffs, then after a short while, not enough time for another cuppa, I was then handed over to the G4S security guards who then drove me to the magistrate court about 45 minutes away. I was locked in another cell, smaller than a toilet cubicle, in the armoured van, with only a small window which meant I could see the sky. It was the first time in days I had seen it. The sky was beautiful. Full of sunshine, full of the most beautiful blue I had seen, with very few clouds. I had never been so pleased to see the sky.

When we arrived at the Magistrates Court, I was then taken into another cell, and kept there for at least another hour. The security guards were really friendly and told me they had been called all the way from Glasgow to collect me and bring me to the court. I asked them how many of us were there that they were transporting. They told me it was just me. The costs involved in this were huge! What were they thinking? All this money wasted. All these resources, all this simply because the police officer hadn't liked me speaking Arabic to my boy? All this because I had left my boys alone for 15-20 minutes. The guards asked me what I had done, so I told them. They just looked at each other and shook their heads, responding with, "We used to be out all day as kids when we were that age. Home before dark, your dinner will be ready."

I said, "Me too."

They then asked me who my lawyer was. I told them Ruben. They said, "Oh dear, good luck." I was asked them what they meant. They responded with asking me if I wanted a cup of tea and a pot noodle. I hadn't been eating wheat or processed food for a long time, and I certainly hadn't had a pot noodle for as long as I could remember. I was really hungry and so I chose the Bombay Badboy, in a sense of irony. I stayed there for at least an hour before being taken up into the courtroom, in handcuffs, by the female G4S security guard.

As I walked up the stairs the first person I saw was John. Sat in the chair directly opposite the stairs where I was coming out of. I had never been so pleased to see someone. The look on his face was one of deep concern, anger and love. I had never seen, or felt that before in my life. I smiled, and then felt the tears prick the back of my eyes. I knew he had my back. Quite literally as he sat directly behind me during the time I was in the prisoner box. I remembering turning around and being told off by the court usher. I was told to look straight ahead.

The female G4S guard had to direct me, because I had no idea when to stand and when to speak. I had never been in this situation before. I didn't like it. It was over in a flash. All that was said was confirmation that Ruben was my lawyer, and that I was being charged with Disturbance of the Peace, and two counts of Wilfull Neglect and Abandonment. I pleaded not guilty of course. If anything I was seeking information to be able to develop the boy's local knowledge. Once the plea of Not Guilty went in, I was taken back down to the cell and I had to wait for Ruben to come and see me. The security guards asked me if I wanted another cup of tea, and yes. Yes, I did.

Ruben eventually came to see me. He asked me a bit about the boys and I, making reference to the point that we had lived out in Egypt, that Inveraray would some like paradise compared to that, and after what we had witnessed. He also advised it would be wise to collect as many character witnesses as I could when I got back to Sheffield. I told him I wanted to see my boys. What had happened to my boys? He told me that they were being cared for by some temporary foster parents and that I would be getting a call from the social services as to when I would be getting my boys back. I told him that as soon as I had my boys back, we were going to see my mum. I needed to see my mum. I needed her right now. He told me that it was fine. I just had to call him when I got to my parents, because I was 'out on bail'. Words I would never have thought would have been attributed to me, and nor would anyone who knew me. I was always the good girl, the 'mum', the one who looked after everyone else, supported others and made sure everyone was okay. Me? Out on bail? How on earth did this happen?

I was released from the handcuffs and led outside by Ruben, to where John was waiting. We hugged each other so tightly. I cried. He wiped my tears and told me it was okay, and to be strong. We said our goodbyes to Ruben and waited for the call from Social Services. It would be at least another two hours until I saw my boys. So John and I went to get some coffee (and his hot chocolate), and then went and got Kelt. John had been to a pet shop to see if they could help out with taking care of him, whilst he came to see me in the courtroom. Kindly the lady agreed. Upon seeing Kelt, he went crazy, so excited to see me. His little tail was wagging so fast. I cried again. I had missed this little fella. He is my little shadow, and has been with me since I rescued him from a pet shop in Egypt. He had helped me heal so much when ramO and I split up. I have nursed him through Parvo[4], travelled extensively with him, taken him to so many meetings and spent hours walking with him. We thanked the lady, and as we walked towards the water's edge, John told me about their adventures together. We looked out over the sea, John's arms wrapped around me. I felt safe. Little did I know it, but I would get to see this sea many more times over the next 18 months.

––––––––––––

[4] Parvo – An extremely contagious disease with a high mortality rate in dogs

SEVEN

GETTING THE BOYS BACK

When the phone rang and the social worker told me he was on his way with the boys, I was sent into another spin of confusion. If they were charging me with Wilful Neglect and Abandonment, and I was getting my boys back, then surely I couldn't be convicted of these charges? None of this made sense. I was not going to question it. I wanted to see my boys again, and I wanted to feel whole again. I still had a HUGE void inside me. I had never felt so empty.

As the moments got closer to the moment I would see my boys again, I told John I was hungry. I hadn't eaten anything but six bits of fruit and two bowls of porridge the whole time I had been inside, and the Bombay Badboy Pot Noodle. He saw the funny side of it and we both chuckled. The pot noodle had already started to activate my stomach and it was churning, but I was hungry, and needed to eat. I wasn't sure if I was feeling faint due to the overload of emotions that was going through me, or the fact that I had eaten so little food, and had so little sleep; but knew it was the combination of all of these things. John asked me what a wanted and at that point I just knew I needed carbs and protein. We got a whiff of some really nice smelling fish a chips. So we asked a local couple if they knew where the chip shop was. We were directed up the hill to this gorgeous chip shop. I am not sure if they were the best fish and chips I had ever eaten, but they certainly tasted like it after the few last days. John and I walked down the street of Dunoon, which is where we currently were. Apparently I had been in Lochgilpead over the last few days. I had no idea where I had been; other than in a variety of different police cells, two in buildings and one in an armoured van.

Whilst we were sat eating our fish and chips, an elderly couple stopped by us and asked where we had got the fish and chips from. When we told them, they said they would go elsewhere; they didn't want to walk up the hill. I asked them what they wanted and offered to go and get them. They sat with John and Kelt whilst I strode up the hill back to the fish and chip shop. I was outside. I was striding. I could hear the birds, feel the sun on my face, see the trees. I wanted to go and sit back where John and I had sat before. I was free to walk wherever I wanted to. When I got back to him and the elderly couple, I handed over the food and said, "Come on John, I want to go back to the sea."

I wouldn't take the money from the couple. The fish and chips were on me. It had been a gift to be able to be able to walk freely, and I had only been inside a cell for a few days, not weeks, months or years like some people. I couldn't imagine what it must be like for people inside for a long time; but then again, long term prisons had TV rooms, toiletries, a gym, a workout ground, kitchens for prisoners to volunteer in, other inmates to talk with. I had a two-and-a-half by three lunge concrete cell with a toilet, which I couldn't flush from the inside, and a tiny slit for a window that let very little light in. Plus many of those inside prisons had done something to actually be in prison. I hadn't. And now I was left actually wondering how many prisoners had actually done something. If I had been treated in this way, and I hadn't even been questioned, how on earth had others been treated? Just how many people were in prison that actually didn't need to be in prison? From the heavy-handed policing I had experienced, I knew there were probably lots of them. I knew I would never trust anything I was told about prisoners again.

I called my mum to let her know I was okay. I didn't know what she knew, I didn't know if she knew anything. But as soon as I heard her voice, I knew she knew something was wrong. She had been called by the social services on Tuesday 28th July at around lunchtime, already 36 hours after I had been handcuffed and put in the back of the police car, and 24 hours after the boys had been placed in foster care. They wanted to know if my parents could have the boys, not telling my mum what had happened. Apparently, due to the Data Protection Act, they were not allowed to tell my mum what had happened to me. My mum had no idea if I had been in an accident, if I was hurt, had been taken ill, arrested or worse. They would not tell her anything. They only wanted to know if my mum and dad could have the boys. When she asked about Kelt, they said they didn't know anything about a dog. They told my mum they would be back in touch later that day, as the boys would be sent back to Sheffield, where they would be interviewed by social services, knowing I wouldn't be present, before they were then sent to my mum and dads. They didn't tell my mum anything about how the boys were going to get to Sheffield, if there was going to be any supervision of my boys or anything. My mum was out of her mind with worry.

They rang my mum later that day, and were asking questions such as where they worked, how long they had lived at the address, if they had any criminal records and other questions to make sure they were suitable to have the boys. They then told my mum that they would call back to let them know what time the boys would be arriving with them, but they never did. This had left my mum feeling confused, concerned and really upset. She was frantic, and couldn't go into work the next day. She wasn't able to sleep that night, and my dad was as angry and concerned as my mum. How could they call with such a request, and not tell them what had happened to me? How inhuman and uncaring is that? What kind of person does that to someone else? Leaving them in a blind panic as to what has happened to their daughter, grandchildren and family dog?

My mum then had an email the next day, on Wednesday 29th, from a detective sergeant asking, "Is this the mother of Dawn Bates, if so, please contact me on this number as soon as possible." When my mum tried to contact her, two or three times, but was never able to speak with the women who sent the email. My mum eventually spoke with a woman who said she would ask the Detective Sergeant to contact my mum, but no one ever did. Again, they left my mum hanging. With no information, not knowing what was happening to me, or the boys, and certainly no knowledge of Kelt. My parents were beside themselves. This made me angry. Regardless of whatever I had done, for the police and social services to leave my parents hanging like this was disgraceful and unkind on many levels. No emotional intelligence at all. So much for protecting and serving the public!

The first my mum knew of anything was when I called her to let her know that I was okay; and to explain what had happened. When she heard what had happened, she couldn't believe what she was hearing. All of this for me being away from the boys for a maximum of 15-20 minutes? And why was I not questioned? Surely that is against the law? And how many parents are they going to arrest and lock up for leaving their children for 20 minutes? There must have been something else. When I assured my mum there wasn't anything else, she couldn't believe it. Especially the bit about me not being questioned and not being able to give a statement. What evidence of neglect had they? The questions my mum was asking were the same questions I had had going through my mind. I told her as it was going to be really late before we got to her, the boys and I were going to stay with my friends Anthea and Roly in Durham, and we would set off at lunch time the next day, arriving with her late afternoon.

I told her not to worry; everything was going to be okay. This was just an ugly misunderstanding, to which she replied, "Misunderstanding!? How can you be so calm about this? This is more than a misunderstanding Dawn. For God's sake! They locked you up in a police cell without questioning, without allowing you to give a statement. That is NOT RIGHT. Not right at all". Then she started crying.

This made me angry. No one upset my mum. No one. What they had done to my mum over the last few days was disgusting. Yes, I did leave my boys in the car, with my dog. And yes, some of you reading this may think this was all my fault. Something I have struggled with because I have yet to meet a parent that hasn't left their children of a similar age, and younger in some cases, alone for this amount of time; whether that is to pop into the supermarket to do the shopping, or collect a younger child from an after-school club whilst they left the older sibling at home to do their homework. Other examples I had from other parents were ones such as they have allowed their children to head off to the park together, or go on the bus or cycle to town. Another one of my friends told me her child was even encouraged to go to the swimming pools by themselves from the age of eight by the local school to teach them to be confident and responsible – a school encouraging this! Friends who camped explained their kids leave the tent in the morning, go off exploring and come back mid-afternoon when their tummies are rumbling. Are they going to arrest every parent on a campsite?

I was soon to realise the depth of disgust people had about what had happened to me, and couldn't believe that I had spent nearly 60 hours in a police cell without being charged or questioned, longer than someone who had committed murder, according to the government website[5]:

The police can hold you for up to 24 hours before they have to charge you with a crime or release you.

They can apply to hold you for up to 36 or 96 hours if you're suspected of a serious crime, eg murder.

You can be held without charge for up to 14 days if you're arrested under the Terrorism Act.

Since I had not committed a serious crime, akin to the status of murder, then why was I held for longer for 24 hours? Or are they saying that leaving my children alone for 15-20 minutes is as serious a crime as paedophilia, gun crimes and murder?

Had I left two young babies, toddlers or young boys alone in the car, or alone in the car in a busy city centre, or dangerous part of a city, full of gun grime and drug dens, then I could understand the police being so concerned. But this was Inveraray! A little piece of idyllic heaven on the beautiful west coast of Scotland! What are the police saying about the local residents of Inveraray? And what would the local residents say about what the police are insinuating about their small village? Not great for tourism in the area that's for sure!

All these thoughts were racing through my mind as John and I still waited for the boys to arrive. We sat back by the sea, just listening to the waves lapping against the shore. His arms around me, cradling me. My worries seem to just disappear for a moment. I looked at him, deep into his gorgeous blue eyes and said, "Not the ending to our holiday I was looking for."

He replied, "No, I guess not. Don't worry, we'll sort it."

Those last words still spin around in my head. Here was a guy I hadn't seen for over 18 years, had only met once or twice before, who I had just spent seven amazing days with, on an island and I had trusted him with my dog, my car, my bank card and he had been there every step of the way. He had walked for hours with my dog to get to the location of the police cells, slept in the porch of his friend's house – as they hadn't been in, organised for a pet shop to take care of my dog so he could come and support me in the magistrates court, making sure he was the first person I saw when I came up into the courtroom. He had contacted a solicitor that he knew from the village he grew up in and here he was with his arms around me telling me 'we' would sort it. Talk about throw yourself into the depths of darkness at the start of a relationship. Would he really stick around? Was he even for real? Did he really mean 'we' or had it been a slip of the tongue? Only time would tell.

We sat by the water's edge for another 30 minutes, then the phone rang to tell me that the boys were 15 minutes away. I looked a mess. I was still in the same clothes I had been in when I was arrested. My hair was greasy and I smelled bad. I apologised to John for being such a mess. He told me I still looked beautiful, and the boys wouldn't care. All they would want would be to be with me. This guy was not real! He was the highlight of a really bad nightmare that I would wake up from any moment. We headed back to the court building to meet up with the social workers that were bringing my boys back to me. As soon as I saw my boys in the back of the car they were smiling at me, I choked back the tears. My boys. My beautiful, handsome boys. I couldn't open the car door quick enough. The boys got out and I held them so tight, kissing them and squeezing them. The void in my soul was filled again. I was doing my best to not cry in front of them, but the tears were slowly falling. I kept telling them how much I missed them. Asking them if they were okay, how were they, where had they been. So many questions. They showed me the puzzle books the foster family had given them and I giggled. That was just the kind of gift I would have given for a long car ride. I realised I had forgotten my manners and thanked the guys from social services. They said it was fine, just glad to see the boys reunited with their mum. I asked where my car was. It was the first time it had occurred to me where the car was! With all our camping equipment, our adventure home on wheels! I was told by the chap called Paul that he and his colleague would be driving me and the boys back to Inveraray to collect the car. I asked about Kelt and John, and John said he would meet me there. He gave me a big strong hug and a kiss on the cheek and one of his cheeky smiles and said, "See you in Inveraray!"

I got in the car and the whole time the boys were telling me that the foster parents they had stayed with were a lot like me, no shoes in the house, healthy food, no processed stuff, bath or shower every night, eat at the table to share news and they really liked their books like I did. I smiled, choking back a giggle. I was so pleased they had been with someone similar to me and that they were okay. They didn't seem fazed by it, which the social services guys said was a testament to me and my parenting. They also told me that is was obvious to them that the boys were very well cared for, and I was a great mother due to the boys good behaviour, level of conversational skills with everyone they met, and the way they both thought about subjects and could hold their own within conversations with adults. Apparently the foster care family had given the social services great feedback on my boys, which only added to the praise Paul and his colleague were giving me. I felt relieved.

When we finally got to Inveraray, and it was time to say thank you and goodbye to Paul and his colleague. They told me that they were really sorry to hear what had happened, and it was obvious the charges being brought about me were unnecessary. They went on to say that anyone spending any amount of time with my boys could see they were very well cared for and not in the slightest bit neglected. His colleague also pointed out that there is no legal age limit on when children should be left alone or how long for. He advised me to make sure my lawyer made that point. It is all down to the parent making an informed risk assessment and the maturity of the child. He also told me that this was one of the biggest wastes on public funding at the moment, and it is only getting worse. His last words to me were, "Make sure you get a good solicitor, and make sure you fight this. Your children are incredible, two of the best young men I have come across in a long time." He then nodded his head, they both shook my hand, and both my boys hands, and said to them, "Listen to your mother, behave and keep up the great work, all three of you." With that they left.

Just as I was about to call John, I saw him walking into the car park where we had been dropped off. I asked him where my car was. He smiled at me and said, "Parked over there."

We walked over to the car, and made sure everything was okay with it, no parking tickets or fines thankfully! I told John I needed to be heading to my mums, but that I was going to be heading to Anthea and Roly's first to break up the journey and not arrive too late at my mums. I didn't want to leave him. I wanted to stay with him, just disappear to a beach somewhere and have another fire on the beach. Just sitting, listening to the waves, closing my eyes and feeling the breeze and smelling the salt sea air... but I knew I had to get going. The boys had already got in the car thinking John was coming with us. John and I kissed goodbye, which made the boys giggle, and Khaalid climbed in the front seat ready to navigate. I was going to miss John; he'd been a real gentleman, and a heck of a lot of fun. We had all learnt a lot about the local area and that was all due to John. He was a fascinating guy, and one I wanted to spend more time with; but he lived in Scotland, and I lived in Sheffield. How would that work?

The boys and I arrive with Anthea and Roly a day later than we had anticipated and when I explained to them what had happened, they couldn't believe it. Again something I would get used to as time went on. We talked into the early hours of the morning and spent a lovely day with each other the next day. Anthea noticed that I had spoken about John a lot and asked me if there was something in it. I said I didn't know, only time would tell, but I hoped there would be. Both Anthea and Roly had known John and his older brother for years too, so knew him to be a great guy. We sat and talked about how the arrest could affect me and my life, my career and the boys; all three of us believing that it would get thrown out of court because it was so ridiculous. Around 3pm the boys and I left so I could get to my mums and reassure her that the boys and I were okay. She needed to see me; I needed to see my mum. The boys were quiet, but seemed to be okay. I was doing my best to not make it into too big a deal, because I firmly believed that once I was able to give my side of the story, this would all be over. How wrong could I be?

---

[5] www.gov.co.uk

EIGHT

MELTDOWN AT MUM'S

On the way back to my mums, the boys and I put the radio on and were singing away. I wanted to get back to some kind of normality. The boys were still a little quieter than normal and about half way back to my mum and dad's, Naasir asked me what it was like in the police cell. When I told them what it was like, Naasir started crying, and told me he was sorry. I asked him when he meant, and that he had nothing to be sorry for. Tears pricked the back of my eyes, and I noticed a layby just up ahead. I pulled over, got out of the car and walked around to his side of the car and opened the door. I gave him such a big hug and told him that it wasn't his fault. We had just come up against a police officer who should have put things into perspective a lot more; and how this was none of his fault. Yes, he had gotten out of the car when I told him to stay in it. Yes, I had left them in the car, but so long as we all learnt from this, then that was the main thing. I reminded him that there was a reason I asked them to do certain things, and it was more to do with others than either him or his brother; and none of this was his fault. I asked him to promise to listen to me and do as I asked in future. He said he would, and we had another big hug and I wiped his tears away, kissing him on the top of his head and went and got back into the car. I was shattered and needed to get to my mums.

After a couple of hours of driving, we finally arrived. Walking into the kitchen was like a flashback to the first time of walking into the kitchen after our return from Egypt. My mum and I hugged each other so much and I just cried. The boys had headed straight into the garden to play on the swings and to play swing ball. I couldn't stop crying, and I apologised to my mum for all the worry I had caused her. She told me to stop being so bloody silly! What I had done was nothing to apologise for; telling me about the amount of kids that came into Tesco (where she worked) younger than the boys, having cycled there on their bikes. Kids played up the village for hours from the ages of seven upwards, me leaving the boys for 15-20 minutes was nothing! And if anything, it should be the police apologising to me for what they had done.

She handed me a cup of tea and fired so many questions at me, just trying to make sense of everything I was telling. I showed her the location on Google images and the distance on Google maps, and then wished I hadn't in some ways, because this made it worse for her. The way in which the police had reacted would be more suited to the inner city ghettos, not this tiny, beautiful area in Scotland! What were they thinking? What was their agenda? What targets did they have to hit? Were they so bored that they had to go around making up crimes? At this point I let out a giggle and my mum shot me a look and asked, "And what is so funny about this? This is no laughing matter Dawn Louise!"

"I know mum, but these are the very same questions I asked, and have been asking myself. Why would they do this? What was their objection? Why didn't they simply tell me 'Look, the boys are fine this time, but don't do it again'."

"Because they wear a police uniform and think they can get away with it! That's why!" My mum started crying at this point and both my dad and I looked at each other.

Neither of us liked seeing mum upset, and my dad's silence throughout all of this had spoken such volumes. The looks of confusion and annoyance on his face had also spoken volumes. He was not impressed. Not impressed at all. Then he said, "What happens now?"

"I don't know dad, I really don't".

And I didn't. I had no idea what happened from this point on. I just knew that I had to call Ruben when I got back to Sheffield, as well as the social services. I refilled my cup with tea, and told mum and dad I was going to go in the garden and be with the boys. I just wanted to watch them play. When I got into the garden, they were playing and laughing hard. I had my shades on, and I glad I did. The tears were falling. Here I was in my mum and dad's garden, watching my boys play. Something I had taken for granted, and something I would never take for granted ever again.

The next thing I know, I heard my mum saying, "Dawn Louise!"

I woke up with a start. My mum only ever used my middle name when I was in trouble. "What? What is it? Where are the boys?" The boys were no longer in the garden and my heart jumped into my mouth and I felt sick. I had fallen asleep watching them play and now they were not here. Where were they? I was frantic! I started crying and panicking. What kind of mother was I to fall asleep and lose my boys? Especially after what had just happened!?

"Don't you dare do this to yourself! They are at the park with the girls. Did you want a cup of tea?"

"What do you mean they have gone to the park? How long have they been at the park? Mum don't you get what has just happened? Where I have just been? What they are charging me with?" I was crying so hard, and my mum just grabbed me and hugged me so tightly.

"Now you stop this! You stop this right now! They've been going up that park, just like any normal child, with a normal childhood, doing what kids should be doing. They are playing outside, in a park, in a village. They are safe! Don't you dare go and start questioning yourself young lady!"

I knew she was right. I knew they would be safe, but the fear and paranoia had already been put in place. I was already starting to question the way in which I parented the boys. Had I been doing it wrong all this time? Had I been too trusting? Was I a good mum?

And yes please, I would love a cup of tea.

NINE
LEFT IN THE DARKNESS

Spending the week with my mum and dad, surrounded by family was great. Hearing all the laughter from the kids, the Bates' family barbeques and catching up on sleep… just what I needed.

I realised that although I had needed a holiday before we went on holiday, I was even more in need of a break now. My mum and dad's garden provided just that. With the sound of the birds chirping away, tractors working away in the fields and the kids playing together, I made the most of the sunshine and the support my mum and dad gave me in looking after the boys. Not that they needed looking after. They were 12 and 8. They were incredibly independent boys. They knew how to cook, clean and take care of each other, I had made sure of that. Khaalid bless him, came to wake me up at one point whilst I was sunbathing in the garden, just to tell me to turn over otherwise I would burn. He'd also brought me a glass of water, telling me I needed to keep myself hydrated. I felt like the luckiest Mummy in the world.

Waking up and drinking my water, my mind drifted back to John, as it had done so many times since leaving him in Inveraray. How had this man come to occupy so much of my mind? A smile broke out over my face and I just knew I had to speak with him. I wanted to speak with him, to hear his voice, and as if by magic, my phone rang and it was him. The electric that shot through my body, and the stupid smile I had on my face… yep… I really liked this guy. Like REALLY liked him. I felt like a lovesick teenager, and what a strangely wonderful place to be in after all these years. We spoke for hours, never running out of things to say. Being in his company, either in person, or on the phone, felt like I was with myself. We flowed together, like an extension of one another; totally at ease in each other's company, and he made me laugh – I hadn't laughed so much in years. Even my mum and dad noticed it, and my mum being my mum, told me so too.

I slept in every day, embarrassingly so. I apologised to my parents every morning, and my mum just kept telling me, "You obviously need it." I did. I hadn't slept until I naturally woke up since before moving to Egypt… and it was getting on for almost two years since we had been back. I wouldn't have been surprised if I hadn't slept until waking up naturally for over a decade. My life always ruled by alarms and disturbed sleep due to either the boys or Kelt, and in Egypt… well just the sounds of Egypt.

By the time the boys and I left my mum and dads, we have all been given a good talking to. The boys were told to do their chores, to listen to me and to keep up with their studies, not that they needed telling, but it was always good for them to hear it from someone other than me, and my mum was probably the perfect person to hear it from. She may be 'Nanny' but she wasn't the kind of 'Nanny' to spoil them or let them get away with anything just because they are kids. No, my mum was very loving – incredibly so – but it was all underpinned with tough love, the kind of love according to all the experts that enabled boys to thrive. Boys need boundaries, but they also need to be trusted with responsibility[6]. They needed to know where the boundaries were so they knew how to push boundaries and innovate, just what I wanted for my boys. I wanted them to push boundaries and innovate, I wanted them to create and take risks. It is the only way to grow and excel in life when there is so much competition out there. I would ask them what Tetris taught us, after having to explain to them what Tetris was! (I giggled when I realised they didn't know what Tetris was, how old did I feel?) Once explained and shown to them, I would tell them that when we fit in, we disappear. Never disappear; never fit in just to fit in. Always be true to yourself. I had always told them that they had a voice and a mind for a reason, and to use them, always.

My mum told me to never doubt my parenting abilities. I was a great mother. My boys were a testament to that. Ask anyone. She told me to not let the bastards get to me and to stay strong. I knew when my mum used the 'B word' that things were serious. It was not a word she ever used, so I knew to take note, otherwise it would be me in trouble with her, and not just the police.

When we left, my dad gave me a really big hug. My dad never hugs me. Ever. He lets me hug him, but it is never reciprocal. So to get a hug from my dad – well, that just made me cry.

The journey home was an enjoyable one. More singing and chatting, and remembering the great times we had had on our holiday. None of us mentioned the 'incident', simply chatting away and remembering the things we had done on our last road trip around Wales and the South West of England. We had had a couple of really great holidays, and even with fuel, neither of them had cost us more than £500 – and that included the activities we had done. I was pleased with that, especially as we had been on the roads for at least four weeks both holidays. I could do this. I could budget. It wasn't something I had had to do for many years whilst being with ramO. With the income from the business and the money I had earned whilst in Egypt, we lived a really good lifestyle. Learning to budget was a skill I was reacquainting myself with.

Once home, we emptied the car and put everything away that needed putting away. I had done all the laundry at my mums, and aired the tent. So it was a quick and easy job to pack everything away.

We were home late and hungry, so the boys went downstairs to Tiffin. Coming in under budget for our holiday, we could afford to have a takeaway for once. The rest of the money was going to be used to fill the cupboards and the fridge for the next week.

I found it hard to get to sleep that night; although I was tired, I knew I had to call the social services the next day. My mind was racing. What would they think of me? Of our home? What would they say about what I had done? I was a nervous wreck, and again, as if by magic, John knew I needed to connect with someone, and he text me to see if I was home yet and if I was still awake. We spoke briefly and he promised to call back the next day, and told me to get some sleep, as I sounded shattered. I fell asleep with a big smile on my face. He had done it again. What was it about this man? How did he do this?

The next day I called social services and a lady called Natasha said she would be over to see me. She explained that she would want to speak with me, and then with each of the boys alone. We arranged a date for her to come over and I felt relieved. She seemed really lovely, and as it turned out, she was. The next phone call was to Ruben. But I only got to speak with his secretary, who took a message and told me he would call me back. I informed her that I had called the social services and gave her Natasha's details and the date she was due to arrive. I was told that Ruben would call me back.

I looked at the mail that was waiting to be opened. There wasn't much, but what was there had Scottish postal markings. I sat at the dining table with a cup of tea, just staring at the envelopes. I didn't want to open them, it would make it all real, instead of it having just been a horrible dream. There was a letter confirming my plea of 'Not Guilty', informing me of the trial dates, what was requested of me in the way of a written narration, character references and the Terms of Conditions of instructing Rubens' Solicitors. The next envelope told me of another trial date, and how I had to send proof of identity for Monday Laundering Regulations, followed by another envelope with an invoice for £360. I read each letter about three or four times. There were terms such as Intermediate diet – what did this mean? My only association with the word diet related to restricting certain foods, and nothing at all to do with the law... not that I knew much about the law. I had never been in trouble with the police before. Ruben had written at the bottom of his letters, "Should you have any queries please do not hesitate to contact our office". I needed explanations to what all this meant, what was going to happen next and clarification to some of the things that had happened.

Why had I not been questioned by the police, or asked to give a statement?

Why had I been left in a police cell for two-and-a-half days?

How is any of this right? No harm had come to my boys, well none other than the psychological damage done due to the actions of the police. I still had flashbacks to Naasir getting more and more upset with the way in which the police officer was speaking with me, and of Khaalid being bundled into the back of the police car, half asleep and looking confused and scared at seeing me in handcuffs and Naasir crying.

Since being back in the UK, I had reassured my boys that the police in the UK were so different to the police in Egypt. That they were a lot more respectful, and the way they spoke with civilians came from a place of understanding, and how the men weren't as vulgar to women as they had been in Egypt. This was our first experience of dealing with the police since returning and all the effort I had put into getting the police to trust and respect the police had been undone. My boys now disliked the police, a lot.

I left message after message for Ruben to call me back and spoke with Felicity in his office many times, often in tears because I just wanted answers, and none were forth coming. She wasn't helpful either, and appeared uninterested in helping any further than passing on a message. I didn't know if she could help, or was so used to dealing with a certain type of criminal that she had become immune to people.

Natasha, the social worker came out to visit a few days after we arrived back, and when I was explaining to her what had happened, the look of confusion on her face said it all. The story given to social services by the police were vastly different to what had actually happened and the time frame given was four times longer than the reality of the situation. The black picture that had been painted by Police Scotland was disturbing. Luckily for me, and the boys, Natasha could see that the person the police had described was so far removed from who I am, and she went as far as saying in her report that she was, "impressed with (me, and the boys), and that she had no safeguarding concerns what so ever… with a good standard of care … and the boys being given a lot of opportunities to learn, which encourages their independence, morals and leadership skills"; further going on to state, "Dawn is a very passionate parent who wants the best for her children". After the initial conversations with both the boys and I, Natasha couldn't believe that the situation has got to this point, and went on further to state that leaving boys as mature and responsible as Khaalid and Naasir alone for the period of time I had, or even as long as the police say I had, in the area in which I had left them, wasn't an issue in her eyes; especially as children younger go to the parks by themselves, take themselves to school, or go to the local shops alone. She even stated that more harm could have come to the boys had I gone to sleep for an hour in my own home, which is perfectly acceptable especially given that I am a single parent, as there are a number of dangers in the home such as knives in the kitchen, cleaning chemicals and the fact that they are of an age where knowing how to use a key and letting themselves out of the house could happen at any time. She then went on to inform me that the law is tricky as there is no legal age at which a child can or cannot be left alone, and it is down to the parent to do their own risk assessment based upon what they know of their children and their level of maturity; and it was very obvious my boys are both incredibly mature and responsible.

Hearing these words brought tears to my eyes, not just because of the acknowledgement of my parenting skills being so high and impressive, but also because I was now angry. All this upset and trauma had been caused for no good reason. I knew I had not done anything wrong and now hearing it from a social worker, as well as my mum, I was angry that I had been thrown in a police cell for two-and-a-half days, without questioning, without good cause, but more importantly I was angry that I had been made to sign my children over to foster care. What kind of people do this to others? Bullies, that's who! People who think they can dictate to others how to live their lives and how to raise their own children. I had seen various signs of a dictatorship arising here in the UK, an ugly nanny state emerging, but now I could see just how far reaching it was becoming. It was like we were starting to live in a passive aggressive dictatorship, and give it a decade or less and it would a fully blown dictatorship. Having just left Egypt, I knew what it was like to live under a dictatorship and I wasn't about to start living under another one anytime soon.

Not only was this feedback and additional information something that made me angry because I had doubted myself, but it also made me angry because the amount of children that need the protection and care from real predators, from abusive parents, I was also angry at the amount of money and resources that had been wasted, and were about to be wasted. I was angry that my boys had been subjected to this. I was angry that my mum and dad had been put through all of this. I was angry that my time and money would now be spent fighting this case, when I should be focusing all my energies and money into investing in the boys and building my business.

I chose to channel the anger into fighting in the dojo and more importantly to clear my name. I chose to channel the anger into researching the law; into the organisational frameworks that made up the police, the justice system and child protection. I chose to find out how much this had cost the public purse already. I chose to look at the behavioural frameworks I had been given as a Police Assessor, and the Code of Ethics that governed the UK police forces. I was angry, because if they could do this to someone like me, who had never been in trouble with the police before, someone who had the tools to create positive change in the community, the knowledge of how to raise entrepreneurial, independent children, and love children so much I taught them and wanted to work with them, then what on earth could they do to people who didn't have such a glowing character. This scared me. I knew from my work in community groups and as a volunteer with some of the BME groups, that had I been from an Asian background, or been 'in the system' before, or a lower socio economic background, I wouldn't stand a chance. I was no longer fighting to clear my name, I was fighting for all those parents that had also been wrongly accused in the past, and also for those who will be wrongly accused in the future. It was time to get my game face on and find out just exactly how the police in Scotland could get away with what they had done; and what I was about to discover was even more frightening than I first thought. The lies, the back tracking, the corruption (as I saw it, and living out in Egypt, having studied politics and organisation dysfunction, I know what corruption is when I see it) and the misogynistic, Masonic attitudes quite frankly disgusted me, not to mention the disjointed and ineffective support systems. This was going to be one hell of a fight, but one I was ready for. I was going to fight this, and I was going to clear my name. I had some work to do; so I made a cup of tea, got out my flip chart papers and pens, and got to work.

One of the first things I did was a mind map of all the areas I needed to look at and research. One being the way in which the police officers had behaved, so I got out the behavioural frameworks I had been given during my Police Assessor training. I went to the website for Skills for Justice, the organisation that develops the professional frameworks for all the emergency services and the military. I went to the website of the National Policing Improvement Agency and I downloaded the Professional Frameworks Personal Qualities documents.

I also spoke with a guy called Steven who was a training development manager at Skills for Justice. I explained to him what had happened and he asked me, "So what do you want to happen? Would you like him fired?"

My answer was a very fast and straight forward, "No! Why would I do that? He needs to be trained in Emotional and Social Intelligence, as well as Cultural Diversity. He has three young children and if he loses his job, it is them that will be affected most. It's a rural area, being fired for this will make it hard for him to get another job in the area. Why would I do that to his wife and children, just because he's made a mistake?" Steven was quiet for quite a while, and his response was not quite what I was expecting. He told me that simply with the response I had given him, he knew I was innocent. He also acknowledged me for my consideration of the office and his family, even after what had happened to me. He asked me what the ideal outcome would be, to which I responded, "Like I said, he needs training, and if you need a great trainer, I'm available!" Throwing this last comment in was done more out of nervousness, and to ease the tension, but he told me that once this was over to contact him again. He acknowledged me for being an incredible woman and pointed me in the direction of other information that I could read in helping me clear my name. He also told me to stay in touch with Skills for Justice. I said thank you and we said our goodbyes. I sat there just staring at the phone. Had that conversation just happened? Had he really pointed me in the direction of all this additional information? Had he really just offered to take me up on my offer of training the emergency services and armed forces? But most importantly, he had believed I was innocent of what I was being charged with simply because I didn't want the police officer to lose his job and have it affect his family? How could someone who had never met me, ask me that one question and totally believe my innocence based simply on my answer? He knew something. Could see something I couldn't. Not just in me, but in the policing and justice system. I snapped out of my thinking and leapt into action.

I downloaded the Code of Ethics for both The College of Policing and from the Police Scotland website. I downloaded The National Policing Vision 2016, The Leadership Review developed by the College of Policing, with Forewords by Professor Dame Shirley Pearce, Chair of the College of Policing and Chief Constable Alex Marshall, the CEO of the College of Policing. I downloaded the Integrity Programme by the College of Policing, along with the Five Year Strategy for the College of Policing. I then went to the website of the Judicial Office for Scotland so I could understand the framework upon which the justice system is built upon, especially The Six Bangalore Principles of Judicial Conduct endorsed at the 59th Session of the United Nations Human Rights Convention at Geneva April 2003. I downloaded the guide 'Getting it right for every child' written by The Scottish Government. I went on the NSPCC websites for both England and Wales, and well as Scotland. I started researching the Children and Young Persons (Scotland) Act of 1939, Section 12(1), and especially the term 'as amended'. My printer was on nonstop print, and the paper that had been stored away from my previous businesses was now coming in very handy. I had a lot of reading to do.

I then got on with collecting the character references from both those in my life who knew me personally and professionally. This for me was the hardest part. The reading and analysing was easy, but reaching out to people to help me, not something I found easy to do. To reach out to them about this was challenging for me on so many levels. Here I was, someone they respected and admired for many different reason, having to tell them I had been arrested for Wilful Neglect and Abandonment of my boys. I had to trust these people with something so personal and damaging to my career and reputation. I had to trust these people had my back, and after what I had discovered about ramO and his behaviour during our marriage, trust was not something I had in abundance anyone, especially my ability to trust myself to trust others. Would I get this right? Would I choose the right people to trust and reach out to? Then there was the angle of knowing I had to get people the courts would take seriously, people that not only knew me, but also who carried weight when it came to children and professionalism. It was time for another cup of tea.

Sitting back at my desk, I smiled and shook my head, I knew who I could trust and reaching out to these people was one of the easiest, but also the hardest thing I had done in our relationships. I chose friends who had careers in Community Outreach, supporting families with young children and in either dangerous situations or severe poverty. I reached out to friends who worked in the NHS who were trained to look for children in danger, a friend who was highly involved in International Human Rights activities, friends who had known me for almost 20 years that knew me both as a parent and as a professional woman. I reached out to friends who were leading professionals and parents, I reached out to Sensei, friends who had lived with me and the boys, seeing me in the day to day parenting role where there was nowhere to hide. I approached the Deputy Head and Pastoral Carer of the boys' school and with each and every single one of them, the support was immensely overwhelming. As I explained what had happened, the level of shock from each one gave me confidence that what I had done was not wrong. They knew my boys, they knew me, they knew our lives and they knew I would never neglect or abandon my children, especially not wilfully.

And how can I be charged for something deemed as Wilful? How can they prove 'Wilful' anything? They cannot see into my soul, my mind and they have no idea of my intentions, and especially as there had been no interview done, no statement collected and there was certainly no evidence of my boys ever being neglected.

My next job was to collect the ID needed and get those sent off to Ruben, and to pay him for his fees thus far. I had asked him about legal aid and he told me that because the charge was a criminal conviction, against children, I wasn't entitled to it. I couldn't believe it. Then the reality of everything hit me… all the money I had been saving, all the budgeting I had been doing… my qualification with The Coaching Academy… the life I was building… this was going to put a HUGE strain on my finances and I needed to step up. I needed to attend as many promo events to promote Vitality as I could. I had to start making cold calls like my life depended on it, because it did. And so did my boys lives. This was not going to destroy the life I was building for the three of us. I went through all the money I had, looked at how much Ruben had charged me for simply arriving at the court and for speaking with John, looked at how much money I owed The Coaching Academy and took a deep breath. I could do this. It was going to be tough, but if I had kept my first business alive and kicking whilst nursing ramO through a brain tumour and recovery, renovate a house and keep the sales coming in, then I could deal with this.

I went back to my flipchart papers, which we stuck to the wall next to all the sheets for my book *The Wife*, and started ticking off everything I had already done, and added the new tasks that had occurred to me whilst I was going through everything. The list was growing. I added target markets, ideal clients, various income streams, monthly payments in and out, tasks to do for the house, the court case and then the alarm went off... it was time to get the boys from school, and I still had not put the chicken in for dinner that night! It was going to be plain chicken that night! The chicken went in and I headed to school. *Today has been hard, but productive, I can do this...* was on repeat in my mind... thank goodness for Heart FM though.. the songs may be mainstream and cheesy but the feel good factor and energy was great! I was singing along, with Kelt sat in the passenger seat, head out of the car window. Life was good, and I felt incredibly lucky. I had some really great people in my life, I had the skills and drive, my health was getting better and most importantly I had my boys and Kelt, my parents full support and a roof over our heads. I was a lucky lady.

And then John came into my mind and I smiled. I had his support too... but did I have him to walk by my side, not just through this, but for as far into the future as I could see? And I could see far into my future. I wanted him in my future... but would he be enough for me? Would he be patient with me as I dealt with all the insecurities I now had? Would he walk this journey with me? So many questions, not enough answers. Only time would tell... and I didn't even know if I believed in relationships anymore, and quite frankly, I still wasn't sure what I wanted. I didn't want to go into this and get my heart broken, or break his heart either. He was such a lovely guy, and I didn't want to start something I wasn't sure about, because like I say, "If in doubt, leave it out," because you have the doubts for a reason, you just have to trust them and work through them.

But I knew these doubts disappeared the moment I saw him, or heard his voice. I just had to get out of my own head.

Seeing the boys coming out of school had started to take on a whole new depth of joy. Seeing their faces light up with big smiles and to have Naasir come running up to me for a hug was one of the biggest highlights of my day; I loved these boys with every fibre of my body, how on earth was it possible to love another person this much. And yet here I was, being charged with Wilful Neglect and Abandonment. My love for my boys is a love so deep, I can't even begin to describe it, a love so deep it sometimes hurts in the best possible way. Going into their room at night, to give them a good night kiss, and just stand there, watching them sleep. A love so deep, you would do absolutely anything to protect them; a love so deep that when they were in school, you miss them. I absolutely love the school holidays because it means I get to spend huge amounts of time with my boys have mad adventures and enjoying each other's company; sometimes I don't even want them to go back to school!

As soon as Naasir was in my arms, having his 'after school' hug, he asked me the question he always asks me, "How was your day, Mummy?"

I looked down into his little face and replied, "It was great handsome, thank you, how was yours?"

He then told me he had had a great day and what he'd been doing. Hearing about his day and everything he had been doing was always something that made me smile because of the way he shared. He was so full of life, so full of expression, a real storyteller... and most definitely on his way to an Oscar!

Khaalid's smile was a different kind of smile; he's quieter, a deeper thinker, very just in his thinking and with so much empathy. Complete opposite ends of the spectrum, sociable and shy, introvert and extrovert, outdoor adventurer and indoor housecat.

At times it was difficult to parent them both, but they balanced each other out and we had a great mix. I am an introvert at heart, but due to business and knowing what I want to achieve in life, I have made myself an extrovert. Going after your dreams, following your purpose, makes you step up. Makes you grow. And knowing what I was about to take on, I knew I would be growing at an incredible rate. All the information I had downloaded and printed off just in this one day, I knew my mind would be expanding, but so would my social consciousness; like I said, if they could do this to me, I would hate to think what they would have done to someone who was already known to the police, the system or had come from a lower socio economic background or ethnicity.

That night the boys and I made dinner as usual but I noticed Khaalid was unusually quiet. I asked him if he was okay, and he said he was. I didn't believe him, I knew there was something wrong. I didn't push it because I knew that he would tell me, when he was ready. He always did. After dinner he took Kelt for a walk around the block, whilst Naasir did his homework and I did some reading of the paperwork I had downloaded. When Khaalid came back, he looked at me and again he looked distracted. I got up to make a cup of tea and asked the boys if they wanted one, Khaalid offered to make it, and told me, "Mummy, you've got enough to do. Let me make it."

I asked him again what the matter was, as we were now away from Naasir, and he just looked at me and told me he had seen the pile of paperwork in my office. He asked me what it was all for, and so I told him that I needed to understand why the police think I did what they were saying I did. If I was going to win this, I had to understand the processes involved. Khaalid then asked me about my business and how I was going to manage both at the same time, with everything else I was doing. So I told him that I would just have to get better at managing my time and that I would need more help from him and Naasir around the house; but whatever happened we were going to win this, and everything would be fine. We were going to be fine; he responded with a nod of his head and then gave me a hug, told me he loved me and then, told me to do as I was told and go and sit down whilst he made me a cup of tea. I don't think I will ever forget this moment. It has even brought tears to my eyes remembering it now whilst I write. My little boy was growing up and was beginning to really grasp the enormity of everything that was happening. If things weren't challenging enough for me on my own, without a steady job whilst I built my business, due to my experience and restricted working hours, I now had this court case to deal with. I asked him if there was anything else bothering him, and he said, "No Mummy! Now go and sit down and I'll make the tea!"

"Yes boss!" I said with a giggle and sat down as I was told to do. That night after the boys had gone to bed, I organised all the information I had downloaded and set about highlighting the areas of relevance. Going through the information I knew I had a lot to do; I needed another holiday. The more I read, the more baffled I was, the more notes I was making, the more I realised how the police officers had failed on so many levels. The more I read, the more I was becoming aware of a huge systemic failure on many levels, and in some respects, a corruption that scared me. I was beginning to feel tired, but I continued. I needed to get this done. I needed to present my questions to Ruben. With what I was discovering, there was no way this should be getting to court. They had to throw this out; the negative implications were too big for them to keep pursuing this, not just for me, but for every parent. I was also not going to allow this to happen to me, or anyone else. I was going to take this all the way. I was going to fight it, but I couldn't fight the sleep. I woke up in the early hours of the morning, sat on the couch, surrounded by the paperwork, highlighter still in my hand, Kelt curled up at my feet. He looked at me and I knew he needed the toilet, so I put my coat and shoes on and off we went for a walk around the block. I got back, tidied up the papers and got into bed, knowing I had to be awake again in four hours… I really did need that holiday.

I was so focused on sales for Vitality, arranging meetings and sending out quotes all the next morning. I needed to generate some cash. Discussing the benefits of having a Vitality policy with one of my potential clients, I was telling them all about the discounts off flights and Mr & Mrs Smith boutique holidays. At the back of my mind I just kept thinking: *I need a break. I need some time to just switch off. Some time for me, in the sun, by the sea.*

As that call ended, my phone rang. It was Michey. As we spoke she told me she also needed a holiday, and before the call was over, we had booked the dates in our diary and by the end of the day we were off to Murcia. My first ever girlie holiday, the first time in my life I had ever been away on holiday with a friend as a single woman. I would be there on the day of the intermediate diet – the hearing before the trial itself. It would be good to be away from home on that date. I could just enjoy the holiday, and regardless of whether the case was thrown out or not, I would still be prepared to go on the 10th November.

I got to speak with John that night as the ship he was on had a scheduled stop in Portugal, on the way down to the Canary Islands. I told him about my holiday with Michey and it turned out he would be in Cadiz at the same time, with time off. We wanted to see each other, so I changed my flight home and booked a flight back from Seville, planning on getting an overnight coach from Murica to Cadiz. I would sleep on the coach so I wouldn't lose any time with him. This holiday was meant to be. I just needed to generate the extra cash to pay for it; so I started delivering leaflets and magazines, whilst also walking the dogs and taking the boys with me. We had great fun seeing who would be the first to deliver all the magazines and leaflets around Chesterfield, whilst also delivering leaflets for Vitality. A firm believer in do what needs to be done to create results in your life, and I wanted to instil this mindset into my boys. You want results; you have to put the hours and the work in. Life is not going to hand you everything on a plate, you have to do the work; put in the extra hours of work… and put the hours in I did.

Fast forward a few weeks and I still had not heard from Ruben. I had left several messages and still had not heard anything. I was getting really anxious. What was going to happen? How was he going to represent me? He hadn't even had a conversation with me since the day I had been charged and released from the police cell. He knew nothing about me, nothing about that night and the events that had unfolded and he was supposed to be representing me? I was not confident, and nor was I impressed. Is this how lawyers operated? Or was this just the way they behaved in Scotland? Acting without knowledge? Or was this the norm across the whole of the UK?

The next time I hear from Ruben was the 7th October when he sent me a letter asking for 'references with regards to my attitude towards my children… my level of caring and interaction with their school and other organisations they belonged to'. He also wanted a reference from 'the child psychologist who would be in a position to provide a reference to indicate (that you are a good mother and also that you have never placed your children, either deliberately or negligently in any state that would jeopardise their well-being'. I got on with collecting the extra references and sent them to him, carrying on with all the research and building a case of my own.

I was still very concerned that I had not yet had a conversation with this guy. I knew I had to pay my bills, including his invoice; maybe this is why he wasn't in touch with me? But the invoice was not due yet, and I was just about on top of everything. I just had this feeling of: *This can't be right. This is my life they are dealing with, the lives of my children. Do they not get the impact of what they are having? Is this how everyone is treated?* Here I was, running a home on my own, with two children, building a business, studying how to be a great coach and selling Vitality; not to mention training in mixed martial arts and swimming almost every day, my time was taken up with a lot, and yet I still wouldn't leave a client without a response to their phone calls, especially given the enormity of the situation. I wouldn't even dream of it. I called again, and this time I was quite firm with Felicity and told her that although they may be used to dealing with this kind of case, I certainly wasn't. I wanted to know what was going on, and when I would hear from Ruben to go over the details for the case. I wanted to know when I was to be interviewed properly about what had happened. We were now heading into October and this had been going on two months, and I still had not been interviewed. I broke down in tears after the phone call. How did this happen? How did I get here?

My holiday with Michey was fast approaching and I was working flat out on promoting Vitality, calling in my clients. I was also making great headway with my studies with The Coaching Academy. Leaflets were being delivered and I was still just about keeping my head above water. But I was still wasn't making enough money. My chosen brother Rob called. He asked me for a quote for Vitality and asked me how I was doing. For the first time since everything had happened, I had a full and honest conversation about how I was feeling, my financial situation, everything. Amongst a mix of tears and giggles, Rob was there for me. Listening, truly listening. I felt heard for the first time in a long time. No interruptions, no advice, no judgements, just listening. He gave me the space to offload and at the end of me offloading, he gave me his advice, his thoughts, his love and the money to pay for Rubens invoice. Me being me, I wasn't about to just simply take the money. I was, as my mother called me 'an independent little madam' and I didn't like taking handouts; I told Rob this.

His response, "Well coach me then. I want to be happier. I am not happy in my job, in fact I fucking hate it. So coach me on how to discover what I truly want, increase my salary and free up time so I can spend more time with my girls." He'd got me. So I agreed. This was a business transaction.

Then it hit me. If I was going to get through this, I had to see this whole situation as a piece of business, as training, a learning experience. I had to distance myself from the emotional and start thinking strategically. If this was something my clients were experiencing what would I ask of them? What would they do differently to what I was currently doing? What could I gain from this?

I went back to my flipchart sheets. I stood there with them for over an hour adding to the lists, adding all the possible outcomes, all the different strategies that I wanted to go over with Ruben. I also added all the impact of his poor customer service, his lack of social and emotional intelligence. I did the same for the police and the prosecutor fiscal. Professionally they had all failed on many levels. Then I turned the tables on myself. What had I done? What could I have done differently? Had what I had done been any different to other scenarios single parents had to deal with daily? Managing time, multiple commitments, and the various situations we were placed in on a daily basis, just because we were single parents.

I was feeling more positive, more empowered and more focused than ever. I was not going to let this go. This was a fight that, although I had already chosen, this was a fight that was much bigger than me. A fight that so many parents were going through on a daily basis; whether it was with the police or with employers. How many parents were dealing with organisational bullying and being managed out of their job just because they had family commitments to deal with? How many parents had to juggle the different commitments of travelling with children? Choosing to go to the toilets in the service stations, leaving their children outside in the car or in the main foyer with hundreds of people going back and forth, simply because their children were of a different gender and too old to go into the toilets with their parent? Surely if they were too old to enter the toilets with their parents, then they were deemed old enough to be left on their own? If they were not allowed to go into the changing rooms with their parents due to being of the opposite gender due to their age, then surely they were old enough to be left alone to go into their own gender changing rooms, to get undressed with adults unknown to them, who were getting changed?

There were so many different scenarios where parents were leaving children alone in the car for a similar amount of time to the 15-20 minutes I had left the boys, and children much younger than my boys. Were the police going to arrest all the parents and charge them with this? When were we supposed to prepare our children for travelling alone to school? To go to the park by themselves? When were we expected to put trust in our children, to enable them to step up to be responsible, to take care of themselves, preparing them for life? Why is it children were being made 'younger', more immature, more reliant on others by the system, the schools and the laws in the UK, then their counterparts in different countries were excelling? Why were the police, the schools and the different organisations of governance encouraging us to wrap our kids up in cotton wool, resulting in a loss of valuable life skills, valuable confidence? Why are we impressed by kids being able to do their own laundry, cook their own meals at the age of ten? Why are we impressed by adults of the age of 22 and 23 working hard and succeeding in careers? This should be the norm.

I was beginning to see how the over praising and over protection, schools against competition (for fear of upsetting the little angels) was debilitating, not just our younger children, but also the young adults. Our kids should know that life is a competition, they should be able to hit the ground running at the age of 16 when they are able to work, and certainly at the age of 18 when many leave home to go to university or getting their own home; and yet we have little boys and girls running around in adults bodies, simply because of the bubble wrap parenting and the suffocation they have experienced growing up. This 'new breed' of parenting is disabling not just our children but also our countries, and we are faced by a generation of spoilt, expectation and lazy '20 somethings' that think the world owes them a living. Businesses are faced with a growing trend in incompetent, lazy candidates for jobs, young adults who lack common sense and the unwillingness to step up, coming in late, 'pulling sickies' due to hangovers and 'can't be arsed syndrome', and so many prefer to employ people from overseas, who show up, do the work and do it well (and as we saw with the Brexit here in the UK, one of the issues was 'foreigners coming over here and stealing our jobs, using our NHS ', when in fact if those that grew up here pulled their finger out of their backsides and did the work, there would be no need to look overseas for employees (but that's a whole different book!).

The combined impact of bubble wrap parenting, restrictive insurance policies for businesses and 'over-zealous' health and safety guidelines costs the UK job market £340 billion every year due to 'disengaged employees' according to The Hay Group. I don't believe this is simply because the employers are not giving the employees the right work culture, I believe it is largely in part down to the attitude of the employees; many I suspect expecting too much for very little effort, and pointing the finger at the employer instead of doing the work on themselves. We wonder why so many small businesses go bust every year, and why so many people are on benefits, and it is because the entire system is broken; from home to school to government; and for the parents, schools and government not to see this link is simply crazy.

Michey called that night and we continued making plans for our holiday, whilst also talking about everything I was learning and thinking. She was in complete agreement with me. As a single parent and Sales Director for the family business, her girls had been walking to school together for years, and arriving home before her. Her girls were a few years older than my boys, but had been walking to school alone at the same ages as my boys were now. She couldn't get her head around it. What we could get our head around though was our up and coming holiday. We were going to meet at my mums and go to the airport together. I was so excited, and we both agreed that we would be taking our laptops to get some work done. We understood that just because we were on holiday, didn't mean business stopped. We were going after our success and nothing was going to stop either of us. We were mums on a mission.

The next day I had a meeting with Nick Clegg, my local MP, and someone I had met a couple of times through business and through

Birkdale School. I explained to him what the situation was and asked him if there was anything that he could help me with. Once he had heard what had happened, and the kind of location we had been in, he was really shocked by the heavy-handedness of the police. He also made the connection that many children of my boy's ages went to the park by themselves, and took themselves to school. He stated that he couldn't help as the case wasn't over yet. He asked me to stay in touch and keep him updated with the progress of the case. He wished me luck and we made another appointment to see each other after the next court appearance.

Back home I sat down with a cup of tea, my highlighter pens and my research. It was time to pull together my own case so I could go over it with Ruben… if he ever got back in touch with me.

---

[6] See the research done by Michael Gurian, Author and Founder of The Gurian Institute; Steve Biddulph, Author, Psychologist and Parent Educator; Dr William Sears MD, Paediatrician and Author of over 30 parenting books; Professor Tanya Byron Clinician, Psychologist, Child Therapist and Author; as well as Author and Lecturer Alfie Kohn who specialises in the areas of parenting and human behaviour.

TEN

BUILDING MY OWN CASE

I had started making progress on pulling my own case together and had received the 'Summary of Evidence' from Ruben. In the summary, it was stated 'you DAWN BATES did wilfully neglect and abandon said child in a manner likely to cause him unnecessary suffering or injury to health and did leave him unattended within a motor vehicle with the keys in the ignition for over an hour while you went away to consume alcohol; CONTRARY to the Children and Your Persons (Scotland) Act 1937, Section 12 (1) as amended'. This was stated for both Khaalid and Naasir before they went onto the third charge against me stating 'you DAWN BATES did behave in a threatening or abusive manner which was likely to cause a reasonable person to suffer fear or alarm in that you did repeatedly shout at your children and repeatedly shout and swear at police officers.'

I couldn't believe what I was reading. I certainly hadn't gone off drinking for over an hour, and I certainly hadn't wilfully neglected or abandoned either of them. For them to have then stated that I had left them in a manner likely to cause unnecessary suffering or harm or injury to health, was again, ridiculous. How was leaving them in a car park next to the castle, in a quiet little village, in the car, with our dog likely to cause them harm or any kind of suffering to health? As for shouting at the boys, I hadn't shouted at either of them, in fact quite the opposite as Khaalid was sleeping and I was trying to calm Naasir down so I could understand why he was upset and so he didn't wake Khaalid up.

As I read through the summary there were so many errors in it, and the timings were so out of sync it was unbelievable. There were holes in it everywhere with regards to the timings, words Naasir would have used, things he would have said and it was obvious they had stretched the times out to suit a story they had fabricated. The initial time stated when a witness called 'Lasek' had first seen Naasir was before the boys had even started to get ready for bed, when John and I were still with them. Had the police done some proper policing and questioned me and got a statement from me, and spoken with the three girls who I had been speaking with, they would have known this information to be false. But herein lays the problem. They had no intention of taking a statement from me, nor did they have any intention of doing any police work.

Further on in the summary it stated that both the witnesses that were assisting the police with looking for me, had all left Naasir and Khaalid in the car alone, for similar amounts of time that I had, so my question is simply this: If it is okay for them to deem it safe for them to leave my boys alone in the car for the same amount of time that I had, why was it not okay for me?

Some of the words that I had apparently used I had to look up because I hadn't even heard of some of the words, and for someone who reads a huge amount of books, crosses many sub cultures of England and has friends across the globe from different English speaking countries this is saying something. Some of the language I was reported to have used as well would never have come out of my mouth, and those who know me really well, would know this.

I was mystified by the threatening behaviour I was supposed to have exhibited, and could not think of why they were saying this. I would need to find this out.

I had this strong sense that I was being stitched up, and it was a deep feeling, one I could just not shake off.

One of the things that really shocked me was a statement I had apparently said to PC Nicola Brindle, "I just wanted one night off. I just wanted to have some wine and go for a nice walk and enjoy the nice scenery with my friend." First of all, it was dark, so I'm not sure what scenery I was expecting to enjoy in the dark. Secondly, this statement had been twisted beyond recognition from an answer to a question PC Brindle had asked me in the police cell when she had asked me what had brought me and the boys to Inveraray. I had told her that we were passing on through and had chosen to wake up overlooking Loch Fyne to the sunrise, and we had stopped at The George as I had wanted a night off from cooking and just wanted to enjoy the evening with the boys and John. How she had twisted it to this statement in the Summary of Evidence was simply outrageous. It was then stated that I had been requested to not speak with my boys in the police car because I was explaining to them what had happened. How could I not speak with my boys in the police car to help them make sense of what was going on? Did these police officers have any sense of humanity or parenting skills at all? As a parent you can't not explain to the best of your ability what is going on to reassure your children, and for someone to ask you to not reassure your children is just crazy. It also stated in the summary that I had gone off to the smoking area of The George Hotel earlier in the night, which certainly hadn't happened. For one I hadn't smoked cigarettes for years, so why on earth would I want to go to the smoking area. The only places we had been in The George was in the dining area with the fire place, the toilet and the bar to pay our bill.

The lies in this summary were very concerning, and I knew that to be able to paint the picture of me white again after all this black had been painted was going to be difficult, but I didn't care. I was not going to stop. They couldn't get away with these lies just because they put on a police uniform every time they went to work, or called themselves a lawyer. The only truth to be told in this summary was the facts that no medical evidence was taken, no blood tests, no breath test to measure my alcohol levels so they could not prove or disprove whether I had been drinking or not, even though I had admitted to drinking two glasses of wine and a mouthful of wine from John's bottle of wine. They also confirmed that there were no CCTV cameras in the vicinity, so they had no way of proving what had happened. When I asked Ruben to obtain the times of the calls made to the police station and the social services, he declined to do so and said it wasn't necessary. How was it not necessary? This was essential evidence that could help disprove their lies. The summary also stated that there had indeed been no interview with me.

I started to look up for the legal age limit to be able to leave children alone, in accordance with what Natasha at Social Services had told me. I looked on the NSPCC website, checked the government guidelines, the social services websites, spoke with the CAB and with Tariq at MAST. Having done all this I knew I had not broken any law, and that it was down to me as a parent to make my own assessment of the situation, and to consider the maturity of my own children as to their suitability to be left alone for 15-20 minutes. So again, my questions 'Why was this being allowed to be happen? If I, as a responsible, loving parent had deemed it appropriate to leave my children alone whilst I nipped up to the castle to check the opening times and cost of a family ticket for the next day's activities, then I was well within my rights, and the law to do so. Had my children been younger, and we had been in an area full of gun crime and drug dens, abandoned buildings in an inner city location, then there would have been no way I would have left the boys. Had my boys been irresponsible and untrustworthy, then again I would not have left them. Had my boys been not been used to going to the local park, or walking Kelt by themselves, then I would not have left them. I had made sure my boys were competent, responsible and trustworthy. I had made a risk assessment, something I was used to doing on a daily basis, and we all had larger than average comfort zones.

One of the pieces of research I had come across was somewhat interesting for me on a business level. It made me wonder how much of what was happening was due to the merger of the eight different police forces that operated across Scotland two years earlier to form Police Scotland. Was this case one of a political agenda within the newly formed organisation? People fighting to prove their worth in this new organisation, trying to flex their muscle to prove it shouldn't be them that gets made redundant or moved to a different location, or their police station that gets shut down entirely. I had seen it many times before, both as an employee and as an entrepreneur. Many people I knew who had their own businesses had gone through the process of merging with another company, and all resulted in a loss of jobs, regardless of how good the original intentions were. I had even considered it when ramO and I were discussing whether to close or sell our first business together. With the west coast of Scotland being incredibly rural, and such a beautiful idyllic area of the world, not just the UK, there was not much for the police to do. This was proven to me when I looked at the crime statistics for the area. With so few crimes happening in the west coast of Scotland, I was alarmed to see the disproportionate amounts of charges being made for Breach of the Peace. They outweighed the other crimes by a significant amount, one of the things as a business owner and mentor I found disturbing. It was a massive red flag for training and development. So I went back to Stephen at Skills for Justice and discussed my findings with him. Again he was very supportive of what I was saying and agreed wholeheartedly with me. He also told me that whilst there was an on-going case against me, he was unable to work or talk with me further; but to get in touch once it was over and let him know the outcome.

I called Ruben and requested to speak with him as I was soon to go on holiday with Michey and really wanted to discuss the case I was building. Again he was out of the office, and this time I spoke with Margaret. She was a lot more sympathetic to my situation and for the first time since this whole ugly situation had happened, I felt heard by Rubens firm. She reassured me Ruben would call me back, and he did, within the hour. I was relieved. He told me that he had not called me back and would not be representing me as I had not paid his invoice. I was shocked. How could he drop me in it this close to the court case? Why had he not told either Felicity or Margaret this piece of news? Why had he not returned my calls, or responded to the updates I had sent him with regards to the payment. I told him I would check my account to see if the money had arrived, as I had just secured the payment, and if it had arrived in my account, I would send it over. I also reminded him that he had agreed to represent me knowing full well my current financial situation, and had been free in his choice to take on my case. He then agreed to represent me in court and said we would meet up before we were due in court to go over the case. When I asked him how would that be enough time to prepare the case with the additional information I had gathered, he again tried to reassure me that he knew what he was doing and I would be okay. I wouldn't get convicted, get sent to prison or lose my children as I had such a good background and my references were glowing. The call ended but there was something that just didn't feel right. I didn't trust this man; but he was all I had and I just had to believe everything was going to go as he said it would.

I then went back to my research and started going through the Code of Ethics, and boy did that make interesting reading. At one point I actually thought it was a waste of time highlighting the points relevant to my case where the police officers had gone against the Code because there were so many points in it they had deviated from. Looking at it with my employers head on, these police officers had not only stepped over the mark, they had sprinted over it and left it in the dust behind them, not even knowing of its existence! The same goes for the Leadership Review. The violations of policing policies was astounding and had this been one of my employees, they would have been sacked immediately, and I would have questioned my own ability as an employer. There was a serious failing on almost every management level that I could see, simply from the behaviours and attitudes of these three police officers. How had these three police officers been able to get away with this behaviour? And how long had they been getting away with it? Their up line manager was either not interest and was as corrupt as they were, or totally oblivious to the behaviours, neither of which were good.

With Police Scotland in its infancy, and looking at the mission statement for the new organisation, I started to look at the history of the other seven police forces that had been operating in Scotland. It occurred to me that Scotland's eight different forces represented the different states of the United States, and then it hit me like a tonne of bricks… the Masonic connection, and how strong it was. Now I am politically aware enough to know about this organisation and their antics in the political world; the devastating effects and the hold they have over many politicians. The agendas they manipulate and the games they play. Some of my friends are even more politically aware than I am. I asked a few of them if they could get me some information on just how deep they operated in Scotland, especially on the west coast. They were only too glad to help. One of them even said, "Why do you want to know? What angle are you looking at?" When I told him, he didn't know how to respond, and told me I probably wouldn't like what I was about to be given.

When John called later that night, I was so relieved to hear from him. So much had happened in the last couple of days and I hadn't told him half of it, just wanting to hear about his travels and talk about our time together when I arrived in Cadiz with him. Just seeing his face, looking into his eyes, I felt like I was swimming in the ocean, free and at peace. I couldn't tell him that of course, that was just for me to know. I wouldn't allow myself to be that vulnerable with him. I was still very guarded and although I knew I had fallen for him hook, line and sinker, I didn't want to come on too strong and ruin what we had. I didn't know how to do this courting process; I didn't know how to be in a relationship anymore. I was scared to show my true feelings. I was scared of being rejected again, and it didn't matter how much this incredible guy showed me he loved me, I just couldn't let his love in. The ice around my heart had melted, but the wall of defence was almost impenetrable. I wanted to let him in, I wanted to just go with the flow, but I had my emotions under lock and key. I also had it in my mind that if I allowed him to see my insecurities, it would eventually start to kill what we had; and that was the last thing in the world I wanted. I felt such a strong soul connection to John, and he was always there at the back of my mind, and whenever I thought of him shock waves ran through my body and a stupid grin would break out on my face. How was it possible to feel so much for someone and yet still be this guarded? Was it just simply a case of 'absence makes the heart grow fonder'? A holiday romance that had blossomed, with the fire still burning because of the distance?

I was anxious in many ways about seeing him when we met in Spain. Would it still be something magical? Would he still enjoy my company? Would this whole Scotland Saga destroy us? It hadn't yet, but I didn't feel like the fun Dawn anymore. I was so overwhelmed by this whole case that I felt as though the carefree, happy Dawn was slowly being sucked out of me. Our conversations were never ending, we just flowed together, for hours, and he always, always put a smile on my face. After the call, I felt safe. I went to bed that night at peace. I was going to see him in a couple of weeks; and I needed to see him. I needed to know how it would be between us, just the two of us, in each other's company all day every day, even if it was only for ten days. I wanted to know how it would be. I didn't want to put my energies into a relationship with someone if it only worked long distance. To me that wasn't a real relationship, that was just two guarded people keeping a safe distance from one another and only meeting up to have a bit of fun together.

I had already had a marriage with someone who was absent a lot of the time, and although the time with ramO was great when he was home, he still wasn't there most of the time. I wanted someone who would be there to enjoy the everyday moments with such as cooking together, walking the dogs and hiking together, shopping together, growing together. I just couldn't figure out how this would work when I knew John's work would be taking him away most of the time. I really struggled with that; but if the feelings for him when I was in his company were as strong, or stronger when in his company, it would be something I would be willing to sacrifice for a future with him; short term sacrifices for the long term gain. I was absolutely certain though, that if he didn't show up in court for me, stand by my side, not just because he was my key witness, but because he was my partner, because he loved me, because he wanted to support me through this nightmare, then it would be over between us. I didn't want to be with someone who wouldn't be there for me for something as serious as this, or only be there when it was convenient for them. It was either 100% from each of us, or nothing. No half measures, no excuses. I was either going to be a top priority or we were over. I knew this with every fibre of my being; but would I have the strength to end it if he wasn't there? Especially given the way I felt about him? I knew it would be difficult, but I also knew I would end it. I had achieved a lot on my own, and if things didn't work out with John, then they didn't work out. I would continue to achieve things on my own. I would continue to build my business, and go after my life at sea. Either John was the right guy for me or he wasn't. I realised I had hardened my heart, some would say too much, but I didn't care. I wasn't going to compromise on this kind of thing in a relationship, no matter how many boxes the person ticked. No matter how much I loved them. I knew what I wanted in a relationship, and if my divorce from ramO had given me anything, it had given me that gift of self-worth.

I woke up the next morning and went over the Summary of Evidence again and started making my own notes on it. It was easier to do after some sleep, even if that sleep was broken; something that had become a regular occurrence since my nights in the police cell. I would wake up in the night worrying about the court case, worrying about the outcome. I would wake up crying, doubting myself as a mother; worrying about the costs involved of travelling to Scotland and staying over in a hotel. The worry of just how much it was going to cost me in legal fees was ever present. I knew I would be looking at an invoice of around £1000 even before we all stepped foot in the courtroom. How many times would I have to appear in court? How many hours work would be involved. Looking at the mileage, the hours in the courtroom and a possible second court date appearance I knew I would be looking at around £5,000. I added it to my list of sales targets. It was the only thing I could do; and if it didn't cost me that, then at least I had put it on my target list and could use the income to pay other investments and bills. I knew I had to focus on the positives, because where the mind went the body followed. If I focused on the negatives, then that is all I would see; like it says in the Qur'aan 'If you look for the bad, you'll only see the bad, but if you look for the good, you'll only see the good'. If only the police had looked for the good in this situation and in the positives of what I was doing with my boys, instead of notching up another arrest and conviction just to keep themselves in a job. I felt the same about the lawyer, or rather the Prosecutor Fiscal. Why had he or she taken on this case when there was no hard evidence, just the conflicting statements of people who knew nothing about me?

I spoke with my mum that afternoon and she asked me how I was doing, and wanted to know the arrangements for my holiday. When would I be arriving at hers, and what I was eating or not eating? She also asked me how the case was going and I filled her in on all the details. Again she used the 'B' word. Twice now I had heard that from my mum. I didn't like it. I told her not to worry and to not get so worked up... then I jokingly said, "You are getting on a bit now mother, don't want you going and having a heart attack."

She came back with, "This is not funny Dawn Louise. This is serious and I wish you would take it seriously."

I reminded her that if I didn't make jokes around it, then I would cry, and I was done crying. I had cried too many tears, and had too many doubts about myself, and I was done with it. Making a joke was a way in which I had learnt to deal with things, a coping mechanism.

Mum asked me how much was left to do on the case and I told her there was still quite a bit to get through, and that I would hopefully have it all done before I left for the holiday. Then she asked me if I had packed yet, at which point I realised I hadn't even got a new suitcase! So whilst I was on the call with her, I got online and ordered myself a new cabin suitcase. I didn't want to take my large suitcase, I was only going to be wearing shorts, vest tops and bikinis anyway during the day, and a couple of lightweight evening outfits. No point paying extra for a large suitcase when I didn't have to. If I purchased extra clothes whilst I was out there, then I would just squeeze them into the suitcase I was already taking, I'd take my large handbag too, making sure it had virtually nothing in it on the way out and carry my laptop in my red laptop bag. Buying my new suitcase was exciting. I chose a Tripp one with blue, pink and purple flowers on it. It was a suitcase for the new Dawn that was emerging, the fact that it was in the sale was an added bonus! I was getting quite good at attracting what I wanted, just had no idea how I had attracted this whole Scotland Saga! My mum made me promise that I would leave all my work at home, we negotiated that I would leave the court case papers behind, what she didn't know was I was transferring all my notes into word documents, and working until stupid o'clock in the morning to make sure I had gone through every document I had downloaded. I would have them all completed by the time I went on holiday. I could sleep at my mums and on holiday, get some proper rest. No boys, no dog, just me and Michey on my first ever girlie holiday! And then my own little adventure to meet John, the new love of my life.

ELEVEN
A WELL DESERVED HOLIDAY

Saying goodbye to the boys was both upsetting and exciting. I knew I wouldn't see them for about two weeks, and when I came back, I knew I would know whether I would have to go up to Scotland on the 10th November or not. I was focusing on the positive that Ruben would manage to get it thrown out of court. I told the boys I would see them in a couple of weeks and gave ramO a quick update as to what was happening. He had been really supportive throughout all of this situation and we were making progress in healing the rift between us. I had let go of the pain and had forgiven him. I didn't want the boys to be caught up between two fighting parents. It wasn't healthy for any of us, and certainly wouldn't help them with their future relationships. I had to lead by example and so I just focused on ramO's positive character traits, of which he had many. He was a great guy, even though he had done what he had done. Taking ownership in my part of the marriage breakdown had helped a lot, and was probably one of the reasons that I was aware of the pressure this court case could possibly have on John and I. Stress was never a good thing for any relationship, and this was the biggest stress I had ever had.

Kelt and I got in the car and headed to Leicester to see my friend Zoe, and her fiancée Adam. They would be taking care of Kelt whilst I was in Spain. I just need it would cheer Zoe up, and I knew she would spoil him. I was so looking forward to seeing Zoe. It had been a while since I had seen her and it was time for some crazy time in the Safehouse as it was known due to her fiancé being DJ Mastersafe, the legendary old school scratchmaster. He was epic! Loved his old school vibe and talent! When we arrived it was time for Zoe and I to head to the shops to get some ingredients for dinner. We were cooking together, something we had been planning for a while. Zoe had been an incredible support for me whilst all this court case had been going on, so had Tina. I knew I could always rely on them to cheer me up and bring me back to earth. I treasured my friendship with both of them. We lived very different lives, but these two ladies would always have a special place in my heart regardless of how different our lives were. Not many people could make me cry from laughing but Tina could; and Zoe, had the biggest, softest heart, but a backbone of steel. They both had so much love to give but didn't take any rubbish from anyone. Zoe, Adam and I had a great night and when it came to me saying goodbye, Kelt looked confused. He had never been left with anyone but my mum before, but Adam soon distracted him and I left. It felt strange not having my boys and Kelt with me, but I needed this time to regroup, to rest, to nourish myself, to heal, and the beach was the perfect place to do that.

On the way to mums, I decided to stop and get myself a bottle of wine. I would share a glass with my mum. It had been a long time since we had shared a bottle of wine together. As I went to pick it up, I panicked. Fear ran through me. I began to realise this court case was having a bigger effect on me than I had realised. I hesitated and then thought to myself: *What the hell is wrong with you woman? The boys are with their dad, you are going to be enjoying the bottle with your mum! Buy the damn bottle!* I let out a nervous giggle to myself, paid for the wine and got to my mums.

Dinner and a cup of tea were waiting for me, and out of nowhere I reached for her tobacco and rolled myself a roll up. Both mum and dad looked at me and asked me what I was doing. I said, "I don't know, I just know I want a cigarette." Dinner eaten and tea drank, I went to my mums crystal cabinet and got two of her best crystal glasses out, went into the kitchen and poured mum and I a glass of wine. I told her about what had happened in the shop, and she told me that I needed to see someone. I needed to see the doctor and that I couldn't allow this court case to affect me so much. Most parents drank wine, pretty much always in front of their children; it was nothing to be ashamed or frightened of. She told me I was being too hard on myself and worrying too much. I knew what she was saying was right, and that there was really no come back, but I just didn't want to risk anything.

This time my dad spoke up and told me, "You can't let them get to you like this. Listen to your mother." My dad NEVER spoke up on things, always preferring to watch and raise an eyebrow here and there. If he had anything to say, it was always to my mum out of earshot of us kids, so for my dad to say something meant something. It was time for me to start listening. Dad had spoken.

The next day I spoke with Michey and we made arrangements for getting to the airport by train. I arrived at Michey's that night and we had a great night. She made me a steak and blue cheese sandwich – and oh my days! It was FAB! The next day we woke up and were on our way to the airport when I realised I had left my purse at my mums! So we had to go via my mum's to get it, which stressed Michey out a tad, but we had plenty of time. We arrived at the train station and I was so giddy. I had butterflies and was now so excited! I was going on holiday! I couldn't believe it. On the flight Michey treated us both to a bottle of wine and from that moment on, we did nothing but enjoy ourselves. I was so glad we had decided to just be spontaneous and book it.

The holiday was great. We sunbathed by the pool, me reading my business books and Michey reading her romance novels. We had chosen a perfect location, no English people! And the locals didn't speak English either. There were a couple of English bars, but we stayed well clear of those. What's the point of us going on holiday to a different country if we were just going to go to places that spoke English and served English food and had English TV channels playing in the background!? Not our bag at all! We went practised our Spanish, went dancing, discovered a local restaurant right by the hotel and went there every day for food. We walked around the local area and I had great fun in the sea, dancing to the music in my head. It was the first year I had worn a bikini and it felt great. All the training and clean eating I had been doing had paid off. I spoke with John most nights and I was excited about going to see him in

Cadiz. As the days passed, my attention was taken up with the date of the court case. How was it going to go? Would the case get thrown out? Sitting on the balcony the night before, Michey and were to witness a storm like no other. It was amazing! The lightning was incredible and the thunder was right above us. I joked, "Well that's not a good omen!"

I called Ruben's office two days later and was given the news that the intermediate trial was being continued and would be the 5th November. The trial itself would still be held on the 10th November, Would John be able to be there? I realised it meant I had to go straight to Scotland on my return to the UK. This would mean I would have to buy another flight and extend my stay in Scotland; more expense, and more time away from my boys and Kelt. I spoke with ramO made the arrangements for the boys and I would sort Kelt out when I got back from my holiday. Michey encouraged me to just enjoy the rest of the holiday; there was nothing more I could do. So I did. We went out dancing that night until the early hours and I danced, danced like my life depended on it. I was the only one on the dance floor for most of the night as we were on holiday out of season, but that suited me just fine. I liked having the dance floor all to myself. It was my space to just lose myself in the music. The next day Michey and I went shopping for some gifts; her for her girls and her dad, and me for my boys, John and my parents. I also got my coach ticket to head over to Cadiz. Holding the ticket in my hand was a great feeling. I couldn't believe I was going to see John. It had been months, and I really missed him.

The next day I got on the coach and headed to Cadiz. I dozed most of the way, but there was a little boy sitting across the aisle from me with his mum. He looked Arabic, and then I heard his mum say his name, Ahmed. My heart sparked. I loved this little boys energy so I spoke with him in Arabic. His little face lit up. His mother looked at me and spoke with me in Spanish. We pieced together a conversation using Arabic, English and Spanish and the lady told me that only Ahmed's dad spoke with him in Arabic and so for him to hear me speak Arabic was a joy for him as his dad was working away, and they were on their way to see him. Seeing Ahmed made me miss the boys so much. I just wanted to hug them. My mind drifted off to the court case and what lay ahead and then I found myself dozing. I woke up at the services and was in need of some coffee. I walked into the café and ordered a coffee in Arabic, not thinking. The guy behind the bar looked at me and smiled and served me coffee, speaking back to me in Arabic. I didn't realise we were speaking Arabic to one another at first; it just seemed natural to me. It wasn't until I was sat outside and a man who was sat at the next table started to speak with me and I replied to him in Arabic that I realised because of the look of shock on his face. He was so surprised to hear a white woman with copper, almost blonde hair speaking with him in Arabic. We talked for a while about Egypt, the state of the Arab world, the beauty of Morocco, and of course Islam. He was a lovely guy and wished me a great holiday. He told me Cadiz was beautiful, and to enjoy it. I told him I would and wished him salaam.

I got back on the coach and saw that Ahmed and his mum were fast asleep and so I settled down to sleep. I woke up as we were about to come into Cadiz and so I looked at the local area from the coach window. As we pulled into the coach station I saw John sitting on a bench. My heart and stomach flipped. I was so happy to see him. It had only been a couple of months, but it felt longer than that. We spent the next two weeks enjoying the sights of Cadiz, a vineyard in Jerez, horse riding on the beach and getting to know the local restaurants. It was a holiday I had always dreamed of, with a man who blew my mind in many ways. I couldn't quite believe this guy was for real. Quite a few of the local restaurateurs started to recognise us and we spent a lot of time by the beach. We enjoyed traditional flamenco singing and traditional family home cooked food in a restaurant right on the beach. It was emotional. I was distracted towards the end of the holiday, knowing what I was heading back home to, alone. John had been requested to write his statement of events and send it to Ruben; again, I was surprised it was only now being requested, after all these months. We spent a night going over the case. John then said we were not to mention it again. We were both on holiday to enjoy our time together, and that whatever happened we would work it out together. He held me tightly in his strong arms and I melted. Several bricks in that wall I had built fell away. He promised me he would be in court for me, he just had to sort out a few things with the ship; he wouldn't let me do this by myself. As tears fell from my eyes, he wiped them away and kissed me. Another couple of bricks fell away.

We enjoyed our last couple of days together, and yet I was distracted because I knew the next time I would see him would be when he arrived in Dunoon for the court case. He could tell I was distracted and kept reminding me 'not to go there'. He'd make me giggle, engage me in conversation and we'd end up just playing, having fun, exploring the areas of Cadiz we hadn't been to yet. Then the last day came and we headed to the train station. He was staying on, going back to the ship. Saying goodbye to him was hard, but as the train pulled away, he mouthed the words I love you and that was it. Tears fell from my eyes and I smiled, and all the butterflies that were inside of me went crazy.

TWELVE
PREPARING FOR THE TRIAL

On the journey home I reflected on all the great memories I had just created, and all the breakthroughs I had had during my time working on my business laying by a pool, and the time out I had taken to simply enjoy myself. I had invested time in me, got clarity on so many things to do with my future. I realised that I didn't want to be tied to the UK, I wanted to travel with my business. Working from anywhere I chose, on the beach, on my boat, travelling and working at the same time. My biggest challenge was the boys. Khaalid still had at least five years in school and Naasir had nine. I wasn't prepared to take them out of school again, and so I would just have to wait another ten years before I stepped into this new reality. That would give me plenty of time to find my boat and crew and make the money the boat would needed.

My mind soon returned to John and the court case. Would he be in the middle of the Atlantic or would he have arrived in the Canaries in time to fly back to Scotland to stand with me in the courtroom? Even though I clarity on where I wanted to take my business, there were still so many uncertainties in my mind around John. Never before had I had so many. Not in life, business or in a relationship. I had been so certain that my businesses would be a success, always believed that the choices I made were the right one, been so certain my marriage would last for life. With the breakdown of my marriage and everything I had seen in Egypt, combined with the experiences I had had since returning to the UK in the business community, the friendships that had broken down and now with this whole Scotland Saga I had so many doubts, too many.

I needed to do the coaching on myself, and I needed to work through what I wanted from my relationship with John. I knew I wanted time alone with my boys, just to focus on them, on myself and on my business; but I also wanted to be with him. His job at sea was providing me with the time to focus on the boys, myself and the business. It was also giving me time to get used to the idea being in a relationship again. I loved the fact that he had a job he loved. I got excited about the life he had at sea, it was the life I wanted, and I had found someone who got it. Someone I could see myself building a life with; but with so much happening, and having to face it alone on a day to day basis, I sometimes wondered why I had chosen someone who was never there when I needed him. Having a lot of time to think, to process on the way home, I suddenly realised I didn't need anyone, because I had the strength within me to achieve everything I have ever wanted within me. I had always pretty much done everything by myself anyway.

As my friend Ali had told me when I first told her of my split with ramO, "You've always been a single mum anyway Dawn. ramO has always worked away." What she said had so much truth in it, but also wasn't fair to ramO. He had been there for me at the end of the day to talk. Sometimes we would be on the phone five to six times a day just touching base with each other, giving each other the space to share what was going on, to support, create and reflect. He would join us for family meal times by me using the speaker facility on our phones. He was always present, even if not in person. Times when he came home, he would take over and I would get to rest. He would cook, let me have a lie in, love on me, and when he wasn't there, he would pay for me to go to the spa for the day. He was a great husband, even though he was distant in the physical.

I knew I had been giving away my own power, my own strength and my courage by passing on the acknowledgement to others that had supported me, but it was me that had done it. Me; I could do this. I could achieve everything and anything I wanted. I just had to trust myself again. I just had to trust in the process and believe that everything would work out the way it was supposed to. I was happier without ramO, had achieved so much and I had some great people in my life; ones that believed in me. I had a supportive mum and dad, even though they didn't understand why I was doing what I was doing half the time; they were always there for me. I also knew that although John wasn't beside me every day, he was still supporting me. He would send me links to information that would help me with the case, messages of support and when he could, he would always phone me on Skype, and always at the time I was at my lowest or buzzing my face off. He was someone who was completely in flow, always let what had gone before go. He never held onto any negativity. Each day was a new day and he was good for me; as I was for him. I enjoyed him on many levels.

With my mind reflecting, creating and developing the plans flying around in my head, I was home sooner than I realised. Arriving back at my mum and dad's on the 2nd November, I told them about my holiday and updated them on the court case on the 5th. I then called Zoe to check on Kelt and arrange to collect him. Mum and dad said they would take care of him whilst I headed up to Scotland. I sorted out the flights up to Scotland, and the hotel. I chose a hotel right on the shoreline, meaning I would get to walk along the beach to the courtroom. It would be my energiser before and after what was to unfold. I was due in court on the 5th of November and I took this as a positive. Guy Fawkes had sent up a rocket, or two, on that day blowing up the Houses of Parliament, going down in history. Would this date be a better omen than the storm in Murcia?

The next day I headed to get Kelt. I couldn't wait to see him. I missed him so much. As soon as I saw him I scooped him up in my arms and he went crazy giving me kisses and wagging his tail. Zoe told me that he hadn't been eating very well and was really sad. He'd missed me, and he needed a haircut! I would take him when I got back from Scotland. I stayed with Zoe and Adam for a few hours, and gave them an update on the Scotland Saga. They couldn't believe I had to go up earlier and be away from my boys for even longer. Zoe made the point of the fact that this whole fiasco was causing more harm to us as a family than the 15-20 minutes I had been away from them. She was right; and in true Zoe style she stated, "It's disgusting what they are doing to you Dawn. Who do they think they? If they are arresting you and charging you with this, then they are going to have to charge nearly every parent in the UK. What happens when you go to the services? You have to leave the boys in the car or in the foyer with hundreds of people whilst you go to the toilet! They're idiots the lot of them!" One of the things I love about Zoe is her passion, and straight forward talking. She's one of those people who wears her heart on her sleeve, and I totally love her for it.

Back at my mums, I noticed Kelt was not himself at all. He still hadn't eaten a day later, so I took him up to the vet's where mum and dad took Ed, their retired greyhound. When Kelt had been examined, the vet told me Kelt had depression as there was nothing physically wrong with him. It is common in the Lhasa Apso breed as they are incredibly loyal dogs and as I had been away from him for nearly three weeks, he was displaying all the signs of depression. He gave me some happy pills for Kelt and some nutrition boosters to help him.

I felt awful, especially as I was about to leave him again for another week. Still, I was going to be with him for the next few days so I called Michelle and asked her if she wanted to head to Holkham Beach, my favourite beach. She jumped at the chance as she'd never been. I knew she would love it, and I knew Kelt would too. He needed to be free to run around the beach and feel the wind in his face.

When we arrived, he jumped straight out of the car. He knew where he was. His little tail started wagging like I loved to see and we headed to the sea. I breathed it in, looked out to the horizon and took my shoes and socks off. I wanted to feel the sand on my feet and the water lapping over them. I charged my soul even more than I had whilst being on holiday. Looking out to sea, my plan of living and working at sea felt so right. I knew it is definitely what I wanted, delivering my coaching at sea and exploring new countries and cuisine. Nothing was going to stop me. I belonged at sea. The mermaid in me was being called home. I never felt more relaxed than when I was by the sea.

Michey and I discussed what was to come in Scotland and I realised I needed to get my game face on. I had to go over the notes and prepare my questions for Ruben. In the meantime though, watching Kelt running about on the beach, and then walking beside me as I was walking in sea, I couldn't stop smiling. I was with my poochie again. God I loved this dog so much! We had been through so much together in his short little life. What with nursing him through Parvo when we lived in Cairo, bringing him home to the UK via Amsterdam to avoid the awful quarantine process the UK imposed, of course all the house moving, the divorce and family changes. He was my shadow, and I was his pack leader. I had missed being woken up by him in the mornings. I had enjoyed the lie-ins and the freedom that I had experienced by not having to do the dog walks, but I was so glad to have him back. I wouldn't swap the wake up calls and dog walks for anything. I loved the routine Kelt and I had created together, it was our time. He could wake me up at any time of the night or morning and I would walk him, hug him and play. He was my baby, my real live teddy bear.

Back at my mum's later that day, I started going through the behavioural frameworks, when something hit me. Ruben had told me not to mention that I had spoken to Naasir in Arabic when the male arresting police officer was standing by the car. I had been wondering why he had said that, but looking at the finer details on the Race Relations Act 1976, Race Relations Amendment (2000), Sex Discrimination Act (1975) detailed in the College of Policing's Recruit Assessment Centre Workbook (RACW), I realised had I mentioned the fact that I had spoken Arabic to Naasir, and then the police officer had told me to stop being aggressive, this would not have been helpful to his career, or this case. It would show his ignorance and prejudices. It would also been seen as racist, something that would have damaging effects on the case being brought against me. Combine this with the fact that there was the whole Scottish Independence scenario happening at that time, so was this anti English feeling combined with racism? The officer has assumed me speaking Arabic was me being aggressive, something that shows a huge amount of ignorance *and* goes directly against the internal policy for Respect for Race and Diversity within the UK wide police forces; something my training as a police assessor had heavily reinforced. No wonder Ruben didn't want me to mention it! I had to speak with Ruben.

The RACW then went on to point out that processes the police officers have to follow, need to comply with the Human Rights Act (2000). How was the treatment I had received complying with the Human Rights Act (2000)? How was keeping me in a police cell for fifty-seven-and-a-half hours, without questioning, or telling me what I was being held for, and only being given several bits of fruit and a bowl of porridge complying with the Human Rights Act (2000)? Not to mention not having been allowed to shower or wash, until I had to beg for one! How was threatening to take my children off me because I could not recite phone numbers and full addresses belonging to friends and family who lived back home in England, and then taking my children off me, in accordance with the Human Rights Act (2000)? How was telling me how to raise my children recognising my rights as a parent? As an educated, independent woman who had helped build and regenerate communities, had taught in schools and done an incredible job raising two very bright and confident young men? The answer in short, was none of these were in alignment with the Acts. I was being discriminated against because I had spoken to my children in Arabic, because my car was dirty after a two-and-a-half week road trip and camping holiday; because I was a strong woman who knew her rights to be heard; because I had told the officer he couldn't intimidate me; because I had requested he allow me to answer his questions. He knew he had messed up, but couldn't admit it, (or wouldn't) as is becoming a common problem in today's society. People are no longer allowed to admit they made a mistake for fear of losing their jobs, being judged or condemned by others; or as in my case, being made into a criminal. I definitely needed to speak with Ruben.

I started pacing my mums lounge; started tapping my 'invisible keyboard' as though I was writing down all the thoughts in my head into a word document. I couldn't sit still for love nor money, and my dad was getting impatient with me, "Will you sit down!" So I went out into the garden.

Then I had another feeling, one that disturbed me on a whole new level. I had the feeling I was being set up, but why? My instinct was telling me there was something much, much bigger at play. The sleazy guy who came into the police cell, a piece of information Ruben had simply ignored. Who was he? Why had things been escalated so much?

Why, had I not just been told, "Look, your kids are fine this time, but next time, don't do it again!" Why were they so eager to take my boys off me? Why were they so keen to charge me without any proper investigations being done? It would have saved a whole lot of police time and resources, public funding, not to mention me and my family a whole load of stress!

I went back into my mum's kitchen, made a cup of tea, cut a slice of cake and went back outside to think. My mind was racing. I needed to get back into the research. Tea drank, cake eaten and I was back in the house with my notes. It was time for round two.

The next day I had to say goodbye to my parents and Kelt again and head up to Scotland. So I caught a train and headed to back to Stansted, to jump on a flight to Glasgow, before catching a bus, a train and then a ferry over to Dunoon. The ferry ride across the Clyde was the best part of this journey, one I would make many times. I would always sit up on the deck, regardless of how cold it was; and it was getting cold. There was snow on top of the highest hills and I was glad to have purchased a coffee before leaving the ferry terminal. The ticket collector smiled at me and asked me what I was doing up on deck. When I told him I loved the sea he chuckled and said, "There are warmer ways to enjoy it love."

We chatted for a bit and when I got off the ferry I said, "See you in a few days!" Walking along the beach to The Park Hotel, I could feel the anticipation building within me. Tomorrow I would need to meet with Ruben and go over the case, but first I had to buy some shoes for court. All I had were jeans and the black dress I had taken to Spain, and I don't think rocking up in court in a vest top and shorts, over a bikini, with my Haviana's would be a wise choice of attire; nor would my walking boots and jeans. I headed into town and got a pair of boots and tights to go with my black dress. Wardrobe sorted, now all I needed was a meal and a great night's sleep.

Over a delicious dinner, I checked my emails and saw an email from Ruben confirming the details of the Intermediate diet and the Trial diet on the 10th November. In the email he stated that "If the Crown can prove the facts as stated in the Summary of Evidence then it is likely that the court will convict me of all three charges" before going on to say "The excellent references that you have supplied will be very useful but only in mitigation of sentence".

Convicted? Sentence? Three convictions? How the heck did this happen? How did I get here? I took deep breathes and went for a walk along the beach. I needed some air. I was gone for at least an hour and when I returned to the hotel, I stopped and had a glass of wine with the owners, when two guys came in for an evening drink. We all got chatting and they asked why I was in Scotland. I don't know what possessed me but I just told them. The reaction was one of shock. They couldn't believe any of it had happened. Then they started to tell me about how many of the rural pubs and family run hotels on the west coast of Scotland were closing because of the problems the police were causing by sitting outside of them each night waiting for punters to leave. Apparently the police would sit outside the pubs and hotels and wait for people to leave before following the guests and pulling them over to breathalyse them. The problem had got so bad that many people refused to go out to the pubs and so the pubs were losing a lot of trade and many had ended up closing. The men started telling me about the Glaswegian footballer Charlie Mulgrew who had been arrested for the same thing. They told me to look it up and mention it to my lawyer. Then they asked me who my lawyer was. When I told them it was Ruben, they said I might as well say my goodbyes now, and prepare for prison and life with a criminal record. Not exactly what I wanted to hear. When I asked them why, they didn't elaborate, but they did tell me I would be wise to find another lawyer. I finished my wine and ordered another one; I was going to go to my room and look up this case against Charlie Mulgrew and run a bath.

Whilst the bath was running, I found out as much as I could about what had happened with Charlie and his wife. Another article came up as a 'related story' about David Cameron and how he had left his daughter alone in a pub. I made as many notes as I could, and then went and got in the bath; just as I did, John called. His timing was perfect. Hot bubble bath, glass of wine and a conversation with my man. We were on the phone for well over an hour, as was becoming the norm. If this is how it would be when he was away at sea, then I could handle the distance and the time apart.

I told him that I would be meeting Ruben the next day and needed to go over the Summary of Evidence again. He asked me when the trial

date was and I told him it was still the 10th November. He told me that
he still hadn't been called as a witness or sent any dates, and that I
needed to find out from Ruben what was happening with him being a
witness. He needed to get the time off work and flights booked. I was so
happy to hear that he was intending to be there with me; and as if he had
read my mind, he told me of course he would be there to support me and
that we'd get through this together. Tears welled up and a couple
escaped, I was so relieved. He would be by my side through this. He told
me to call him as soon as I was out of court the next day as he was
heading off to the Canary Islands the next day. I hoped I would be out of
court in time to be able to call him before him and the crew set sail. I was
so happy for him to be able to do this journey, something he had wanted
to do for a very long time. I just wanted to be sailing with him. I wanted
to be on the ocean. Sailing, with the wind in my hair and the salt sea air
in my lungs and the motion of the waves rocking me to sleep; I would
just have to settle at the moment for my walks along the Clyde.

The next day was court day. I woke up, showered, had breakfast and
went over the summary notes I had sent Ruben. I was confident that
when I met with him later that day, I would be more confident about how
the case would progress. I had produced a document about how the
accusations being made against me were very detrimental and a
defamation of character. I had also produced an analysis of the Children
and Young Persons (Scotland) Act 1937, with additional notes about
David Cameron leaving his daughter alone in a pub – and how nothing
had happened to him. I also mentioned the footballer Charlie Mulgrew
and how his case had been thrown out of court. I looked at myself in the
mirror and repeated my affirmations for the day and got my mind in the
right place to be able to deal with whatever came my way.

Walking along the beach, I breathed in the sea air from the Clyde.
Passed lots of dog walkers and I wondered how Kelt was. Was he okay? I
text my mum to find out. I looked out to sea as I left the beach and called
on the universe to help me. Walking into the courtroom, the energy was
heavy. It was an oppressive energy, one that was suffocating. I didn't like
it. At all. I had been there about ten minutes before I saw Ruben. He
acknowledged the emails but didn't go into detail. He told me what
would happen and then he told me to go through the double doors and

sit in one of the chairs. The energy in there was even more negative. I felt sick. The last time I had been in here was when they had brought me up from the cells below, dirty, unwashed and lost. I had been away from my children for two-and-a-half days. Had had them taken off me, put into foster care. I wasn't just fighting to clear my name today, or to have this case thrown out, I was fighting for my children, for all those who had been in this situation and not had the power, the tools or the voice to fight the system. As I sat there, I got my book out *Understanding Management and Organisational Dynamics: The Complexities of Diversity*, a book I had been reading to develop my leadership coaching programmes and training courses; a book that was proving to be very helpful indeed.

I got the feeling that someone was staring at me, and when I looked up the court user was looking at me and the book, and looked confused. I smiled at him in my usual friendly way, and he smiled back. He was the first person to smile and show any warmth towards me. I had been so absorbed in the book, I hadn't seen all the other people come into the courtroom. I was told by the usher to put the book away. When I asked why, I was told that it was not allowed in the courtroom. I couldn't understand why. None of the other cases had anything to do with me, so why was I allowed in there? By absorbing myself into the book, I was at least giving the person on the stand as much privacy as they deserved. But no, this whole setting was to belittle and shame those who were in the stand. Public humiliation, a form of deterrent, to obey and fear 'the system'. No wonder my energy didn't fit in here. I looked at my watch and realised that the judge, or rather Sheriff as they are known in Scotland, was over 20 minutes late arriving in court. Where was he, or she? Why were they running late? All these people in the courtroom waiting to get on with their day, and the judge was this late? I wasn't impressed, but the caring side of me hoped something bad hadn't happened.

As I looked up and to my right, I saw Ruben going through some paperwork. I wondered if it was my paperwork he was going through; and at that moment my name was called. I was asked to go and stand in the box I had stood in previously. My heart was racing, my mind pounding and my hands shaking. The charges against me we read out and I could hear the gasps and murmurs from those behind me in the seating. The judgements had already been cast. I was a bad mother to everyone in the courtroom already, or at least that what I felt. Ruben read out my response of 'not guilty' to each of the charges. The judge looked at me as if I was a piece of dirt. He then started speaking at me, telling me that what I had done was not acceptable, and asking me if I understood the charges being brought against me. I said I did. Ruben attempted to put forward the evidence gathered, but the judge was not willing to hear about it, or my excellent references. It was then a matter of discussing my witnesses and the trial starting in five days. My only witnesses were John and the boys.

The judge and Ruben were discussing things that I couldn't keep up with, simply because my head was swimming. I needed to get out of here. The feeling of nausea kept sweeping over me. Ruben then turned to me and told me that John had to be there, I told him that John was at sea and about to cross the Atlantic, and that he wouldn't be back until April, May at the latest; but that he should be arriving in the Canaries end of November. The judge didn't care. He stated the trial was going to have to go ahead in five days' time and John had to make it back. I looked at the judge in disbelief. The last I knew, there were no airports in the middle of the Atlantic ocean; nor was it possible for a tall ship that travelled on average at five knots per hour to arrive anywhere soon. John would be setting sail in a couple of hours and I needed to breathe. I was appalled at the attitude of the judge, the way he spoke at me and had been so dismissive.

I was then told to leave the courtroom and Ruben told me he would meet me outside. I couldn't get out of there quick enough. I felt as though I had a hand around my throat and my legs were like jelly. I made it down the stairs and as soon as I opened the doors to the outside, I gasped and gulped in the air. My head started spinning and I felt faint. I had to lean against the wall of the building, waiting for Ruben to appear.

He finally arrived after what felt like ages. He told me that the trial would still be going ahead in five days and that I was to make sure I was there. I told him that I was not impressed by the judge's attitude and that it felt as though he had already made up his mind. Ruben dismissed these thoughts and told me not to worry. He wasn't convincing. He then said he had to go and would be in touch, and that he would see me in five days' time.

I headed back to the beach, ready to head back to the hotel, but needed a cup of tea. I stopped at the café by the ferry terminal and ordered a cup of tea to take away. Sitting on the bench outside, looking out over the Clyde I reflected on what had just happened; the attitude of the judge, the way he spoke to everyone in the courtroom, not just those of us who were there in the docks, but also his colleagues, especially the lady who was recording everything. His whole attitude was dismissive and arrogant. The way he had dismissed everything Ruben had said and how he had expected John to get back from where he was in five days, just wasn't possible. I wanted to look into the behavioural frameworks of the justice system and the principles that underpinned it. There had to be something on the internet regarding this, so I started to walk back along the beach ready to dive deep into this new area of the law.

As I walked along the beach, listening to the waves crashing, I thought of John. I needed to call him and see if he had already left port. He didn't answer, so I sent him a text message, hoping I hadn't missed him. I then called my mum and told her what had happened and told her I would be back the next day about 8:30-9:30pm depending on whether my flight was on time. I then called Tina to let her know how things had gone and she agreed I had to look into making a complaint about the judge. I called Rob and let him know how things had gone and he wasn't impressed either.

I arrived back at the hotel, hungry and ready to eat. I had a couple of hours before dinner was to be served, so I had a couple of shortbread biscuits with a cup of tea. Everyone who I needed to contact had been contacted and updated. I sat on the bed of my room and started to research the complaints procedure for the Scottish Courts. I called the Judicial Office for Scotland and spoke with a guy called Ryan who pointed me in the right direction. So I downloaded the Bangalore Principles of Judicial Conduct which were endorsed at the 59th Session of United Nations Human Rights Convention in Geneva in April 2003. I then spoke with my friend and confident Robert Keston, a Human Rights Specialist who is funded by the Swiss Government for his working around the world about the judge's behaviour and attitude towards me and my case. It was a very informative afternoon and also very draining.

I had decided to have a soak in the bath before dinner, just to relax and unwind. If I couldn't be on the sea, then I would open the window and listen to the waves crashing whilst soaking in hot water. I must have dozed off as there was a knock at the door asking if I was going down to dinner. I sat up and said, "Yes please, give me 15 minutes!" I was so hungry I had a starter, main and dessert, all washed down with a glass of pinot grigio.

After dinner, I was sat with the hotel owner and his wife who asked me how it had gone in court that day. They were shocked that it had not been thrown out and were incredibly kind. I told them I would be back in a few days, and we booked a room for two more nights as it was cheaper for me to fly home, than to stay; plus I wanted to get back to Kelt, as well as my mum and dad. Back in my room I wrote out my notes on the Bangalore Principle and started to fill in the complaint form. Starting to feel tired, I decided to finish it off the next day whilst waiting in the airport and flying home. It would be done before I landed, ready for me to send it as soon as I could hook up to a WiFi connection.

The next morning I was blessed with a beautiful breakfast of poached eggs, smoked salmon and Scotch pancakes, it was delicious! I had a long day ahead of me and my ferry would be leaving soon, so I said my goodbyes and walked along the beach, knowing that I would be on the sea very soon. Again, once on the ferry, I went straight up on deck. My new friend wasn't on the ferry, but he was there when I arrived at the other end in Gourock. He asked if I had had a great time and I smiled and said, "Not so much, but I'll be back in a few days." He looked intrigued and I said, "I'll fill you in next time." We said our goodbyes and I headed home, looking back over my shoulder to the Clyde, taking in a deep breath of the sea air before I boarded the train.

I arrived at the airport in plenty of time, only to find out the plane was delayed by half an hour. Great! I had time to complete the complaint form! Positives from the negatives! As I read the guidelines for the complaint form I shook my head, and let out a chuckle of disbelief. The guidelines were so strict, and had been written in such a way, they themselves acted as a deterrent to people wanting to complain. So much for growing from feedback, wanting to offer a great service to people and improve moving forward! As I read through the Bangalore Principles, switching from them to a new word document, I knew I had a strong complaint, and the judge had failed to adhere to the guidelines, it was just whether I would be able to navigate the complaint form's guidelines and get the complaint across. I managed to get a lot done before boarding the plane, text my mum to let her know I was boarding and the time I should be back, but would of course give her a call when I arrived at Stansted.

I closed my laptop, and my eyes, settling down on the plane for a power nap. I would finish the complaint on the train back to my mum's. Then the announcement came over the tannoy that we had to wait for the runway to clear. The next thing I knew we were touching down in Stansted. I had missed the whole flight. I looked at the time and realised that I had missed the last train back to my mum's. I checked the prices of hotel's locally and just knew I could not afford one, so I went to grab a coffee and resigned myself to the fact I would need to sleep in the airport. There was no option of the airline paying for the hotel, as the flight had not been delayed by three hours, and it was RyanAir.

Still, I had spent two and half days in a police cell, the airport was luxurious compared to that! I was cool with it, and motivated to make sure I made so much money it wouldn't matter whether I would have to pay a taxi all the way home or stay in a hotel I deemed expensive at this moment in time. I was going to change my life and my money story and go for it. As I found a nice quiet seating area, Rob called to ask how things were. I gave him the update and then he read me the riot act. I was not going to stay in the airport; I was going to stay in a hotel. He hung up and ten minutes later gave me the address of the Premier Inn nearby. He had booked me a room and breakfast. No arguments, no crying with gratitude, just told me to get my arse to the hotel and let him know when I had checked in. I felt truly blessed to have Rob as my friend, and loved him dearly. His friendship over the years had meant so much to me, and he had always stood by my side, whether we were messing about on the dance floor pretending to the hoovering or staying up for hours chatting about everything and everything. He was one of the coolest guys I knew, if not the coolest. The love he had for his friends was deep, but the things I loved about him was the way he spoke about his partner and daughter. The love he had for them… beautiful. The way he spoke about them, they were very lucky ladies indeed and I was looking forward to meeting up with them all soon.

I woke up the next day and headed home to my parent's, knowing I would be back here in the next two days. Still it would give me time to see Kelt and my parents. I had been in touch with the boys daily hearing about what was happening with school, letting them know everything was going okay, doing my best to not worry them. Khaalid had the most interesting questions and Naasir was just not impressed with the police at all. Khaalid, well his opinion of the police and the courts was through the floor. He just couldn't understand it, and was telling me that whenever he saw anything on the news about people being arrested he didn't believe it was as bad as the police and the media made it out to be. He had so little faith in the police now, and it made me sad. I had told them things would be better in the UK, and now this had made them both believe otherwise.

"Why can't they just leave it Mummy? Nothing happened to us, you weren't gone that long and we were safe. It's just stupid," was the comment that they both kept repeating to me. What could I say? I agreed with them. It didn't matter how many similar situations I thought about, as a single parent travelling or holidaying with two children of their age and gender, I would have to leave them unattended for a similar amount of time on many occasions. If I took them fishing, or camping, or on a road trip, me simply going to the toilet or for a shower would mean they would be left alone for the same amount of time. If we were at the park together and they were playing on the Parkour equipment, me walking to the toilet or to going order lunch, would mean the same amount of time away from them. None of it made sense in my head. How was I supposed to prepare them for being responsible and getting about on their own if I couldn't leave them alone in these situations, showing them I trusted them and had confidence in them? How could I show them that people are trustworthy if I myself didn't trust anybody?

They both asked about Kelt and I told them he was much happier, and Nanny had been feeding him so much he was already putting on weight. They told me to give him big hugs and to tell him they missed him. Then they told me they loved me more than anything and really missed me. They wanted to know when I was going home. It had been ages. Battling with my emotions I told them I would be home soon, I just had to go back to Scotland for one more day and then I would be home. Naasir then told me he was sorry. Sorry for getting out of the car. I told him it wasn't his fault and the tears flowed, quietly so he couldn't hear them and I repeated that it wasn't his fault. There were just a series of events that no one could foresee. It was a combination of things, and everything would be okay. My heart was breaking. Here was an eight year old boy taking all the blame on his shoulders. I told him that I was the one that left them in the car alone, and I was responsible for that; that the policeman had chosen to arrest me and that he had made that choice.

"Yeah, it was a stupid one Mummy," Naasir butted in.

"Yes, it was, but it was what happened, and I am dealing with it. Don't blame yourself Baaba."

"But I got out of the car Mummy, when you told me to stay in the car. I'm sorry I didn't listen to you, but I needed a wee."

"Baaba, it is fine. Nothing happened to you and you are fine. You are free to make your own choices. You are free to listen to me, and why I want you to do or not do something, and that you have to make up your own mind about things. Haven't I always told you that?"

"Yes Mummy, but I didn't do as you asked. And now you are in lots of trouble."

"I am, but you know what Baaba, everything happens for a reason. We may not know or understand the reason, but everything happens as it is supposed to and we just have to make better choices."

"I promise I will listen to you more Mummy."

"I know you will Baaba, and thank you. Just remember, whatever happens, I love you, and I don't blame you. You are not to blame okay? There are adults involved and we are all responsible for what happens. I promise I will do my very best for you always. I am doing my best to make this all go away."

"I know you are Mummy, you always do do your best. You're the best Mummy ever. I love you. Hahaha! I just said do do – does that make sense?"

"Made sense to me Baaba and I love you too, so much."

"Okay then Mummy, I love you. Talk to you later."

And with that he hung up. And then I sobbed. I made my way up to my bedroom and cried. I cried for so many reasons, but mainly because I felt as though I had let my boys down. My mum came up the room with a cup of tea, and told me I handled it well; before stating that neither I nor the boys were at fault. Yes, some people would blame me, but they were probably going to be the parents that wrap their kids up in cotton wool or who distrust everyone and everything. Parents leave their kids alone; have done since the dawn of time. Parents have to make things work, especially single parents, and anyone who doesn't understand that needs to step into the world of what it is like to be a single parent, and not be so arrogant as to think it could never happen to them. We chatted for a long time, had loads of hugs and I realised I was hungry. Like really hungry. As I don't eat wheat, there was very little to eat as mum hadn't gone shopping yet, so we headed to the local farm shop. Memories of playing in the fields and riding my bike when I was younger came flooding back to me, a big smile breaking out over my face. Mum asked me what I was smiling at, so I told her.

She came back with, "Yeah, and you didn't have a mobile phone, or a crash helmet. Kids are too pampered these days and people are too paranoid. Do you think I knew where you were when you were out playing or riding your bike? You were gone all day with your sandwiches and a drink. Being kids. Exploring. Having fun. Growing up. Just like you are teaching the boys to do. More parents should do it, so stop being hard on yourself. You're doing a great job. Don't let them get into your head. Those boys love you, they are doing really well at school and have everything they need. Anyone who can't see that needs their bloody heads looking at."

Listening to my mum when she got off on one, made me giggle. I knew where I got it from. I loved her for it. I didn't always agree with her, but seeing what I saw happening with employees, kids in school and the attitudes of other parents towards their kids, I had to agree with everything she was saying. I knew I had to believe in myself and trust that I had done nothing wrong. I had not broken any laws. There was no legal age limit to leave kids alone, and I had made a risk assessment based on my own knowledge of the world, my boys and what I had gleaned from the local area. The only thing I hadn't taken into consideration was an over-zealous police force and the depths of the passive aggressive dictatorial nanny state the UK had become.

Later that day I had a phone call with Ruben to say that he had received the complaint and would ask his colleague David Watts to call me later to go over it with me, but would advise me to not send it. Ruben was to be in court for the whole day tomorrow, and he wanted to make sure I would still be in court on the 10th. I told him yes of course, flights and hotel were already booked. I told him that I was going ahead with the complaint, and would be confirming it by email later that day. I also told him I had updated the Summary of Evidence. He told me David would be calling me later the next day before 4pm to go over the case, and that he was still going to see me the next day in court. He ended the call with, "Don't worry, everything will be alright."

I was really annoyed with him. I had so many questions and needed them answering. I would be in court in two days and I still had no idea what was happening. I was not impressed at all. Surely there had to be a Code of Conduct with the Legal Society on how lawyers treated their clients?

I left early the next day to head back up to Scotland, and the only things I was looking forward to were the ferry crossing and being by the beach. This time I had brought more of my research with me, my notes and my game face. I hadn't spoken to John for a few days as he was in the middle of the Atlantic, sailing on a beautiful tall ship, learning about all the intricacies of the boat ready to take on his next qualification. The closer I got to the Clyde, the more I felt closer to him. It was great to have a partner who loved the ocean as much as I did, well more so. He had made it his life, been on the ocean for years. I was so looking forward to making my childhood dream of being on the ocean a reality. Thinking about him made me smile; sent shockwaves through my body. He was a great distraction to have. The day went really well. There were no delays to flights, trains or ferries, although the wind was up and the crossing would be a bit choppy. I couldn't wait! I loved it when the weather was strong. I chose to stand up on the ferry, looking out at the sea from the railings, watching the waves crash up against the hull. The ferry was bouncing around and it was great! Then my new friend appeared, "You back again? You know, I don't think I've ever seen a woman like the choppiness of the sea the way you seem to be enjoying it. It's good to see."

"Thanks, I do love it. Makes me feel the power of the sea, makes you humble."

"Aye, does that. Puts you in your place so it does. Been on the sea all my life, a fisherman in my younger days, too old for that game now though." I told him about John, and he said, "So the fisherman has caught his biggest fish yet then. You know there's a mermaid out there for every fisherman… just depends on whether he can handle her or not. He's a brave man your John. You've got some power in you young lady. I don't need to know you to be able to see that. You keep that power, you harness it. You'll do right in this world. The world needs some strong women, ones like you."

I blushed, smiled and said thank you, and looked back out at the Clyde. He headed down to the stern of the ferry to prepare it ready for us all to leave. I stayed up on deck until the very last moment, savouring the moment. I now had a very long bus ride ahead of me, and the weather wasn't great. Apparently there were some roads closed due to some floods, but I remained positive.

I chose to sit down on one of the benches that looked out across the Clyde. Staring out to sea, knowing I had at least half an hour before I caught my coach. I went over the conversation I had had the previous week with the men in the hotel. What had they meant about Ruben? Was he really as bad as that? Yes, his customer service was awful but was his legal representation as well? I would find out tomorrow in the courtroom.

I started going through the research I had brought with me, I delved deeper into the behavioural frameworks, I came across Patterned Behaviour Description where the police officers are assessed on 'How one has responded to situations in the past', a strategy based on the premise that past behaviours will predict future behaviours. With this in mind, and Ruben telling me the references were excellent, I was confident that my character references were going to hold me in good stead, but it also concerned me. If the male police officer had jumped to the conclusion that me speaking Arabic to Naasir was aggression; and he and his female counterpart had been so eager to arrest me, based on assumptions and jumping to the conclusion that I was a neglectful mother, simply because the car was dirty and I had left the boys alone for the same amount of time it would take me to have a shower, then who else had they arrested based on ill informed, prejudiced assumptions? Then something else hit me. What else were they assuming about me?

I had also managed to speak with my friend Robert about the Human Rights perspective on this whole fiasco. He told me I needed to get information on previous cases both the judge and the male police officers had been involved with before; what crimes they had been arrested for; what the results and rulings were; and told me I needed to push for the name of the male social worker who had first arrived in the police cell. He told me that considering it was a male judge, ad male arresting officer, combined with what had actually happened, there was an obvious systemic lack of fair treatment that I was receiving as a woman, and as a single mother – an independent, educated woman with a global outlook and experience. He also told me to consider the pro Tory government and it's conservative, non pro-women stance, even though Nicola Sturgeon herself was a woman, she was also a childless woman who wouldn't fully understand the tough choices and the decisions parents have to make, especially lone or single parents. He further recommended I get in touch with Women's Rights groups and cause public outcry at the way in which I had been treated, not only by the judge, the prosecutor, the male officer and the male social worker.

On the coach to Kilmartin that night, through the heavy rain, I was mulling this entire situation over. It was disgusting the way I had been treated, and those that knew had been shocked, maybe there was something in going public with this. To go public though would mean exposing myself and the boys to trolls and vile, nasty behaviours and comments. People would be judging me without even knowing me. I had to consider the impact on the boys more than myself. How would they feel about this all going public? Would I be strong enough to deal with whatever came my way? Then there would be the likes of Piers Morgan, but I figured if I could put Robert Kilroy Silk in his place on BBC's Question Time, I could handle Piers Morgan, and he would be the worst of the worst in my opinion. As for the nasty trolls, and people judging me, well that would say more about them, than it would say about me. As the bus continued through the heavy rain, it was almost as if the rain was washing away the fears I had of going public with this. I knew I wasn't just fighting this for me, but for all the other parents who didn't have a voice. I knew that I was fighting this for my boys to be able to parent their children the way they wanted to. If I didn't stand up and fight this publicly, then what real difference was I making? None. Absolutely none. The bullies would win, and I hated bullies.

I arrived at the hotel around 10pm and the owners had been so lovely, they had come to collect me from the bus stop. When I walked into the hotel, there was a really lovely woman called Magda working behind the bar. We hit it off instantly. She showed me to my room, took my food order and when I returned downstairs, there was a glass of pinot grigio waiting for me with my dinner. Perfect! I sat by the fire and chatted with Magda and the other customers sat at the bar. I overheard a few of them moaning about the police sitting outside another local hotel, commenting with, "They're not going to be happy until all the pubs and hotels are out of business. They even got Mac the other week…"

As I listened I couldn't quite believe what I was hearing. An old guy, who never had anything more than an orange juice, had left the pub one night and tripped over the carpeting on his way out of the pub he was in. He got on his bike and had cycled up the road only to be pulled over by the police and arrested for being drunk in charge of a vehicle. The police had been sitting outside the pub all night. I got out my laptop and started taking down notes of what I was hearing. I then asked if this was for real or whether they were pulling each other's legs. They said it was very real. Many of the pubs had been the target of the 'sitting police men' and especially now that the legal limit had been so drastically reduced. A glass of wine was too much. A pint would put you over the limit, so people just weren't going to the pub anymore. If they couldn't have a glass of wine or a pint of ale with their Sunday lunch or after work, then what was the point? I couldn't believe first of all the legal limit was so low, and that the police were being so heavy-handed. With everything I was learning about the police up here in Scotland, I was having serious doubts about the actual level of intelligence, awareness of their actions and whether they actually cared about anything other than their own egos. I had another glass of pinot grigio and asked her for the WiFi password. I wanted to see where the ship was that John was on. Had he arrived in The Canaries yet? And I also wanted to get my thoughts together to send the email to Ruben on the conversation I had had with Robert. I wrote Ruben the email and sent it at 23:39 that night, explaining I wanted to discuss all of this with him when I saw him the next day.

I arrived at the courtroom early as promised and yet there was no sign of Ruben. I was then told to wait in the reception of the police station. I didn't recognise the location at all, but I did recognise the man who had told me to wait. It was the arresting officer. My hands started shaking and my heart was racing. I took deep breaths and sat down. Oh the things I wanted to say to that man! I knew they wouldn't help matters so I kept quiet.

Then a lady walked in and was all smiles with me, "Hi Dawn, how are you? You look well!" I had no idea who she was. Then she said, "I'm Heather, the social worker."

Flashbacks of the first night in the police cell came flooding back to me. She was the woman from social services, and in a dazed response I said, "You're the woman who made me sign my children over to foster care." I was just gazing at her, not really looking at her, but just gazing.

I felt sick, I needed air. So I got up to leave and I was ordered by the arresting officer to remain where I was. No change in his attitude then. I then saw another chap come in and go through some other doors, and then more people. I couldn't see where they were all going, but I knew I needed air. I didn't care what the police officer had just said, if I didn't get air soon, I would pass out. So I stood up and went and stood outside. I noticed the usher from the courtroom from before in Dunoon. He told me I needed to go around the back of the station and go through a side door and up some steps, as that was where the courtroom was. So I followed him and there we waited and waited. I still hadn't seen Ruben and my thoughts flashed back to what the guys had said at The Park Hotel in Dunoon about him. As we were all led into the courtroom, I was approached by an incredibly overweight, ill looking guy in a black gown. I wondered what he wanted. He asked me if I was Dawn, and I said I was. He told me he was David, the chap I had spoken to previously on the phone.

I was shocked. "Where is Ruben?"

"Did he not tell you? I am representing you today."

"No, no he didn't."

"I'm sorry he didn't inform you. I have a copy of the complaint here with me that you sent over last night, so I will need to mention that in court today."

At that moment we were all told to take our seats. A few moments later the judge walked in. I didn't like this man. His energy wasn't nice.

We all sat down and there was a woman who went on the stand, a very well-spoken woman. She was representing herself and boy did she have a lot to say. She told the judge she was disgusted with the treatment she had received and that they should all be ashamed of themselves. She mentioned that what had happened had been blown out of all proportion and the law had better wake up and check themselves. I didn't know who this woman was, didn't know what had happened, but she had a fire in her belly that I admired. I also happened to agree with the statements she was making. Her case was then dismissed and she was given a fine of some kind.

Next up was another woman, who had apparently gotten behind on some payments of one kind or another. David was representing her and I was looking forward to seeing him perform. As soon as he stood up, I could see he had no power. He was like a scared little boy standing in front of the judge. I knew there in that moment the outcome for this lady was not going to be a good one. David stood and explained the lady's situation had become worse as she was unable to work and was in therapy to which the judge responded with "So you're telling me she is insane?"

I could not believe what I had just heard! Insane? Where had he got that from? David had just said she was in therapy, not admitted to a mental health hospital. David responded with "No, your honour, she is in therapy."

"So you are telling me she is insane." I sat there in shock. How on earth had no one else working in the courtroom said anything? Why was this man allowed to be sitting up there as a judge?

The gasp from the people behind me, whoever they were, was one of shock too. A female voice said, "He can't say that can he? So everyone in therapy is insane? That's awful!"

"He can say what he likes; he's the judge, unfortunately!"

A look from the usher told them to be quiet, and David retreated into himself and mumbled something. This was not looking good for this woman; or me. I had a mouse representing me instead of a lion. Not good. Not good at all.

I was the next one to be called up and state my name. The charges against me were read out and my plea of not guilty delivered. David stepped up and said that I was there by myself and that my key witness was still in the middle of the Atlantic. He then mentioned the complaint I had written and sent to Ruben, of which the judge had no knowledge of. The look the judge gave me was one of shock and offence. He adjourned the case for a period of time and went away to read the complaint that David had handed him. The murmurs that went through the courtroom and the look the usher gave me were ones of surprise. Behind me I heard, "About bloody time someone complained about this arsehole."

The only female worker in the courtroom, the secretary who was doing all the note taking, and passing pieces of paper to and from the lawyers and the judge, setting dates etc glared at me. She was not impressed by me at all. We had to wait for about 20 minutes, and when the judge came back into the courtroom, he was a very different man. His arrogance had subsided and he seemed gentler. You would have had to have been asleep not to have seen the change in him. The way he spoke was kinder too, not by much, but a noticeable difference. He directed his next words towards David, "It seems Mr Watts that Mr Murdanaigum has done his usual trick of leaving you ill prepared and not able to represent your client properly, a paying client who deserves much better service and is entitled by law to proper representation."

"Yes, your honour. Ms Bates and I only met this morning."

"Ms Bates, your key witness is still at sea I believe."

"Yes, he is. He should be landing in The Canaries in a few days."

"Well, on this basis and the fact that you have not had the representation you have been paying for I am adjourning this case. You are still to adhere to the terms of your bail and a new court date is now to be set."

After going back and forth between the courts secretary and David, it was agreed that the new court date would be the 14th December. In

Dunoon. I was relieved. I would get to be by the sea, and John had plenty of notice to be with me.

David and I went into the witness room after we were excused from the courtroom and I told him I was not happy in the slightest with the way Ruben had behaved. I was also mentioned that I was not impressed by the comments the judge had made about the woman in therapy. David apologised to me for the way things had turned out and I told him it wasn't his fault; his boss had failed us both. He did say that my complaint had very obviously shaken the judge and made him think twice about the kind of person I was. It was very obvious from his tone of voice and his behaviour towards both me and to him. He said he had never seen that kind of change in the judge before, and he was very impressed with me. David then told me that the best person to represent me was a guy called Gary McAteer, and his firm Beltrami and Co. He helped me locate the number and I called them straight away, making an appointment for two days' time, when I was back in Glasgow on my way back home. It was almost as if I knew this was going to happen, as I had booked an extra day in Kilmartin just in case the court case went on for an extra day. I was told this wouldn't have happened and another court date would have been set, so I had an extra day in the hotel. David was kind enough to give me a lift back to the Kilmartin Hotel and wished me the very best. He also told me that the standard of my research, the work that I had produced would have left many professional lawyers with years in the industry in shame. He told me I should consider a career in law. I thanked him for the compliment, and said I could not work in a place like a courtroom day in day out, it was too oppressive and negative. In my head I was saying much more, because I knew I certainly couldn't work in a career where I had to deal with the arrogance of people like the judge, the way the law didn't have space for emotional or social intelligence, or that it was an inhumane system created to control people and dictate how individuals lived their lives. Every time I went into the courtroom I felt dirty and felt that a cloud of darkness hung over the place. It reminded me of life in Egypt during the Uprising. So much darkness.

When I arrived back at the Kilmartin Hotel, Magda was just setting up for the evening and the owner was clearing out the front dining room.

They were about to redecorate. I offered a hand the next day, and told them I was hungry. They told me dinner service would be starting in 30 minutes so I went upstairs to change. I came back down to a glass of pinot grigio, and laughed with Magda. She asked me how the case had gone, and I told her what had happened. She was pleased that I wouldn't have to go to court alone and that John would be back in time to support me. She then said she had told her friend about what had happened and he couldn't believe it either. Back in Poland this would never have happened, in fact quite the opposite, it would have been the police officer telling Naasir off for getting out of the car and not listening to his mother. I replied, "Yeah, that's what England used to be like too."

Dinner was served and I ate well. I had not eaten so much but then I hadn't been mentally and emotionally drained as much as I was feeling at the moment. The bar was quiet and so Magda and I had a game of pool, I had another glass of pinot grigio and then I helped her close up the bar afterwards. I took another glass of pinot grigio to my room and ran a bath. I lay in the bath just going over the day's events in my head, knowing I had just sacked Ruben as my representative, given the judge a wake-up call and promised to help out with the decorating in the hotel the next day. I put my music on through my Bose and relaxed. For the first time since the holiday I was able to relax and take deep breaths. "Baths are great!" I found myself saying to no one else but myself. Then I remembered the bath at The Park Hotel in Dunoon… I would be back in it with the sound of the waves crashing in about four weeks. I was looking forward to it, and the ferry crossing. But for now, it was time to sleep; and sleep like a baby I did.

I arrived in Glasgow ready for my meeting at Beltrami and Co, with a guy called Frasier Matheson. I explained everything to him, and told him about my financial situation. I told him I was in the process of building a business and so funds were tight. He said that was fine, he understood my situation and we signed contracts. Neither Frasier or I mentioned legal aid as I had already been advised by Ruben that because this was a criminal case against children, my own children no less, I would not be entitled to legal aid. Frasier didn't offer legal aid representation, and nor did he suggest I seek out a legal aid firm. I had to pay £1000 on account to them within the next seven days and then they would get to work on my case. I also had to provide a copy of my bank statement, as this would give them a much better understanding of my finances, as well as prove that I was resident in the UK, helping them to do fraud checks on me. He also advised that his colleague David Fitzpatrick would be working on the case with him. Another David I thought… great. This is not going to get confusing at all! One name, two men and two different law firms, I could deal with this.

THIRTEEN

NEW LAWYERS, NEW HOPE

I arrived back home to be with my boys; I couldn't have been happier. They asked what had been happening and I was torn between telling them exactly what had happened, and sticking to the terms of my bail; which stated I was not allowed to speak with them regarding the case. They had questions. I was their mother. I chose to be their mother above and beyond being someone out on bail. Being a mother won hands down every time. No court in the land would stop me from answering my boys' questions, especially when it gave them the reassurance of what was going on and helped them to gain understanding of a situation such as this, one that had our futures hanging in the balance. When it came to questions from children, I had always believed if they were old enough to ask the questions, they were old enough to be given an age appropriate honest question. I had never lied to my boys, not even when it came to things such as the tooth fairy and if Father Christmas was real. "No, he's not," I would tell them. "But Saint Nicholas is. Santa Claus comes from Saint Nicholas, but instead of wearing red and white, he wore green. The red and white comes from the coca cola branding because Santa Claus is a marketing character for Coca Cola." Some told me that I was killing imagination, and I would disagree, the amount of books my children read and the amount of stories we made up around the campfires, during the power cuts in Egypt, sat around a candle; my boys had imagination, in abundance.

As we sat around the dinner table that night, an everyday occurrence in our home, Khaalid was quiet. Naasir was chatting away as usual, when Khaalid told him to shut up. Shocked by this outburst, I asked him what was the matter. He just started crying. Now Khaalid is a sensitive lad, one who has a very deep sense of justice and empathy. He has the kindest soul I've seen in a child, but he also has a deep passion for sticking to the rules and fairness. Seeing him in tears told me that something much deeper was going on besides him just wanting Naasir to be quiet. I asked him if he wanted to share anything, or if he just wanted to be by himself.

He blurted out, "Why didn't they just wake me up? I could have told them where you were and none of this would be happening! Why didn't you just stay in the car Naasir? Then this wouldn't be happening! Why are we not allowed to be left alone in the car for a short time? We are good kids! We are sensible! We can be trusted! This is just stupid! You're a great mum! You give us freedom to grow, to explore and learn. Just like the kids in the Famous Five. Why are they doing this? Why can't we have a proper childhood?"

I let him just offload, my heart breaking, whilst still being really proud of what he was saying. I agreed with him wholeheartedly, apart from the statement about Naasir getting out of the car. It wasn't Naasir's fault. The policeman was just being incredibly heavy-handed and over the top. You see the thing is, I have always taught my boys they are free to choose what to do based on the information I give them. I am not here to control them, just guide them. They can either listen and trust me, or they can go against me and we'll deal with the consequences... as we were doing now. Everything in life is a learning curve, and provided we work together and support each other when things go wrong, then we can achieve success, because the best team is family. I've taught my boys to fail forward. I have taught them it is okay to make mistakes, and that success comes from failure.

I got up from my chair and gave him a very big hug. "You are great kids, and I do trust you. I wouldn't have left you alone if I didn't. I also trusted the locals, felt that it was safe. And yes, you deserve a proper childhood like the children in the Famous Five books. As for Naasir getting out of the car, yes, he should have done as he was told. Yes, he should have stayed in the car, but if he needed the toilet, then he needed to get out. At the end of the day Khaalid, we are learning just how strong we are, and how sometimes the way of life we, and others choose, just doesn't fit with others. They get challenged, and they respond in a negative way, sometimes in an aggressive way."

Naasir was now crying, so I hugged him too. I reassured him it wasn't his fault that all of this was happening. It was just a series of incidences that occurred, and it all started with me. I made the choice to leave them for the 15 minutes that it would take to check the opening times and ticket costs. I made the risk assessment of the local area. I was the one that the police officer was confronted by. But it was also the police officer who was being over-zealous and heavy-handed. I reassured Naasir that it was not his fault. He was the child in all of this and I was the adult, so was the police officer. We were the ones that had to set the example.

To which Khaalid stated, "Yes but Mummy, you did nothing wrong! It was me! I should not have fallen asleep. I should have stayed awake, but I was tired. I'm sorry I fell asleep, but why didn't they wake me up? I don't understand why they didn't wake me up. And anyway, Kelt was with us. We were safe. It's not like when we lived in Egypt. That would have been stupid, but where we were was lovely. Why did they have to go and ruin our holiday?"

I told him it was not his fault; that he had every right to go to sleep. He was tired, why would he not go to sleep? I also confirmed that he was a great big brother, and I also didn't understand why the police officer hadn't woken him up. I told him I would ask my new lawyer this question. And yes, Kelt was with them, and as the windows were blacked out and no one could see inside, Kelt's bark would have put off any intruder; and yes, leaving them in a car in Egypt, or in downtown Glasgow, or any inner city or busy town would be foolish. I would never have left them in that kind of location. Parking up in the overflow car park of the castle, in a quiet little village gave me no concerns whatsoever, especially given their ages, and the time of day and the day of the week. I told him that this is why I teach them to be streetwise, why we must always do a risk assessment, why we should learn about risks, and be aware of our surroundings. It was one of the reasons I have encouraged them to explore our local neighbourhood on their bikes and go to the park by themselves, to learn how to be streetwise. Far too many people are not streetwise these days and are very good at pointing the finger at others and suing councils, employers and local public organisations, instead of taking responsibility for themselves and their actions.

The boys and I finished dinner and snuggled up on the couch and read a book together. I had missed them so much having to go back and forth to Scotland. Never before had I been away from my boys so often. In the 12 years I had been Khaalid's mother, I had spent more time away from him in the last six months than I had ever been away from him. Naasir more so. The longest I had ever been away from them was ten days, when I went to visit friends in Morocco just after I had finished breastfeeding Naasir. ramO had been away and so it was father and son bonding time, and time for Mummy to recharge her batteries. I hated time away from my boys, hated it. Spending time with them playing games, reading books, cooking and playing was what nourished me. It made me feel whole. Being a mother was the biggest pleasure in my life, so much so I hated it when they would go back to school after a holiday. I was building a business around them. I am first and foremost a full-time Mummy, and everything I do revolves around my boys. Some would say I'm obsessed with my boys, and I'm all good with that. I love spending time with them, listening to their thoughts and ideas, encouraging them to be the very best version of themselves, however they choose to be. I love our crazy, random conversations about everything and anything, and I find it strange that so many parents buy into the modern day take on the Victorian school of thought that children should be seen and not heard – with the modern day approach of shoving a tablet in their hands or shutting them up in the car with video screens in the back of the front seats. Engage with your children, converse with them, create and learn with them. Children are our biggest teachers and will lead our countries, communities and businesses one day, so starting to develop these skills now at a young age is essential.

The next week the boys and I spent a lot of time cuddling up and talking. We snuggled up on the couch and watched movies together, went to the dojo and did our MMA training. Naasir slept in my bed and we spent the evenings cooking, and the weekends baking bread and cakes. Then it was time for me to head back up to Scotland. I had to spend time with the 'new' David going over the case and preparing my defence.

Arriving at the Buchanan Coach Station I grabbed a coffee and started walking to Beltrami and Co's offices. Five minutes off the coach and the heavens opened. I was drenched by the time I arrived, and was greeted by two women who gave me the impression I was unwelcome. Not so much as a friendly greeting or a cup of tea or coffee offered. Not that I wanted one, as I had just had one, but to have been offered would have been nice. Even a towel or tea towel. So much for the wonderful Scottish hospitality I had heard so much about. I thought back to the really friendly people I had met at the ferry crossing in Oban, those friendly restaurant owners at Cuan Mor, the friendly locals we had met at The George Hotel in Inveraray; and the many individuals who had helped us on our wild camping trip. I had to focus on the positive people rather than the growing trend of negative people I was encountering. I knew that the circumstances I was now venturing into was going to bring people into my life who were used to dealing with criminals, some of them really nasty pieces of work, genuinely bad people, but going through this experience was also teaching me that really great people get caught up in this criminal system for a variety of reasons and they are judged harshly and treated badly by people who have no knowledge of the individual cases these people are involved with. I also wondered if the way I was being treated was due to the fact I was English, especially given the current political situation. I also knew that the negative reputation of the English was growing on a global scale, and to be honest I didn't blame Scotland for wanting to step away from England. Our combined history was painful and ran deep. Scotland wanted their independence, wanted to break free… and a smile broke over my face. Here I was wanting to escape from Scotland, after having initially wanting to find out about my Scottish grandfather, and the Scottish legal system had a grip on me that kept dragging me back. The irony of it all.

I had been sat in the reception area for a good ten minutes when a young man called me through. This was David, and I liked his energy; and I liked the no nonsense approach he had. As we went through the case notes and the research I had done, David stopped and told me that he was highly impressed with the quality of work I had done and it was refreshing to work with a client who had a good grasp of what was going on. I was shocked to some extent as I didn't think I had a good grasp of what was going on, it was all so confusing to me as to how we had actually got to where we had. How had this happened? Why was I being charged with disturbance of the peace? Why was I being charged with Wilful Neglect and Abandonment? David told me I was being charged with disturbance of the peace because I had waved my arms around in a threatening manner and been verbally abusive to the police. This is why I had been charged with Breach of the Peace? Was this for real? I sat there in disbelief. I had not been waving my arms around in a threatening manner in the slightest. I had been 'speaking with my hands' as anyone who does public speaking or is highly animated does; combine that with the 'Arab' in me of having been part of the Arab world for the last 20 years and there was no wonder I spoke with my hands. I asked him, "Were the police saying gesticulation was a violent behavioural trait? Were they going to arrest every animated European, Mediterranean, African and Arabic person on the planet? Would they arrest speakers such as Tony Robbins and Gary Vee if they came to the UK?"

David understood what I meant and could see that I spoke with my hands. This was to be part of my defence. I also asked him how I had been verbally abusive to the police. What was it I was supposed to have said? When I read the statement he had got from the male arresting officer, I had to ask him what the words meant, and he could tell I didn't know what the words meant, and that I was not the kind of person to have spoken in the manner I was being accused of.

Later that day I looked up the phrases I was being accused of saying on the Urban dictionary; and even the milder form of the phrases I was accused of saying would not have come out of my mouth. It was just not a form of vocabulary that I had within me. The further we went through the statements, the more I could see the police were clutching at straws. They accused me of being incredibly drunk, and yet they also stated that I ran to the car. If I had been incredibly drunk, how would I have been in a fit state to run to the car, and where was their evidence for this? They had not breathalysed me, nor done a blood test. They had no way of knowing whether I was drunk or not. The witness statement from Lasek stated that I had 'appeared' drunk. How could she say this? She didn't know me, had no point of reference upon which to base her opinion, she wasn't a behavioural expert, and she was nowhere to be seen, so was not in close enough proximity to me to know whether I was drunk or not. How could she be used as a reliable witness? The answer? Because she worked as a receptionist in a hotel and had seen other drunk people.

Having been known on the Sheffield business scene by one or two ladies as the 'pissed woman who didn't drink' I had to share this information with David. He looked amused. "Why did they call you that?"

"Because I giggle a lot and because I am an animated person."

He noted that down as well.

The more we went through statements, the more I sat there in disbelief. I was being accused of several different things and all of them contradicted each other. In one part of the arresting officers statement I went off drinking with a man and was nowhere to be found. In another part, I was sat on a park bench (the only park bench was less than three metres from the car). I was also accused of being neglectful because the car was in such a state... and after two-and-a-half weeks on a road trip around Scotland wild camping, surfing, cooking on our little portable fire pit, no wonder the car needed a good clean. We had however kept it clear of rubbish, an achievement by most parents' standards. David could see the inconsistencies and would work these into my defence.

We then moved onto previous cases in law that had set precedence, and David had some strong ones. I could see why he had used them, and combined with the complaint I had made about the judge (which he felt had been a very bold move) we had a strong case. David was also in agreement with a lot of the research and arguments that I had put forward, especially the point that there was no legal age limit at which children could be left. Due to the fact we had lived in Egypt during the Uprising, the ages of the boys and the rural setting, he could see why I had not had any reservations about leaving the boys. He did state however that because I had left the keys in the ignition, to prevent the alarm from going off, and we were parked up by water, the danger had been in the boys driving the car into the loch. I looked at him with disbelief. Really? Seriously? Driving the car into the loch? First of all there was a wall in front the of the car with a metal barrier which would have prevented this, secondly the speed at which the car would have had to be going to break through the wall would have been impossible give the distance behind the car. As for my boys being stupid enough to drive the car in the water, I would have bet my life on it that they would never have done that. They had been cleaning the car at home by themselves to earn their pocket money with the keys in the ignition since we had been back from Egypt, and helping me to clean the car with the keys in the ignition since they were toddlers. They had been taught the consequences of playing with the key by me demonstrating to them when I started the car, by using videos on YouTube. The only reason the key was ever left in the ignition was to prevent the alarm going off, and when cleaning the car, was to listen to the music and to prevent the car from locking them and or the keys inside the car.

David looked at me and asked him to give additional examples of how I had instructed the boys around things that others might consider dangerous. I said, "What, other than living in Egypt during an uprising? Well they have been cooking meals with me since they were old enough to sit on the worktops, cooking omelettes since they were five or six, been around kitchen knives, the cooker and the gas hob since they could sit on the counter top. They climbed trees, they went into the woods at the back of our house before we went to Egypt to collect firewood for the barbeque and fire pit. They made campfires, they cooked on the barbeque.

The more examples I gave him, the more he seemed impressed and could understand why I had not been fazed by leaving the boys for the 15 minutes I had been gone. I asked him how they could get away with the accusations they were coming up with, and he told me that the witness statements were proof. When I said, "Well that's not physical evidence! It's just police officers corroborating each other's story, and taking statements from others who really cannot be trusted as witnesses. They've been in a pub all night. This is highly fabricated!"

"That's evidence I'm afraid Dawn."

When we went over the timings on the individual statements, there were lots of inconsistencies. I said to David, "All you need to do is get the statements from the three girls I spoke with, and they will tell you they were with me until 11:30. Then all you need to do is gather the times of the calls made into the police station. And how come a police officer had been so quick to get to the scene?"

David dismissed the request to discover who the girls were, and gather the times the calls went in, and informed me that apparently the arresting officer had been on his way home, which is why he had not been in police uniform. I told him that he had been, but not in a police car. Again, another inconsistency in the evidence.

The next area of the case was the location of all the officers and the cars in the area. David could tell that I was recalling the scene as it was. I could pinpoint everything. I have a good memory for things, especially locations and people's phone numbers. As anyone from my business networking days and they will tell you I could recall which companies they worked in, who they worked with, where we met and what they did. I had a reputation for having a good recall. Not great when people wanted to argue with me, but very useful in recalling situations and introducing people. The scene laid out by the police was highly inaccurate and each of the officers had given differing descriptions. How could the prosecutor fiscal have even entertained the case with such inaccuracies in the statements?

David said we were not to focus on that, we just had to work on proving I had not wilfully neglected or abandoned the boys. I came back with, "Well first of all I never abandoned the boys because I had every intention of returning, which I did, within 15 minutes. And the next thing is no one can prove or disprove anything wilfully, because that comes from within, an intention. I had intended to find out information so I could give my boys another day of fun education in around a castle the next day. I had intended to wake up the next morning with them to watch a beautiful sunrise." I had no intention of neglecting my children, ever; and with all the character references from those who knew me, all David had to do was present the character references and these would backup my story.

He informed me that my character references would not be used, and could not be used. When I asked why he told me that anyone could provide excellent character references from people they knew and Scots Law wouldn't accept them. So here I was, a fantastic mum, a woman with some incredible character references, ones that had humbled me so much, from childcare and health professionals employed by the government, the NHS, business owners and International Human Rights Experts willing to put their name and reputation on the line, and not one of the references could be used 'because anyone can get good character references'.

I was not only incredibly disappointed, but I was angry. These police officers could say what the heck they like, paint a very black picture of me and I had to stand up in court and paint the black picture white again. How on earth was I supposed to do that when I wasn't allowed to use character references? And why had I been told to get them in the first place if they could not be used in court? Not only had my time been wasted, but so had the time of my friends and colleagues willing to support me. It seemed to me that there was a lot of time and resource wasting going on within the Scottish policing and justice departments, costing HUGE amounts of public funding; just to fuel egos and the bullies operating in uniforms. David told me he understood my frustrations and agreed that when it came to situations like the one I had found myself in, not using character references was not a good practice, but it was the law in Scotland and we had to work within the legal framework. I told him I don't know how he could work within such an awful, unjust and corrupt environment, to which he answered, because to make it better, you have to be part of it. He also told me he didn't like to lose, and with the amount of research I had done, and the case law he had pulled out, I had a strong case. He was confident but couldn't guarantee I would win.

We went through the case law, the remaining statements and summary of evidence and did all we could. I had to leave mid-afternoon to catch my flight back to London and because David had another meeting. David told me he would continue working on the case and call me if he needed any further clarification. I left his office and headed towards the coach station when my stomach growled at me and demanded I ate. I hadn't eaten anything since I had left my mum's that morning at 6:15. It was now 2:30pm. I stopped off at All Bar One and had lunch, went over my notes, which I had taken throughout the meeting with David and started writing down more questions, more thoughts and then wrote down the following thoughts: *What's the worst that could happen? What's the best that could happen? What's most likely to happen?* I had done this previously, but now armed with all this new understanding of case law and the insights into how Scots Law worked; I had a much more powerful journaling session to do. I had terminology to also look up further and understand, and I just had this feeling that the judge was going to do something spiteful in order to get back at me for the complaint I had made.

I still had a fear about him residing over my case. He wasn't a pleasant man, and his attitude towards women was very negative. There was also something I just couldn't put my finger on about him and the prosecutor fiscal. They both gave me the creeps for different reasons, and they both had a very arrogant air about them; and if there was one thing I hated, it was arrogance. I had brought my boys up to know that arrogance is ugly, and so is ego. I had two men misogynistic arrogant men trying to prosecute me, a woman – and a single mum at that, who was an independent, educated, successful woman, everything they appeared to not like about the female of the species, and I knew deep down there was a stitch up going on. I just couldn't understand why, other than the fact that the police officer had exhibited racist and sexist attitudes towards me. Was it because he realised he had made the wrong assumptions about me and couldn't back track for fear of losing his job? Was it because he was a Mason? I had a strong feeling this attitude from the police officer, the judge and the prosecutor fiscal were all Masons. I was their worst nightmare. Except they didn't care about me and my boys, or the impact this case was having on our lives, they all only cared about their own egos.

Eating my chicken salad and enjoying a glass of pinot grigio, I had this wave of determination sweep over me again. These were my boys. I had the right to raise them as I saw fit to do so. I had read countless books on how to raise confident, competent, happy and successful children, and my study had started when I was 14 years old when I took Child Development as an exam option. My thinking was, if I need to study to become a doctor and save lives, then I need to study and understand child psychology to help guide my children through life. Plus the powers that be had not grown either of my children inside of them, or kept them alive on breast milk alone for six months, and up to the ages of 11 and 13 months. Nor had they invested every waking moment and every penny available to make sure the children had had the best opportunities I could give them. They were not going to tell me that leaving my two boys alone for 15-20 minutes was Wilful Neglect and Abandonment – especially as neglect is something that is stated as something that happens on a regular basis over a period of time; and abandonment means I left them with the intention to never return. Who were they to tell me what was safe or not safe for my children? There are some adults I wouldn't leave alone for ten minutes, nor would I allow them to cook a meal for me, but my boys? Yes, I was confident that they were street wise and competent enough to be left alone for that amount of time; and not just because of the confidence, skills and awareness I and their Dad had instilled in them, but also because of the confidence, skills and awareness Birkdale School and Sensei Joel had instilled in them at martial arts training. My boys were and are great lads, and I am a great mother, and I am not going to have anyone tell me otherwise; especially someone who knows nothing about us and the life we have led.

What this case was bringing up for me though was what was it the police knew about the local area? Was Inverarary a dangerous place? Were the local residents a volatile and crazy group? What had the ITV team missed when they took the Dowager and Grantham Family there to film Downton Abbey? Was there a paedophile ring living close by, and if they knew about it, why were they not doing something about it? Why had the police officer been so early to arrive on the scene? It was a bit too convenient that he 'was just passing by' within the 15-20 minute window 'on his way home from work'. And why would him admitting that he had made a mistake and retract his course of action be so problematic? Was he on a final warning? Was he up for a promotion and this would affect it? Was there a particular target he had to meet to get his promotion? And why was the prosecutor so eager to convict me? How much did he get paid per case? Was he just interested in lining his pockets rather than acting in integrity and ethics? Was he expecting a bonus? Or was his conviction of me a target too? And what about the judge? What was his intention? Why had he entertained this case in his courtroom? How much was he getting paid per case? Why was he wanting, and happy, to waste so much public funding? Or was he close to a milestone in the amount of people he convicted?

I later found out that the arresting police officer was in fact acting Sergeant and was due to be promoted; something he wouldn't get had he backtracked on his actions in this case. I could not find out anything on the prosecutor fiscal, but I did find out that the judge had previously put away a paedophile in quite a large case of offences. I knew there was something more political going on than met the eye. I just couldn't prove it, but my intuition was becoming stronger and I knew there was something much bigger than this at play. There had to be. I also found out that eight children a day are taken off their parents by the social services in the UK. Eight children a day! I have worked on enough community regeneration projects in my time with families from lower socio economic communities and worked with people across all of the class systems to know that parents today are not that bad that eight children a day have to be taken off their parents. I found this figure disturbing, very disturbing! Talk about a nanny state and passive aggressive dictatorship being in the UK! I knew as soon as I saw David Cameron meet with Sisi, I didn't like the way the UK was going... and the more research I did. The more I couldn't wait to leave the UK. But go where? Everywhere was great until you went to live there and got under the skin of the place. The ocean was the only place I wanted to be anyway. I just had to wait for the boys to grow up and be more independent and then I could go. My place was with my boys before anywhere else. My duty was that as a mother, before business, before my new relationship, before anything. I would have my time alone to travel when they were with their dad on their visits with him. That would be when I would fill up my cup so much so I loved my boys from the overflow; and for now, I was good with that.

FOURTEEN

COMPLAINT REJECTED

Opening up the mail was becoming a daunting task. What was I going to find? I dreaded opening my emails, my mail and answering the phone. This was the impact this case was having on me. I dreaded speaking with people. I was really turning into myself to protect myself, to protect my boys. Opening up the mail in the morning was becoming a nightmare. Being in the process of building a business, applying for contracts – which even as a consultant I was told I was too over qualified! Seriously! All I want to do is put food on the table to feed my boys! Hence why I carried on selling Vitality and I was only just keeping my head above water financially. I dreaded opening a letter which only confirmed what my bank account told me – that payments hadn't been made due to insufficient funds in my account. No of course they hadn't been paid, my money was going on trips to Scotland and on legal fees. I was determined that I would make it work. ramO had started to pay for the martial arts gradings that the boys had, so that was a help, and I was pulling in a few sales, but nowhere near as many as I needed to pay for all these legal fees.

I was due in court on the 14th December, John was due back on the 10th Dec, and would be meeting me in Dunoon. Days before I left to go up to Scotland, I collected the mail. My heart and stomach swapped places when I saw the Scottish postmark. My hands started shaking; I broke out in a cold sweat. I knew before I even opened it, it wasn't going to be good news. The Scottish postmark tends to have that negative energy about it for me these days. I started to open it, and then put it down. I went into the kitchen to make a cup of tea. I would open it over a cup of tea.

I sat down and took a sip of tea and finished opening the letter. I could see it was from the Judicial Complaints department in Scotland. As I read the letter telling me the complaint had been rejected, a nervous giggle escaped. Of course it had been thrown out. What was I thinking? With all the rules on how to submit a complaint, instead of just being given the freedom to complain in a way that suited the case, the treatment and the complainers personality, there was no wonder my complaint had been rejected. Even with the amount of information I had included, with the Bangalore Principles that were highlighted, cross referenced and detailed, they still rejected the complaint. I had broken down the language used in their rules for making a complaint; so much so, I felt I was learning a different language. I had broken down the criteria for complaining just to make sure I adhered to all their rules, and yet they had still rejected it. How many complaints were actually accepted, if any? I sat there and felt this feeling of anger rise up within me. Thinking back to my time living in Cairo, before and during the Uprising, the Regime were in charge, and who were we, the citizens, to question them? The Masons were in charge in Scotland, especially on the west coast; and here I was, an independent, educated single mum, travelling alone with two kids, giving them the holiday of a lifetime, an educational one at that, doing all the driving, everything that would normally be the combined roles of a dual parent family – and I stood up for myself against the bully of a police officer, and then had the nerve to question the judge? Who on earth did I think I was?

I used to know who I was, but this case was making me doubt myself in many ways. The pressure of the travel logistics; the learning curve of the law, and how different English and Welsh Law is compared to Scots Law; the drain on my finances; the delay in my business, the sleepless nights. I was managing, but I was only getting maybe five hours sleep a night. I would go to bed exhausted and then I'd wake up worrying about the case, or having woken up from a bad dream about the social services taking my boys off me. I had so many bad dreams about losing my boys, that I would wake up from them on what was becoming a weekly occurrence. I had to work out physically so that my mind would shut off. I would re-read the references that my friends and colleagues had written about me, just to remind myself I was a great mum. I looked through all the photos of our previous years road trip holiday, and the photos of Scotland before my arrest. I had given the boys a fantastic holiday. A fantastic couple of years since being back in the UK; even with the bullying at Birkdale Senior, the breakup of my marriage to ramO, moving home twice… the boys and I had had a great time. I reminded myself I could do this. It may not be how I envisaged it, but I could do it.

Fraser, my initial lawyer had told me that even though my references 'cast me in a very positive light' they were not strictly relevant to the charges being made against me. Something to this day I do not understand why, because each of the references go into detail as to what I am like as a mother, an educator, business woman and community developer. I knew the references were great references, and had they been allowed in the evidence, then I am sure the judge would have had a better opinion of me; again it made no sense as to why I had not been questioned or interviewed, and as to why my references were not allowed. Why was it okay to attempt to prosecute someone without finding out all the facts of the matter first? Why is it okay for the police to paint a very black picture of someone, that bears no resemblance to the person under suspicion, and then have the accused do their very best to paint it white again? You'd still end up with a murky grey colour, one that has many negative on the lives of the individuals. It affects trust issues within families, communities and can go a long way to preventing people from working; and recovering mentally from the lies and deformation of character. Just because they put a police uniform on to go to work, they should still be made to abide by the laws of Human Rights, which I firmly believe they had not adhered in this case. I have a right to speak with my children in Arabic and not be told I am being aggressive. I have a right to make choices based on what I know about my boys, the knowledge and the life I have given them, I have the right to make my own risk assessment as a parent and I have the right to stand up to bullies, regardless of the outfit they are wearing.

The more this whole Scotland Saga went on, the more I began to hate Scotland; and that upset me because I had met so many amazing people in Scotland, my new partner at that. A part of me felt sorry for the people of Scotland, but I knew this didn't just happen in Scotland. This happened all over the world. Corruption and denial was everywhere; and I now truly believed there was an even deeper underlying corruption in Scotland, than I had first believed. I know there is corruption in every government. With the big egos, backhanded deals to trade arms, protection of politicians, kill many unknowns to save profit or the face of an influential, it isn't just the stuff of movies, it is the stuff of everyday life. I just couldn't believe it was happening to me, but in some way I was glad it was happening because I was learning, and I am now sharing it with the world, to help others protect themselves; to help others understand that they are not alone in this, that they too can rise up and fight the injustice that is happening to them, their family, their friends and to others in their communities. It was a big weight to acknowledge and an even bigger one to carry, but I know I am strong enough and have some incredible people around me to support me; but I still felt alone. How could I share this with others just yet? How could I expect them to understand or make sense of all of this when not even I could make sense of it all?

I sat there in the chair and thought back to the two ladies in the courtroom who had also been dealt with in a nasty manner by the judge. I wondered if either of them had made a complaint. As I wondered my phone rang. It was John; and a huge smile broke over my face. This man's timing was impeccable. He asked me how the boys and I were and I gave him an update. He was so attentive to the boys, would speak with them to reassure them everything would be alright. I wanted to hear all about his adventures around the Canary Islands. As he told me about his escapades I laughed, thinking about all the fun he was having. A pang of envy flashed through me. Here I was dealing with all this, and struggling to building a business – and here was my partner away at sea living on a beautiful tall ship and watching the sun rise and set, eating on deck, feeling the wind on his face and being ricked to sleep by the motion in the ocean. I longed to be with him travelling around the world on our own ship. It wasn't just a longing to be with him, it was a longing to be on the ocean; and each time I went to the beach, or heard his adventures, the stronger the pull was. Whether John and I stood the test of time together, I would live at sea. No question whatsoever in my mind. John told me his plans to return, and my heart flipped. I would be seeing him in just over a week! A rush of emotion came over me, tears fell and I pushed them back down; but he knew. He told me not to worry. Told me not to let them get to me; or inside my head. Told me that I had not done anything wrong and we would get through this. I thought of his strong arms around me and instantly felt better. Then I had a fleeting thought: *I need to be able to do this for myself, by myself.* Which was closely followed by: *No one is an island Dawn, this is too big to deal with by yourself. Accept the love and the support.* Something I had struggled to accept over the years. How many years was anyone's guess, but I was learning. John and I stayed on the phone chatting for about an hour, sorting out arrangements and catching up. We said our goodbyes and knew I wouldn't get to speak with him until he landed in Glasgow as they were heading over to another island in the Canaries ready for him to fly back.

Speaking with David at Beltrami's later that day we had conversation about the boys being witnesses for me, as Fraser had mentioned in the meeting I had had with him on the 2nd December. David said he would need to speak with them individually and needed my permission. I had nothing to hide and knew my boys would say the truth of what had happened. I gave David permission to speak with them and told him it was up to them if they wanted to be in the court as witnesses. I told him that I had nothing to hide and I was not going to tell the boys to be in court or not to be in court, it was entirely their decision. They were smart enough, and strong enough, to make their own choices.

I called ramO to tell him that David would be contacting the boys to speak with them about what had happened; and that they would possibly have to be witnesses for me in court on the 14th December. I asked to speak with the boys to let them know and asked him if he would support them making their own choice, of which he said he would. Of course he would, he was a great dad in that respect. He gave both sides of the coin and then allowed them to make their own choices. One of the things that had appealed to me about ramO was his ability to play devil's advocate, annoying at times, but it always gave food for thought and perspective.

I know some would say leaving the boys to choose whether they would appear in court as a witness, is a decision too big for a young child to make, but I say that depends on the child and how the parents raise them; combined with the information shared with the child. We were unbiased, factual and non-emotional when it came to preparing our children to make choices. We included how different emotions came up and what they might expect or experience, nothing more and nothing less. We have always believed it would be unfair to colour their judgment and pass on any fears or beliefs we had; even when it came down to religion. They were free to choose, or not choose.

I also told him when the court case was and asked him to make arrangements for him to bring the boys to Scotland in case they were expected to be witnesses. He said of course he would be there to support me and the boys. With everything that had happened thus far with this court case, I had to acknowledge ramO for being the man I had originally fallen in love with. He was still there, even though I wasn't in love with him anymore; he was still the kind, thoughtful and supportive man I had known for 18 years. The reference he had given me spoke volumes, even though it was not to be used within the courtroom.

It still bugged me that my references couldn't be used, and I knew that had the court even been bothered to find out the kind of person I was, the fact that I was still amicable and building bridges with my ex-husband after his betrayals, would have spoken volumes – because it was all for my children. And here in lies the problem with the legal and justice system. They are only interested in the here and now. They are not interested in the events that led up to the actual incident in which they choose to persecute and prosecute someone; and this shows a huge level of ignorance and lack of emotional and social intelligence. An analogy I like to use is this: Even granite, if you chip away long enough at it, will crumble. The same goes for people. Unless the police and justice system are willing to put the event itself into context, then they are carrying out a huge miscarriage of justice. If a woman defends herself from her husband in yet another attack or rape, and this time grabs a lamp and smashes him over the head to get him off her, and kills or disables him, is she done for murder? Or manslaughter? Or grievous bodily harm? Or should she be let off and supported to help her deal with the trauma of having an abusive husband who raped and attacked her? There is always a back story, and there is always a reason people do what they do, and if we are going to have ethical and moral policing in this world, then prior knowledge and character references have to be seen and taken into consideration.

I made another cup of tea then purchased my train and flight tickets back up to Scotland. Heading into my bedroom ready to pack my suitcase, a huge sense of tiredness came over me. I sat down on the bed and fell asleep. I woke up to a phone call from Birkdale asking if I needed Naasir to go into after-school club. I then had a call about collecting Khaalid from Forge Valley. I quickly washed my face and jumped in the car to collect Khaalid as Ms Roper at Birkdale Prep had said she would put Naasir into after school-club. I was so incredibly grateful to the ladies on reception at Birkdale, as well as Matron, and of course Mr Leighton. Mr Oakey was another great teacher there. They all knew of the situation I was facing and the support they gave was just wonderful. They knew these allegations were idiotic at best, so stood by me in any way they could. I told them that Naasir would need to be out of school for a couple of days as he had to make an appearance in court. Mr Leighton was surprised and yet not. He shook his head and said of course, whatever needed to happen to see the end of this sorry affair. Getting Khaalid permission to be out of school was a very different affair. Permission slips and authorisation from the Head of Year... how very different the state and private school rules were... and how different the support; but then again, the team at Forge Valley had not known us long, so their coldness was – I guess, somewhat – to be expected.

I apologised to the boys for being late, and as always asked them how their day was. Khaalid just dismissed my question and told me, "An apology is not needed Mummy. You are doing a lot. Like you say to us 'Don't be hard on yourself' okay? And yes, my day was fine, thank you." The way he said it, and the way he looked away told me that something was going on; but I respected his space and asked him if he was going to see his friend Mark after school on the Friday. It was becoming a regular thing for Khaalid and Mark to hang out together, and it made me feel comfortable that Khaalid was making friends.

Collecting Naasir, I was welcomed by his arms thrown around me.

God I loved this boy! So incredibly generous with his hugs, and I was the lucky Mummy to be on the receiving end of most of them!

When we returned home we made dinner together and the next thing I know, Khaalid was waking me up as Naasir giggled. I had fallen asleep at the table and nearly put my face in my dinner... much to Naasir's amusement. Khaalid told me to go to bed and he set his alarm to remind them of the time to go to bed. I woke up in the morning fully clothed and crashed out on my bed. I panicked and then remembered Naasir giggling. I checked the time and it was time for Kelt's walk. As I went into the kitchen, there was a note from the boys telling me they loved me and how Khaalid had walked Kelt around the church before going to bed. These boys. They were so grown up and responsible, so caring, so loving. How on earth was I being charged with Wilful Neglect when I had raised these two boys, pretty much single-handedly, into these fine young men?

I was heading to my mum's that day, as ramO was having the boys for his week with them. I said a very big goodbye to the boys and told them I would possibly see them up in Scotland on the 14th December. They immediately asked if 'Uncle John' would be there and I said he should be, to which they replied, "Good!"

I spent so much time at my mums sleeping. Both my mum and I talked about what it was like for her as a single mum, and how she had mentioned what had happened to a couple of her friends. Each of them disgusted at what had happened to me. It seemed everyone who had been told had all had an equally shocked and disgusted response.

I knew I had to go public. The police should not be allowed to get away with this. One of the things that occurred to me, whilst talking with my mum about the choices she had to make when she was a single mum, was how very little had changed in the way of systems and support. Having spoken with friends who were single, and everything I had experienced since arriving back in the UK, I had learnt a lot about how blasé many married couples are, and I had been, with regards to life as a single parent. Yes, I had raised the boys predominantly on my own over the years, but I always had the backup of being married. And yes, there were lots of initiatives who claimed to help the single parent, but many were not inspiring, or enabled the single parent to rise up. There were a lot unnecessary hurdles and blockages in the way, when all you wanted to do was get going and rebuild your life.

There was still a lot of judgement around the single mum, but one thing I had begun to learn was the negative reactions some of my male friends had had. One of them had been out with his daughter to get her first ever bra; and what should have been a lovely experience for a parent to share with their child, turned into a nightmare shopping experience. Shop assistants and shoppers alike had seen a man in the underwear section with a young girl and assumed the worst of him. Scornful looks, people tutting, and no one prepared to help.... But no one prepared to do anything else other than pass ignorant comments and looks his way. I was surprised the shop assistants didn't offer to help out, and said I would be happy to go back to the shop and help his daughter, and say something to the shop manager; I even suggested he ring up and report the incident, but he just wanted to forget the whole thing. I told him if he didn't say something, other dads would get the same treatment. I left it at that. It was his choice and only he could make it.

It was startling though how in 40 years, nothing much had changed in the way of social and emotional intelligence; and as a subject that I love and regularly study, I find it frustrating to say the least. Our phones, cars, homes, workspaces and hospitals have improved greatly, but the work we do on ourselves as individuals and as a community, very poor to say the least. As humans we are so much more capable of social and emotional evolution, but we remain rooted in the past, in suspicion, in fear and lacking self-confidence. With so many controls and pointless pieces of legislation – just because something happened once and the powers that be want to prevent it from happening again – we are suffocating. We have very little confidence in ourselves – just bravado. Scared to say what we truly think. Overwhelmed by so much information that we don't absorb any of it, staying stuck. Remaining in ignorance; eating, working, sleeping, getting drunk, taking drugs, totally unconnected to our souls and living in our heads.

I sat there looking at my mum, listening to her words, seeing her mouth moving, and yet, I heard none of what she was saying after a while. I felt like I had shifted something. I felt like my soul had awakened, just by acknowledging how very little the human consciousness had evolved. My mum shouted, "Dawn Louise"… the only two words to snap me out of anything. I knew my mum had been saying my name a few times, not just because she used Dawn Louise but by the look on her face. "Did you hear anything of what I just told you?"

"Yes mum. I did, some of it. I just can't believe how little we have evolved. What with what I saw and experienced in Egypt, and now this? People need to wise up and wake up. Just like Matt Ridley says…"

"Who?"

"Matt Ridley, he's an author. He wrote *The Red Queen Theory* and in it he states that 'The more we evolve, the more we stay the same. It's a great book'."

"I'll take your word for it, now, do you want to go to Hunstanton in the morning?" I looked at my mum with the biggest smile. With my mum looking straight at my dad and telling him, "See I told you she hadn't heard a bloody word I was saying."

I gave them both a big hug. I was going to the beach, with my mum and dad and Ed, their dog.

"Cup of tea?" I asked with a big smile…

"Yeah, go on then."

FIFTEEN

THE TRIAL

I arrived in Greenock on the 10th December, ready to board the ferry over to Dunoon, when I ran into the chap from my previous trips. He asked me how things were going and as I told him, he just couldn't believe it was still being entertained. "Bring back the old days when kids were expected to be responsible and given the opportunities to be so. Too many namby-pamby[7] youths these days who expect everything done for them and who can't think for themselves. You do right love. Anyone meeting you can see that you are a great woman, there's just some things you know about people, and I can tell you're a good 'un."

I blushed and thanked him for his high praise.

He said he was going to make a cup of tea and asked if I wanted one. I gladly accepted and he told me to stay where I was, outside, looking out over the Clyde, and he would bring me my cup of tea. He walked away shaking his head. When he came back I could tell that he was slightly troubled so asked him if he was okay. His response wasn't one I expected, "I just want to say that I am really truly sorry that a lovely lady like you is having to go through all this; especially when there are people out there that do serious harm to kids. It makes me blood boil it does." I told him I was sorry that I had upset him with my news, and thanked him for the cup of tea. He came back at me with, "No need for you to be sorry love, it's those arseholes who think they know better than we do about our own kids, and think they can tell us how to raise the wee bairns. Sat in central bloody government, in their ivory towers, that's what makes me angry love, not you. I feel for you, I really do. And you'd better drink up that tea, the ferry will be in in a few minutes." He nodded to me and then went back to his work.

I finished my tea and then walked towards the ferry platform, handing my mug to the other chap that welcomed me and immediately asked, "You going back up top then love?"

At which point I giggled and said, "Of course!"

"Be a bit cold up there today love, plenty of snow on top of them there mountains."

I looked over the water and noticed the snow topped mountains and a massive smile broke out across my face. Oh how I loved the scenery of the west coast… If only all this hadn't have happened, I would have been happy to settle here in later life; but not now. Not now all this had happened.

I sat up on the deck and closed my eyes, just feeling the wind and sea spray on my face. I took deep breathes to breathe in as much of the air as possible. It was cold, but it was a refreshing cold. A cold I enjoyed. As I closed my eyes I could see me on a ship at sea. I could feel my hands numb from the cold, tough from hoisting the sails, I could feel myself being rocked to sleep by the motion of the sea. I focused on the sound of the water slashing against the hull of the ferry, and before I knew it we were in Dunoon. My new friend nodded to me as I walked off the ferry and said, "Thought you were gone for good up there. Thought we'd need to get the smelling salts out!" To which we both laughed. I told him I'd see him later or in a few days, to which he nodded and said, "Aye, that you will."

I smiled. I loved it when John said "aye"… I am not sure if it is the vibration at which his voice resonates or what it is, but hearing him say "aye"… hmmm say it again please, John.

I headed to The Park Hotel and received a very warm welcome from the owners. I was shown to my room and left to settle. I said I would come and join them for a drink when I had finished unpacking. As I walked in the room I smiled. I would get to spend time in the bath, with the windows open, listening to the sound of the waves crashing and know that John would be here shortly. Even though it wasn't the best circumstances to meet up under, it was still time together.

I walked down to the bar and smiled as there was also a glass of pinot grigio waiting for me, on the house. I thanked them and also acknowledged them on the work they had done on the hotel since I had last stayed. They were really making a difference and it showed.

I asked them what time dinner orders stopped as told them I was going back to the ferry terminal to meet John. They said they would make sure we ate, and I was not to worry about anything during our stay.

I arrived at the ferry terminal and John was already off the ferry and looking for me. We walked back to the hotel with him telling me about his trip back and the lady at the check in desk in Spain getting mixed up with 'Dunoon' and 'Don't know' when she'd asked John what his final destination was. It had also been quite an easy journey, everything flowing as it should do. We arrived back at the hotel and the Tennents I had ordered for John and my pinot grigio was waiting for us on the bar. We went to the room, dropped John's stuff off and then headed back to the bar for dinner and drinks. I couldn't stop looking at him. He looked great. Being on the ship had been good for him physically and being on the sea, great for his energy. I couldn't stop smiling to myself about how sexy he looked. (He's going to tell me off for putting this in the book, but hey, it's my book and he needs to learn to take compliments positively. He is sexy and I don't care if the world knows I think my man is sexy; and a whole lot more besides).

We had another day before I was due in court and so we walked around the town and just enjoyed each other's company. Catching up on many of the things we had been up to since Spain. The court case was only touched on a few times, and there really wasn't that much more to add to what we had already discussed. This was a day to relax and find my zen space; before getting my mind ready for the next day. We enjoyed a lovely meal, some delicious wine and a night together. John ran me a bath and put some music on. I lay there in the bath with a big smile on my face. He had made it to Scotland to be with me. I felt supported, loved, and protected. I must have dozed off as John knocked on the bathroom door asking if I was okay and if I wanted more wine. I noticed the water wasn't as warm as I liked it, so I knew I had been in the bath at least an hour, so I got out and had a final glass of wine before sleeping; which I only managed about a couple of hours. I lay there, still in John's arms and wondered what the next day would bring. I must have been awake for quite a while, when John kissed the back of my neck and told me to stop worrying and go back to sleep; again putting a big smile on my face. This man!

I woke up what seemed liked ten minutes later, but I knew I had slept for at least another two hours. The sun had come up and the first thing I heard was the waves crashing on the shore. I loved this room by the sea. Smiling at the thought of living at sea, and when not at sea, waking up in a beach hut or a cottage by the sea... *Yep, most definitely what I am working towards*, I thought. I was still lying in John's arms, and as I woke up properly, I remembered what the day meant; a day in a courtroom. Proving my innocence; when by law I was innocent until proven guilty – and how could they prove me guilty when I had not done what they say I had done. If anything, today was going to be an interesting learning curve for me; if we managed to get it all done today.

Meeting David in the courtroom foyer, the boys arrived and there were big hugs all round. I thanked ramO for bringing them to the court, whilst John caught up with the boys and got the cheeky banter underway with them. I loved seeing the way they all interacted, and sometimes had to pinch myself that I had found a guy who not only ticked all the boxes on my list, but was so much more than the list itself. There were my non-negotiable items on that list, and the more work I did on myself, the more I added to the list, the more John stepped up – without even knowing what was on the list. The more I added the more I realised that it didn't matter what was on the list, because I had found a guy that was much more than I had anticipated, and although he went about things in a very different way, the outcomes were pretty much the same. We were both up-leveling, both wanting the same things, both unwilling to negotiate on certain things, and both growing together... as confronting as that may be for me when I went into my head and my insecurities decided to show up again. Each time they showed up though, one look or hand hold from John, a recall from a memory, the use of one of the new coaching tools I'd learnt, the quicker they disappeared.

David asked me to go to the interview room with him and discuss a few items on the agenda. It turned out that two of the witnesses were not able to be in court today, so it would mean I would have to come back at a later date. He apologised as he knew this was more expense for me and more time out of school for the boys. I knew that this needed to be done, so I said, "Look, whatever needs to be done for me to be found not guilty – because *I am* not guilty – then we'll do it."

David nodded and told me to make my way to the courtroom as we were about to start. I must have gone white because I felt quite faint, my heart started racing and my hands shaking. I felt sick. The closer I got to the courtroom the more negative energy I felt. There was a really oppressive air about this place and I couldn't wait to get out of there. But I knew I was there for the day. Whilst waiting for the judge to arrive, I went through some positive mindset work in my head. I wasn't able to write down positive affirmations in my journal, so I simply repeated them in my head over and over again. The judge walked in and we were told to rise from our seats, as a mark of respect. I for one did not wish to rise to respect this bully but I had no choice, as I didn't want to add contempt of court to the list of charges being bought against me. Just looking at him, his energy was dark, the total opposite to mine. I was a happy bunny who liked to giggle and help people, empower them, help them fulfil their own potential, and here I was in a room with a guy who took away people's freedom on a day to day basis (admittedly some of the people he had put away, were best kept off the streets – yes, I'd done my research on this judge and the cases he had worked on, along with the outcomes of the cases, but filling up prisons with people who have a different world view and anti-establishment mindset wasn't a good enough reason in my eyes).

The judge looked straight through me. He didn't even have the decency to look me in the eye, or to look at me, only through me. What had happened to this guy over the years to make him so unable to connect with those in his courtroom? Or had he seen so many nasty people, everyone he met was guilty of nastiness and illegal behaviour. Just like a mortician, so used to dealing with death, they become immune to it, and are indifferent to those who turn up in their mortuary. I felt sad for him. Sad for those who surrounded him. I wondered what he had been like as a young boy. Had he been happy and joyful? Or had he been a bully? Liking the power over others as he had no power in his own life? Sometimes I wished I hadn't done so much work on personal development and psychology, it always made me wonder how people had ended up the way they were now. An occupational hazard, like the judge presuming everyone who walked into his courtroom was guilty before he had even heard the evidence. My complaint may have been rejected but I knew this judge was going to be hard to convince of my innocence.

As the trial got started the witness Beattie stated that when he approached my car and tried to open the door, Kelt had barked so much, he backed away. My first thought was: *Why are you trying to open the door of my car?* The judge and the lawyers didn't even pick up on this. His evidence was so haphazard and the timings so off, it was as if I was hearing evidence about another incident. He also had a dark energy; there was something just not right about him. I didn't like him. Not one bit. Then the arresting male sergeant as he now was, PS Wilson, took the stand and he bumbled and stumbled along, with his timeline not matching the timeline of the witness Beattie. Why was David not picking up on the inconsistencies? Don't get me wrong, I was impressed with David's demeanour in the courtroom but there were so many inconsistencies in Wilson's statement, even from the summary of evidence that I couldn't help wonder why David wasn't picking up on them. PC Brindle was the next to take the stand and she brought the case against me for Breach of the Peace and Wilful Neglect crumbling down. She was obviously under duress to say the things she was saying. It was as if she had a big neon sign above her head shouting out my innocence; and her fear. She couldn't make eye contact with me. Her energy had changed. She was a shadow of her former self; and I found out she had relocated to another station shortly after I had been arrested and charged. She was so confused with what she was saying, and recalling what she had obviously been told to say that the judge had to ask her to clarify what she was saying; because on one hand she was saying I had been rude and abusive and then on the other hand she was saying that she was too far away to hear me, when in fact she had been less than 50 yards away from me the whole time.

I turned around at one point as I could feel this immense anger feeling coming from behind me. I turned around I looked at PS Wilson.

He had a face of thunder, and I was quickly urged to turn back and face the front of the courtroom. I knew why he looked so angry, because he knew that PC Brindle had weakened the case against me. As she left the stand in a deeply flustered way, I wanted to reach out to her and ask her what on earth had happened to her, but it wasn't my stuff to deal with. She had made her choices, whatever they were, and although it was obvious they were not serving her on a deep level, she had made the choices to lie on the stand. Her conscience was deeply troubled and anyone with any knowledge of human behaviour would have been able to tell she was deeply uncomfortable with what she was saying. As PC Brindle left the courtroom, PS Wilson was hot on her heals and from just outside the courtroom doors I could hear stifled voices – very unhappy voices. The usher also heard them and got up from his seat and headed to the doors. PS Wilson was obviously VERY upset with the testimony that PC Brindle had given. His anger and negativity energy could be felt all around the courtroom, and when he left the atmosphere lifted. Now to some all this talk of energy maybe a little too out there, but consider when you have just had a disagreement with someone, or you have walked into somewhere and you just know that someone is not feeling great. This is the energy I talk about, the energy that triggers our empathy, sympathy or joy for someone. To dismiss it, would be to dismiss our very essence of being human.

John was up next and he was the most confident of all the witnesses. Something the prosecutor and judge obviously didn't like as they were looking at him with a wary eye. His timeline of events were only slightly off, but then John doesn't know what day it is half the time as he lives his life at sea and away from the regimented time-keeping of the world on land. He makes me laugh when he shakes his head at me for being so organised and able to tell the time by 'what I feel is the time'. I say to him, "It's like you, you know the time of day by looking at the position of the sun and the stars in the sky, I know the time by being in tune with nature." Growing up in the countryside, I got used to knowing what the time was by just looking at the sky. I feel the time. I have got so used to measuring time since doing the Paul J Meyer Success Motivation International Goal Setting programme when I was 21; and planning my day in five minute increments. My time keeping and ability to know how long something should take, and has taken has become something those that know me have always been impressed with. It's what makes me great at enabling others to manage their time; and why my morning routine with the boys works so well, even if we have overslept – which is a rarity.

John's testimony took us to the end of the day and the boys never got heard, so by the time I had left the courtroom, ramO had already left with them. I was gutted. I wanted to see my boys and give them a big hug. David instructed me to go to the witness room to give me an update. He said that the fact PC Brindle had made so many errors was a good sign, but not conclusive. He also said that there were enough conflictions during the timings for him to use with the next lot of witnesses. He apologised that the boys would have to come up to Scotland again, but their testimonies were now very important. He said he was hopeful, but couldn't give me any guarantees. I was hopeful that he was hopeful; but it was just the way in which the judge kept looking at me that made me uncomfortable. A thought flashed through my head that he should never play poker, because his conviction of me was written all over his face, and that would never be a great thing in a game of poker... not that I play poker, but I am very used to the phrase 'poker face' and understand what it means.

As John and I left the courtroom, he held my hand. I realised I had tears escaping. I was tired. I was drained. I just wanted a hot bath with the windows open so I could hear the waves, and a glass of pinot grigio. I wanted to lie in John's arms and fall asleep. I wanted to hug my boys, and was pissed off with ramO for having left without saying goodbye. I knew it was because they had a six hour drive ahead of them and he wanted to get them back so they could be fresh for school the next day, but an hour would not have made that much of a difference with the boys as they had got used to sleeping in the car, in tents, on couches and in luxury hotel rooms. My boys could sleep anywhere. So yeah, I was pissed off at him.

As John and I were heading back to the hotel, our tummies rumbled. We hadn't eaten at lunch, and so we went for a walk around the supermarket, trying to figure out what to eat. There was so much we couldn't eat, due to me not eating gluten, pig or processed food, and we were both health conscious, so in the end we settled for a rotisserie chicken and we brought a bottle of pinot grigio. It was quite dark when we left the supermarket, and as we headed back through the town it was nice to see it lit up. We ate the chicken on our way back and then got to the bandstand. We were giggling at the fact we were having a classy meal and loving every morsel of it. I joked with John saying, "You really do know how to show a girl a good time." Because he did. I loved the way John made things more about the experience rather than the expense. A car drove by and I heard the music and started singing and wiggling around the bandstand. We both started laughing and ended up in each other's arms. I was totally in love with him. I couldn't deny it. He made life so much fun, and stimulated my mind, body and soul. I felt like the luckiest woman in the world.

The next day we made sure we had a hearty breakfast at the hotel and sorted out some of John's admin before heading off. We were heading to my mum's, the first time they would all get to meet each other. I knew they would all get on, but I wasn't expecting them to all get on as well as they had done. My mum and dad loved John, and my dad had more conversation with John in the first two hours of meeting John, than he had said to ramO in about 18 years. Mum and I stood in the kitchen making dinner and giggling with each other. John had made a great first impression. I was happy, very happy, especially as I had made a point of wanting to be with a guy who would get on with my parents this time around. There had been too many 'tenderhook' moments with ramO over the years; and as my parents and I had become really close over the last two years, I didn't want a relationship with a guy to damage that.

I needn't have worried; John had won them over; and my mum really liked him… and his cheeky nature. Kelt was also really pleased to see John, and their little adventure together on the night of my arrest had bonded them both. Kelt also listened to John more than me now, which I was not impressed with, cheeky little monkey! Kelt was MY dog, not John's! As I cuddled Kelt, I asked him why he was being a little traitor, at which point he tilted his head to say, "Who me? Never!" At which point we all laughed and Kelt rolled himself further into my arms. God I loved this dog!

Heading back to Sheffield with John, knowing I had him home for at least a week was great. I was slightly nervous at arriving home with John, because it was a special moment for me. Meeting my parents, arriving in my home, he was getting to see the depths of me not many see; and for an old fashioned kind of girl, these were big steps for me. He would get to see our life, how we truly lived. He would see me and how I organised my life. He had stuck by me this far, seen from afar this happy go lucky woman, who was so driven, focused and proper on one to provide for her children. He had stuck by me through this awful court case. He had met my parents, and if my mum's crazy ways hadn't sent him running, then there was hope.

One of the things I love about my mum is her full on 'take me or leave me' attitude. She speaks her mind, is completely herself, whilst dancing around playing 'silly buggers' with the grandchildren. John had warmed to her immediately; and could see where I got a lot of my full-on 'up for it' vibe.

But now he was in my home, the home that was still in transition from my previous marriage. Items that didn't belong in my future but were there out of necessity rather than choice. A layout that hadn't really been thought about as I hadn't made the time to get it sorted out whilst building my business and all this court case was going on. It didn't matter though. John just settled in, and it felt right. With John being in my home, with my boys and Kelt, it felt right. Why did it flow so seamlessly with him? Why was I still second guessing? Why couldn't I just accept that I had a guy that loved me and wanted to be with me? Had he not proven himself enough over the last six months? Why did he have to prove himself at all? Man this 'new relationship' business was an interesting one. At first it was exciting, whilst being incredibly nervous about kissing someone new after 18 years with the same guy. But now deeper feelings were entering the mind, body and soul, it felt scary. I had already let a guy into my life and had children with him. I had told John I didn't want another child, unless it came with sails and a deck, it was a boat or a baby. If he wanted a baby, he had to find someone else. He was still with me. A boat it was then.

After a couple of days of being at mine, John got sick. REALLY sick. His temperature was so high, so much so I had to take him to the hospital. He was out of it for days; and I was quite worried about him. As it turned out he would miss his flight back to the boat; and that resulted in the captain telling him not to bother going back. I couldn't believe her attitude. Here was a hard working guy, who had so much experience at sea, and who was incredibly safety conscious, really sick in bed, on antibiotics and unable to fly, being told if he didn't make the flight he would lose his job. So John stayed with me; and was able to come back to Scotland with me for the next trial date, which was set for January 11th. The day I would take to the stand. The day I would hopefully get a chance to finally say what had happened that night, set the record straight, and walk away from this nightmare leaving it all behind in the past as an ugly situation that had provided so many insights in the system that tried to control the lives of others, when they had no right to; they just assumed they did, and because they believed in their own hype so much, and their own egos, the public had gone along with it; convincing themselves these bullies in uniform, black gowns and wigs, and the ones in suit and ties were what was needed. A massive case of Stockholm Syndrome if ever there was one; and reminded me so much of the Egyptian mindset of 'needing' a dictator to keep the country stable, even though the regime kept the country unstable and full of fear just so they could profit from all the uncertainty.

Once John was feeling better, he was up and out of bed and into action. I had been writing some ideas up on my wall about places to tap into, different offers, and marketing ideas to blog about when I heard all this noise. I went through to the lounge and saw that John had emptied a cupboard that I used to store things in, that led through into my bedroom. He had pulled everything out and was re-organising it. Then he moved onto what is now known as 'John's shed' – aka 'the cupboard' with all the DIY tools and gadgetry needed for the home, the vacuum cleaner and the dog's clippers, food and medications. He'd organised the lot and it all made so much sense. It was like he had read my thoughts... or rather, he had listened. He had heard me. Through all the white noise of the last year, he had still heard me.

I remember sitting down at dinner that night with a massive smile on my face. Khaalid asked me what I was smiling about, and I simply said, "What Uncle John has done around the apartment today, it feels great." And it did. It felt great, not just because things were organised and furniture had been rearranged, but also because he had heard all the things I had been sharing with him over the last few months about what I wanted to do with the place, and he had just implemented so much of what I wanted. I felt heard. I felt understood. I felt seen. I felt supported. I felt loved.

We sprang into action to find him more work, and working out what he wanted to do, achieve and what he needed to do to achieve it all. He sent off a few emails, but there wasn't much about as it was the 'off season' unless of course he headed over to Australia or Thailand... something exciting for him, but that took us further apart, for longer periods of time, and meant he wouldn't be able to attend the trial with me. I knew this trial was having a negative impact on many areas of my life, and it was putting me in places emotionally and mentally which were not good; I was also very aware that it wasn't just me going through this. John was as well. So were my boys, my parents and the friends I had confided in. Not wanting to be a burden on anyone, I kept a lot of what I was thinking and feeling to myself, and every now and then I would have a meltdown. John saw me have a meltdown and recommended that I go to the doctor to see if I could get some help talking to someone.

So I went, but was told that I had all the tools and coping mechanisms I needed, and didn't qualify for any help; even though it was obvious to the nurse that I was in need of help, the process of the 'eligibility scores' meant I didn't score high enough on the depressed scale, and so I was on my own. Great! More processes that overrode the human ability to make sound judgements and support fellow humans in a time of need. When had the UK population become so dependent on following systems and unable to tap into humanity? When had this shift happened? When would people wake up and see how capable they truly are instead of living in fear and doubt of themselves? When would they realise that following processes was numbing their souls and brains to such an extent that they were now part of a very big problem that was allowing a passive aggressive dictatorship to evolve and emerge?

When had people tuned out and become so totally numb? When had they chosen to follow fear of losing their jobs instead of stepping up to create their own job security? When had people become so afraid of making mistakes? When had they stopped doing what is right and human? When had we as a species stopped stepping into abundance? With so many jobs being lost due to automation, why were people so afraid of up-levelling? If they were so scared of losing their jobs, why were they still playing small? Why were they not innovating? I was becoming more and more disillusioned, and not with all things Scotland either. Still all I had to do was get through the next stage of the trial and then I could kiss goodbye to this whole nightmare and just get on with my life. Start implementing all the business ideas and really get down to work, instead of being totally consumed by this nightmare and wanting to hide from the world.

I was a shadow of my former self. I was not in a good place and I was feeling trapped. I had to escape. I had to figure out a way to departmentalise this whole process... and this is where I guess it is easier to be a male... departmentalising is such a male thing. I knew I had to step into my masculine energy to be able to deal with this issue, whilst also remaining in my feminine. Oh, the challenges; the drain. I just wanted to disappear. I just wanted to get on a boat and disappear. I just wanted to leave everything behind. I knew the boys would be fine with ramO, I knew the dogs would be fine with me, or my parents. I just needed to disappear. Where no one knew me. Where I could just live simply. Pull veggies, eat clean and just be free to walk, sail, climb do whatever...

And as if John had read my mind, he said, "Let's go walking tomorrow. Let's make a soup, some flapjacks and just go walking with the boys and the dogs."

I looked at him, almost suspiciously. "How on earth do you do that?"

"What?"

"That! How do you do that?"

"Do what?" He replied innocently.

Hmmm... John. What a guy you are; how blessed I feel to have you in my life. Reading my mind without even knowing it.

---

[7] Namby-pamby is a phrase used to describe people who act younger or less capable than they actually are; who are weak of mind and resilience; and who also use a feeble act of behaviour to get themselves out of doing something.

SIXTEEN

THE VERDICT

Arriving back in Scotland on the 10th January, the day before the trial, I was a bag of nerves. John had done his best to calm me down, to reassure me, but it wasn't him on trial. It wasn't him that was about to step into the courtroom and have more lies told about him and the way he had treated his children. I was a devoted mother and of all the things in this world anyone could accuse me of, being a neglectful mother was probably the very worst thing they could accuse me, other than hurting a child. I loved kids, especially my own boys. I had made a conscious effort to raise two young people into people I wanted to be around. I loved their minds, their humour and everything about them, so to be accused of Wilful Neglect and Abandonment hurt me to the very core of my existence; and anyone that knew me, knew I was, still am, devoted to my boys. They were my world, and my devotion to my boys probably played a part in my marriage breaking down. I made little or no time for ramO. His needs went unmet; if his needs were met, then he would have stayed faithful. But he didn't. That was his choice, but one that made me feel inadequate as a partner. I didn't want to make the same mistake again. I wanted to be all I could be as a mother, as a partner, whilst also honouring my needs. Never giving up who I was to fit into the world any more. I was here to shine, but feeling rather blemished at the moment, it was hard to even flicker, let alone shine.

Dunoon was becoming a place I loved to hate. I loved the crossing over from Gourock. I loved the views from the ferry as we crossed the Clyde. I loved the little café by the terminal... especially their Scotch broth. I loved the walk along the beach to The Park Hotel, and I loved that even though Dunoon should hold some very sad memories, I couldn't help remember all the beautiful memories that John and I had created together. Eating a roast chicken from the wrapper together, cups of tea in the harbour café... his beautiful blue eyes... soothing me, making me feel at home, every time I closed my eyes. Falling in love all over again at the age of 38 was such an amazing feeling, and anyone who resists it, after having a failed marriage, I highly recommend it. Learn from the marriage, allow yourself to trust another. Allow yourself to be loved. It is a beautiful experience. And if, like me, you always have this thought at the back of your mind about it not working, let go of trying to control it. Just go with it. It is a hard thing to do, not saying it is easy, but learning to love, and be loved... a beautiful experience. And if it doesn't work out, then you're another step closer to knowing what will work.

John and I woke up the morning of the trial. ramO and the boys would be there again. Another two days off school... will the schools send the £240 fines for having four days off school to the court? I doubt it very much. The systems are all in it together. Make the parents paranoid, make them fearful and then punish them, for things they are not even aware of. I wondered how many people would actually have children if they knew they had to study the books of laws for each and every country they visited, especially given that they are so different.

I mean let's face it, how many parents, lone, dual or single actually know the laws that govern them? I mean, it's not like we have to sit an exam before the baby is born, or we get given a copy of 'The Law – and the impacts on your parenting' in the bounty packs alongside the tub of Sudocrem, pampers samples and breast pads. No one gets given a copy of any law book, until they have broken the law; and as I was finding out, the laws in which we are governed by are so out of date with the life and level of consciousness many of us are living now. I mean, come on, imagine driving a car from the 1930s.... or living in conditions from the

1930s… and yet here I am being put on trial for breaking a law from the 1930s. It just doesn't make any sense. The law needs massive reform. The police officers need to be trained in emotional and social intelligence. The police in Scotland need to get over the fear of job losses, which are common in any merger. The eight different police forces becoming one, after years of being a law unto themselves, and the focus on American police brutality, meant that many of those who have been getting away with heavy-handed policing, were now having to be extra careful; something that PS Wilson had obviously not cottoned onto. Police personnel like him need to get over their own ego, their own insecurities and start acting from a higher level of consciousness.

The world is becoming more aware, and the general public are finding ways in which to get their messages out there; as I found out in Egypt when the regime tried to block the internet. We found ways around the blackout, those from outside Egypt, helped those of us in Egypt find a way, and just in case the powers that be try to silence me, or squash this book, I have also made provisions for it to be released.

I thought back to the statistics of crimes actually committed on the west coast that I had looked at to see what the crimes were like in the area I had left the boys. Thinking there must be a really big culture of violence and kidnapping; but when you look at the statistics of crime, these show a HUGE amount of training issues for the police. I looked at the crime figures for the west coast of Scotland, I looked at the crimes percentiles for the area Argyll and Bute and saw that the amount of crimes committed by the public in all areas such as violent crime, damage to local property and theft, were less than nine incidents per crime… as opposed to over 300 'crimes' of 'disturbance of the peace'. If these figures didn't place a HUGE RED FLAG against the police in the west coast of Scotland in the region of Argyll and Bute I don't know what would. Looking at these figures from a business owner's point of view, a trainer's point of view and a human point of view, there were so many areas of development that needed looking at. There were so many things wrong with the picture that the Police Force's own figures displayed; and here they were for all to see, and no one taking action against them.

I thought back to the conversation I had with the chap Stephen from the Skills for Justice, there was massive work to be done on the west coast, massive work, but as John reminded me, "This is not about them, this is about you. Focus on you and the boys."

The only problem with doing that was it became too personal. The only way I could cope with this issue, was to look at it from a professional development point of view. It felt safer. It was made distant. It helped me get my feelings in check. Kept me somewhat sane in what had become a very insane situation. I mean, seriously, you just couldn't make this stuff up…. well, apparently Police Scotland and the Scottish Judiciary could.

I thought back to the Code of Ethics for Policing in Scotland on the way to the courtroom:

-'Encompasses the values of the organisation and our commitment to Human Rights' – Failed

-'I recognise my role in policing as being a symbol of public faith and trust, and the obligation this places upon me to act with integrity, fairness and respect' – Failed

-'I shall not behave in any way, on or off duty, which shall bring discredit upon the police service' – Failed

-'I shall act as a positive role model in delivering a profession, impartial service, placing service to communities before my personal aims' – MASSIVE FAIL

-'I shall avoid all behaviour, which is or may be reasonably considered as abusive, bullying harassing or victimising' – MASSIVE FAIL

-'I will demonstrate and promote good conduct and I will challenge the conduct of colleagues where I reasonably believe they have fallen below the standards set out in this Code' – MASSIVE FAIL from all the police officers, especially both the female officers!

As I went through this Code of Ethics in my mind, with the above points only reflecting on the integrity side to the Code, without even venturing into the Fairness, Respect and Human Rights elements of it, but the one that I really resonated with me was:

-'I will respect individual freedoms of thought conscious or religion, expression, peaceful assembly, movement and the peaceful enjoyment of possessions.'

So where had he done this in regards to me speaking Arabic to my boys? Where had he done this in respect to saying because my car was messy and a little smelly due to the damp tent and the fire pit, I was wilfully neglectful – instead of simply being a mother who wanted to raise competent and responsible adults, giving her children a holiday on zero budget? Where had he respected my thought consciousness when it came to knowing the world as I did, both as a multi-cultural family member, as well as an avid traveller (not a holiday make that frequented holiday resorts but a proper traveller? Where had he done this as a woman who had worked on various community programmes, getting to know many cross cultural, socio economic backgrounds? Where had he done this in regards to me being a single mother who travelled alone with her children and doing the job of two parents? He hadn't; and therefore had broken pretty much every ethic posted publicly in a non-protectively marked document anyone can find on the internet. PS Wilson had FAILED miserably, and yet here we were about to sit in a courtroom again, wasting the time, money and resources of at least eight people, not including those who were not employed by the state such as ramO, John and myself – and of course my two boys missing out on school work. This was a HUGE waste of public spending, just so PS Wilson could have his ego rubbed and his promotion protected.

The fact that Scottish judges are the highest paid in Europe, five times more than the UK's average salary, didn't actually have a bearing on the case as I originally thought it would. I was under the impression that they got paid by the cases they resided over, but no. They are given an annual salary, regardless of whether they are just in their findings. I also found out the female judges only represent only 21.6% of judges in the UK[8], with Azerbaijan the only state with a worse gender balance of 10.5%. I wondered how these figures actually contributed to the amount of women prosecuted, especially after Judge Ward's comments about the lady in therapy being insane, and the way in which he spoke to every female I had seen him converse with. None of the interaction I, or my boys had had with the police or Scottish judiciary this far had met any of the ethics outline in the Code of Ethics, and here I was on trial.

Sat in the dock waiting for the judge to come into the courtroom, I felt my hands start shaking. My heart started racing and I felt sick. I was no longer able to look at this from a professional point of view. My self-imposed protective armour had gone; not that it had protected me from near financial ruin, or the emotional and mental stress; or that it had destroyed the faith the boys had in the police – something I had worked hard to instill after leaving Egypt. I felt like I was on a merry-go-round, spinning out of control. I wanted to throw up, but I couldn't. I was to sit there in the dock for the remainder of the day, until it was my time to give evidence.

I listened to the Witness Lasek give her evidence and she had confirmed that Naasir was not at all upset about me not being with him in the car, but had confirmed that he was out of the car. She praised him for being very confident, chatty and polite; but not once did she say he was upset. She even admitted that she had also left him alone to go back to the pub to gather help to try and find me. When you consider that the hotel she went to was less than a two minute walk away, and the timeline she gave, it was obvious there were more discrepancies in the timeline the police and their witnesses were fabricating. Why could the judge not see this? And why was David not pulling her up on the conflicts of time with the evidence given on the previous court date? I was getting frustrated. I wanted to speak with David about all these discrepancies; but I had to sit tight and be quiet.

I listened to how this woman, who didn't know me from Adam, who had no professional training in behaviour, who had only worked as a hotel receptionist, was given the opportunity to give her professional opinion of my behaviour. Someone she has never met before, someone who she has spent no time with, someone who she had never witnessed in any other circumstances than apparently from a distance that would take her two minutes to get to me. This woman, with no professional or academic expertise in behaviour specialism was allowed to stand in court and say that I was drunk and that I was waving my hands around in a threatening manner. David didn't ask her how many people she knew who gesticulated with their hands, he never asked her how many people she had met who were public speakers, or from the Arab world, or who were animated; he just let this one slide as well. How can this woman's observations of me be classed as reliable? She'd been in the hotel drinking; and it wasn't established how much she had been drinking… but then she was a police witness and wasn't on trial. How convenient.

I was then told the boys would be up next to give evidence; but they had to give evidence from a different room by camera link up. After wasting about 30 minutes of time, I was asked if it would be okay for the boys to actually come into the courtroom to give their evidence. The discussions back and forth were almost laughable. Would it be appropriate for the boys to be in the courtroom? Would it be better if the prosecutor and David removed their gowns, jackets and ties? Would it be better if this was removed, if this was done and I began to realise just how these adults placed so much fear in the way when there really didn't need to be.

David looked at me and then asked me what I thought. I just looked at him and said, "My boys have been seeing men in suits and ties since they were babies, they have lived out in Egypt David, come on, seriously? My boys will be fine; it's just you adults that are making such a song and dance about everything; but thank you. I appreciate the gesture."

It made me realise just how much kids were protected from life, and how as adults we add far too much meaning to things without explaining to children what to expect. I had already told the boys that the judge would probably be wearing the gown and a wig, shown them photos and explained that it was a uniform just like any other; the only difference was this person had the power to send people, innocent or otherwise to prison. When the boys were eventually brought into the courtroom, the judge, the prosecutor and David had removed their gowns and wigs. The police officer that had been sat guarding the door, just in case I made a run for it, was removed, as were a couple of other guys, who I had no idea why they had been there throughout the trial they didn't seem to participate in anything, they just sat there, for hours. Not a job I would like, that's for sure; but each to their own.

As the boys walked into the courtroom in their shirts, ties and waistcoats, I was not only incredibly grateful to ramO for bringing them up to Scotland, but for also buying them some new cloths and having their hair cut. They were so handsome, the pair of them, and they looked super smart. Their smiles when they walked into the courtroom and saw me were huge. They were so pleased to see me and when they were escorted to the desks in front of me, they both turned around to speak with me, which David asked them not to. Khaalid frowned as if to say: *She's my mum, I want to speak with her.* Instead he just winked at me and blew me a kiss. I loved that boy!

Naasir, had to be told a couple of times to not turn around and smile at me, and he too winked and blew me kisses. I couldn't help but smile and David reminded him again that he needed to face the front. The only thing I could have complained about was the way Khaalid sat in the chair with a slight air of contempt for the judge, but hey, his mum was on trial for neglecting and abandoning him, which he knew was a load of rubbish. He'd see the effects of what this system had done to me, had cost us, and he'd seen the police brutality in Egypt. This wasn't an ordinary 13 year-old boy sat in the courtroom. This was a very smart, very perceptive young man, who was head and shoulders above most adults when it came to understanding the political games we encountered in the world. Some of the comments he made during the elections, comments he made following the news coming on the radio or an article he had been asked to discuss in English at school; this boy had every right to have an air of contempt for the judge. The boys did themselves proud, not just me. They spoke clearly, articulately and anyone with any kind of awareness would see that these boys were well cared for and had never been neglected. But then again, if the character references had been read and acknowledged none of us would be here now. Instead, there was a lot of, 'If this had happened…', 'If only they had…', 'If only I had…'. There was no point going there. We were where we were and it was about making the most of it all.

As the boys left the courtroom, they looked at me again, smiled, blew me kisses and waved. I knew in that moment that ramO would do as he had done last time and take them home before I had a chance to hug them and tell them how proud I was of them. Even now, writing this, tears are welling up because walking out of the courtroom, verdict known and not being able to hold my boys, still brings tears to my eyes.

I was next up in the stand, and even though David did a good job, the prosecutor was a really smarmy, slimy character. His arrogance towards me was vile; his whole demeanour, one of a very nasty individual, made me want to scrub myself clean. He had already decided I was guilty, even though I am supposed to be innocent until proven guilty. I was guilty and he was going to prove it. His line of questioning was obviously built upon the fabricated timeline that the police had given him, and I just wish that my legal defence had paid more attention to the distorted timelines that had been given throughout because it would have been easier to prove the fabrication of the so-called facts the police and prosecutor were working on; something I later said to David. I was hardly given space to explain what had happened; the judge looked at me with utter contempt, as did the prosecutor throughout the whole time I was on the stand. I spoke clearly, stuck to the facts and answered the questions as they were put to me. Some of the prosecutor's questions I had to ask him to rephrase because I didn't understand his question, or more importantly, his angle, and even David had to call out objection quite a few times. But the seeds of doubt that the prosecutor wanted in the judge's mind was already sown. I could feel it. I wasn't given the benefit of the doubt, nor was I able to represent myself properly. I knew as soon as I stepped into the courtroom all those months before that I wouldn't be given a fair trial; and with the way I was treated during the questioning here in the courtroom, my faith in Scottish Justice and Policing had just been wiped out. I had hoped, maybe foolishly, maybe naively, that the trial would prove me wrong in so many ways about the men that ran this courtroom, and this side of Scotland, but I was wrong. Everything I thought would happen happened; and I felt broken.

Waiting to hear the verdict felt like forever; and as the judge weighted up the 'evidence' he had heard, he looked up at me. I felt like I as the worst kind of person he had ever come across. The look on his face still haunts me. His scowl, the frown, the look of absolute disgust, I had never before had anyone look at me in this way. Ever; and nor do I want someone to look at me like it again.

The feeling I got was one of dread, of having let down absolutely everyone I knew, especially my mum and dad, and the boys. He was going to find me guilty. I knew it. As he read out the charges, the first being the charge of Breach of the Peace, they found me not guilty, of course – how could they. I breathed a sigh of relief.

On the charges 2 and 3, the ones of Wilful Neglect and Abandonment of Khaalid and Naasir, where David submitted a plea of no case to answer, the judge came back and cleared me of the charge against Khaalid, but convicted me on the charge against Naasir, stating I had left him alone. How could he say that when the whole time throughout this case it was obvious I had left Naasir with Khaalid, and for no more than the 15-20 minutes I said I would be gone? I hadn't broken any laws. I could actually have left the boys alone for longer as Khaalid was 12 years old, paying him to 'babysit' his younger brother. There was no legal age limit at which children could be left alone and I had asked David to stress this, but he didn't. I was not happy. Although the judge found me guilty of Wilful Neglect and Abandonment of Naasir, he admonished and dismissed the charge against me. What did that mean? I know we were not in England, but some English please? I broke down in tears and in one of the most patronising voices I have ever heard in my life the judge told me, "You've brought it all upon yourself, young lady. Take proper care of your children in future; and let this be a lesson to you." I was apparently free to go.

I spoke with David after the trial and asked him to explain everything to me. He told me that I would now have the conviction on my record for 11 years, but wouldn't be fined, or have to do any jail time, community service or anything like that. It was just the conviction for 11 years on my record.

JUST the conviction? 11 YEARS? But I hadn't broken any law! How could I be given a criminal record for 11 years when I hadn't done what these people said I had done? How was it right? So using the logic of this case, it was okay for me to get a group of people I knew to say that someone had done something, when they hadn't, and then get them arrested, with no physical evidence, just by getting a group of people together to say something had happened. That's how the law worked these days is it? Great. What a fair, just and honest society we live in! David told me he was very disappointed with the outcome and didn't like to lose. He told me we could appeal against the decision but he would advise against it. I told him, "But I'm innocent David, why would I not appeal against it? I am not going to accept a criminal record on my file for all to see, when I didn't do something, especially something as terrible as Wilful Neglect and Abandonment. Do you really truly fully understand what that means to a mother? A mother who loves and cares as deeply for her children as much as I do?"

He couldn't say anything other than, "I'm sorry Dawn, I truly am."

I was devastated.

A dedicated mother pigeon holed into a world of parents that didn't care about their children. A world of parents that thought of other worldly, sinful gain rather that the beauty of being blessed as a parent. A world I did not belong to. I loved my children. Had done everything I could to enable them as adults, and here I was with a label, a conviction that told the world I didn't value our greatest teachers.

I was determined to fight this. It had never mattered to me before what others had thought of me; but to have people think I was a bad mother.... never. Not ever. Forget that. It was now time to clear my name properly. It was time to appeal this and appeal this with everything I had in my arsenal. Except I was the one who blocked it, and it would be something that I would not realise for months to come.

Back at home, I sat and cried. I felt I had let everyone down. I felt like a failure as a mother. I felt like I had let myself, my parents, my children, my friends and my community down. I was not the person I thought I was. I was a convicted criminal. What a low place to be. What a shameful place to be. I had never felt so invaluable. I had never felt so worthless in all my life. I had never felt such shame in all my life. I was now a criminal; and what on earth did that mean? What had I made it mean? Did I look so poorly upon criminals? Did I think it would not happen to me? How arrogant and disillusioned had I become? Becoming a criminal, as I was finding out, could happen to any of us at any time... even with the best of intentions... even with the purest of backgrounds. If the law wanted to make an 'example' of you, or wanted to 'get you' then they would. No questions asked. They were in control, and you were merely a pawn in their own little chess game. I had come to question how anyone could work in this environment, in this dark energy and with so much corruption; because whichever way you wanted to look at it, there was corruption within the system. There was no hard evidence to prove what had happened, no police investigation, no challenging the lack of procedures followed... all to hide something bigger; I just didn't know what it was. The timings given by the police and their witnesses were all wrong. Were they covering up a lock in at the local hotel, protecting the license agreement? They were definitely covering up the racism exhibited by the male arresting officer, and the lack of leadership shown by the female arresting officer who had not followed the Code of Ethics; they were also covering up the various changes in their story, all designed to make something fit, just to get a conviction, just to hit certain targets... at the expense of my life, and the life of my boys.

My gut instinct also told me that there was something else at play.

I just couldn't figure out what it was.

I just knew I was being set up.

But why?

Would I ever find out?

Leaving Scotland and heading back to my mums with John, I allowed myself to breathe, knowing I could take a breath. The fight was not over, but round one was. Now I had to focus on round two; clearing my name of this awful conviction.

I was quiet on the way home, going over in my head what it meant to me to have criminal conviction. What did it say about me and my view of criminals? I kept having this though, and I knew I would never ever believe the details I would hear on the news again about someone who had been convicted of a crime. I was doubtful of what I heard anyway, having made a documentary with Channel Four some ten years earlier, but now with this insight, I knew my belief in the police and judiciary system was gone; and it would take a lot to restore it – if it could ever be restored again.

John held my hand and asked me if I was okay, and told me to put it out of my mind. Easier said than done John! Having John there to hold my hand, to rest my head upon his shoulder was so comforting; he made me feel safe, but also scared all at the same time. Why was I not able to feel safe by myself? Why did I feel I needed someone else to make me feel safe? I always told my boys to stay together, that there is safety in numbers; was that why I felt safe? Or was it the old fashioned view I had of being in a partnership, that a man was there to protect his woman. I wanted a man to protect me, but I knew I also had to protect myself. I drifted off for a moment. I was exhausted. It was time for a coffee. I needed to stay awake, and then I could rest when I got to my mum's. Sleep had been broken now for six months. Being tortured by the Chinese involved a sleep deprivation technique, how was this any different to that? It was a bit like when the boys were babies, not that they kept me up at night as they were great sleepers. I let out an ironic little chuckle. This court case had caused me a greater lack of sleep than either of my two boys had when they were newborns. No wonder I looked tired, exhausted as some had told me.

This court case had delayed my business, caused delays in writing my books; it had consumed me and caused me so much upset. I was going to appeal. No question about it. I just needed to sleep, recharge and now learn about the appeal process, but first I needed sleep; and sleep at my mum's I did.

---

[8] Report by Council of Europe on the European Judicial Diversity & Efficiency 2014

SEVENTEEN
APPEALING MORE THAN JUST THE VERDICT

By the time I arrived back in Sheffield, David had written to me to confirm my conviction and that we would be discussing the appeal process. There was also an invoice for £7,849.76 for the professional fees in connection with the case… with £217.40 for expenses which ramO had requested. I couldn't believe it. With everything else that was going on, he had submitted a request for his expenses to be paid. Talk about a blow to the stomach and the heart! I get that he had supported me by taking the boys up to Scotland, paid for the fuel and the hotel, but for him to issue a request for expenses, I just couldn't get my head around why, when he knew I would have huge legal fees, and had been paying my own travel and hotel accommodation, he would stick the knife in like this.

"Really, ramO?" was all that I could say whilst tears rolled down my face. I was beginning to realise he was so hungry for money, and I felt sorry for him. His humanity, his respect for me as the mother of his children was non-existent and came second to his love of money; he was just like his mother in this respect and I was disappointed in him. I never thought, even with everything he had done, that he would stoop this low. But he had. And the invoice was sat there in front of me to prove it. I had hoped we were building bridges between us, but with this, he had set fire to the whole timber yard, not just the bridge. It would take a lot for him to earn my respect or trust again and just as we were starting to communicate again. Why, ramO? Why?

I set about setting targets and working on my business again. I needed a distraction, and I threw myself into my work. But I was scared. What would happen if people found out about what had happened? I just wanted to hide, but I knew I couldn't. I got back into my study with The Coaching Academy and worked on the values and beliefs module; I needed to go deep into myself and coach myself on this self-doubt. I need to clear my blockages, and I also wanted to work on my beliefs around what it meant to be a criminal. Journaling also helped. It was confronting, but it helped. It shifted a lot, and shifting these doubts was also freeing. I was beginning to feel brighter. John was staying with me, and whilst I was working, he would make me cups of tea, lunch and remind me to take a break. He would also ask me about my business, offer feedback, make suggestions and share interesting websites that may help me. He was amazing, and so supportive. It was great to have him there working on my business with me. It cemented the feelings that I was in a real partnership, 100% from each of us. It was balanced. Supporting each other and building each other up, as it should be.

I loved the fact that he would pick up on my mood and tell me to stop working and get a packed lunch together so we could go hiking, just the two of us, without Kelt. It was Dawn and John time, and I loved it. It was so nice to be taken care of, to have him tap into my energy and know I needed to re-energise, in nature.

On the 4th February I opened the mail and what I read made me fall to the floor. There was a letter from Disclosure Scotland, the Protecting Vulnerable Groups Scheme. Due to my conviction 'of a relevant offence (which) requires that under section 11(2) of The Protection of Vulnerable Groups (Scotland) Act 2007' I was being automatically considered for listing in the children's list; and that the decision was made on the 21st January. For a period of six months, if I applied to work with children in schools, as was my intention as a career coach, Disclosure Scotland would inform anyone doing checks against me that I was under consideration for inclusion on this list. The letter also stated that the period of six months may take longer, depending on a judge aka a sheriff on the application of Scottish Ministers.

I was told I was not being barred from doing regulated work with children during the period whilst Scottish Ministers were considering whether to list me or not. I felt sick. The room started spinning and I cried from a place within me I never knew existed. I made my way to the bathroom and threw up. How could I be even considered for this list: a list that includes child rapists, abusers and murderers? How is this even possible? All I did was leave my children alone for a short period of time. I got up from the bathroom floor and went back into the lounge to find my phone. David needed to know what I had just received. When I told him about the letter, he said I should not have been sent this as the charge against me was admonished; and he told me this is one of the reasons he disagreed with admonishment of convictions. He told me to forward him a copy of the letter, so I took a photo of it and sent it to him. I had to collect Khaalid from school so I made myself a cup of tea and washed my face; took deep breaths and headed out the door. Once in the car, I turned up the radio and sang my heart out. I needed to sing. I needed to release the negative energy; and Heart FM was just what I needed to listen to: cheeky banter and songs that I could sing along to.

I got a call from David the next day and he told me he was going to be writing to Disclosure Scotland and informing them that under no circumstances was I to be added to this list as I was not a threat to any child. Then it was playing the waiting game to hear what would happen.

Receiving this letter had knocked me for six. I just didn't want to get out of bed, talk to anyone or do anything. John talked me round and told me to rise above it. This is exactly what the system wanted, and I was not to let them get to me. I snapped at him, "It's alright for you to say that, you're not being considered for addition to a list of people who are the sickest people on the planet. I can't get added to this list John, I just can't. I'm not that person." And I broke down and cried again.

I had cried more since this whole ugly fiasco than I had done in my whole life. My steely resolve that I had built throughout my life, and deepened whilst in Egypt was gone. I was so broken. How did I get here? Why was this happening? What had I done to deserve any of this?

I went back to Nick Clegg's office and we had another meeting. He was shocked things had got to this, but again couldn't help because we were in the appeal process. I realised it was becoming pointless having a local MP, especially as there was nothing he could do for me. He was really lovely and told me if he could support me he would, but his hands were tied. I thanked him for his time and his support, and left his office feeling completely lost. Where did I go now? How did I clear my name? More research. It was back to researching the law; and more walks in nature. I needed to surround myself with trees and water. A holiday would be great, but how could I take a holiday with £8000 worth of legal fees to pay? A holiday was out of the question. I had to throw myself into my work and make the money. But with my head in the space it was, work was the last thing on my mind.

I kept pushing myself though and I made calls to potential clients for Vitality, promoted my business by making calls to existing contacts, cold calling from directories, magazines and the internet. I promoted my business on social media, doing what I am best at doing – putting on a brave face. I didn't want the wider community to know what was going on, so it was all smiles and business as usual. I was ashamed of what had happened. I was angry that the police, justice system had done what they had, and I was disgusted with the fact I was under consideration for this Disclosure Scotland list. How many parents, like me, had left their children alone for 15-20 minutes, would the justice system need to add, and how many had they added for similar convictions?

Throughout my research I found out that even joking around with your friends and dropping your trousers to show your backside, a moony as we called it at school, could result in you ending up on this, and other similar lists. How many school boys would they have to arrest? And would they extend this to those on the beach who wore thong bikinis? I mean, the same amount of flesh is on show, so logically speaking anyone who wears a thong bikini needs to be added. Logic is logic, right? So just how far were these organisations prepared to go?

A few days after speaking with David with regards to the Disclosure Scotland letter, I received another letter from him regarding the adjustments to the reported case for the Appeal, because the judge had stated that I had put the boys up to their statements simply because they were articulate and well spoken. Oh my apologies for raising smart, polite and articulate children who speak well! Having attended Birkdale, one of the top 15 private day schools for boys in the country, read books endlessly, had an English teacher and tutor for a mother and parents who travelled extensively; parents who understood that for our children to be understood better, speaking with a neutral accent when in different countries would help them to connect, and get further in life; something that irked us, but that was the reality of the world sadly. I know that when I neutralised my accent, I was able to win more contracts with clients overseas than when I spoke with my Fenland accent.

There were several errors in the Judge's report, such as:

-vehicle details

-the witness Lasek had gone looking for 'the young boy's brother' (when Khaalid was in the car), rather than me, his mother

-he had stated the incorrect times yet again

-he included statements that had been dismissed in court with regards to the breach of the peace charge, something that in my opinion should not have been included

-he had stated that Naasir was not crying, but was fairly docile – something that had not been mentioned, proving he was fabricating more stuff to prove his point to uphold the conviction

-he stated that there was a cushion or pillow up against the car window, which would not have been seen due to the blacked out windows, and something dismissed in court as irrelevant

-he stated that the arresting male officer had turned up in his police vehicle, when he hadn't; it was his own personal, unmarked car

-there were additions such as me shouting at the public, even though there had been no public about, and this was not even mentioned in the courtroom

-I was stated as being more intoxicated than John, but this had not been proved, and no evidence had been collected; and if I had been breathalysed, or had my blood taken, they would have realised that I was not even over the limit to drive, let alone be intoxicated.

I was hopeful that judge had mentioned the fact that the arresting officer was friends with one of the witnesses, something I found highly suspicious, and backed up my theory, in my mind that this was a setup, because surely the appeal judges would see this was unreliable evidence. I was also hopeful that the witness Beattie had mentioned Kelt had barked and acted as a deterrent to him opening the car door. I was also hopeful that the judges would question why the police had not woken up Khaalid to ask where I was, rather than just leaving him to sleep. With further inconsistencies of the timings, I was also hoping the appeal judges would see through all of this. There were so many additions such as PS Wilson, the arresting officer 'giving the young boy a choice to get out of the car'. How is this a choice for a child of eight-and-a-half? When a law-abiding adult is asked to get out of the car, they do it. Smarter adults would ask why, and probably still oblige. But a child of eight-and-a-half going up against a police officer, there is no choice there. He stated that PS Wilson, "Didn't know why the boy was apprehensive." If he had bothered to let me answer his questions on the evening, he would have learnt that we were all afraid of the police having lived out in Egypt. The police were the enemy in Egypt, and now they had become the enemy here in the UK.

Point 14 in the report was entirely fabricated and contradicted the above points of 10, 11 and 13. In point 16 of his report there was more lies concerning my location when the two female officers arrived at the scene, and further comments about gesticulation and talking with my hands being aggressive.

In point 17 of his report his says I was cautioned and charged at 6:20am with a contravention of Section 38 of the Criminal Justice and Licensing (Scotland) Act 2010 and further charges with the contravention of section 12 of the Children and Young Person (Scotland) Act 1937 which was a massive lie, and now I realised this was to cover up the fact that they had kept me in a police cell without charging me or telling me what I was being arrested for; giving them the 57.7 hours that I was locked up to fabricate this whole case, and avoid the breach of procedures of releasing me within 24 hours for a crime lesser than murder, and the 48 hours of being charged with murder or a similar charge, and longer than the 48 hours is restricted for those who are held under suspicion of terrorism. This was a massive set up and cover up; and I am angry with David at Beltrami for not pulling them up on it at the time. Who was the slimy, overweight guy from social services, the one with the dark energy? Why was I not given any paperwork as to who had looked after my children; or that they had taken my children from me? So many things just did not seem right to me.

Point 19 of the report went on to refer to how the witness Lasek had passed judgement on my behaviour even though she had no prior knowledge of me or my behaviour. Apparently I had the 'voice of someone who had consumed alcohol'. When this woman wasn't in a close enough proximity to me, and didn't know anything about me, how could she say this? And was my fear and frustration of the situation not something to be taken into consideration? She wasn't a behavioural expert or therapist either, so why was she being given the authority to comment on my behaviour?

In point 22 of his report he referred to the opinion of the Lord Justice General Hope in the case of H vs Lees; and D v Orr where it was stated, "A reasonable parent, in all the circumstances, would regard as necessary to provide proper care and attention to the child." Insinuating that I was not a reasonable parent and had not provided proper care and attention. He then went on to reiterate that Naasir had been left alone, when everyone involved in this case knew that Khaalid was with Naasir, so how could he be alone?

In point 24 he stated that I had been away from the car for at least 50 minutes, but again there is not physical hard evidence to prove this, and this was a physical impossibility, and had proper policing been done, they would have known this.

He also failed to mention that during the trial Naasir had admitted that I had told him where I was going, he just hadn't listened to me and chose to go against my instructions. He stated the local area was deserted, even though it was not a deserted area; and anyone who knows Inverarary would know this.

He stated he did not believe my evidence, even though the boys had both backed me up. In his notes, he mentioned in point 4 that he believed Khaalid to be lying when Khaalid had backed me up.

He further went on to state that there was no reason for me to have done what I had done, reiterated that I had gone off to consume alcohol, again something that could not be proven. He mentioned that there was no reason for me to leave a child alone in a car at night, to which I asked David, "So even if the toilets had been open and I had gone to the toilet, and this had happened, would that not be a reason?" David had no answer to this, and simply shrugged his shoulders.

He then went on to reiterate that my behaviour was that of an intoxicated person, even though this had been dismissed in the court. So why mention it? Just to colour the views of the judges on the appeal and to paint a black picture of me, as a bad mother. Reading his report, I knew I stood no chance of winning the appeal. I was angry. The judge had filed a false report and used elements of the charges dismissed and had covered up the mistakes of the police officers by lying in his report.

Needless to say the appeal was rejected. Not just the first time, but also the second time. My fate was sealed. I was a mother with a criminal conviction of Wilful Neglect and Abandonment. I was heartbroken, but not broken. I was determined this book was going to be written and I was going to expose them for what they had done. This was now much bigger than me and my case. This was corruption and it was having a really negative effect on my life, and no doubt the lives of so many others; and as someone who believes in human rights, I was not going to let that happen. I was going to have to figure out what my next move was, but I need to refocus, and regroup. I needed to take a break from all of this. I needed my mum. I needed a getaway… and John was about to deliver all over again.

EIGHTEEN

CONVICTION COSTS MORE THAN A RECORD

I threw myself back into my work because with all the trips back and forth to Scotland, and the court case having taken up so much of my emotional and mental energy, I was now broke AND BROKEN. Money was incredibly tight and I was constantly having to live on borrowed time when it came to paying my bills, something I was not used to. Other than having had a loan to buy a car some 20 years earlier, I had never had more than a £50 overdraft, and couldn't remember the last time I had used it. Since ramO had had his brain tumour and I had rebuilt the business back up, I had always had money in my account, I always knew there was more than enough for what the boys and I needed and wanted. I could shop for whatever I wanted, whenever I wanted, not that I wanted for much. I lived quite modestly, wasn't extravagant, but did enjoy travelling, eating out and being able to buy designer clothes and accessories for the boys and I. We had had a good life; and here I was broke.

I was struggling to buy food. I had been forced into a position where I would tell the boys I wasn't hungry, or had eaten lunch late so wasn't hungry at what would have been our family mealtimes. I often went through the day on just one meal of salad sticks and a pot of hummous; or a bowl of pasta in the evening with them. I spent days going over my finances and cutting cost where I could. There were the non-negotiables such as the life insurance, the gym and martial arts, luxuries for some, but not for me. If anything happened to me, I knew the boys would be taken care of financially with the life insurance, and the martial arts was not just for our fitness, but our social life and our chosen family to give support locally. It was positive male role models for my boys. It was my support mechanism, somewhere I could release the pain, the fear in a positive and constructive way. The gym was a place I could just swim, be by myself, lose myself in the water, it was me time. It was a place to work, to network, and to meet up with friends. Plus it was such a minimal cost, and the benefits we received far outweighed the costs involved.

I had a few bags of lentils in the cupboard, spices, rice and I could cheaply buy fruit and veg from the supermarket, and my mum gave me her Tesco Club card vouchers so I was able to get some food with those. Then there were the friends who actually saw through my smile and came over with bags of food, or took me shopping for food. Some gave me money to get some food, and I felt embarrassed and ashamed. I felt as though I was failing my boys. What kind of mother was I who couldn't bring in enough money to provide for herself and her boys? I struggled with the fact that I was choosing to remain at the gym and the dojo instead of using the money to pay for food, but I knew I just couldn't give them up. I just kept believing that everything was going to work out, and that we would be okay.

As John wasn't working, he wasn't able to contribute financially either; but what he lacked in finance, he made up for in supporting the boys and I emotionally. He took on the role of step-dad with such ease, and the boys really responded. He took the pressure off me, would teach the boys new skills, would sit and talk with the boys, play cards with them and helped them find activities to do locally that didn't cost anything. He took them to the local BMX track and spent time with Khaalid teaching him how to repair the garden gate. He encouraged us to get out of the house and we would go hiking for hours, teaching the boys about the local wildlife, how to make a great campfire, much better than the ones I had shown the boys! He used his own knowledge of cooking in restaurants and living on boats to show us how to make the food go further, spent hours teaching the boys how to manage time and plan how to cook meals. He would diffuse the bickering between the boys; He showed them how to respect me more and I would often sit there and tears would fall.

I had called in my soul mate, a man who got me, knew what I needed, and delivered time and time again, even though I was in the depths of the darkest days of my life, and here he was, standing beside me; loving me, even though I didn't feel as though I was worth loving sometimes. I felt like a complete failure. When he saw me in tears, he would wipe them away and tell me I was beautiful, tell me not to let them get to me; that we would get through this. He would remind me of who I was, of my strength and he would hold me so tight, I felt like I was being put back together again. He would share ideas with me for my business, send me links for different opportunities he came across, one of which was *The Excelsior*, a tall ship that would give me the opportunity of taking my coaching business out to sea, something I was longing to do.

I contacted Mary at *The Excelsior* and we had a very positive conversation, many in fact, and then she offered me a trip sailing over to Copenhagen with then crew, learning the ropes, quite literally, and seeing how I got on with the crew before we went ahead with the deal of me chartering the ship for my coaching clients. I was heading off to sea! I was about to sail on an authentic tall ship and fulfil a dream I'd had since I was a little girl, and John had been instrumental in that. He heard me. He saw me. I was falling harder and harder for this guy and I just knew that if he asked me to marry him, I wouldn't hesitate. We may not have been together for very long, but I had known him from afar for 20 years, had seen him grow, had watched his life at sea and longed for that life, and now we were building it together. I had to keep pinching myself. He would do whatever it took to make me smile and laugh, and I loved watching him with my boys and hearing them talk, giggle and play together. I loved watching him cook, watching him think, connect dots, be silly. We were coming up to the end of our first year together and I had never been happier, even in such darkness.

I remember sitting at my desk and cold calling, reconnecting with contacts, following up on leads and John came in with my lunch and told me to eat, put things away we were going for a walk. So we went to the Botanical Gardens, taking a bag of peanuts and some fat balls with us;

and this is where I fell even deeper for my squirrel whisperer. He placed a load of peanuts in his hand and crouched down, waiting patiently, whilst squirrel after squirrel came and ate out of his hand. He was mesmerising. I felt like I was in a dream. I thought back to my list of qualities I was looking for in a guy, and here was a guy who had not only ticked every single bloody box on it, but was writing his own boxes! He supported me in so many ways personally, made me feel like a woman, complimented me, set my soul on fire, and more! He supported my business, shared what I was doing, encouraging others to work with me, and passing ideas my way. He was the man I was looking for to help be there for my boys, as an additional father figure I was hoping for; and the future we spoke about together was so in alignment with each other, I just couldn't believe he was for real… but he was, and I felt like the luckiest woman alive.

As the financial problems continued I kept looking for solutions. There had to be another solution rather than just cutting costs and selling things off. But that's what I was doing. I sold furniture, toys the boys no longer played with, gave away clothing to the charity shops, freed up so much space in my home and allowed energy to flow better through the house. Plus the weather was looking up so I had most of the windows open allowing more fresh energy to flow throughout. With the sun shining and the birds singing, buds appearing on the trees, I started to connect deeper with nature and feel energised… and then I realised that I needed to take drastic action. I needed to focus on the business to bring in the money.

I spoke with ramO and asked him if he would be willing to take the boys for a month because I couldn't afford food for us all. I also needed to focus and work like a badass on bringing in the money. He was more than happy to take the boys for the month and a date was arranged for him to come and collect them. I was going to use this time wisely. I was going to use this time to work on building my strength, saving and making money.

The day came for the boys to go to ramO's and I started to realise what I was doing and the situation I was in. I couldn't afford to even keep my boys at home with me. My heart broke. My spirit plummeted and I felt awful. What had seemed like a good choice at the time, you know the boys being with their dad, spending quality time with him, giving me a break, time to build the business, the reality hit me. I was so broke because of all the travelling to Scotland, broken due to the emotional and mental trauma I had been through, the time taken away from my boys and my business, and ultimately myself, and here I was, sending the boys to their dad. I leant against the wall in the kitchen and cried. I cried my heart out, made noises that I didn't know were possible. I was shaking and almost hyperventilating. How had I got here? How could I be sending my boys away? What kind of mother was I? Were the courts right? Was I bad mother? Was I now abandoning them? So many thoughts flashed through my mind and feelings of regret enveloped me. I sat there and cried for over an hour and fell asleep due to the emotional outpouring.

It wasn't until Kelt started to tap me and lick my face that I realised I had fallen asleep. Lying there on the kitchen floor, I was a mess. I got up, washed my face and took Kelt for a walk. I needed the walk just as much as he did. Seeing him run around and play with the other dogs, feeling the spring air and sun on my face, I closed my eyes and turned my face up to the sky, soaking in the sun and the warmth. A couple of people asked me if I was okay as I had just stopped dead whilst I was walking. I smiled and said, "I will be, thank you." Kelt was still running around chasing dogs and then I bumped into my friend Jorja, who I had met nearly a year earlier when her dog Solo was just a puppy peaking his head out of her coat jacket. We had connected quickly and to see her today was just what I needed. Her smile made me smile back and we spent the next hour drinking coffee in the park, on her, and talking about where we were both at. She had just had to leave work due to ill health and was in the process of figuring out what to do next. Before we knew it, an hour had passed and it was time to say our goodbyes to get the boys from school. She gives some of the best hugs does Jorja, and she is a great listener. I felt truly blessed to have her friendship, I still do, because no matter how bad things get, we always find something to giggle about. Jorja, I love you darling.

Back home that night, I kept thinking about the car. It had given us so much joy, but now it was haunted with bad memories. I had loved that car once, but now, it was just a reminded of that night. I lay in bed with John the next morning and we were discussing our options. He was off to start work on a super yacht for a private family, having been given a contract a week earlier. He first had to go and attend a training course back up in Scotland, and I was so happy to see him excited about things again. He was going to be put through training courses to get him where he wanted to be and sail around the Scottish Islands and Highlands, something he had always wanted to do; but first he had to collect the boat from Greece and renovate it so it was fit for the new purpose of hosting Exclusive Whiskey Evenings and tours for high end clients on it. We celebrated that night with an egg, chips and beans dinner; a far cry from our first meal out together of a lobster and seafood salad at Eesk in Oban with some nice ice cold pinot grigio.

I told him the next day what I had been thinking about the car. I wanted to get rid of it. But I had had a new turbo and a new exhaust fitted. Then the gear box finally gave up the ghost. The guys at Mr Gearbox in Sheffield were life savers and helped me so much when it came to getting the car back on the road in the quickest most cost effective way possible. They were angels in the form of mechanics; but the car had got to a point where I had to get rid of it, not just because I was throwing good money after bad, but I just didn't want to be reminded of what I had happened every time I got in it. Plus I needed the money to pay my rent, and I realised that the monthly savings would be really beneficial to my monthly cash flow. I calculated how much all the new parts would be when sold for scrap or second hand parts, costed up the alloys, and then set a price that I was not willing to negotiate on. One or two garages offered me £50, as if I was numpty that had just fallen out of the sky. I had set the minimum price at £950, a very fair price on a 57 plate VW Sharan with blacked out windows and all the new parts on it.

I realised that garages were not the route I had to take and so started approaching some of my male friends who knew mechanics, including the guys at Mr Gearbox. They sent a few guys my way, but it was my friend Danny who recommended a guy who offered me £750 and I said no. He told me it was a good price and I told him, "I don't do good, I do great; and I've already costed up the parts, checked how much you could sell it for, either as a job lot or as scrap and I am not accepting less than £950."

He handed the cash over straightaway. No arguing, no more negotiating, and he did it with a smile. "You're a shrewd business woman!"

"I know!"

We both laughed. Having done the deal I felt a surge of the 'old Dawn coming back' and went straight into my office to get cracking on some work. I had to stay in flow. I had to use this motivation to propel me forward. I booked two more meetings for that week just from cold calling businesses in the local business directory. I then started looking at the plans on the large A1 sheets pinned to my office walls. Which ones had I achieved? Which ones did I still want to proceed with? And which ones was I in the process of? I had achieved a lot more than I thought I had, was well on my way to achieving more and there were a few that I just looked at and didn't feel inspired by. I stuck up some fresh pages and created more lists. It was game on time.

John left a couple of days later so it was just me and Kelt. The house felt empty without the boys and John, but it gave me the time to focus on what needed to be done. It gave me the space to just cry, to just dance around the house, to just be by myself with my thoughts and to do lists. I walked to martial arts and saw the boys every night. I couldn't wait to get there, and as I wasn't able to be with them at home, I would train for two to three hours each night, one session with Khaalid and a session with Nassir. My fitness went through the roof. Khaalid started to do bootcamp with me too, and it was great to see him growing in confidence and mixing with the adults in the adult classes. Sensei was a really positive influence still and during bootcamp, he and I would 'rave' to some of the old school tunes that came on during the mix.

We developed what I thought was a really deep friendship, and it was wonderful for me to see a man so in love with his wife. The more training I did, the more I wanted to enter a fighting competition. Sensei and I discussed it at large and it wasn't really the fight I wanted, I was fighting myself and I had to become at peace with myself before he would let me fight, and I totally respected him for that. Some of the guys in the dojo called me scrapper and I loved training with Ady and Bute... both old school ravers, so lots of banter. It was great to connect with people that got my vibe. Bootcamp night was my going out, my clubbing sessions, as well as my fitness time. I was the happiest I had been in a long time, especially since I had made good friends with Leanne and Phil, two fab ladies who the boys took a shine too as well. I was so glad I had not chosen to cancel the £50 per month fee to keep going. That £1.66 per day was a great investment. It pulled me out of what could have been an even deeper depression, and considering I didn't 'qualify' for help from the doctors, even though they could clearly see that I was struggling, this was cheaper than any therapy session, and a lot more positive in so many ways. I had always believed in positive action and looking forward, rather than having therapy or taking anti-depressants, but I had succumbed to both a couple of times; but not this time.

I was investing in coaching, whether it was of the fitness variety or the business and personal variety; and whilst the boys were away I started reading my leadership books, my personal development books. I started listening to Gary Vee, and started unfollowing people on Facebook that I termed as 'vague-bookers' and those who shared their dirty laundry in public. I didn't want negativity in my life any more. I just wanted to move on, and move up. I had had two weeks away from the boys at this point and John was in Greece. I was succeeding and had started to create some great results. I loved working and studying, it was part of my geeky nature, something I had learnt to embrace about myself rather than deny or hide away from. I didn't want to take 'a day off' because I loved what I was doing. I enjoyed learning. I enjoyed developing myself and stepping up.

I also started to realise a big change was happening to me. I couldn't quite tell what was happening, but I knew there was something stirring deep within me. I was tuning into myself again, and it felt great! I wanted to step away from the local business market because it was just too negative. I had been to so many events whilst the boys and John had been away and in each and every single one of them people were just not inspiring. They were either putting themselves down, or others, incredibly overweight and unhealthy – looking like a heart attack waiting to happen or stuck in the old boys network way of doing things. I knew this is not the world I wanted to do business in anyway. Those days were over for me.

But where would I be able to draw my clients in from? I started to

REALLY hear what Gary Vee was saying (thanks for the heads up on this one Ciaran!) and I realised that taking my coaching business online would be the way forward for me. So I started to play around with figures and I realised the earning potential and the amount of time it would free up for my boys, for me to get my books written and the amount of freedom I would have to do all the things in my life that I wanted to do.

I was starting to get excited and I remember telling my friend Jay, one night before we went out to TLI, the techno rave night he put on, that I was going to take my business online. I was making him a cup of tea whilst he did some last minute promos and tasks, and remember getting really excited about the income I could generate. I started to do a little jig in the kitchen because it wasn't just about the income I could generate; it was about the amount of people I could positively impact around the world. I had always had a global mindset, and always wanted to impact the world in a positive way, and now I had just discovered a way of doing it… I just didn't know how to pull it all together. I knew it was just a matter of time before I figured it out though, I just had to keep making my lists and getting the work done, working backwards as it were, because something would click, and everything would become clear. It always did, well in business anyway.

One of the things I got really present to though was just how much this court case had cost me. Not just in the cash spent, but also the amount of income lost. Looking at these figures, the fact that I had planned to have two books written by this point, and none of it had materialised. It had cost me time with my boys, my car, mine and the boys freedom, it had cost the boys time with me, it had cost us all happiness, it had stolen a year of our lives – lives which were happier than we had been for a long time, even with the divorce between ramO and I. The impact this last year had had on the boys was immense. They no longer trusted the police. Khaalid had lost his smile, had become really angry. There was a disconnect between the boys, and Naasir was more emotional than I'd ever seen him. It had cost me time with my boys, which is ironic in so many ways. The things they convicted me of had cost me more time away from my boys than anything else that had happened in our lives, including the 12 days I had spent in hospital when Naasir was born.

I wanted to sue the police, the justice system and the social services, so I started looking for law firms that would take the case on, on a no win-no fee basis. It was like looking for a needle in the haystack; but I was not going to give up. But first I knew I had to have my boys' home with me again. I spoke with ramO and told him I was ready for the boys to come home. I missed them too much. So the boys were going to be coming home in a week. That was my deadline to make more money. So I listed all the ways in which I could make money in the next week. All the things I needed help with and set to work. Again, I told myself nothing was going to stop me. This time, the power that came with that statement sent goosebumps all over my body. There was a power there that I had never felt before, and it excited me. A lot.

NINETEEN

THE EXCELSIOR TRIP

With conversations going back and forth between Mary at The Excelsior Trust, she introduced me to David one of the Trustees. He had been one of the Chief Executives at Bernard Matthews and we hit it off really well. We discussed plans for the different ways in which we could work together, and the similarities between us personally. Things were getting exciting, and it was agreed that I would join the crew in Lowestoft and sail over to Copenhagen, returning by plane once we arrived. All I had to do now was organise everything with the boys and Kelt. I had two weeks before we set sail, and ramO wasn't going to be around to take the boys and Kelt.

I spoke with my mum, my dear friends Laura and Debbie (if you've read my other books in this trilogy, you'll know all about Debbie and the deep love for her that I have). I also spoke with my friend Sophia and everything was organised. The boys were going to be having a big adventure between these four people! Khaalid would be staying at Laura's for a few days, Sophia would pick Naasir up to take him to school for an Outward Bound trip I had managed to gather enough money to pay for, before both were collected by Debbie to go home for a couple of days, before my mum took over for the remaining few days, bringing Kelt back with her after I had dropped him off there on my way to the marina where the ship was to leave from.

I had been doing quite a lot of research on *The Excelsior*, and she was a beautiful ship. She was quite small when it came to Tall Ships, but still very beautiful in a very authentic way. The fact that she was used as a fishing boat in her early days appealed to me, especially as it was sat on the beaches of Weybourne and Cromer, whilst my dad was fishing as a child, that my love of the sea, and my desire to be out at sea, had first presented itself to me. I was beyond excited and meeting Gavin the Skipper, or Captain as was his official title, was something I was looking forward to, especially as we had connected whilst on the phone.

A couple of days before I was due to set sail, I said goodbye to the boys and headed to mum and dad's on the train with Kelt. He too was going to be having a great little adventure, and would no doubt come home a few pounds heavier due to all the treats that my mum and dad would be spoiling him with. Kelt had begun to know that I was leaving him whenever we got on the train, and this time he stuck to me like glue. So many times, he would look up at me with his cute little face, and those beautiful dark eyes. Seriously if this dog was a man, he'd be the perfect partner! Seriously loyal and so loving. Dogs really are such beautiful souls.

Arriving at the marina, with my yellow fisherman wellies and cerise pink thermals packed in my rucksack, not forgetting my shorts and bikini – well, a girl has to make the most of every weather opportunity – I was feeling on top of the world. I felt as though I had really turned a corner and couldn't wait to set sail. As the rest of the crew turned up, and we got ready to set sail, I started to get an idea of where and how I could deliver my training on board. I was excited to learn about all the rigging, how to plot charts, read the weather – something I had never done because I was just someone who took the weather as it came. If I got caught out in the rain, just embrace it and enjoy the rain on my face. I was excited to learn about how to steer the ship, about the history, and to see how the group gelled on board. Living and working in such confined spaces, for days, weeks, months on end was something that intrigued me, and would make me realise either way, whether a life at sea was for me.

The crew was a great one, of all different ages, backgrounds, socio economic backgrounds and we all gelled, well nearly. There was one or two that just annoyed me due to their laziness and resistance to get stuck in and work together as a team, willing to allow the rest of us to do the work, whilst they hid downstairs in the galley. Cleaning was also something that they didn't want to do, but other than that, it was an amazing experience and I could see how perfect coaching at sea on a proper sailing boat would work for my business.

When I wasn't on watch, I would be either cooking, cleaning or writing out business ideas, and also stealing moments to sit and just look out across the ocean. I was on night watch with Gavin every night and it was such a beautiful experience; just being on deck at night, under the stars, navigating by the stars and learning about each other. We had so much in common and our favourite topic of conversation was food. We both LOVED food and the same foods no less! By the end of the week I had grown very fond of Gavin, and I was looking forward to developing a business relationship and friendship with him. He was a very funny guy and I nicknamed him 'kappa boy' a reference to a past shared interest that we had. When I called him this for the first time on our second night watch together he giggled his head off, and walked up to the bow of the ship, shaking his head as he went, whilst I stood at the helm giggling away to myself. After a while I realised that I was steering the ship. It took me a few moments to realise the magnitude of this. Yes Gavin was on deck. Yes he was an experienced seaman. Yes he was moments away should anything go wrong, but here I was steering a tall ship! I did a little dance in my yellow fisherman wellies and was giggling away to myself when I looked up and saw Skipper. He giggled at me again and asked me what I was giggling for and I replied, "I'm steering a ship Gavin! OMG! This is so AWESOME! Hahahaha!"

He told me to carry on and returned about 20 minutes later carrying a mug of coffee for us both and some nuts and biscuits. He apologised that there were no gluten free biscuits and offered me the nuts… at which point he laughed to himself and I asked him why he was laughing. He replied, "Just the right thing for you those nuts!" And he walked back up to the bow of the boat giggling to himself again. The smile on my face made my face ache after a while and I just couldn't get enough of the whole experience. Seeing nothing around me but ocean, lit up by the moon, staring at the sky, checking the compass, knowing that in a few hours I would be witnessing the sunrise, as Vinnie, the bosun came up on deck to relieve both Gavin and I. Vinnie was also a really lovely guy and I had a lot of time for him. A real sweetheart. I just knew I wanted to work with these guys in the future, and it couldn't come soon enough.

The next night I came up on deck and had quite a shock. Instead of being met by the darkness of the night, I was met with lights everywhere, like some kind of fairground out in the middle of the ocean. "What? Where are we? Why are there all these lights?"

Gavin laughed and told me, "Brace yourself Dawn, you're about to navigate us through the TSS."

"The what?" And then it dawned on me… A TSS was the equivalent of spaghetti junction in the middle of the ocean with ocean liners, tankers, small boats and any other vessel that happened to be navigating across the shipping channels. And Gavin wanted me to sail the ship through it. "You're having a laugh Baldrick! You seriously want me to do this?"

"Yep." Was his only response, other than giving me the co-ordinates.

I panicked a little. Could I do this? I was only three days in and here was Gavin aka Kappa Boy aka Skipper handing over the ship to me.

"Don't worry, you can do it, and I will be right here to help you." His belief in me was comforting, and I stepped up to the helm and took the tiller[9]. He could tell I was nervous and sent Vinnie down to make me some coffee. Then we all got a surprise. The back sail started flapping and all of a sudden one of the rings fell, just missing someone's head. Vinnie, Anton (another regular member of the crew who was volunteering) and Gavin all sprang into action to sort the sail out, and I moved out of the way, whilst still steering the ship. In my efforts to move out of the way, I let go of my grip on the tiller and we started to go of course, NOT what you need as you are navigating your way through a TSS. Gavin was annoyed by what had happened, swore at what had happened and got cross with me and it really shook me up. I knew the consequences of going off course. I knew he had trusted me to sail us through. Yes I had let go for a brief second, but the degrees off course, even by a couple could have disastrous implications. I felt I had let Gavin down, the crew down, and myself down. We managed to sort everything out but Gavin was not happy; and I felt it. We all did. I felt myself welling up. I could have just steered us into a liner, or a tanker, I could have just caused a massive accident at sea. Yes, I was a novice. Yes, I had moved out of the way to avoid getting hit by the sail, but I had taken my eye off the thing that mattered and that was the compass direction and my task. I was racked with guilt; not just for the rest of the watch, but all the next day as well.

I kept out of Gavin's way all the next day and spent time writing in my journal about how I felt and what I could learn from it. I spent a lot of time by myself that day, and avoided speaking with everyone. I did my jobs, but went deep inside myself. Vinnie and Anton came to speak to me and they both very kind and sweet. They reassured me that everyone makes mistakes, and my reaction to moving out of the way of the beam was understandable, especially given that there were four men dealing with the problems with the sail. They told me not to worry, but it had got me incredibly present to the dangers that can end lives. Don't get me wrong, I was aware of them before, but it is not until you are in the danger, that it actually takes on a whole new meaning, and depth.

I avoided Gavin for the rest of the day and was not looking forward to the night shift with him; so when I wasn't sleeping, journaling and reflecting in the folks haul, I was down in the galley cleaning and prepping for dinner. I needed my space; space to come out of this and deal with it by myself in my own way. By the time it came to night shift I was ready to stand at the helm and steer the ship. I could have shied away from it, refused to do it again, but like the old saying goes, 'You just have to get back up on the horse and ride it'. I was so focused; I was determined to not let it happen again.

I hardly spoke with Gavin that night, choosing to keep conversation to the job in hand. He felt the distance, and he apologised for swearing at me, and getting cross with me. He shared with me that over his career he had had many close shaves, and many experienced crew members he had had over the years had made similar mistakes. It also hadn't helped that what had happened had happened at the very beginning of the watch when I was thrown into the deep end of navigating through the TSS.

I accepted his apology, and I made mine, but I still kept my distance. He disappeared downstairs to check on the engine room and the control room, and came back with a coffee and some more nuts as a peace offering. I couldn't help but smile and my distance melted away instantly, especially with the look in his eyes, which I will admit were very beautiful eyes. He had a very kind soul, and my mind drifted ever so slightly back to John and his beautiful blue eyes. His gentleness, and how much I missed him. I had wanted to learn so much from him, but I was learning from Gavin; either way I was still learning and it would benefit my future at sea.

The rest of the night was beautiful, the sea was a little rougher than it had been the previous nights, and we even had a spot of rain, to which I turned my face up to the sky and allowed it to wash away and fears and doubts I had. I really wanted this life, I mean really wanted it. Sailing the oceans, both night and day; being exposed to the elements and able to witness the stars in their absolute, clearest beauty. With no light pollution, just the moon and the ocean, not even another boat that we could see, the sound of the ship breaking the water, the gentle rocking of the ship, this is where I wanted to be. Surrounded by the Universe in its most natural form, on a boat which was made of wood; the most authentic tall ship, with the most traditional methods of restoration available. This mermaid was home, albeit without a fish tail and bare breasts, swimming deeper than man could ever swim... this was the closest I was going to get for now... until I was in scuba gear and a bikini swimming deeper in the ocean than I have ever swam; then I would be home.

The next day we entered the Keel Canal through Germany, and the sun was shining hot. It was time for some bikini top and cotton shorts action, and boy did I get an amazing tan that day! Feeling the sun kissing my skin, with the cool breeze taking the edge off the heat, lots of relaxing, banter and laughter, this truly was a great day. Other crew members were busy working away and Gavin and I were at the helm again... talking about food, especially tiramisu... it was agreed that I would make one when we got a chance to get all the ingredients.

Serephina, one of the volunteers from the States, laughed with us, "Do you two only discuss food?"

To which we both laughed and said, "No! We discuss coffee, past lives and more food." For us both to come out with the same things, in the same order, made us look at each other and burst out laughing... or rather for Gavin to chuckle to himself, lower his head and shake his head. He was too cute when he giggled! He was such a sweetheart and I grew very fond of Gavin over the time we sailed to Copenhagen. I also admired him a lot for his seaman skills. His ability to navigate the ship through some of the tightest entrances to marinas, keep patient with some of those who were not pulling their weight in the team and the connection and communication he had with the second mate was incredible to watch. Really incredible. They both made a great team.

Throughout the seven days at sea I was put through my paces to learn as much as possible. I sailed 575 miles at sea and learnt enough to pass my competent crew, but sadly my certificates were never sent to me, so I have no way of proving my nautical miles and my competence. I did confuse Gavin with my knot tying though, because although they were correct, it took him a while to realise it because I had tied them 'backwards' or rather back to front. They were still valid knots where me being me, had tied them from a different perspective.

On the final night, having arrived in Copenhagen, we started drinking. Much of it went on through the night and continued until the next day. We were treated to a barbeque and continued drinking through until after I left to board the plane. I had never had a drinking session like it and to be as clear headed as I was, I am sure I drank myself sober... if that is even possible! It was a great night and day. The rum was great, the wine was fab and the atmosphere and connections made we celebrated in a beautiful way. I was going to miss Gavin a lot. We had learnt a lot about each other and yet, in the grand scheme of things there was still a huge amount to learn. I knew I would be back on board *The Excelsior*, I just didn't know when.

Saying goodbye to Gavin was harder than I thought it would be. I just didn't want to leave him or the boat. I knew I had a lot more to learn from him, and I felt that we had created a very strong connection, a friendship that I wanted to continue. When we said goodbye and hugged each other, we hugged again. We kissed each other on the cheek and said, "See you soon." I added, "kappa boy," to the end of my sentence, which left him giggling away and as I walked away I looked back, and saw him turning back too. He tipped his cap and I smiled, deeply, and blew him a kiss and carried on walking to the train station. It was time to go home.

On my way home, I started to journal about my future life at sea, about taking my business forward and how John and I, with our combined knowledge and skills sets could create an incredible lifestyle and business; which for me, were one of the same. There was no going to work, to escape home, and no going home to escape work. My work was, and is, an extension of me, and I loved myself. I didn't want to stop being me, it had taken me a long time to like myself, so why would I not just be me in all moments of time and get paid for doing what made me *me*?

I called John from the airport and he asked me how the trip went. I spent at least 20 minutes just gushing about the whole trip, and I could feel him smiling, heard him giggling and I could hear his relief that it had gone so well and I still wanted to live at sea. I told him I had been journaling about our future together at sea, and had loads of ideas I wanted to share with him about our business together – him doing what he loves and is great at, and me doing what I love and I'm great at. The figures stacked up and it was more than possible. All we had to do was find the right boat. My flight was then called and we said our goodbyes. I couldn't wait to Skype him when I got back home to Sheffield, to see his face, to look in his eyes and hear his voice. Man his voice... sent shivers through my body like a hot knife through butter, especially when he said things like "aye"... hmmm.

This trip had confirmed so many things for me, especially the fact that I wanted to spend the rest of my days sailing the world with John. Now all he had to do was ask me to marry him, because I had already been looking at wedding dresses on the internet, and chosen the style of dress I wanted. He made me giddy, he didn't just love me, he loved on me, and this is something that I had learnt from being married to ramO, you can love someone, but unless you love them in the way that they need loving, and ensure they feel your love, it will never work. To love someone is not to simply love them from afar, it is to make them feel loved by meeting all their needs, and understanding their love language, and acting upon it. Anything less than that just isn't going to work, and you might as well forget about it. John made me feel loved, he made me feel heard, we wanted the same things, and we were working towards a future together. I had never been happier. I honestly felt like I had found my soul mate.

---

[9] A tiller is the equivalent of a ships wheel but more like a long wooden arm that you use to steer the rudder.

TWENTY

CHILDHOOD CONTRADICTIONS

Having had time to rest and go into myself to heal after the final verdict, I started to look at each and every area of my life.

I started looking at my business and what was missing, what needed to happen and what I truly wanted. I realised that with this whole court case, my focus had changed. My energy had been drained and I had learned so much about police corruption that unless I shared this knowledge someone else was likely to go through it. So I went back to all the research I had discovered. I looked at all the information that I had previously not been aware of, AND I was one of those on the planet that was AWAKE! If I had not seen this information, then what chance did those who were asleep stand?

I knew I had to do something, and as this book had started out as a book about empowering single mums, how to create a life you love after divorce; and how to learn to love again, it had now taken on a life of its own! I mean come on seriously, you couldn't make this shit up if you had tried! Yes, I am an author, yes I am a dreamer, but the stuff I had gone through over the last couple of years since coming back from Egypt, man – just give me a break Universe! I need a break! Little did I know that a break was coming, in more than one way!

Going over the research I had done, and then considering what I was reading, I couldn't help thinking what a massive contradiction there was between those who governed us and those who encouraged us to raise empowered, responsible adults, and those who advised us on how to overcome mental health issues. You see as a 'Yes! Parent' I was someone who believes in giving our children challenges and exposing them to situations that enabled them to think about everything they have ever learnt, been taught and wanted to achieve, is a great thing. Steve Biddulph, Dr William Sears, Dr Tany Byron and countless other experts all espoused the same thing, especially for boys. Boys needed boundaries, but they also needed trust and situations that tested them; hence why many remote tribes and villages around the world, still have the tradition of sending their young boys off on 'initiations' – days out in the wilderness making their way back home; a little like Richard Branson's mum, who incidentally only left him alone for several hours to make his way only a few miles home at the age of four years old. This had enabled him to become resourceful, independent, street wise, and now look at him. Did I want to raise my boys to be like him, or David Cameron and the other cronies that sit in parliament? Hmm let me think about this… for all of half a second! I want my boys to be capable, innovative, strong of mind, body and soul. Bear Grylls wasn't wrapped up in cotton wool either; and look at how incredible his life has been! David Attenborough, another great explorer, and one of the greatest inspirations we have for understanding the natural world.

I was also convinced that enabling the boys to stand on their own two feet, to do all their own laundry, ironing and sewing was preparing them for a future of independent manhood. We cooked together, took it in turns to cook and watched MasterChef together. Their food was great when they took the time to think about it, but as typical young lads, sometimes thought just went out of the window and although the food was healthy, it wasn't always the best they could do… and trust me, my boys can cook when they put their minds to it! (They really are going to make great husbands one day!) One of the things that I was also adamant about was not being a maid, or pack horse for my boys, as I see so many mothers have become. Their stuff, their responsibility. They need to take something to school, or something needs carrying, then they need to remember it and carry it. It is the only way they will learn. I am their mother, I am not their maid, and neither am I their servant. The way I allow my boys to treat me, and the way I allow other men to treat me, will enable my boys to think they can treat women in similar ways, and I have to set a good example to them. I will not have them disrespect women, nor will I allow women to disrespect men in my company, or in front of my boys, as I want my boys to be respected by women. Boundaries are so important, and sadly very few people set them, or even know what their own boundaries are, and so allow people to walk all over them. Not on my watch boys! Not on my watch.

One day when I was going through all the research about extending boundaries and thinking about my work as a coach, expanding people's comfort zones, a comment that Khaalid had made came back to me, "Mummy, schools encourage us to read 'one of the best children's authors the world has ever known' and yet we are not allowed to do the things the Famous Five are allowed to do. Why get us to read Enid Blyton if not to inspire us to be more responsible and to be resilient?" The questions this boy asked! He blew my mind constantly. I just knew that Khaalid was a special soul, and would go on to achieve great things in this world, in the most humble of ways. Naasir on the other hand, although very much a special soul and who will also go on to achieve great things, would also charm his way through life in the cheekiest, funniest way possible, with a huge amount of intellect behind him. If there was one thing I was immensely proud of my boys for, it was for taking the coaching I gave them. Their paths in life, their intellect, their persona's, everything about them was simply down to the choices they made as individuals from the lessons, analogies and guidance I gave them; and of course their father and those who had stepped up for them. They either took the coaching or they didn't, I as their mother could only share my wisdom with them, and then leave it up to them to choose; as I had done whilst in Inverarary.

Rebuilding my life, and the life of the boys, was a struggle, I don't mind admitting it. Not being able to do things with the boys without checking the bank balance beforehand; not being able to just go out for dinner or buy what we wanted, when we wanted – it really got to me. Not being able to jump in the car and go off on an adventure got to me the most. I missed our weekend road trips. I missed the freedom that having money gave me. I missed the freedom of choice that money had given us. It wasn't the money I wanted, it was the freedom that money allowed and when I sat there journaling one day, creating business projections I got so totally excited about taking my business totally online. I could create a heck of a lot more income by myself with an online business than ramO and I had ever generated together, and the freedom that gave me and the boys, had me excited…. And I mean really excited me. I declared right there and then in that moment that I was going for it. Money was not the objective, it was the lifestyle I wanted…. And the learning I could give my boys along the way to positively impact the lives of millions, whilst also creating millions. The three of us were going to remain humble, whilst also generating more money than we had ever had before. It was time to tap into multiple income streams and go after my first million. I had less than 18 months. It was game on time. MASSIVELY!

Going back to the research, knowing that I was going to sue the police, I started to look at statistics. According to statistics (whether we like statistics or not) 10% of women are going to be criminals by the age of 53; and 25% of men are going to be criminals. Nice. Thank you. Thank you for having so much confidence in us as human beings, rather than human doings. The government and the police are not wanting to 'Protect and serve' they are wanting to achieve targets and get paid more in budgets from the powers that be. The system isn't for free thinkers, it was designed to create 'sheeple' – people who follow like sheep. These are the people who are happier to remain ignorant to all the information available to them – even though it is impacting their lives in negative ways, whether they realise it or not, now or in the future. People who are happier simply watching others live life, instead of living their own life. People who are happier to numb themselves with all the poisons in the processed foods they eat, sitting for hours in front of a TV screen, or scrolling through their social media platforms, not engaging with life, simply believing whatever is put in front of them rather than taking a moment to think about what all this information means to them, and their children. Why have so many people forgotten what life actually means?

I know everyone has a choice, and a right to live their lives in whichever way they choose, but with this freedom comes responsibility. We have to be responsible for our actions, and our lack of actions. By not being responsible, we become a dead weight in society. We see it with the NHS. People don't take care of their health, they don't exercise, or eat properly, and due to the bubble wrapping of ourselves and our children, our immune systems are getting weaker, so we become more and more ill, placing unnecessary burdens upon the NHS. We see people who are, and let's be honest here, so stupid and unwilling to think, unable to place all the jigsaw pieces together that people run to the hospital for a temperature, instead of drinking cold water, placing a cold compress on themselves or their child; or not taking care of the foods they eat, the amount of activity they do and so they get bigger and bigger, putting pressure on their joints, their organs and their mental and emotional well-being, and then wonder why they end up with illnesses such as Diabetes 2, expecting the NHS to fork out for treatment after treatment, and get their meds for free. I have several friends who work for the NHS, a couple who work in the A & E departments, and they are always in disbelief at what people will go to A & E for. Hardly ever do they have a REAL accident or emergency, and many things could be avoided if people just took better care of themselves and did the basics, such as the things I mentioned in with regards to the temperature. People have become so dependent on others, so paranoid about the plethora of 'consequences' of 'Dr Google' and self-diagnosis, but have little interest in using this very same platform to figure out ways to protect themselves from the illnesses and symptoms in the first place. The NHS provides such a valuable service, but like many things, people just abuse it. They take better care of their mobile phones, their laptops, looking good for everyone else, instead of taking care of their own well-being.

Having lost a huge amount of weight following the illness I suffered with Naasir during and after the pregnancy, and the lack of activity I could take part in whilst living in Egypt, not to mention being unhappy in my marriage, I know how difficult it can be to lose weight, but it all comes down to how much you love and value yourself. How much you respect your body, and ultimately it is a choice, a very easy choice. So many people will disagree, but it is the excuses, reasoning and the love of a victim story that keeps them stuck where they are. I was determined that although things were tough for me with this whole Scotland Saga, I was not going to become a victim, or wallow in self-pity. I was not going to allow what was happening to drown me, and stop me from achieving all the goals and dreams I had for me and the boys.

The boys were handling this whole situation with Scotland so well. I would often explain to them where I was at with the whole thing, where I was at with my business, because children see things so clearly. There are no complicated scenarios, just simplicity that things had got way out of hand and went against our freedom and human rights to choose how to raise our children in a way that enabled them to be happy, confident children – were also street smart, as well as socially and emotionally intelligent.

With some kind of normality returning to our life, not the normal of others, but our kind of normality, I told the boys I needed a holiday. I was adamant that I wanted to stick to our original plan of travelling around England and Wales in our first year back, Scotland in our second year and with Ireland being our road trip the third year back. However looking at costs of hiring a car that we would be allowed to take Kelt in, and all the logistics, not to mention costs, I was stuck on how we could make Ireland work. I spoke with John about his time off and what his plans were for the summer. I wanted to see him, even if it was for a few days during the holidays. It turned out he was due a week off work, so I spoke with the boys about whether they were happy for John to join us for about a week. They were more than happy for John to join us, and were excited about the activities we would do.

The figures just were not stacking up for Ireland and so we considered going back to Scotland again, but this time just heading straight over to the Isle of Tiree where John had his house. Doing this would mean he could sort out all the paperwork and give it the once over, as he hadn't been back in a year. I had a long conversation with the boys about going back to Scotland. It wasn't something any of us wanted, but as the court case had drained me financially, a holiday on Tiree and then some wild camping on the Isle of Bute seemed like a good idea. Khaalid joked that I shouldn't get arrested again, at which point we all laughed and realised that we had arrived in a good place. It was still raw, but being able to laugh at the situation and the absurdity of it all, felt good. Now all I had to do was shake off the fear of actually going to Scotland.

After deciding that we would go back up to Scotland, I started to figure out how I was going to deal with this appeal process, and how I could make people aware of what was going on – other than writing this book. I knew I needed to approach people who were in power. I had to contact strong independent women in Scotland, in the field of law and in the media. Nicola Sturgeon and Mhairi Black were both making headline news with the pro women policies, and the pension debate. I was also looking at Lorraine Kelly, nicknamed 'Oprah North' due to her daytime chat show on TV. I had also been searching for contact details for Baroness Helena Kennedy, TV and radio shows, as well as which female/parenting magazines I could contact with my story. I was on fire, the list was growing, now all I had to do was follow it all up; little did I know things were going to take another step back… and the break I wanted, wasn't just in the way of a holiday, but a break from the whole Scotland Saga all together.

TWENTY-ONE

FORGING AHEAD

Whilst all this Scotland Saga had been going on, I had noticed Khaalid's mood had been going down. He assured me that everything was okay, but both John and I knew it wasn't. I had asked Khaalid on many occasions about how things were with school, wanting to eliminate the different possibilities. ramO and I had been getting on better so I was wondering if it had anything to do with that, whilst reassuring him that although ramO and I were getting on better, it wasn't a sign of us getting back together.

I asked him if he was upset or concerned about anything regarding John and I, he said he was fine with it. He really liked John, and how he spent time talking with him about different aspects of life that had helped him grow into a strong-minded man. He said he also liked the way John made me laugh and did stuff around the house, made the effort to play games and take them to the BMX track. He enjoyed the hikes that we often took with the dogs and how John helped him understand timings better when cooking.

So if it wasn't Scotland, ramO being around more, or John, that left the school environment. I knew it wasn't the food he was eating, or an overdose of screen time, or lack of exercise, so that left martial arts at Pride and school. I spoke with him about Pride and he was happy there, and he was enjoying the extra bootcamps and adult sessions he was now attending. So that left us with school. I knew he had a good friend Mark, and one night Mark stopped over. I asked him how school was going for him. He told me it was okay, but then dropped a bombshell, "I don't know why you keep sending Khaalid back to school with everything that he is dealing with. I wouldn't want to go back." I asked him what he was referring to and he told me that Khaalid was being badly bullied, and had been beaten up and kicked to the ground many times. He told me that Khaalid was often referred to as a terrorist, a member of ISIS, and told that his tablet was a link to ISIS. I was devastated. Mark made me promise not to tell Khaalid he had told me, and said he was surprised Khaalid hadn't told me. He also told me he didn't know how Khaalid had put up with it for so long. When I asked how long it had been, he told me that it had been going on pretty much since the beginning of the school year. At that moment I was so incredibly proud of the strength and resilience Khaalid had shown, but also deeply saddened he hadn't said anything. I was also angry with Forge Valley School for not informing me of what had been happening.

I spoke with John that night about everything Mark had told me and told him I didn't know what to do. Khaalid had obviously not told me for a reason, and I didn't want to break Mark's trust, but my loyalty and motherly instinct was far stronger than anything else. On the Sunday evening, John and I sat down together and spoke with Khaalid about what Mark had told me, making sure that Mark was concerned he had broken Khaalid's trust, but reassuring Khaalid that Mark had shown himself to be a great friend and had only let it slip by accident. We spoke with Khaalid at length and asked him why he hadn't said anything. He told us that I had had enough to deal with and didn't want to bother me with anything else. He said he could handle it. When I asked him why he had allowed a group of boys, or rather thugs, to kick him to the ground and he had chosen to not doing anything, he told me, "Mummy, if I had fought back, I wouldn't be able to train in martial arts, then all the money you have worked hard for and invested has been wasted." I was yet again so incredibly proud of him for being so thoughtful, understanding the implications of fighting back, but really angry with the whole Scotland Saga for taking away my son's voice in a time of need. I called the school, demanded a meeting with the Head of Year, the Safeguarding officer and told them that regardless of whether I had a meeting or not, I would be at the school on Monday morning and would sit and wait until I was seen. A meeting for 10am was booked.

On the Monday John and I turned up at the school ready for the meeting. I explained what I had been told, omitting who had told me, and as soon as the safeguarding officer Rob Holladay and the Y9 Head of Year Natalie Coddington. Both were very dismissive of what had gone on and said that Khaalid was always seen smiling around school, and that there had been no serious incidences that needed to be reported home. When I asked about the beatings Khaalid had received, they went quiet. In that moment I knew they knew they should have mentioned these incidences to me but wanted to save themselves and the school's reputation. They then turned their attention to John and asked him who he was and what had any of this to do with him. He told them he was my partner and then he said something that took me back but made my heart flip… "and it's up to the boys if they want to call me dad or not."

He had made hints about us growing old together and restoring an old property, telling me he would do whatever I wanted him to, but this was a public declaration, to someone outside of the pair of us. I was taken off guard for a few moments and then regained my focus. Rob Holladay told us that there was nothing serious that we should be worried about and if there had of been, they the school would have told us. I asked them what their definition of 'serious' was? Khaalid had been beaten up four times, had been subjected to daily racism and Islamophobia, with the teachers in every class being aware of the situation to such an extent the perpetrators had all been given daily sanction warnings; and yet not one of the teachers or the head of year had put all the jigsaw pieces together and realised, or cared enough to do anything about it. Now I know the teachers are swamped with paperwork and targets, and there is bullying in every school, it's almost a rite of passage through your teenage years as you find your place in society, but for the length of time, the seriousness of the verbal, mental and emotional abuse, and the constant harassment in the classrooms, combined with the four beatings, enough was enough. The school had to do something about it, and I told them that if these children were to remain in the school without being reprimanded than I was taking Khaalid out of school.

Natalie Coddington warned me that if I took Khaalid out of school, they would mark it down as an unauthorised absence and I would be fined £60 per day, for each day that he was absent. I laughed. I was so in shock that she had the audacity to tell me that they would fine me for protecting my son. Was this woman for real? I told her that she had the choice to either deal with the racist ignorant thugs in the school, that were a cancer in society, or I would remove Khaalid with immediate effect. I gave her a week.

The week came and went and nothing had been done so I informed the school Khaalid would not be returning. That night Khaalid built a fire using his school uniform, and watched as it went up in flames. My love of fire and using it as a healing tool had been something Khaalid had witnessed time and time again, and he had now chosen to use fire in the same way. Sending negative energy, thoughts and emotions up in flames was a powerful release, and I was glad that Khaalid had chosen to use this as a method of healing.

Three days later I was called to a meeting at Forge Valley School to see the Welfare Officer and Rob Holladay as Khaalid's absence was 'a problem' and if I did not return him to school then matters would need to be taken further. So John and I returned to the school and had the meeting. John was amazing. The way he stepped up for Khaalid and I. I so wanted to kiss him! We both told the school there was no way Khaalid was returning to the school and I had already started homeschooling him. If they wanted to pursue the matter further then they could go ahead. I was not returning my child to a school where he was being bullied based on his father's religion and his ethnicity. I also went on to tell them I was not happy with the comment made by Natalie Coddington regards to Khaalid becoming 'more of a normal child, one that hangs out at Meadowhall and plays online with other kids his own age on his Xbox'. I wanted my child to be who HE wanted to be, not become a sheep and follow the mindless masses. How this woman got to be a Head of Year was beyond me. This kind of attitude is part of the problem with parents and teachers, and is resulting in a disillusioned, bored and lazy nation of young adults. Instead of telling Khaalid to conform to the masses that hang out at Meadowhall, why not celebrate the fact that he loves to read, enjoys archery, is a green belt in mixed martial arts? Show him for the leader he is, instead of trying to crush him into yet another stereotype of 'youths' and encourage him to 'hang out' online or in a shopping centre where groups of youths are always the first target for the authorities when it comes to any vandalism or thefts that occur. I knew the instant Khaalid told me what she had said, regardless of anything else going on in my life, I was not allowing Khaalid to return to Forge Valley.

As the meeting progressed it turned out the Welfare Officer wasn't a welfare officer at all, he was an attendance inspector. He had no concerns about the welfare of the child, no interest in why I was removing Khaalid; all he wanted to do was make sure Khaalid was in school to make sure the numbers looked good for the school. When I said this to him, he even confirmed that he wasn't there 'to do deal welfare as such' but did need to know if I intended to return Khaalid to school or not. When both John and I said no, unanimously and together, the meeting ended and they informed us they would be in touch. I told them I had nothing further to say to either of them and that whilst they allowed the bullies to remain in the school, they were condoning racial hatred and Islamophobia.

Back in the car, I just sat there. How on earth could they sit there as a safeguarding officer and a welfare officer and yet have no real interest in the actual welfare of the children in the school? How could they not actually remove these bullies from the school, and defend them by saying, "Everyone is entitled to an education." Yes, every child is entitled to an education, but allowing these bullies to continue with their schooling, whilst the victim of their onslaughts struggles to focus, becomes withdrawn and drops grades, is akin to supporting the theft of the victim's education. Thankfully, Khaalid is not a victim, he is a silent warrior and has developed a very thick skin, an astute mind and has an incredible soul.

When we returned home after the meeting, it was time for a cup of tea and a hug with John. Oh how I loved this man, his hugs, his presence, everything about him. A hug from this man was like an instant recharge. I had learnt how to recharge myself and nourish myself following the divorce from ramO, but John's hugs were on a different level. They were so powerful for me, like they penetrated right through to my soul. And those arms of his! They were so strong and the way he just wrapped them around me, I felt like I had a force field around me. I felt so safe in his arms, and then when he kissed me on the head during our hugs, I just melted. Even with him being away, only having a relationship via Skype or phone call, and our holiday in Spain, we were strong. I couldn't wait for the day that he proposed, I knew I would accept in a heartbeat, I just had to be patient due to his crazy five year marker point. I didn't get it, because to me you either know or you don't. I knew, he had his reasons, and I just had to accept those.

Once the cups of tea were made, we spoke with Khaalid, who whilst we had been at the school for the meeting, had been at home doing some work that I had set him. Khaalid asked how it had gone and I told him that from now on, he would be homeschooled by me until we could get him into Tapton. He smiled and relaxed instantly, and said 'Okay, cool!'. He then showed me the work he had been doing, all of it correct and to a good standard. The three of us sat and discussed what we were going to do education wise, and I said I had already been looking at the learning objectives online for his year group, and the year above. I had already worked out a learning plan and said we would go over it the next morning with him. I just needed to have a lie down, gather my thoughts and process the fact that I was about to launch my business, John was about to go off on another boat and I was now embarking on the journey of homeschooling all over again. Lots to do, but I was looking forward to it. Seeing my boy learn again and grow in knowledge and confidence right there in front of my face. Yep, this was exactly what I needed, and with the plans I had developed in line with the learning objectives and my business plan, we were going to build a family business... Dawnee Stylee!

TWENTY-TWO

PREPARING TO LAUNCH

With John now off to Greece to bring back a super yacht, it was just me the boys and Kelt again... the travelling trio and one dog as we had become known as; a name Khaalid and Naasir had come up with on our first road trip, and I had started to use on across the social media platforms to connect with family and friends based across the world.

It was strange John not being around, as he had been so involved with the boys and the household. He'd taught the boys how to measure up and build the back gate, taking them to B&Q to look at materials and go over with them the pros and cons of each material and method. He'd had my back when the boys had misbehaved, explaining to them calmly and respectfully why they should not be speaking with me in the way they had been or why the behaviour was not acceptable. He sourced activities for them to do locally such as going to the local BMX track. We'd spent meal times preparing dinner together, cooking and enjoying conversations around the table, and when the boys and I went training down the dojo, he would have dinner prepared for when we got back.

We would play cards, board games and watch movies together. Often I would have to pinch myself at having found a guy who was willing to step up and get involved with the family as much as he had. I loved the way he would spend hours with the boys talking, the playful banter, the wrestling and giving each other dead legs... proper boys stuff, toughing them both up for the school environment. I was incredibly happy. I had a man who not only made me laugh, had ticked off every single box on my list (and then added a load of his own!) he also supported my journey into discovering more about my place in the world on a global scale (whilst he wished to remain anonymous). Watching his eyes and seeing his mind tick over as he read news articles, especially the environmental ones; the smile that would break over his face, or the frown before he burst into a dialogue about where the idea/issue he had read about would end up. His love for the environment, especially the ocean was a massive attraction. His generous nature of giving to others, his deep voice and his strength on all levels just added even more to the appeal.

Our conversations were stimulating, and the more he shared his mind with me, the more I fell for him. His words of encouragement, ideas for my business, the way he asked questions about what I was doing, showing an interest in my mind, and the things I wanted to achieve. It was almost as if I was living in a dream. I loved the way he looked at me, encouraged me to be the best version of myself, encouraging me to go out with friends; and as I've said, when he wrapped his arms around me I felt like there was a force field around me, around us; something no one and nothing could penetrate. I felt like Batfink[10], with a shield of steel wrapped around me. He made me feel so safe, allowing me to be all of myself, a space to let my guard down and be vulnerable, a space where I could just be all of me; something I had not had before. I had always had my guard up, and that wasn't due to ramO, it was due to the fact that I hadn't believed in myself as much as I did now. I was still finding myself, learning how to let go of the values and beliefs I had grown up with, that had been compounded by the head space that I had ended up with, due to never really feeling like I belonged anywhere, even though intellectually I knew I belonged everywhere, on a soul level I always felt like I didn't belong. John and I were so connected, even when he was thousands of miles away at sea. It didn't matter about the physical distance between us, it was all the other connections between us that mattered, and of course the physical when he was home. I loved the thought that whenever I was by the sea, he was making his way home to me, to us; to our home.

As Khaalid and I worked our way through the learning objectives he needed to achieve, we were motoring on with the launch of my business. His IT objectives were met by producing the powerpoint presentation for my launch; he completed his excel and word document objectives by doing data entry of business cards and exporting them into an email marketing system. He worked through his English and PHSE objectives by reading Dale Carnegie's *How to Win Friends and Influence People*, Stephen Covey's *The 7 Habits of Highly Effective Teens*, whilst he read *Great Speeches that Transformed the World* for History, came out with, answered the phone for my business taking messages and sending emails on my behalf. Working with him, watching and listening to him liaise with all those connected with the launch of my business made my heart soar, and his confidence was building hour by hour. To tackle other objectives for school he would read books such as Predators, watch David Attenborough programmes and TEDx Talks on all things science. We managed to cover all the objectives in no time at all, going deeper each day in his understanding of what he was learning and how he could expand on it. We enjoyed walking Kelt together and choosing what we would be having for dinner that night. Sometimes he would walk to Birkdale Prep to get Naasir, chatting with Mr Leighton and Mr Oakey. With each passing week his confidence grew, and he smile got bigger, and his eyes started sparkling again.

Khaalid's progress, his ideas for my business presentations, his cheeky and deep nature made spending time with him so enjoyable. Seeing my boy grow into a young man, seeing him explore his own mind and deliver such great results was something magical, and I knew that the appeal process to get him into Tapton, just 15 minutes' walk away and with many families of a similar diverse background, outlook on life and success mindset was my most important mission at this moment in time, along with launching the business. Khaalid would have some amazing opportunities at Tapton in the way of sports, expeditions and friendship groups, so I needed to make sure that I bought in the money to pay for all his school trips, team strips, the Duke of Edinburgh's Award... and the collection of Adidas trainers for his ever growing feet! Not that I minded, it just meant that I got to share some of his trainers whilst he flew past size seven!

We both set to work on the appeal process, downloading documents from the internet, highlighting and legal tagging the relevant pages and paragraphs, putting our case together. We knew it was a done deal, there simply wasn't going to be anyone or anything going to stop us. We make a great team the two of us, and I loved working with him. He impressed me so much with the way he created things on a computer. Quick and creative thinking was something he excelled at, and the ideas he implemented and tried out before dismissing them or going with them impressed me no end. This really was a young man who knew his own mind.

Each and every time John called, which was daily and for at least half an hour, some days a couple of hours, he would ask how Khaalid was doing. He would ask how the launch was coming along and he was proud of how Khaalid was progressing and all that he was stepping up to be.

He would then tell us both how he was rebuilding the yacht, explaining stuff in different details to both of us. I was fascinated with everything he was telling me, the things I was learning from him about how to fix things, the wiring nightmare in the engine room and some of the mishaps that happened along the way. He would speak with Khaalid, encouraging him, guiding him. He'd chat with Naasir about school and tease him about girls; this made the boys felt included, which was so important to me. I didn't want to be in a relationship with someone who didn't connect with my boys or my parents. I wanted my family to be a family, a happy, connected and supportive family.

With my business presentation finished, the school appealed case ready it was now time to dive deeper into what results we wanted to create as a family. The summer holiday was the one we all wanted to get sorted out, but with finances at a minimum due to the court case expenses, I was struggling to fund the holiday we desired in Ireland. We wanted another road trip, but that would mean driving over and jumping on the ferry with all our camping equipment. The cost of the ferry wasn't too bad, but the cost of the insurance was just stupid – especially considering we would be driving on the same side of the road, with the signs in English! I could understand it if we were driving on the opposite side of the road with signs in say Italian, but the same driving conditions? Come on, really! Another stupid bit of legislation and corporate greed in action.

Khaalid and I looked at lots of different options whilst Naasir was at school, and when he got home we would go over the ideas together whilst we cooked dinner or ate at the table together. There was just no way I could make it work financially. I looked at taking another part-time job, booked more appointments for Vitality and put offers out for coaching, all before the launch, but nothing was delivering before we were due to leave. Speaking with John one night we discussed the idea of going to Scotland again. I still wasn't keen, nor were the boys, but we all agreed we'd had such a great time on Tiree that it was worth considering.

With the only way of dealing with the past years' experience being laughter, because I had done enough crying, the boys joked, "Let's go to Tiree again Mummy, just don't get arrested again!" I didn't know whether to laugh or cry with pride and joy. Here were my boys using humour to deal with a really painful situation and proving they had already moved on, proving to me that children are more resilient than we give them credit for. In fact, they are so much more resilient than us adults; less ego to deal with for a start.

So after several conversations with the boys, looking at the figures with Khaalid (fulfilling all his maths objectives), I spoke with John and it was agreed we'd pick him up in Greenock and then head to Tiree. It would be a great chance for us to relax, surf, cycle and spend time together as a family; and hopefully meet John's daughter, if she was up for it. We didn't push it on her, she had to make up her own mind, but I was looking forward to the day that I got to meet her. The way John spoke about her, the way he loved her; the photos I'd seen of her growing up and the adventures they had both had together, I was more than ready and willing to include her into our family life, so were the boys. I knew it had to be on her terms. The boys had met John as my friend, not as my partner so they had seen us both evolve into partners. With John's daughter it would be different. She would be meeting me as her dad's new partner. A delicate situation for some teenagers to handle; but John trusted her, and he trusted me. With my own parents having got divorced when I was younger, and being torn between two dads, or rather a father and a dad as I see it now, I was aware of hormonal teenage mood swings and identity. Couple that with the work I had done professionally, I knew John and I had to be sensitive to his daughter's feelings. He assured me that she was a smart girl, and that I had nothing to worry about. I trusted him, so we made plans for Tiree and with him having told her about me, it was agreed that I send her an email to say hi, asking her permission for us to meet one another. I never heard anything back, so took that as a no.

About a month after sending John's daughter an email she also communicated with him that she needed some space, and that she didn't want to see him when we came up to the Island. He was gutted by this, especially as he hadn't been able to see her since he had got the job on the *Bessie Ellen*. With only 12 hours to pack his stuff up and get to the boat, and her being off the island, he never got a chance to say goodbye to her; so to be told she didn't want to see him was a massive blow. I didn't know how to support him, but I knew he had his own way of dealing with stuff, so left him in his man cave to process his thoughts and emotions; being ready to support him where I could.

The day finally arrived for Khaalid's school appeal meeting, so I set him some work to do, and headed off into the city centre for the meeting. I hadn't been this nervous for a long time. I knew that it wasn't me that would be affected by this decision of the local authority; it would be Khaalid, and his happiness meant the world to me. I didn't want to see my son be refused from Tapton, for his own sense of well-being, social life and education. I knew I had what it took to teach him, but we both wanted for him to be in school. Sitting outside the appeals office in the City Hall, I waited, and waited and I waited. Oh how different it was going to a meeting with the local authorities! If I had kept a client waiting that long, I would have lost them, and quite rightly so; but as a parent wanting to get my child into the right school environment for them, I was understanding that the parents that were in there before me would be fighting their case, so sat there going over our case notes and our 'why'. I would walk out of that meeting victorious.

The meeting went really well, it was both reassuring and insightful. The appeal judges were the nicest people, and totally understood why I had to remove Khaalid from Forge Valley and why we both wanted him in Tapton. What was surprising though, was the way in which the school boards chose the schools. I was baffled as to why they chose to allocate Khaalid into Forge Valley in the first place. It just didn't make any sense at all. The criteria used showed no emotional or social intelligence at all! They had chosen the school based on the fact that the school was the closest as the crow flies. So regardless of whether there was a river, train tracks or mountain range I guess if we had one, that would be the school they placed the child. As the crow flies it would only take Khaalid 15 minutes to get to school, but using public transport it took him over an hour on public transport, using two buses and a tram, with a good walk. The great thing about it was he was growing in confidence using public and getting even more street wise; the only issues I had was the amount of time it took him, and the racist thugs on the bus that went to Forge Valley School. I also had the niggling worry that the conviction I had for Wilful Neglect and Abandonment would raise its ugly head again. I mean, if I couldn't leave him alone to check out the opening times and the cost of a family ticket to improve his knowledge on part of Scotland's history, then surely sending him to school on a bus every day for an hour each way was also Wilful Neglect and Abandonment? Just shows how stupid the police, Prosecutor Fiscal and Judge were in arresting me, and then going on to convict me! Hence why the system is messed up. It doesn't work because there is no alignment and communication, or understanding how the different parts of the governing bodies and organisations work… and as this school allocation process shows, no common sense what so ever.

I spent nearly an hour in the meeting with the team, and was told that I would get a letter within the next ten days to say whether Khaalid had his place or not. The meeting had gone so well, I knew he would be offered the place. Like I said it was a non-negotiable. He would be going to Tapton in September. I called Khaalid as soon as I got out of the meeting to tell him how well it had gone and why I was longer than expected. He told me he had started on more work and had taken a few more messages, and that he would have a cup of tea ready and waiting for me. Hearing this was music to my ears… a cup of tea was certainly needed! Before I had even got home, a 20 minutes bus ride, I had a phone call from the school allocation team and it was confirmed that

Khaalid was going to Tapton! RESULT! I was so overjoyed that happy tears pricked my eyes and then the kindness of the lady who told me was just so wonderful. She said she just couldn't leave me over the weekend or for the next ten days, she and the team felt I had to know straightaway. Less than 30 minutes after I had left the meeting, and as soon as I walked in, and started grinning, Khaalid knew. He gave me the biggest hug, and as I write this now, the emotions I felt that day are rising up again, the smile on my face and the tears pricking my eyes; because I know the really positive impact Tapton has had on my boy ever since. He had grown exponentially and had totally stepped up into an incredible young man. The theory of the school, home and pupil relationship working together to accelerate children, couldn't be more proven. Tapton is an incredible school and the leadership, administration and support teams are just simply wonderful!

And now Khaalid was in at Tapton, it was time to launch the business! And with only a week to go it was game on time... again!

My friend Kirsty and I had arranged to hit the cash and carry for the wine and lagers for my launch event at The Oakbrook Coffee House. Sam, the owner, was putting on some great gluten free food, but just didn't have an alcohol license. Kirsty arrived mid-morning and Khaalid chose to stay behind with Kelt so they could go for a long walk, with a note in his pocket as to why he was off school, should he get questioned by a truanting officer. Kirsty and I had met many years earlier when we were in ante-natal classes. He son was the same age as Khaalid and we had been friends ever since Khaalid was five months in the womb. The thing I loved about Kirsty is her larger than life personality, her drive and ambition, not just for her, but for everyone. She talks as much as me, if that is possible! And we both enjoy good wine. She is also an incredible friend, always there to kick your arse out of victimhood and make you see sense. Everyone needs a Kirsty in my opinion, and I feel so blessed to have her friendship. So thank you Kirsty. I know you are probably not expecting to read about yourself in my book, but to not mention you wouldn't be right. You have supported me so much over the last 15 years through various guises of our lives and I love you dearly!

Having purchased the drinks, alcoholic and non-alcoholic drinks, it was back home to do a radio interview about the launch and to send off the latest press release and email to all my contacts, putting out a last minute call to those on my database of contacts. When I got home, I was careful who I invited. I wanted to thank those who had been with me on the journey since I got back more than those who would be clients, or who could bring me clients. It was about surrounding myself with those who meant something to me. Sadly my parents and John couldn't be with me, but my boys were there, and boy did they shine their lights! Nassir dressed up in shirt, trousers, tie and dinner jacket and was my 'security' for the night, making sure those who were invited were the only ones allowed in, and then in charge of making sure everyone handed him a feedback form before they left. He was hilarious! And oh so cute! In many ways the star of the show! Khaalid was there to make sure all the music and presentation worked properly, as well as encouraging people to eat and drink. What was really impressive for me was the way in which he walked up to everyone he didn't know and shook their hands introducing himself, and how he just flowed around the room so naturally networking with the adults. Very proud Mummy moments from both my boys… so much for being a neglectful parent! But then if the police had bothered to do their job properly and read the twenty plus character references, and the impressive social services report that was completed, they wouldn't have convicted me, or even taken the case to court in the first place. We tell our children to do their homework, but the 'powers that be' often forget to do their own. Anyway, I digress.

The launch was, in my opinion, a great success. The people I wanted there were there; apart from John and my parents, and my friend Martin Manning; but all were unavoidable and understandable absences. I was happy, incredibly happy. DawnBates.com was now live! Website and launch complete it was now to get down to business; and start putting the whole Scotland Saga behind me. Now the boys and I could really rebuild and accelerate our lives; and to say we were excited is an understatement! We had been making a list of all the things my business would be able to provide for us, and the list of adventures was BIG! My boys had so many adventures planned for us, even I was excited! I loved their ideas, because they were BIG. They were unlimited; and they were experiences not things. What more could a parent want? I fell asleep that night with a massive smile on my face; having kissed my boys goodnight as they slept and with Kelt lying at the foot of my bed; the only thing missing was cuddles with John; and low and behold he phoned to find out how the night had gone. Of course he did. Why would I ever doubt that?

---

[10] Batfink was a cartoon character in the 1980s who was a bat who had 'wings like a shield of steel'.

TWENTY-THREE

TIREE BOUND!

With Naasir about to finish the end of term, I realised I hadn't told my mum we were heading backing up to Scotland. It wasn't something I had wanted to tell her. I knew she would be worried. I had already told Tina and she had already told me to "be bloody careful!" The only thing I had to do was tell my mum. I was a little nervous but it had to be done.

Once the deed was done, Mum wasn't too happy. The look of concern was written all over her face, "I can't believe you are going back there. After everything? Just be bloody careful!"

The more people who found out I was going back to Scotland, the more people responded the same. "I can't believe you are going back!" "I wouldn't go back" "There's no way I will be going to Scotland, and you are going back?" The disbelief friends and family, as well as colleagues had, was overwhelming. Was it really a good idea to go back there?

I had my doubts, but chose to believe that the racist, ignorant mindset I had experienced the first time wouldn't happen again. "Don't put the negativity out there. Everything will be fine." I had promised them both the boys and I would be fine. Nothing bad would happen. We were going back to stay at John's house and we had enjoyed so many happy memories there the first time. What could go wrong?

Naasir ran out of school on the final day and with the car already packed, he jumped into the back of the car and off we went to Greenock to collect John. We arrived at the super yacht he had been working on and he showed us around the yacht, with the permission of the owner's son. He showed me all the work he had been doing, and I was impressed with all he had achieved. He, and the team he had been working with, and directing, had done a great job. I was so proud of him. We enjoyed time up in the saloon with the owner's son, and getting to know another member of the crew, and then it was time to head off again.

When we arrived at the ferry terminal the next day, we were all looking forward to having some relaxing family time. Surfing was most definitely on the agenda and so were a few barbeques on the beach. We arrived on the island about midday and headed straight to John's house. Kelt needed to run so we let him off the lead and as he headed straight to John's house, my heart soared. Even Kelt knew he was heading to our second home. It was wonderful to be back on the island, and the first order of the day was to get some food in. So as John and I went through the cupboards to clear out all the dried food stuff he hadn't had time to deal with a year before, making a list of the things we would need, the boys got themselves unpacked and settled.

We all then walked to the shops, giving Kelt a good run, and run he did! He loved being free to run, and here on the island, he was as free as he wanted to be. We all were. Whilst in the shop, I noticed people looking at us. I didn't think anything of it; why would I? We were strangers to the island and even in small villages on the mainland of the UK, locals would look at new people on the island. But surely they must remember John? He hadn't changed that much. I put it to the back of my mind and we walked back home. It felt so easy to call what had been John's home 'home' because he made it feel that way. Wherever he was felt like home. He felt like home.

Cooking in the kitchen that night I noticed people walking passed the end of the garden and didn't think anything of it. There hadn't been anyone in John's home since he had left quickly to take the job on the Bessie Ellen a year before. Now there were lights on and people moving around in there. Of course the locals were going to be looking in. That's what local's on a remote island did. I'd grown up with it in Friday Bridge, a Cambridgeshire village, why would this be any different? Especially four hours off the main land on a remote island? The next day it was time for John to go through all the mail that had accumulated and I cleaned out the cupboards in the kitchen whilst the boys played a board game called Stratagem. John had taught them how to play it the year before and they had loved it! Then as the sun came out, the boys and I went out into the garden with Kelt. I lay there sunbathing and the boys were playing with Kelt, when several young children came by on their bikes staring at us and then bursting out laughing. Then several cars drive by, all of those in the car turning to stare at us all. It made me a little uncomfortable, but I told myself it was because the locals were not used to seeing a woman sunbathing and young lads playing in John's garden. But it kept happening, so much so I told the boys I was going inside. I was feeling a little insecure about sunbathing in John's garden so chose to go and put some shorts and a t-shirt on, hoping that would stop the staring. Then it became overcast anyway, and we all went in and I started reading and the boys started playing on John's Xbox. John was still going through all his mail, and I noticed he had a frown on his face. I offered to make tea and as I gave it to him, kissed him on the forehead and asked if he was okay. He mentioned that he felt like someone had been in his house, and said he would call his friend who had a key to his place to check out when he had last been there. What with the staring from the neighbours and this, I was starting to feel uneasy. I put it down to the previous years' experience and chose to do some mindset work. I felt as though I was being paranoid, but why would John feel like someone had been in his house?

Thinking back to John's daughter, I asked him if he was going to see her. He replied with, "She's asked me not to go and see her, so I'm respecting her wishes. She'll know by now that I am home, if she is here on the island, so if she wants to see me, she'll come over." I encouraged him to go over and told him she probably said it whilst she was hormonal, but he was adamant. He knew his daughter, I didn't. She also knew that he was respectful of other people's wishes, so would know if she had asked him to stay away, he would. I hoped she would stop by, because I really wanted to meet her. She was part of John, and looked so much like her uncle, John's oldest brother. I felt that it would be a good idea for us to meet, at least for a barbeque on the beach with Kelt and the boys, but I let the situation go. It wasn't my place to go over or invite her any more than I already had done. It was her choice – and, like John, I had to respect that.

The next day, we'd agreed to go for a walk and then have a barbeque on the beach. The boys were being a bit resistant and annoying each other, so we told them where the opening in the field was, and that we were going to start collecting the wood for the fire. Kelt came with us and was having a great time, especially when he started chasing the sheep… which wasn't a good idea. I tried calling him, but I had come to realise that when John was with me, it was John who became the pack leader in Kelt's eyes… little traitor! The boys soon joined us, after we had collected the firewood (typical hey!) and then we all started looking for the crabs and other rock pool animals. Khaalid and John started building the fire whilst Naasir and I continued to play and explore with Kelt. The sun was out; the water was warm-ish… as well as can be said for the seawater on the west coast of Scotland! I wanted to swim but it was too rocky, so I simply enjoyed playing and climbing over rocks. With the fire going, I poured John and I a glass of wine and the boys some juice, whilst Kelt was still having loads of fun sniffing around the rocks and being chased by the waves. I was so happy, we all were.

I wanted to take some photos, so Khaalid ran back to John's and collected my phone which was on charge. He was back within 15 minutes, just in time for the next round of drinks… and to put the minted lamb steaks, that I had promised him and Naasir, on the fire. Junk mail was a great fire starter if ever there was one.

After a few hours, as the tide was starting to come in, and the air was turning cool, we put the fire out and started to head for home. I reminded John that I wanted to see the seascape change, and that we needed a few more items from the shop. The boys didn't want to come and see the seascape change as it was "boring!" and they were wet from messing about the sea, so they turned into the cul-de-sac where the house was and John and I continued to the shop about five minutes away. As we walked back, we headed to the bench, just up from where the house was and sat down looking out to the distant islands, with John explaining which was which, and us spending some much needed alone time together. The tide came in really quickly, so we headed home knowing the boys would be just finishing off in the shower and would have the movie *In Pursuit of Happyness* ready, and hopefully a cup of tea.

That was when it happened. The 'Scotland Saga' was about to take on a whole new level of crazy. As if the four of us hadn't had enough to deal with.

TWENTY-FOUR

LIGHTNING STRIKES TWICE

Walking back home, a couple of bottles of wine in hand for that night and the next day, John and I were just enjoying a silly walk home, bumping into each other on purpose, kissing and tickling one another when we heard shouting coming from behind us. We looked at each other and I said, "'Cor blimey guvnor! Glad they are not shouting at us whoever they are!"

We continued to walk the rest of the way home, ready to enjoy a cup of tea before cracking open the wine and settling down as a family to watch the movie, when all of a sudden we heard, "What kind of father returns to the f***ing island and doesn't come to see his daughter?" At which point there was a guy right behind us, so we turned around to see who it was. Neither of us knew who he was, and tried to walk away, choosing to ignore him. But he was adamant we were going to hear what he had to say. "What kind of an f***ing a***hole are you? You're a f***ing waste of space!" All directed at John, before he turned to me and said, "And you! You dumb f***ing blonde have been brainwashed by this f***ing c**t!" Now not being dumb, or brainwashed, I would have normally laughed at his ignorance, but this guy was frightening me. So it was a case of trying to remain calm, and to get this guy to calm down and understand that the situation between John and his daughter had nothing to do with him, whoever he was. His whole attitude was one of someone wanting a fight, and the alcohol on his breath was enough to make me feel drunk just breathing it in, especially after the two glasses of wine I'd had over the last couple of hours on the beach watching the seascape change by the lighthouse.

When I asked him to not speak at us in that way, he had positioned himself only a couple of inches away from my face and was what we call in the UK 'squaring up to me'. I gently pushed him away to put more space between us, and he went to punch into the right of my face. At this point my MMA training kicked in, and the fears I had developed living in Egypt of the violence I'd seen in Cairo at the time of the Egyptian Uprising. I was shaking, but remembered Sensei's words in my head: *Keep calm, remember to keep your guard up and step back*. I brought my arms up to block the punch. I managed to block the punch, even though he'd thrown it with such force that it connected with my face (leaving me with a slight swelling and painful jaw movements for a couple of weeks, as well as swelling to my right wrist and pain for nearly five weeks). At this point, I slapped him and told him to go away and leave us alone. He continued to use the same vulgar language and then he started on my boys' ethnicity. I was so glad the boys had chosen to go home and shower, make the pot of tea and get the movie ready. He stood there in my face repeating over and over again, "And who the f*** do you think you are bring your Paki sons to this Island?" He spat in my face. My blood was boiling, and I really wanted to unleash all my MMA training on him, but knew I couldn't. I wouldn't be allowed to train again, and like they say about arguing: Never argue with an idiot, they'll beat you on experience. This guy was not worth me getting in trouble, or my energy. I knew from the training I had been given by Sensei I could have dropped him to the floor, but what would be the point? Especially after I had seen how corrupt and incompetent the police had been the year before. So many of these things were flashing through my mind, and all I wanted was for us to be back home with the boys and Kelt.

I was hoping they were not able to see what was happening from John's front window, because I really didn't want them to know about this incident which I was hoping would diffuse itself very quickly. I was wondering where John was and why he wasn't saying anything, or trying to protect me. Where was he? I didn't understand what the heck was going on, and I was doing my best to keep this guy in front of me from hurting me further. He then grabbed my right bicep, and I slapped him around the face, thinking it would help remove his grip due to the shock of being slapped. It didn't work, so I pulled my arm back as if I was going to punch him, and he still kept up with the aggressive verbal abuse.

At this point I saw John's daughter come running up to the scene screaming abuse at me, "You're not wanted here! Why don't you just f*** off! Leave us alone!" I couldn't believe it. Here was John's daughter behaving in a way that I knew would break his heart. He didn't even raise his voice in front of children, let alone swear in front of them. I put my arm out to stop her getting any closer to the situation as I did not wish for her to get hurt, nor did I wish for her to hear the way this man was speaking with me – even though her own language was also vulgar; but she came at me lashing out and kicked me several times in the legs. I told her to calm down and watch her language. I also reminded her that it was her that had asked her dad to give her some space to think about things and not to visit her, and that John was only respecting her wishes by staying away.

At this point I saw recollection in her face and she then continued to shout at me, "What the f*** do you know? Who the f*** do you think you are? You're not welcome here!"

The first man who had been verbally and physically abusive towards me had now turned his attention towards John, who I could now hear was asking this bully to stop verbally assaulting me. My first thought was to try and get home to the boys, but there was now a second man who I saw was kicking John to the ground and shouting at me, "You're a f***ing dumb bitch if you believe anything this t*** has to say to you! You've been brainwashed by this f***ing a***hole – he's a f***ing useless piece of s***! You and your Paki sons are not welcome here! Why don't you just f*** off?"

Where had all this come from? The previous year we had been on the island, we had not seen or spoken with anyone, other than Marty Larg down at his surf school Blackhouse Water Sports, and John's friend Sam; who to be honest, I didn't trust. There was just something about him that

I didn't like, and John knew I didn't trust him. I didn't know Sam, but I did know my own instincts, and I trusted them.

The two men who had been verbally abusive to me, were now focused fully on John when a much younger blonde haired guy came over to me blocking my path. I recognised him as one of the neighbours that had been walking around John's property laughing whilst looking in our direction the day before. He continued with the same racist comments towards my boys as the other two men, also adding that I was a 'Paki lover'. He started to strut around in front of me, and when I asked him to repeat what he had said and to ask him why he was being so vulgar and racist when he knew nothing about me, he fell over whilst laughing in my face. The first two men were kicking John about his body and to his head, with John trying to protect himself in the foetal position.

All I wanted was to get back home to John's so I walked over to him, and for some reason the three guys all of a sudden started walking away. John got up and started walking back to his and I remembered the wine, so did a quick glance around and couldn't see anything. John's daughter had also disappeared. I was in shock. What had just happened? I'd never been in a fight in my life except in the dojo; and why all the racism? John called out to me to come home, and I saw there was some blood on his face. I felt like I was in a daze. What the hell had just happened? It all felt so surreal. One minute we're on the beach with the boys and Kelt having a lovely family afternoon, and then we're having a nice romantic time together and then this! From out of nowhere! I remember walking back to John's thinking: *I really am beginning to hate Scotland!* And then I started crying.

At one point I was excited to learn more about Scotland, especially as my grandfather on my mum's side was Scottish, but now? Then the dream of John and I living on the west coast together went up in a puff of smoke. How could I live in Scotland by the sea now? Giving me the best of both worlds, living on the sea and by the sea? I couldn't. And why hadn't John jumped in to stand between that first guy and me? So much started unravelling in my head. Seeing John's daughter standing there watching how the two men had kicked her dad about the head and body, not once asking them to stop; what had this little girl been told about her dad? What had John not told me about himself? My head was spinning. I realised I was in shock, and I realised I was just standing there with tears running down my face. Then I snapped myself out of it as my boys faces flashed through my mind. I tried to compose myself as I didn't want them to see me in this state. I had about a minute before I walked through the door. As I walked through the back door, the boys were getting ready for bed. I looked to John, who had cleaned himself up, and he said, "I've told the boys we'll get an early night as we've got surfing tomorrow, and we'll watch the movie afterwards." I felt relieved. It gave me a few more moments to compose myself and say goodnight to the boys, who were excited about going surfing; as was I.

We had been home for just over an hour and I let Kelt out for his final walk of the night as he had returned back home with the boys. Kelt got out of the garden and I went to get him back, noticing there was a police vehicle outside of the property where John's daughter lived. I went to get Kelt, and as I did, another man, one of the neighbours, started shouting the same kind of racist abuse at me. I saw a female by the police car and she asked me what the matter was. Forgetting that this would probably be 'one of them', I tried my best to explain to her what had happened, whilst putting Kelt on the lead, when another neighbour also started shouting racist abuse at me, telling me, "F*** off with your Paki sons! We don't want you here!" I asked this man why he was being so rude and offensive. I started crying, not just because of the abuse, but because the pain that was shooting through my jaw when speaking.

I picked Kelt up, and went back to John's house. It was no longer a place that felt like home. I just wanted to get away as soon as I could, but didn't want the boys to know, so knew I had to put on a brave face for them in the morning. When I got back, making sure the boys were fast asleep instead of reading, John and I discussed what had happened and what was to be done about it. I told him I just wanted to forget about it. They had said their piece and done what they had done, and there was no way I was ever coming back to Scotland, so there was no point reporting it, plus I didn't want to have to deal with the police again and have all this turn into a trial having to spend more money and time that should be invested in moving forward with our lives. People like that love the glory and the drama, and I wasn't prepared to give it to them. At the back of my mind I was wondering why this had happened, what was the purpose of it all?

The following day it was raining, so we stayed in. I was still trying to make sense of what had happened. Why had they come and attacked us like that? I was still shaken up, so kept myself busy. I remembered the last time we had been there I had made some bread, or at least attempted to, so I thought I would amuse the boys by making some more. So I made some bread in the morning, and whilst cleaning away, I then went on to clean the kitchen, whilst John and the boys played Stratagem and cards. Realising I was hungry, I asked them all if they were also hungry, they all said yes, so I made lunch… and a victoria sponge cake, to enjoy whilst we all sat down to watch a movie together. Whilst I was making the bread, I saw the three men who had assaulted us and a woman with ginger hair walking around the edge of the garden. The man who assaulted me first took it upon himself to urinate into the garden, shouting abuse which I could not fully hear. Not only was I disgusted, but I was hoping John had the blinds closed. I stood in the kitchen wondering what the hell was wrong with these people. I mean who does that? It wasn't as though John lived in an area where you would expect to find that kind of behaviour, or at least it didn't look like it. Not having met any of the other neighbours, other than saying hello to the couple who had two black labradors at the end of the road whilst out walking Kelt, you would think it was a pleasant enough little community. Oh how wrong I was turning out to be.

After the movie, Kelt needed to go for a walk. I didn't want the boys to go, and I needed some fresh air, so I took him. I decided to walk toward the ferry terminal away from the houses on the left where the attack had happened the day before, thinking this would be a safer option, but alas, I was wrong again. On my way back to John's, the man who had abused me first approached me again swearing and repeating much of what he had said the night before, along with accusing me of stealing a phone, which he threatened if I did not return to him, he "would f*** (me) over".

I told him "Just leave me alone. I don't know why you're all being so aggressive and nasty. Just leave us alone; and I don't know anything about your phone. Get yourself a life and stop trying to ruin other peoples."

To which he replied "F*** you, you blonde bitch!" When I got back to John's, I went straight into the kitchen and made a cup of tea and stayed in the kitchen to drink it, after having taken tea through to the boys and John. I was shaking and crying again, just wanting to leave the island and Scotland all together. John knew something was up and came through to the kitchen and just held me. He asked me what had happened and so I told him. I could feel his energy change. I had never seen John angry, but I felt it rise in him. He hugged me tighter. I felt safe, but now I had niggling doubts in my mind. Where had he been when the first guy had assaulted me? Why hadn't he stepped in? Did the other guy arrive on the scene earlier than I thought? I didn't remember seeing him arrive, he was just there. I shook the thought away as I stood there in John's arms, fear just falling away. I could tell from his embrace that he was feeling guilty about bringing us into this, and then I remembered John telling me the night before that this was not the first time his ex-partner, the mother of his daughter, had one of her previous ex-partner's set upon him in a similar manner. That time he had informed the policeman on the island, a PC Steph(en) Tanner, but nothing was done about it. No surprise there then.

Seeing how John's daughter had behaved, and the way I had seen the people behave around the garden over the last few days, I was becoming very aware of why John had felt the need to terminate the relationship he had previously had with his daughter's mother, and chose to keep himself to himself whilst he was on the island. These people were not coming across as the kind of people that John had in his life; but then again, how many people had I met in John's life? Not many. I knew some of them, as we had mutual friends, and none of them behaved in the way these people were behaving. Why was I having so many doubts? John immediately picked up on my thoughts and asked what was going on in my head, telling me not to put myself in a place I didn't need to be. We spoke at length whilst the boys played on the Xbox. He answered every question I had, and didn't get upset or offended by my questions.

Kissing me on the forehead, he told me to go wash my face, as he was going to go back and be with the boys, deal the cards for a game of Ace-Two-Ten aka 'Shithead' amongst the raving friends I had back in the day. The boys were getting really good at it, and we all loved playing cards together. We had a few games of that, a few games of Blackjack, Fish and

Rummy before choosing another film to watch. Then I made myself giggle thinking of Jack Sparrow saying, "Why is all the Rum gone?" thinking to myself, *Where is all the wine gone?*

Then I remembered seeing the second guy who verbally abused me, grab them off John and throw them away, only to hear them smash. *What a waste of good wine, he really is a moron.*

The next day was sunny and so John, the boys and I walked to Blackhouse Water Sports to spend some time on the beach and to do some surfing. There was no way I was going to allow the events of the previous days to ruin our holiday. We walked the two hours to the beach, going a different way to the way we had gone the previous year. John gave us more local knowledge and history, and Kelt trotted along beside us happy as Larry *(Who is Larry by the way? Does anyone know?)*. We laughed so much on that walk; it was hard to believe the events of the previous day had happened. This is one of the things I love about John, he is able to shift really quickly, he never holds onto anything. It happens, it's dealt with and it's gone; simple as that.

Whilst down at Blackhouse Water sports we caught up with Marty and I started chatting to a really nice lady from Europe who was working on empowering kids, and had worked on some really great initiatives. We swapped notes and then it was into the water. I found it really hard to get both my wet suit on, and to stand up on the board proved difficult because I couldn't put much pressure on my right wrist as I pushed myself to stand up. Bruises had also started to show up on my wrist, as well as my upper arm. My jaw was swollen, and thankfully the bruising just looked like the shadow from my hair and the light; so no explanations needed to anyone. There were also some people there whom we had met the previous year, with a cousin who was over from America. With Marty's boys now in the surfing championships, everyone was having a happy time catching up. After Khaalid's lesson, and Naasir, John and I body boarding and playing rather than surfing, it was time to head home. We said our goodbyes and started walking. We had been walking about 30 minutes when Nassir started asking John about the times he'd hitch hiked. Naasir asked if we could hitch hike and stuck his thumb out, for us to only be picked up by the guys we'd just left down the beach who had their cousin with them. They had one of those really cool motorhomes, and John and I were learning all about the holidays these boys had had in it, and then went on to ask the boys if they fancied a road trip around Canada one year with their cousins. Both were up for it and so we considered that as a good holiday in the years to come.

We asked to get dropped off at the shops, so we could get supplies for dinner, including some wine, and then arrived home just as the rain came down. Whilst the boys showered and got themselves into their pyjamas, John and I prepared dinner, stealing hugs and kisses as we went about it. It had been a great day. I then showered and John got the boys to get their bags ready to leave the next day, and then when he showered it was my time to pack. Tomorrow we would leave Tiree, the day after the boys and I would drop John off and leave Scotland for the last time, heading home to my mum and dad for a couple of weeks.

After we were all showered and packed, it was time for dinner and a movie, and wine; and although my wrist and jaw was still hurting, and the bruising was showing up more, John and I had put the whole ugly incident behind us. The boys didn't know a thing about what had happened, and that is exactly how I wanted it to stay. They didn't need to know. They'd had a great holiday, even if it had rained more this year than the last.

TWENTY-FIVE
ARE YOU DAWN? TAKE TWO

It was the 25th July that we headed to the ferry terminal on Tiree. John had to return to his job as Head Engineer on the super yacht, whilst the boys and I were going to continue with our road trip. We were going to go over to the Isle of Bute to do a spot of camping before returning to see my parents on the East coast of England, but I no longer wanted to do this and just wanted to get home to my parents in Norfolk; plus the thought of putting the tent up with my wrist the way it was, didn't seem all that appealing.

On the ferry ride home, John and I were discussing sleeping conditions because he knew the boys and I were not going to be allowed to stay on the yacht. He offered to put us up in a hotel as he didn't want me driving all night. I said it was fine, the boys and I would camp out in the car. He wasn't keen on that idea, as it was such a small car, unlike the VW Sharan we had had the first year. This led us onto discussing what car to get, our first purchase together. We both liked the Audi Q5 and Q7 ranges, and we discussed the figures and decided to lock in April the following year. The boys were obviously going for the bigger Q7, so it was a done deal. Everyone was happy, so it was time for some silly games and to critique the food on the TV show that had come on in the area we were sitting in. We were all in high spirits, but my wrist was still really hurting, especially when I was picking up the luggage. Khaalid had noticed a few times I was in pain and asked what I had done. I had simply told him that I had hurt it when John and I were at the bench watching the sea scape.

As we were walking off the ferry in Oban, I noticed two police officers. I didn't think anything of it. That was until they asked if I was Dawn Bates. My first response was "Yes. Why?" They told us not to worry we weren't in any trouble. My heart started racing. My mum and dad hadn't been very well, and so the next thing out of my mouth was "Is it my mum? Is it my dad? Are they okay?" They then said they couldn't tell us, but that there were two other police officers coming over to speak with us. I again asked them if it was my parents and if they were okay. They said in a really friendly toned that everything was fine, and the other officers would explain everything when they got there. I thought: *How could everything be fine? Here were two police officers, with another two on the way; that is not a 'fine' situation.*

The two male police officers then escorted to an office in the ferry terminal, offering to get us a drink of tea or water. At this point I could see the boys looking scared and confused. I told them "It's okay boys, they are saying not to worry. Everything is going to be fine." Khaalid looked at me in disbelief and with his left eyebrow up with the look of, *Really Mummy? You believe that after last year?* Naasir had pretty much the same look on his face too. Both of them had very little faith, trust in or respect for the police now. The police, lawyers and Judge had done a great job of destroying those the year before. I then looked at John, trying to read his face. There was something going on in his mind and I didn't quite like the look of it. I asked the two officers if it would be okay for the boys to taken into the kitchen as I didn't know what this was about and didn't want them to hear any bad news about my parents, before I could process it myself. I told the boys not to worry and again they look at me with doubt. I hated it. After all we had witnessed in Egypt, and then all we had been through the previous year, it was no wonder really.

When the two officers arrived, one female and one male, John and I were told, "We are just here to confirm your identification and nothing more."

I asked, "What's this about? Is it about my parents?"

John then asked, "Why do you need to confirm our details?"

The female officer then informed us, "Due to an incident which happened on Tiree, there was a public disturbance and we just need to confirm your details. You are not in any trouble. Please don't worry."

I responded with, "But why do you need to confirm who we are if we are not in any trouble?" The male officer then informed us that we needed to be questioned separately.

John asked, "Do we need a lawyer present? Are we being charged with anything?"

The male officer replied, "No you do not need a lawyer, and no you are not being charged with anything. But we do need to confirm your details. It's just a formality."

John looked dubious and said, "Well if we are not being charged with anything, and we are not in any trouble, then we should be free to leave."

The male officer, PC Hogg, quite sternly told us that it was a procedure that needed to be followed and it was in our best interests to confirm our details. I then said, "Look I don't want any trouble, if you are saying we are not in any trouble, then I'll confirm my details." John tried to protest, but I said, "Look this is my choice. I have nothing to hide. We were the ones who were attacked John, we have the injuries to prove it and I just want to go back home to my mum. Let's get this over with."

John was then taken into the room with my two boys by one of the officers who had met us at the ferry terminal. I was then asked by PC Hogg to confirm my name, the name of my boys, the name of their school and their father's name. I found this strange as my boys had nothing to do with it. So I asked, "Why do you need the names of my boys? And their school? And their father's name? They were not involved in this."

"It's just for identification purposes," responded PC Hogg. The female officer, confirmed again that it was simply a procedure and that I wasn't in any trouble and all I had to do was confirm my details. So I did. Reluctantly, but I didn't want any more hassle from Police Scotland so I gave them the details they wanted. As soon as I did, both PC Hogg and the female officer looked at each other and I knew something was not right; and then in the next moment I was told I was being charged with three counts of assault, one against two men – neither men I have heard of before and who I presumed were two of the three men who had verbally and physically assaulted me, and I was also being charged with assault against John's daughter. At this point I felt physically sick. My head started spinning again and my stomach was churning. The back of my jaws were tingling and that acidic taste started rising. I was shocked and furious!

I went on to tell the two police officers that we had been attacked physically and verbally; that I had been spat on and the racist comments made against me and my boys. I also reminded them that they had both just sat there and said we were not in any trouble, and that this information had been obtained by lies and deception. I also told them that if I was being charged with assault it was akin to charging a woman who was in the process of being raped for defending herself. I informed them they had just told us we were not in any trouble, and that we did not need a lawyer and that these charges went against what we had just been told. My head was still spinning; my stomach was still churning and the acid still rising at the back of my mouth. The thought of me getting charged with assaulting a child when all I had done was try to protect her from getting hurt whilst defending myself made me feel so physically sick, I actually threw up. I only just made it to the toilet, and when John heard me throwing up, he came over to check on me. When I heard his voice from behind me I just didn't know what to say. How could I tell him what I had just been told? That his daughter was accusing me of assaulting her when I hadn't even laid a finger on her? John was straight down the line with the truth; hated liars just as I did. This wasn't going to sit well with him; none of it was, especially not this. My heart broke for him, as well as my boys; and myself. More incompetence on display by Police Scotland! Did they ever do any investigation work, or did they just pick a target and go all out to destroy that person they had randomly chosen?

After having thrown up, I went into the room where my boys were and stood there in disbelief at the poor policing and investigation work that was yet again taking place. No investigation just heresay from a group of people who had attacked John and I, and who were obviously backing each other up with their malicious story; with the support of the local police officer PC Steph Tanner. I was disgusted. The boys were looking really worried now, and both came over to me and hugged me. They asked what was happening and I just didn't know what to say. How could I tell them what was happening?

John was questioned whilst I was in the kitchen with the boys. The two male officers who had been waiting for us to get off the ferry offered me a glass of water and a cup of tea. For the first time in my life a cup of tea during the middle of the afternoon was the last thing I wanted. I was called back into the office where we were asked to confirm our details, and the female officer told us that we should attend Oban police station over the road and make our statements of what had happened.

John and I made our way from the ferry terminal, went to have a coffee to explain to the boys what had happened and then headed to the police station in Oban. When we arrived we informed the Sergeant on duty what we were there for and he refused to take a statement from us before asking me, "And where were your children at this point? Had you neglected and abandoned them again to go off drinking and starting more fights? We don't take statements from women like you who go to islands, neglect their children, get drunk and start fights." I was shocked that this statement had come out of this man's mouth and could not believe what I was hearing. When I told him he had no right to speak with me in that way, and that I wanted his name and number, he refused point blank to give it to me. I then requested he take a moment to notice my children were in the reception area hearing a police officer speak with a civilian in this manner, not to mention a man speaking with a woman in such a disrespectful tone; he refused several times to give me his name and number. I later found out he was Sergeant Brown, and that I was unable to prove what had been said to me because apparently there are no video cameras in Oban police station, and even if there were, it would be visual only (not doubt to cover up the poor attitude the police officers had towards members of the public and to hide the way they incited a lot of the responses and behaviours they faced).

We then left the station without being allowed to give a statement, and headed to the hospital to get my wrist and jaw checked out, as well as John's head; as he'd had a headache since the beating. We were both examined and our injuries recorded, photos taken and John was advised to attend a hospital in Glasgow to undergo a CT scan due to the head injuries he obtained. I was told my jaw were badly bruised, and would probably hurt for quite a while, but to just keep using them as normal (No peace and quiet for the boys, John and my parents then!)

I drove through the night to Glasgow and waited in the car with the boys whilst John went into the hospital for his CT scan. I was getting tired and yet the adrenalin was coursing through me like anything. Why on earth had these guys taken it upon themselves to come and attack us? What on earth did they think this kind of behaviour would prove, and how would it benefit them? I just couldn't understand this mentally at all. John's relationship with the mother of his daughter had ended years before, they had both moved on, or at least he had. She was obviously still stuck in anger, resentment, hurt and ego; failing to realise this kind of behaviour wasn't good for her own daughter. My relationship with ramO may not be perfect, but at least we were working together and had reached a point of maturity that would show the boys that regardless of what went on between us, they were our main concern. Bitching and bad mouthing eachother would only hurt the boys. Violence never solves anything and the kind of behaviour these guys had exhibited was obviously something John's daughter had witnessed before, otherwise she herself wouldn't have behaved in this way. I know I was deeply troubled by what I saw and experienced at the hands of these thugs, and what I had seen in John's daughter. With the way John had been so quiet since the attack, I knew he was hurting, and processing. I couldn't imagine what he was going through, but I knew he had his way of dealing with things, so I left him to deal with it in his own way, in his man cave, simply letting him know I was there by his side; and we would get through this together.

He came out of the hospital several hours later and told me the doctors had given him the all clear. What a relief! I had already been through brain trauma with my ex-husband some 15 years earlier, and really didn't fancy going through it again. With the boys still asleep in the car, I told John I needed coffee, and water before we set off back to the super yacht in Greenock. With a hit of caffeine inside me, music on and the window open for some of the journey, we made it back to Greenock. Again, we were not allowed to sleep on the yacht, so the boys and I slept in the car. I wasn't too impressed with the owners of the yacht to be honest; there would be no way I would have refused the family of one of my crew's family from sleeping on board, but hey, not everyone is the same; and with all the hotels in the local area fully booked, the boys and I got comfortable and slept.

The next morning John came walking up the pontoon, empty handed. I was a bit pissed off at that to be honest, I had hoped he would bring me a morning coffee, and the boys a juice or something, but apparently he wasn't even allowed to do that. Were the owners of this multimillion pound yacht really that stingy? Or had John simply not asked them? Or even thought about our needs? My mind had been racing all night. What had I gotten myself into? Was this relationship really worth all of this? Why was it okay for the boys and I to sleep in the car, and not on board the yacht? This wasn't the life I wanted. I was rebuilding, wanting to thrive, not survive. Why was this happening? What was it I was supposed to be learning from all of this? What value was I placing on my own life? My boys' lives? I knew I was tired, but even so, there are certain standards of life I wanted to live, and sleeping in a car, whilst my partner slept on a multimillion pound yacht less than 20 metres from me and my boys, was not the life I wanted. I had some serious thinking to do.

And then he walked over, apologising for not bringing me coffee, and for us not being able to sleep on the yacht. He also apologised for everything that had happened since we had been together. I'd never had an apology like it, nor a hug like it. Was he simply charming me? No, I don't believe so, and if he was, he was a bloody good actor. I wasn't sure whether my heart was breaking because I was considering walking away, or soaring because he had been able to read my mind. I just didn't know anymore, and tears started gently falling. He noticed them and wiped them away, kissing me on the forehead. I wanted to push him away, but I couldn't. His arms were wrapped so tightly around me now that I felt his apology. The energetic connection we had was intense, powerful; and once again I felt like I was wrapped up in a shield of steel.

After a short while, he had to get back to work, and so we said our goodbyes. Not knowing when we would see each other again in person. What a way to end our holiday. The boys were quiet during the start of the journey, so I asked them how they were feeling. With the words,

"Why does Scotland and the Scottish Police hate us Mummy?" coming out of my Khaalid's mouth, I felt angry, and deeply saddened. How could I answer that? I couldn't even make sense of it all, so how could they? How do you explain these kinds of attitudes and behaviours to an incredibly smart 10 and 14 year-old in a way that makes some kind of sense? I told them that I had no answer for that question, other than it wasn't the country that hated us, it was simply the attitudes and behaviours of a few; then went on to remind them of all the lovely people we had met in Scotland the year before.

I then asked Khaalid to get my notepad out and we started writing down everything we felt, and ideas for how to tackle this situation. I was going to write a mandate to the government, to the College of Policing, to the European Court of Human Rights. I was NOT going to allow this to happen to others either. The darkness that resides in the Scottish Police force in the way of racism, sexism and corruption has to be stopped, because it has no place in today's society.

I could tell my boys are very badly shaken up at this second incident involving the police in Scotland, and I hated the police for the way it had impacted my boys. They really had messed with the wrong mum this time. How dare they! To have them ask, "Why does Scotland and the Scottish Police hate us so much?" broke my heart and had instilled a very damaging idea into my boys, and I wanted an explanation for them, FROM Police Scotland AND from the First Minister; and that is exactly what I was going to get; whether I had to go public or not. They BOTH had to be held accountable for the actions of the people representing the country, and accountable they would be.

TWENTY-SIX
YOU WHAT!?

On the drive back to my mum and dad's I couldn't stop worrying about how they were going to take the news that I'd been arrested again. I was more afraid of hurting my mum than anything the police could do to me. I just didn't want to break her heart, or worry her. Khaalid called her to let her know our ETA after we'd had the radio on a bit, and been singing. That always boosted us. When she answered the phone full of cheer, Khaalid and I looked at each other. He knew I just couldn't bring myself to tell her. He gave her our ETA and said we'd see them all soon; but she knew something was wrong. She could always tell. She knew I was pregnant with Khaalid before I did, and that was from a photo published in a local business magazine. (When they say mums know everything, with my mum, they are not kidding!)

She asked me what was wrong and when I said I'd tell her when I got there, the first thing she asked was, "Are the boys okay?" Khaalid replied they were fine, and Naasir confirmed it from the back of the car; it was pretty much always a speaker phone call between us. When I said we were all okay, she insisted I tell her what had happened, and she used a tone of voice that I knew if I didn't tell her, I'd be in more trouble than I was in with the police. So I told her. Hearing my mum's voice tremble whilst telling my dad, and then hearing her tears, and then the fear in her voice made a fire rise up within me. Not only had they messed with my boys twice, they had now upset my mum twice; I was not happy. She wasn't well, neither was my dad; and now they had this to deal with. I fought back the tears, but I could still feel the storm rising within me. I knew I hadn't done anything wrong. I knew they were trying to stitch me up a second time, and with the first conviction, it would be even easier for them, or so they thought. A plan was forming in my head, and all the law study I had already done, was now going to be expanded upon. They were not going to win this. They were not going to beat me, and the nasty, vicious little game John's ex was playing, was not going to divide us. If anything, it was going to make us stronger. If for some reason John and I ended up apart, it wasn't going to be because of some vindictive, spiteful ex-partner; it was going to be because we weren't right for each other.

After the call, I had to pull over. I was too angry to drive. So I got out the car and told the boys to stretch their legs and take Kelt for a walk in the field next to the layby. Then I cried. Not tears of sadness, but tears of anger, of rage. I allowed the rage to escape in roar like screams and paced up and down. There was no way I was getting back in the car until it had died down. How dare they charge me and John with assault when it was those thugs that had come out of nowhere and attacked us? How dare they! I know about close knit communities, I grew up in one. I know about rural racism, I wrote about it in my first book *Friday Bridge*. I know about small minded mentalities, I have dealt with them all my life, and now everything I had ever done on a professional basis was falling into place for me to win this.

Then it hit me. This wasn't happening 'to me', this was happening 'for me' – for me to take the professional work I had done to a whole new level; to really create a powerful and positive change in the world. Naasir's name was no accident either, nor was the fact he had gotten out of the car in Inverarary the previous year. I had chosen his name four years even before Khaalid was born, knowing that if I had two boys, these would be their names. With Khaalid meaning 'mortal or eternal' depending on the context in which you use it, and Naasir meaning 'the one to bring about victory' these weren't Muslim names, or simply Arabic names, they were powerful names with legacy attached to them;

and legacies we were all here to create and leave behind. The rage inside of me started to subside and a strange feeling came over me. One of strength, of knowing and of light; and if I had to choose a metal to describe it, I would say it was titanium. I felt instantly calmer, and as I turned around I saw the boys walking back with Kelt. Khaalid was the first to give me a long, deep hug, and then Naasir. Kelt made us all laugh as he wanted in on the action too; so we had one of our 'family hugs' – all four of us together, with the three of us holding Kelt up in the middle, with him giving us all kisses.

After a few minutes, we all got back in the car and carried on driving, and just as we set off, that Titanium song came on the radio, by Sia, and I couldn't help smiling to myself. The rest of the drive was of the boys and I remembering the holiday we'd had in Wales two years earlier, both boys leading the conversation. Then all of a sudden Naasir said he never wanted to go to Scotland again; with Khaalid agreeing in quick succession. I had to agree with them, I didn't want to go back, even though John and I had discussed restoring a coastal cottage together, had even looked at a couple of the derelict properties on Tiree and discussed what we could do with them; but now I didn't feel safe returning. I knew I would have to go back to Scotland if these stupid charges were not dropped, but I wasn't looking forward to the thought of it at all, not one bit.

With a text message to my mum by Khaalid telling her to put the kettle on, Kelt started to perk up. He knew exactly where we were. He knew he would be getting spoilt rotten with biscuits, titbits of my parents' plates and a cup of tea in his bowl whilst at my mum and dad's. Even spending a week with them he always gained weight! Plus he had Ed to play with, or rather torment by always attempting to hump his back leg; which is not good as he is a retired greyhound. Poor old Ed!

Walking in through the door, I saw mum in the kitchen and dad in the garden. I opened the garden gate and let Kelt run around, hugged my dad and went in to see my mum. She stood there with worry written all over her face. Again the determination to win this took over and beat the anger from rising up. We held each other in a tight hug for ages. I could feel the tears shaking through her body. My jaw tightened. The determination strengthened; and just as I was thinking it my mum said it,

"Those bastards!" Again, the shock of hearing that word come out of my mum's mouth was enough to know the depth of her anger towards them. I sat down and rolled her a cigarette, and without thinking I rolled myself one and lit it. I'm not a smoker of cigarettes, but right then, at that moment, I smoked that roll up and joined my mum whilst she asked question after question about what had happened. When I had finished telling her, the first thing she said was, "Well, you'd better let John know you've arrived, he'll be worried about you."

I couldn't help but smile. She'd taken to him completely, so had my dad. So I called him and told him we'd arrived and he asked to speak with my mum. I handed the phone over to her and the next thing I hear from my mum is, "What are you apologising for? Did you stitch her up?" He'd obviously said no, because she came back with, "Well you've got nothing to apologise for. So stop being so bloody silly." Consider yourself told John! To know he had apologised to my mum for another situation happening with the police whilst the boys and I were in his company made my heart flutter; but made me wonder why both things had happened? Was it coincidence? Was it an energetic thing that belonged to him? Or was it one of the purposes for us to come together? Regardless, it had happened and I was going to fight it. I rolled another cigarette for both mum and I, and we went out into the garden to be with dad.

My nieces and nephew turned up a little later and the boys disappeared up to the park with them all, whilst my sister walked in and said, "Hiya! Are you alright?"

She didn't know what had happened and so I said, "Yeah, I'm okay, got arrested again, but I'm alright."

"You're joking!" she laughed back.

"I wish I was Ellen, I wish I was." And then the tears fell. The boys weren't around, mum and dad were in the garden and I just let all the emotions release themselves with each tear drop. Then I laughed, "I think I have cried more in the last three years than I have ever cried in my entire life!"

Mum came in and said, "You can pack that in! You said they were not going to beat you, and they're not going to. Sort yourself out and get your bloody laptop out and start doing what you do best. Get it all down in that word document thing, have a cup of tea and then you can help me make the salad for the barbeque."

Yes mother. So that's what I did.

I didn't last long that night, and was in bed way before the boys were. I slept a solid 19 hours, then had an afternoon nap the following day, followed by another 12 hour sleep the following night. I was mentally, emotionally, spiritually and physically drained.

I kept wondering how my life had ended up how it had. What had I done to get me to this point? I also kept playing the whole thing over and over in my head. Why hadn't John stepped in and stopped the first guy from punching me? How did he not know about the level of racism in the local area? Or did he? And if he did, why did he take us there? I knew he had kept himself very much to himself, and I knew there had been more lunatics killing themselves and many others in so-called 'Islamic terror attacks' so maybe the racism and Islamophobia attitudes had grown whilst he had been away, but for him to not step in whilst this guy was verbally and physically attacking me... I couldn't get that out of my head. He hadn't had my back. He hadn't protected me; or stood up for my boys; and that was something I couldn't live with. I wanted someone who would fight for me, protect me; and my boys.

But then I remembered what he'd said to me before about how he'd been dealing with the second guy. Then I remembered how he had spoken with my mum and how he'd apologised for what happened; and the embrace we'd had by the super yacht, and all the support he'd given me throughout the last year. My head was a mess. I wanted him beside me. I wanted to curl up in his arms, but he wasn't with me. He was up in Scotland, at work, and I didn't know when I would see him again.

And just as I was in this headspace and wondering when I would see him again, he called me on Skype. As soon as he saw me, he knew where my head was at. Told me not to put myself in places I didn't need to go. He held space for me to just release, to say what was on my mind, and when I looked at him, I knew. I knew I had nothing to worry about. That look in his eyes said it all, and I'll never forget it as long as I live.

TWENTY-SEVEN
AVOIDING THE DISTRACTIONS

I knew I had to keep focused but with this new distraction, I was finding things difficult. Here I was trying to build a business, to provide for my boys, and not just the nice to haves, the essentials; and at every turn there was one curve ball after another. I was getting worn down. I was becoming more and more disillusioned with everything. I just couldn't believe I was attracting so much bullshit into my life. I had always been a loving, giving person. Someone who not only built myself and my boys up, but others too; people I didn't even know. I supported others to fulfil their dreams, to believe in themselves and here I was having to deal with the evil that resided in our policing and justice system. It seemed everywhere I looked there was police brutality, miscarriages of justice, corrupt government leaders; all doing their best to put out another's light to make their own shine brighter. I saw shootings, wars, people living in dire conditions. I saw pain and suffering; I saw the news manipulating people at every turn with carefully timed news articles that built fear and paranoia in people. I saw political agendas causing fear of others from different countries, people not giving a monkeys about anyone but themselves, and in some cases people not wanting to even care about their own health and progression, ready to blame others for all the misfortune in their own lives; and I kept coming back to the quote 'When you point the finger at others, there are always three pointing back at you.'

So what was I missing? I knew I had not assaulted these people, and I knew I had never laid a finger on John's daughter. So why was I being targeted by Police Scotland yet again? Why were they not doing proper investigations into what had actually happened? Why were they being so incompetent? What was their end game? I knew if I was going to beat this latest challenge I had to focus on the only thing I could control... the way I dealt with it. I had to get clear on what was going on in my own life, go after the things that really mattered to me, get out of my own head and go after the life I wanted, whilst also going back to studying the law even further; regardless of how much other stuff I had going on, I needed to understand the law in terms of Human Rights, Family and Criminal law.

My main focus was the boys first though, making sure they were not badly damaged by this latest incident with the law. I had to make sure I wasn't badly damaged by it too, but with complete exasperation with it all, I had no idea of even how to start building them. I had to build the three of us up at the same time and just suck it up and get on with it. So that's what I did. And it was hard. Very hard, but I had no choice. Our sanity depended on it. My boys' future depended on it, especially as there was so much anti-Arab, anti-white going on in the Western world; and Khaalid was still in a place of recovery from all the Islamophobia that had gone on in Forge Valley and Birkdale Senior School. He was my main concern, and I didn't want Naasir taking on any more guilt than he already had for getting out of the car the year before. Knowing it was going to be easier for the Police to pin these latest charges on me because of the year before, was swimming around in my head; and I DID NOT want that becoming a thought in Naasir's mind. He was only nine, and this was a burden no adult should carry, let alone a child of nine. I hated the police now, and I don't use that word lightly. What they were doing was totally irresponsible and careless; and given the fact that the state's main purpose of existence is protect the family[11], and all they were trying to do is destroy me and my family, they were doing a pretty poor job of fulfilling their sole purpose.

I made sure I kept the boys positive by focusing on Khaalid's new start at Tapton, getting his uniform ready, and making sure Naasir was ready for his final year at primary school. I took them to the cinema, went on hikes with them through the Peaks, played board games with them, spent quality time with them laughing, cooking, dancing, singing, playing in the park, discussing the future plans and holidays. I acknowledged them for the incredible humans they are and encouraged them to keep being their awesome selves. We put it behind us; and then when they were at school, asleep or with ramO, I would dive deep into healing from this latest phase of the Scotland Saga, my fitness and my business.

Whilst on one of my daily calls with John, he completely took me by surprise and told me we were going on holiday. To Italy! A country I had always wanted to visit. He had heard me talk about my desire to go to Italy, seen me go all dreamy when I talked about it, and now here he was telling me to book flights, as we were going in October. He was paying. I couldn't believe I was actually going! I was so excited! Yet another dream was coming true. I was on cloud nine, especially as I was also making plans to go back on board *The Excelsior*, this time around the Channel Islands, a part of the UK coastlines I had never been to, but always wanted to go.

Having been out on *The Excelsior* back in May, I knew it was time to get back out on the boat. I needed to be back on the ocean. My soul needed it, especially with this latest curve ball. I wanted my coaching business and my life of an author to go to the next level, I wanted my clients to join me on the ocean, away from the distractions of their own life so they could up-level their lives. I wanted to share the beauty of the ocean with them, to enable them to plot a course for boat, and use it as a great way of enabling them to set a powerful and positive course for their own lives and go after the life of their dreams. I also wanted my dream of living on the ocean writing books to come true. I wanted to travel the world in the most environmentally way possible, to enable the boys to enjoy travelling without Khaalid suffering from hay fever as he did when we travelled around the country by road; and I wanted to spend my life with John on the ocean.

With the trip arranged, and Kelt coming with me this time, I had both the trip to Italy and the Channel Islands to look forward to, positives to look forward to. A time to just reflect, build on my sailing knowledge and experience. It would be a chance to be on the ocean, a place where my soul was at peace. Just being me, and seeing how Kelt would handle being on the ocean, because it was to be his life too... when John and I eventually got our own boat. The time was getting closer to leave. The boys were going to be with ramO and everything was ready.

In the September, a month before the trip, I started to do an online course with an incredible woman named Regan Hillyer; a woman who would enable me to change my life in more ways than I could ever anticipate. The course was called Online Empire Builder and would take me closer to live my life at sea, being location free and impacting the world in a more powerful and positive way. I had put the events of Tiree to the back of my mind. I hadn't heard anything from Scotland and believed it had all been forgotten about. I had already made massive shifts in my thinking, in the way in which I was developing my business, had met some incredible women on the course and these women I knew got me on so many levels. I had actually found a space where I felt like I truly belonged in the business world. I had never felt like I belonged in the business community in Sheffield; I either wasn't taken seriously enough because I laughed too much, or was too outspoken, or not 'professional enough' whatever that was supposed to mean. I also found there was a lot of lipservice being paid; people promising this project was going to happen and then due to the 'powers that be' funding was cut or not made available. It was almost like the business community in Sheffield was relying on benefits to keep their businesses going or make a project happen, rather like those who don't work and rely on the benefits system to keep them in food and shelter; or just not willing to work with solopreneurs, or startups because we had 'no proven track record' or 'x amount in the bank' or 'x amount of years accounts'.

I also found a lot of the coaches somewhat hypocritical. At one meeting in particular, the language of negativity and scarcity was just too much. Here were these people supposed to be transforming lives and businesses, and yet they themselves were negative and stuck. I just felt there was too much scarcity, too many 'traditional' ways of doing business, and too much negativity. Even women I had looked up to in my early years of being in the Sheffield business community were in scarcity, and no longer inspiring to me. I had changed. I had evolved, and stepped into the next level of business that I had been looking for, whilst the others around in me in Sheffield kept talking about how things were hard, how there was not enough business out there, how they could never employ or work with others overseas. They were struggling and it showed in their faces and the language they used. I felt sad and uninspired in their company, apart from one lady, Lesley. I don't think there was one thing Lesley was negative about, and I just loved being in her company. I loved her energy and the time I spent with her. We had become friends' years before at a business lunch and had giggled our way through most of it. She had lived in the Arab world, had a lot of the same interests and was a huge bag of energy, so much it was infectious. We were kindred spirits, and she was someone who had been supporting me through the first phase of the Scotland Saga. She was disgusted at what had happened and had written a character reference for me, one that left me speechless.

I looked forward to my weekly online training sessions with Regan, some nights staying up until two in the morning just to take part. I was dedicated to making my location free, online business a success and if it meant I had to stay awake, or go to bed and wake up again a few hours earlier than that was what I was going to do. I would do whatever it took to realise my dream and to build a business that would not only give my boys, John and I a life that we all loved, but also impact as many people positively, around the world; people I wouldn't be able to access if I remained in the old school ways of doing business. The world was changing, my audience wasn't in Sheffield, and it wasn't simply limited to the UK. I had a global vision. The world needed healing and I wanted to be part of the global change that reduced mental health problems, gave joy to people and shone a light on the darkness so as to help eradicate it. I may only be one woman, it may be a big goal to have, but it was one that motivated me and one that inspired me. I wanted to lead my boys by example, lead them into thinking that they too could make a positive difference in the world and be anything and anyone they wanted to be.

So putting off sleep for a few hours was no big deal. Some friends didn't understand it. Some friends didn't like the way I was changing my life, and they are the ones who fell by the way side, but the ones that really mattered, such as Rob, Alan and Tina, they cheered me on and supported me in ways I didn't anticipate. Rob, Nikki and Chris were also incredibly encouraging and supportive, not just with the Scotland Saga, but also with this new business I was creating, all whilst still selling Vitality with them. Seeing Nikki's smiling face whenever I saw her was just beautiful, such a big cheery smile. She just radiates light, joy, and so much energy! And her giggle! A truly beautiful sound to hear!

With positive people, driven to succeed around me, cheering me on, getting me on multiple levels and the new investment I had made into the business, I was feeling content. I had found a solution that was going to be the perfect single mum solution and I wanted to internalise this training, make it work for my life and my business, combine it with all the other knowledge I had and then take my training and coaching to a whole new level. I knew I had turned a corner. I knew this was the right path for me, and my business; now it was all about implementing it all and calling in the business. It was time to up-level my life again and I was excited. I loved the way I kept shifting through all the blocks I had, the way I kept diving deep into the stuff that was holding me back. The more I looked inwards the more I saw results. The more I took myself on, did the mindset work, the more I was able to shift and grow, letting go of stuff from the past that I didn't even know was holding me back. It felt great to release all this 'stuff', it felt like weights were being lifted off my shoulders. I had more energy and was finally making money to pay off the legal fees from the court case, and invest in much needed clothes for the boys.

With so much going on in my life, and so many changes happening within me, a deep awakening was taking place, I went back to my 'list' of qualities I wanted in my future life partner. Did I still want the same things on that list? Did I still want to be with John? Did he fit into my higher vision? I felt that it was an almost pointless exercise because I knew that I wanted to spend the rest of my days with him. Not only did he meet all the existing qualities on the list, but all the new ones too... and then so many more. Being with him, thinking of him, just him... I still felt like a lovesick teenager; and it felt great. I felt spoilt, loved and treasured. It excited me, and scared me; because the more I fell for him, the more I wanted us to last forever. Did forever exist though? Would John commit to me forever? Only time would tell, and although I wanted that ring on my finger, I wasn't under any illusions.

---

[11] www.worldfamilydeclaration.org/WFD

TWENTY-EIGHT
TRAVEL, TRAVEL AND MORE TRAVEL!

With my trip on *The Excelsior* less than a week away, and then Italy less than three weeks away, I was pulling together ideas for my Coaching at Sea sailing trips and VIP Client retreats. With all the knowledge and breakthroughs I had been having since starting the Online Empire Builder with Regan, I felt unstoppable. All areas of my life were falling into complete alignment and I was succeeding in all areas. I had clients showing up out of nowhere and had already had some speaking engagements booked. I had been registered as a mentor with the Sheffield City Region's Mentor bank and things were looking good.

My fitness was the best it had ever been and I was really enjoying walking the three miles to and from the dojo with the boys. It gave us an hour each way to giggle and discuss stuff going on and our goals for the future, both as a family and as individuals; I loved these walks. Getting to spend quality time with my boys made me so happy. They were really awesome young men and so much fun to be with, I felt like the luckiest woman in the world to be their Mummy. They made me so proud of them. Do make me so proud of them.

With the boys at ramO's, it was time for Kelt and I to set off to the train station and head down to Portsmouth. I was really looking forward to seeing how Kelt would cope with being on the ocean; was he going to be okay? Would he be seasick? Would he be tempted to jump overboard into the water or would he be fine? He'd already flown back from Egypt, been on ferries, bikes, in cars, on buses and trains with no problems whatsoever, so I was pretty confident he would be fine. He was totally spoilt by all those sat near us on the trains, his cuteness just sent people into moments of weakness, and he lapped it up.

Arriving in Portsmouth and heading to meet Gavin and Vinnie I was excited. I arrived and saw a glass of pinot grigio waiting for me. They'd remembered! Then Vinnie noticed Kelt and fell in love with him. Big hugs all round and straight back into the banter and giggles. I had missed these two and was looking forward to spending the next seven days sailing with them around the Channel Islands. I was introduced to another couple of guys and told they were the only other crew members for this trip. The boat would feel so empty! Plenty of room for Kelt though, and he loved it! He found his little spot on the sheets (ropes) that were stored in the dinghy and Gav was totally smitten with him, making him pull toys and snuggling up with him. Kelt milked every single moment of it. He wasn't sick once and loved sitting at the stern of the boat looking out at the ocean. So now my goal of living at sea had another tick on the list – thank you Kelt!

The trip was so different to the one before and this was a good lesson to learn so early on. I knew my life at sea would be so transient and I had to get used to it one way or another. No longer would it be staying in the same place, seeing the same people day in day out. I didn't like living in London due to the transient lifestyle, but that was totally different; London was a major city, and not the place my heart called out for. When I was on the ocean, my soul rested. Felt like it was home, so the transient life at sea was something I was looking forward to experiencing. The trip passed so quickly and plans for my future business were written and projections made. Gavin was so helpful making sure I knew the costs involved with The Excelsior and how they generated the cash needed to run the day to day, as well as the repairs and moorings; not to mention how I could save money. He truly was a God send. Little did I know it would be the last time I would see him and Vinnie.

Arriving back in Sheffield, I couldn't wait to see my boys, but first it was laundry on, a walk through the woods with Kelt, grab a bottle of wine and run a hot bath. Kelt lay beside the bath, his usual space and started snoring louder than I had ever heard him snore before! Sea air must have done him some good!

The boys arrived home the following day full of hugs and questions about how Kelt had been; wanting to see my pictures, and wanting us to cook together. These boys! They just made my heart burst with their enthusiasm and desire to do things together as a family. What more could a Mummy want? They were even asking me if I had been practising my Italian, in preparation of meeting John and heading off to Italy. The encouragement my boys gave me was so heart-warming, I felt so blessed to have such supportive boys. We spent so much time together practising Italian on the Babbel App on my phone, which left us in fits of giggles as not one of us could even get the word 'Si' correct with the app! I mean seriously! How hard is it to say 'Si'? We resorted to making up words that sounded Italian and it reminded me of the languages I would make up with my sister when we were younger. The boys got into full on Italian mode, "Mummy, let's have pizza tonight!" or "Mummy, I think we should have lasagne for dinner tonight," and then, "Mummy, I think we should go to Gigi's for dinner tonight." A local Italian restaurant owned by my friend Gigi. Before the time came for me to head to my mum's the boys and I had got so into Italian mode I felt sad they were not coming with John and I; but John and I needed time by ourselves; quality time to just be the two of us.

The boys went to ramO's on the Friday night from school, so I headed to my mum and dad's for a couple of days, then to London for a night in a hotel close to Stansted ready to meet John the next day. I had started another course with Regan called the 15 Day Wealth Creation Intensive, and only had a couple more of the Online Empire Builder sessions to do, one of which kept me up until 2am to begin and then I was buzzing so much I didn't sleep until 4am! I was loving the energy Regan's courses gave me due to the blockages I was releasing. I didn't care that I might be tired! I had work to do. I had legal fees to pay off, boys to invest in, as well as my future to invest in. Like my Nanny would say 'Idle hands make the devil's work' and my mum would say 'Do your best, because then no one can ever ask anything else from you'. So it was game on ALL the time. Never stopping, because not only had the Scotland Saga court case cost me thousands in money, it had also prevented me from building my business, resulting in lost earnings of a sizeable amount, not even including the emotional and mental suffering the boys and I had been through. But that was beside the point for the next two weeks. This time was for me and John. I never saw him as I walked into the airport, but I felt him walking towards me; and when I turned to him I saw a huge smile on his face. Feeling his arms around me and his lips on mine was such a magical feeling. He took my hand and led me through the airport. We checked in and as soon as we were on the plane it was a bottle of Champagne to celebrate everything I had achieved, and life itself.

Arriving in Puglia, we headed over to the car rental place and collected the car we had booked for the two weeks. I was to drive and John was to navigate; and within about 15 minutes the map was thrown in the back of the car and it was just go where the roads and the universe took us. We travelled across from Bari Airport to Napoli, Roma, up to Tuscany, across to Perugia, down to Vieste before heading down to Ceclia Messapicca. 2,587 kilometres in two weeks taking on olive picking with a wonderful lady called Alba in Tuscany, which was interesting and not just because Alba is the Scottish name for Scotland and Italian for Dawn… another bloomin' Scotland connection! We went foraging for Chantarelle mushrooms in Vieste on a AgroTourismo with a guy called Lino, and learnt so much from him about the local and national history. We only intended to stay with him for a night but ended up staying four nights. Things didn't go to plan with this holiday though as John got robbed in Roma and that really put us both under pressure; another test for our relationship. Would they ever end? I was starting to have doubts about us again, and yet I pushed them down; I wanted to enjoy the rest of our holiday, and enjoy it I would.

At the end of our holiday, John had some bad news, although I thought it was more of a blessing. The couple he had been working for on the super yacht demanded he end his holiday early and return by the Monday. If not, he would lose his job. Needless to say he lost his job, and now he was free to find another contract where he would be respected more and the boat owners had the integrity to deliver on the promises they gave upon signing contracts. It put a downer on the end of our holiday and I just couldn't help but look at the connection between me doing a 15-day Wealth Creation Intensive and John getting robbed, losing almost £4000 and then losing his job. What was the universe telling me? Was this the right relationship to be in? Only time would tell.

We arrived back in the UK, and as I headed back up to Sheffield, John stayed with his friend Sam in London. John was to work at the sailing club Sam managed and then he would come back up to Sheffield to be with me. The two weeks had been so eventful, a roller coaster of emotions, and then they were over. I had been to Italy, had an incredible time, and yet come back with doubts about my relationship when the trip should have strengthened us. Why was I having so many doubts? I had come to trust my instincts and yet here I was not walking away; just diving deep into the feelings and working them out. I couldn't just walk at the first time of struggle between us. Yes I had experienced two awful incidences in Scotland since I had been with him, but neither were due to being with him. He hadn't set me up, but was it the universe warning me? I just didn't want to think about it right now, I just wanted to get back to my boys and Kelt; and start implementing everything I had been working on during the holiday. Yep! Even during the two weeks I had spent on holiday with John, I was still working on my business. I attended every training, bunching them up into a couple of hours, every other day. I was committed to achieving my dreams and just because I was on holiday didn't mean I was going to stop working. If I wanted to have a location free business then I had to see how I got on with that... and my work is an extension of me, and why would I take a day off from who I am? It just didn't make sense to me. It also gave John his own time during the day to do his thing. We may be a couple but we are also both individuals.

Arriving back in Sheffield I noticed all the mail, but I just wanted to sleep before the boys came back the next day with Kelt. I fell into bed that night and slept like a baby, so deeply and rested; the first time in a long time, which I hadn't noticed until I woke up the following morning. Relaxing into the day, I chose to open the mail... and then wished I hadn't. There was a letter from Scotland. A letter detailing all the charges being made against me; and ONLY ME! WTF? Why is it that there were three guys attack us, and I am the only one to be charged? And why wait all this time to send any kind of paperwork through? My hands started trembling, my heart was racing and my legs went weak. I ended up sat on the floor with Kelt beside me giving me hugs and kisses, climbing on my knee. I was furious! This was akin to charging a woman with self-defence because a guy chose to rape her. Were Police Scotland REALLY that stupid? Obviously they were. I made my way to the kitchen, made a cup of tea and then called David, the lawyer at Beltrami & Co who had represented me during the last case. He asked me to send through the paperwork sent so he could have a look at it and advise me what to do next. I told him I had already written up a testimony of the attack when I had arrived at my parent's just two days after we had got off the ferry. He told me to send that over. So I sent that over, then I called John. He had to know what was happening. There was no answer, so I messaged him in case he was sleeping or working. I knew he had started working on transforming the kitchen, the menu and the restaurant at the sailing club in South London.

I had a shower and got myself together so I could be fresh for when the boys got back. I had over an hour so it was time for Kelt and I to go for a long walk. I needed to be in nature, I needed to hear the water in the streams and the waterfalls. I needed to hear the wind in the trees and feel the wind on my face. It was also good to wrap up warm in my winter jacket and scarf, to feel protected, because right now I felt vulnerable.

How could this all be happening again? What the hell was Scotland's problem? Other than a police force which it seemed did no police work and Prosecutor Fiscal's who had no common sense or emotional and social intelligence when it came to choosing the cases they took on. I mean come on seriously, anyone with any ounce of humanity would have seen this for what it was: A bitter ex-partner who was either still in love with the father of her child, resentful of the fact she had been a single mum, or in fact a mum, or hated the fact that she was stuck on a small island four hours off the mainland, who had caused countless problems not just for the father of her child, but also messed with the mind of her own daughter. This had nothing to do with me and everything to do with

John's relationship with his ex-partner, the mother of his daughter. I was simply collateral damage, in the wrong place at the wrong time....

Or as I needed to think about this whole ugly situation, I was indeed in the right place at the right time to expose the incompetence within Police Scotland even further. I had to think positive, take the positives from the negatives, because if I didn't, I wouldn't be able to focus on my boys and helping Khaalid to choose his options for his GCSE's, or get Naasir ready for his SAT's, or take my business to the next level. I had to get smart, legal smart and so it became my mission to study the law even further.

I went onto the websites of both Sheffield University and Sheffield Hallam University, as they both had Law Faculties; one of which was named after Baroness Helena Kennedy, who sits in the House of Lords and works tirelessly for the rights of Women and Children in the field of Social Justice. Sheffield University also has a very good reputation of being one of the best Law Schools in the UK, so being in Sheffield was a great opportunity to study the law: and attend the different events open to the public as well as students. We also had an incredible range of libraries in the city, so it was time to renew my library card and get stuck in: Human Rights Law, Family Law and Criminal Law. I had a very little amount of time to study, so I had to get to the guts of this case and focus directly on the relevant areas of law. I also added in Professional Incompetence and the impact on the state. I contacted friends of mine who were in Law Enforcement, called organisations such as Skills for Justice again, The College Of Policing, The Independent Police Complaints Commissioner's Office and Human Rights Organisations, as well as spoke with my friend Robert Keston, who was a Partner of the PDHRE[12], a global movement in the education of Human rights; and the author of the foreword in my second book *Walaahi*.

It had been a few days since I had left a message for John, and it wasn't like him to not contact me back. In the 18 months we had been together, he had always replied to my messages. So I tried calling him again, and sent him another message. I understood how hard he worked, and knew he was working shifts, so wasn't really that concerned, but given the nature of the reason I was calling, I was really surprised at his lack of communication, even if was just a quick five minute call to check to see how I was coping with this latest curveball. It was the first time he'd behaved liked this and so long as it didn't become a regular thing, I wasn't too bothered. We were, after all a partnership; and partners are supposed to, in my book, support and be there for each other in the best times and the worst times. I had been in a marriage with a lack of communication and I was not going to continue in a relationship where communication wasn't present in difficult times. I had been there and got burnt before. My two prominent love languages are communication and touch, and so far John had ticked the boxes in both of these love languages. I had also done a lot of work on myself and had set new non-negotiables. My needs either got met or they didn't. And if they didn't, it was about discovering why, understanding the possible reasons behind it and weighing up whether it was worth carrying on.

I waited until that evening, knowing that John would have at least stopped for something to eat, or at least woken up from the previous night's shift. I called him and got through to his voicemail. Then I sent him a message to ask if everything was okay. It just wasn't like him to not respond so quickly. Was he sick? Had there been an accident? So many things went through my mind, especially given the difficult time we had experienced in Italy.

I decided to call his friend Sam who he was staying and working with. When I spoke with Sam, I was shocked at the response I got. I either stopped calling him and leave him alone or lose him forever. I felt as though I had been sucker punched. Here I was dealing with shit from John's past and now being told by the guy he was staying with to leave him alone. I held it together on the phone and told Sam he had no right to comment on my relationship with John and if John felt that way, he should at least have the balls to tell me himself.

I hung up and broke down in tears of anger and hurt. I felt angry that I had been left to deal with this by myself, hurt that I had been left to deal with it myself and that Sam had become the messenger of John. Allowing myself to fall in love, and so deeply had been the biggest challenge over the last 18 months, not just because of ramO's cheating, but because I had boys. Whoever came into my life was also in theirs. I had been through hell and back since I had been with John because of the events that had happened with Police Scotland. My personal journey of learning to trust myself to trust another man with my heart had been immense. I was still confronted with it all, and now I was dealing with this next round of the Scotland Saga, my guards went up. If I was going to get through this, I had to realise I was on my own. If John couldn't even respond to my messages, just to check on how I was, then how was I going to trust him to have my back when we lived at sea? Was it going to be him simply looking out for himself? Leaving me to fend for myself? NO. I wasn't going there. I wasn't going to put any more of my trust in him; and those wings of steel just turned into titanium, my own shield, for me and my boys; and it would take a lot for him to penetrate my force field again.

It did occur to me several times that it was just Sam shit-stirring, I had an uneasy feeling about him anyway, but if John chose friends who did that, then that was just as equally a good reason to step away. I didn't want, or need that kind of mentality in my life. I had learnt the hard way that environment was, and is everything; and you are the sum total of the five people you spend the most time with. I didn't want Sam anywhere near me; but John trusted him. It was time for me to turn inwards and trust myself, and only myself.

The boys and I walked to MMA that night and man did I let my pain and anger out on the punch bags. I squatted as though my life depended on it and kept myself very much to myself. Sensei knew something was up and called me into his office. He had been my mentor for the last couple of years and he knew where I was at, with the Scotland Saga and the whole learning to trust myself to fall in love. He knew I was in deep, had met John and was a great role model for the boys. I trusted him, so I explained what had happened. Was I being too needy? Was I asking too much? Sensei was shocked I hadn't heard back from John just as much as I was. He even went as far to say that if a man is truly in love with a woman, he would do everything he could to help and support her; and there was no way he would have left a friend to deal with what I was going through let alone someone he had chosen as a partner. He made me a cup of tea, then told me once I had drank it, I was to go and release everything on the punch bags, kick punch do whatever I needed to do to get the feelings out, the frustrations and then go home have a hot bath and then sleep. There was no point dealing with what I was about to embark on in the head space I was in. So I did just that; and woke up the next morning with a body so sore from such a workout that it felt great! Man it felt great! There really is nothing quite like a punch bag workout when you are in a certain frame of mind.

The next day I realised it had been almost five days since I had spoken with John, the longest we had gone without speaking with each other, either voice to voice or at least by messages on messenger or Skype. Even when he had been away at sea, he always made the time to contact me. I just couldn't figure it out, and the longer it went on, the more my defences were growing stronger. Harsh to some people I know, but I was not going to allow myself to get hurt again by any one. As I was cooking with the boys that night, Khaalid put his arm around me and asked me if I was okay. I said yes I was, and he replied, "No you're not, and I know John hasn't called you. Have you broken up?" I wasn't ready to answer that question, nor was I wanting to discuss it with my 14 year-old son. But he knew I was hurting, and had noticed that John hadn't called. Before I could answer him, he said "It's okay Mummy, the three of us and Kelt make a great time. You're beautiful, smart, funny and lovely so he's an idiot if he doesn't want to be with you." Well that was it! Tears of gratitude sprung into my eyes and I gave him the biggest hug. He was such a loving boy and very perceptive. I was absolutely sure he would make a great husband and father. I was so proud of him.

We continued to cook dinner, ate and then the phone rang. It was John. I didn't want to answer it. I just wanted him to go away, but I knew that was my ego talking and so I answered it. The first words out of his mouth were, "I'm sorry I haven't called, I've been so busy with work and sleeping; and haven't had my phone on. What's going on? What's all this with these messages?" I didn't know whether to believe him about not having his phone on, he always checked the news and what was happening with his friends on Facebook; or he was watching a film. I chose to tell him what the paperwork had said, and then told him what Sam had said. I told him if he wanted to end it, he should have the decency to end it himself, not send his minions to do his dirty work for him. He was shocked by what I had said, and told me quite firmly he didn't want us to end, had been working and sleeping, and that he would be having a word with Sam. I told him I wasn't happy with the lack of communication and told him where it had put me in my head and what had come up for me. He told me not to put myself in that space, I didn't need to. He loved me and we were going to get through it together. We chatted for about an hour and I chose to trust what he had said, and the way in which he had said it; but I still had doubts in my head. Had the damage been done? Would I be able to get past this? Only time would tell.

The next night I turned up at MMA with the boys and we had a great couple of hours with each other. ramO collected the boys and I stayed on for the technical and sparring session, so had three hours of MMA training. During this session, the rest of the girls and I had been giggling and laughing – especially when it came to training on the TRX system. I just couldn't keep a straight face when working out on it, it reminded me of a bondage set up and with my mind where it was due to writing *The Wife* (which included quite a bit of erotica) I just couldn't handle it.

Sensei's wife was in the class and she told me she would love to read some of my work, so I said I would write something for her; and within 30 minutes of saying that Sensei walked into the dojo in THE most gorgeous red Adidas trainers. I got distracted and got punched in the side of the face by one of the other girls I was training with. Everyone laughed and then I had an idea. I would write a short piece of erotica using the trainers as a metaphor.

So that night when I got home, that's what I did, posted on Facebook, tagged Sensei in it; not realising the impact it would have on mine and the boys' lives. I was asked by Sensei if I could meet him, and so I agreed. When we met, he told me that his wife was really not happy with what I had written and so I was no longer welcome to return to MMA, nor were the boys allowed to attend either. I couldn't believe it! All because I had written a short piece of writing, like she had asked for, she was now demanding I leave the dojo. A place where the concept of family and belonging was the mantra; a place where building each other was the encouraged practice and here I was being asked by my mentor, my Sensei, to leave because his wife thought I had the hots for him.

Firstly, he was my Sensei – a line I would never cross, even if I did fancy the pants of him (which I didn't, he just wasn't my type).

Secondly, he was married. Another line I would never cross. You don't mess with relationships, especially ones where marriage and children are involved.

Thirdly, I was in a relationship, albeit on shaky ground at that point.

And fourthly, he was my mentor. I had never shown any interest in him as anything other than my Sensei and mentor. She had asked for an example of my writing, and with my love of Adidas trainers resulting in me getting punched in the side of the face due to being distracted, I had delivered something that had a level of privacy for all of us who had enjoyed a giggle at my expense. The sad thing was, she had now set a precedent for the dojo. Whenever she felt threatened by another woman in the dojo, would this woman (and her kids) be asked to leave the dojo? I was devastated to tell you the truth. Another guy in my boys' lives had now just walked out on us.

They were confused when I told them we had been asked not to go back, but they were pleased in quite a few ways. That night as I lay in bed, I just couldn't believe what had happened. The thing that also disappointed me was that Sensei had asked me to lie about why I wasn't going to be there anymore. He asked me to say I was focusing on my swimming more. Why would I lie when one of the key things taught at the dojo was to be honest? And when I was honest to the core... sometimes too honest for some people, but always honest, how could I lie to people who I had considered family over the last couple of years?

I soon realised, after not having been in the dojo for a couple of weeks, the lack of depth this concept actually had within the dojo. There was no family the boys and I were part of, we were just members of a private MMA club; we didn't fit and hadn't fitted for longer than I had realised. How naïve could I have been after all these years and after all the experiences I'd had? My desire to have leaders for my boys, being able to enjoy a sport – which was also a great self-defence technique had overshadowed the truth of what was really there; which as nothing but lip service and a false sense of family. Time to move on, find another dojo where we could continue our training. We were only four belts away from black belts, and I wanted my black belt. Something I had always wanted. Having looked around, there were no other options. The closest MMA classes we could attend were in Chesterfield, but with not having a car, that wasn't an option as it would take an hour-and-a-half to get there, but nearly two-and-a-half on the way back. Plus the boys were not feeling it anymore, so that was it. Our MMA sessions had come to an end. I was gutted; and it would go on to impact me in more ways than I anticipated.

Towards the end of November I was talking with my new friend Amity, who I had met on the Online Empire Builder course. We had a lot of synergy between us and so we made plans for me to go off overseas again, this time to Brittany.

I had spoken with John a lot more about what was being said about the charges. David from Beltrami had told me that he could no longer represent me as the fees to fight this court case would run into the thousands and as I already owed them money, his directors wouldn't support him in representing me. He did however pass me over to another guy called David who did legal aid work. David had already spoken with him and he had agreed to represent me. Speaking with this new David, I found him to be rather abrupt and dismissive. I felt like I was guilty before even being heard. Something I was becoming accustomed to. He told me he would arrange for the legal aid forms to be sent to me. They would be with me in a few days and then he would discuss the way forward. John was still in London and working with Sam. Our communications were getting better but I was still very guarded. I wanted to protect myself, and yet whenever I saw his face I was smitten. I told myself not to let the heart rule, listen to sense, but the heart was winning every time. I was in love with John and nothing was going to stop it; even if the walls were up.

I arranged my trip to Brittany and was due to go just after my birthday, John had said he was coming up for my birthday on the 6th December. I was half expecting him not to come, but so excited all at the same time. It wasn't until the end of November when he confirmed his train times with me that I believed he was coming. Sam had really got into my head. I didn't want to call John in case I was bothering him, or pushing him away. I didn't want to lose him, but I wanted to feel free in my relationship, and I didn't. It was not a healthy place to be in at all. I needed to do some deep work on myself. I needed to get to the root of these feelings and so I arranged a coaching call with Vicki, my coach on the Online Empire Builders Course. We dove really deep and I got present to the rejection that was coming up from years before when my father left at the age of four, and the fact that my mother worked so hard that she very rarely came to my school plays. I knew she was working and doing her best to provide a great life for us and so never really put pressure on her to be there but I always wanted her there and was jealous of my friends whose parents were there. I now got how that was playing out in my adult life. Now I had access to this, I could make a choice, let it go, or allow it to keep preventing me from moving forward. I chose to let it go, and chose to move forward with John without the negative thoughts in my head, to really step into my heart space and just feel into the future with John. It made such a huge difference.

Whilst all this was going on, all the study, the business building I was also planning on writing my next book *Walaahi*, ready to release on the 25th January as a paperback and as an eBook on the 1st February, in line with the anniversary of the start of the Uprising and the Million Man March. It was going to be tight but I knew I could do it. I told John my plans and he said if that was what I wanted to do, he would support me. The boys also gave me their backing and so it was time to add another project into my already busy workload. I always liked being busy, and having a butterfly brain, true to being a Sagittarian, I always found it easier to have multiple projects on the go at once. It kept me interested, and motivated.

With arrangements made for the boys and Kelt, I set off to Brittany to see Amity and had a great week with her. We went to the standing stones, went walking in the forests and of course we went to the beach. It was so wonderful to spend some time with her and work on our businesses both independently and separately. Amity was also interested in empowering women to follow their dreams and did more on the marketing side of launching a business. I was more involved in the whole process of setting up and moving through the different areas to launch the business and grow it. We had a lot of synergy, but with everything going on in our lives, we knew we would work with each other in the future, rather than the present. I interviewed her for my business but never got to promote the interview as things changed quite dramatically for us both. It was a case of family first for both of us, and as single parents it was essential for us both to focus on our children and our individual businesses.

Whilst I was in Brittany, I had another email from David at the new law firm, McCusker McEllory & Co, he wanted to know more about what had happened so I sent him the testimony I had already sent to David at Beltrami & Co. I then didn't hear anything back from him for what would be another couple of months; enough time for me to return to the UK, head back to my parents, with John, the boys and Kelt, in ramO's car. It was nice for me to be able to be in a place with ramO where we were working together, and be in a space where John was also able to travel with us. ramO dropped us off and headed on to Cambridge. John, the boys and I had such a lovely Christmas at my parent's, and it was, for me, a perfect Christmas. I even got to spend New Year's Eve with my friend Jaime and her husband Kevin, the first New Year's Eve Jaime and I had ever spent together in nearly three decades of friendship. It was also great to spend the evening with John, him meeting Jaime for the first time. I was feeling incredibly happy. Even with the turmoil and stress with the latest court case lingering in the background, I was still content; I had my boys, my partner, my oldest friend, my family and my health.

I just wish my business was in a position to be able to pay off the legal fees, even though I wanted to take action against Police Scotland and the Scottish Judicial System for the hell they had put me and my family through, the costs I had incurred, the slander on my name and the lost earnings, and that was all without calculating the mental and emotional abuse they had inflicted upon me and the boys. The problem was, taking legal action against them meant I needed a Scottish Law firm, but as they had employed every different law firm in Scotland to work with them on various different cases, not one of the firms who worked on professional indemnity cases would take on my case due to a 'conflict of interest'. Police Scotland had been very clever, whether intentionally or not. They had stitched up the entire population in more than just one way, and protected themselves in the meantime. I even went as far as contacting the lawyer, who had worked on the Stephen Lawrence case, but they wouldn't deal with it due to it being based on Scottish Law and they didn't have anyone in the firm qualified to take the case on. My only option I felt was to keep moving forward and study the law myself; win this latest case and then publish this book, calling them all to account and exposing the professional misconduct, inadequacies and corruption.

———————

[12] PDHRE: The People's Movement for Human Rights Learning, www.pdhre.org

TWENTY-NINE

WHERE'S YOUR HEAD AT?

As the New Year set in, I knew I had to implement all the things I had been planning. I had to get *Walaahi* written, get my head around the relevant laws (and their sub clauses and amendments!), I had to up my game when it came to calling in clients and find a new way of working out and keeping in shape. I also had to find time in all of this for the boys, John and myself.

Although John was now staying with me, he was distant. There was a space between us that hadn't existed before, and I felt like I was losing him. With so many outside pressures such as work and the court case, I realised I had started to neglect time with him. He was so supportive of what I was doing, and never once moaned about the amount of time I was putting into my business, but I began to realise the amount of time was becoming too much when he started to criticise a lot of what I was doing. I didn't understand it to begin with. I was building this business for us, the boys and to make a positive and powerful impact on the world, to leave a lasting legacy that would positive impact others afters I was gone, especially the generations of my family for years to come. Building my business and writing my books would pay for the boat we had discussed owning between us; would pay for the life we wanted. I began to wonder if he actually wanted that life with me anymore, so as I journaled every day I focused on building my confidence to be able to have the life I wanted with or without him. He either wanted to be with me or he didn't. I had made it very clear to him I wanted him, I just had to get through this court case and get *Walaahi* written and then I could breathe again. I had to win this court case. I had to. There was no way I was going to be found guilty of these charges.

With the timeline to publishing *Walaahi* set, I sat down and wrote it... within a week. I knew what I had to write, and so I sat down and wrote for about ten hours a day, with dog walks and breaks in between. John was sat beside me and would encourage me to have a break and play cards, or watch the series Vikings with him. He would make all our meals and encourage me to stop writing at the end of the day. I felt so supported by him during this week than I had for a long time, but there was still a distance between us; and it was pushing me further and further away. I felt rejected on many levels and I just didn't need this distraction. He kept telling me 'stop putting yourself in that place Dawn, you don't need to go there' but without the closeness or the communication coming from him, I felt my head had nowhere else to go. For me, what he was withholding was fundamental to a relationship, and without, what was the point? My heart felt like it was breaking every day and was causing me a big distraction.

I sent the manuscript off to my publishing consultant Linda, and we prepared the marketing campaign for it. When she told me within less than a week I had made a bestseller list on Amazon I couldn't believe it! I had written a book within a week and within a week it was an international bestseller on three continents! I was over the moon! I was so excited! And I couldn't believe it had happened. I walked around with a stupid grin on my face for days. John was pleased for me, so were the boys.

But when I told a few friends I felt a void of energy develop between us. One of these friends now doesn't have any contact with me, refused to reply to messages and has put a massive distance between us. That hurt. The fact that I had been successful in what I had set out to do had resulted in losing a friendship brought home the fact that those we surround ourselves with has to be a careful choice. Environment really is everything. It made me realise that ego for some, is so much more important than a deep supportive friendship.

I also realised that I had to be careful with who I chose to celebrate and share my future success, and what could possibly turn out to be a lonely road, if I didn't choose carefully from that moment on. When I then chose to have a celebration dinner, at one of my favourite restaurants, and only a handful of people came to celebrate with me, I realised even more who really had my back. It was time to up-level again, this time with those who showed their true support, instead of keeping those in my life to those who simply talked about supporting me. Actions speak louder than words, and sadly a lot of actions didn't back up the words people spoke about. I felt disheartened, but even more determined. If people were going to walk away simply because I was becoming more successful, or because I was going through a difficult time, then they were not my people. I also felt incredibly lonely, and started to isolate myself; staying home, not calling people and refusing to answer the phone. I didn't feel I could trust people anymore. When a few friends who lived nearby called to ask if I wanted to go out, I would stall them and make excuses not to go out. The night of a friends 40th I had a really bad anxiety attack. I didn't want to meet new people. I didn't want to explain the work I did, or tell people I was an author. I also knew I had to get my head into studying the law, but with everything I was learning, I felt like I was drowning.

With so many of the laws we are governed by and expected to live within, with *all* clauses and sub-clauses amended all the time, I didn't know how any of us were not criminals all the time. What was really becoming apparent is that people are simply criminals just by living life to the full, and it was simply a matter of time before we were discovered. It was sickening. It was scary and it made me realise why lawyers all look tired, stressed and ill by their 40s. Just keeping up with the law changes would be stressful enough, let alone working in the dark energy of a courtroom, the modern day equivalent of a medieval marketplace. Police officers, lawyers, the judges, the public in the public gallery, all of them putting judgement on people whom they didn't know, basing what they knew on small snapshots of someone's life, not what had led them to this place. The law professionals know they have the power to destroy innocent people's lives, and yet they still choose to play games with the other lawyers and see who can win... sometimes forgetting they are actually dealing with other people's lives. The more I studied the more I realised the laws were so screwed up[13] and the lawyers had to work within a game of manipulation of words[14]. It was a chess game, and although some lawyers probably go into the profession to help others, I didn't see anyone practicing the law who looked happy. They all looked tired, drained and ill. I had walked away from the IT industry because I just didn't want to keep up with all the changing technology and knowing that by the time the manufacturers had released the products, they were already out of date. It wasn't a healthy industry, but like law, it paid well... but is life simply about living for money?

Part of my research included the books *Learning Legal Rules, PACE (Police And Criminal Evidence), Civil Rights, Police Law, The Criminal Justice Act* as well as going further into The Bangalore Principles, which Scottish 'Justice' is based upon; and refreshing my knowledge on *The Declaration of Human Rights* and how that applied to this case. I was seeing patterns that baffled me, quotes in books that confirmed that lawyers 'can't keep up with the law', 'all areas of law are in a constant state of flux. Innovations in the use of technology, European Legislation and case law demand constant changes' and one of the scariest comments for me was from the Statute law which stated 'Parliament is the most important modern source of law' – oh boy! We're doomed! Unless of course we are welcomed into the fold by the likes of David Cameron, Theresa May and vilify people such as Jeremy Corbyn!

With so many acts of corporate manslaughter covered up and ignored, financially corrupt deals and hidden directorships of certain individuals and their spouses in major organisations, which dumb down and restrict nations from free speech, a right to educate their children in a way they deem fit, medicate themselves (or not) in their own natural way and instigating restriction of movement, failing education and health care systems, how on earth can we trust the government to be the modern source of law? It reminded me of a phrase, 'You are free to do as we tell you' because how are any of us supposed to know how to be law abiding citizens when those who study and practice the law cannot keep up? How are we supposed to understand the delicacies of the law, when someone who studies law, then has to choose a particular subject in law to practice in, but cannot represent someone in a different field of law? For example: If someone chooses to study law, and then chooses criminal law, they are not allowed to represent someone in family law, unless they do a further couple of years in the area of family law. Interesting to know, don't you think? Especially in the case I was now facing. Here was a family issue, that was not being dealt with by the family law courts, even though the police knew of the shared custody, constant harassment and the time wasting of courts time by John's ex, which had now spilled over into a Criminal Law case where I had been physically, verbally, racially and religiously attacked by a group of small minded islanders who had nothing better to do in their lives other than cause upset and misery to others, simply based on the colour of their skin, hair colour and association with another. The more I continued to study the law, the more the Linkin Park sound 'Guilty by Association' came into my head. I found myself listening to this sound, and the album over and over again. I was guilty of whatever the police and courts deemed me to be guilty of simply because I was seen as a middle class, English woman who had betrayed the English by having children with someone of a different ethnicity, demonised by the western governments and media channels (to suit various agendas) and who the islanders didn't want on their island. Looking at the figures on the document 'Tiree Profile[15]' I became even more aware of why we had suffered the racism we had.

•On page 2 of the 'Tiree Profile 2014', under 'Headline Findings', it states the total population of Tiree is only 653 in 2011, with only 316 households being occupied, with 16.1% of the homes on the islands being second residences and holiday homes

This statement itself further backed up my observation that those who have colluded together to bring these charges against me, feel threatened by an outsider coming to the island and purchasing property, taking it away an opportunity for the younger generation to own, or rent, their own home on the island.

•With 57.9% of the Tiree population aged over 45 years, 13.9% being under the age of 14

When I came across these figures I was left wondering why PC Steph Tanner took three days to take statements from those involved in this case, as it is unlikely that there is a huge amount of work to do on the island that took his attention elsewhere; thus giving those who have produced 'witness' statements time to collude and create a fabricated story. It also gave him time to bring up my previously admonished conviction, and use that to slander and create bias when approaching the Procurator Fiscal.

When I looked at the employment figure in the blue collar sector, as opposed to the white/pink collar sectors, it is also safe to assume that there is an element of resentment, which is a well-known factor in most community and organisational challenges that arise; very much akin to the North/South Divide. This can be further identified by the lack of qualifications gained by those on the island

•49.1% have lower than a higher grade of education, and only a further 15.9% of the island have a higher grade at GCSE/SVQ

A key indicator in people's behaviour and their mindset towards people of my standing in the community and those of different backgrounds.

•With 99.4% of people on Tiree being 'white' and 85.8% of those being 'white Scottish', and only 2.1% of those on Tiree being born outside of the UK

This goes a long way to back up my statement that there was a level of racism involved, even though unbeknown to those attacking me, my grandfather on the maternal side is Scottish. Not that it would have mattered in this case. I was a mother of 'Paki's' and a threat to their lifestyles, more so than ever as I was in a relationship with John; and how dare the pair of us think we could bring 'Paki's' into their family or neighbourhood community? Reading these statistics and thinking back to the quote 'Legal reasoning is an exercise in constructive interpretation' made by Ronald Dworkin, Oxford Jurist and Legal Philosopher, I felt somewhat encouraged; because if they can use legal reasoning in constructive interpretation, then so could I... and the lawyer that would eventually represent me. I had zero faith in the new lawyer David at Beltrami had sent my way due to the lack of communication and delivery on the actions they said they would deliver on. I made another call to them and left a message with reception again. Would I get a response this time? Only time would tell.

I was taking a break one day and decided to check in on some of my friends on Facebook, as well as access one of the training videos in one of the many groups created by Regan.

Within the first few seconds I noticed a video being shared by *The Guardian*, featuring Libby Liburd, the powerhouse of a lady whose words you read at the start of this book. Her video was powerful. What she had to say about the views of single mums from the wider society REALLY resonated with me. So I contacted her, I just had to acknowledge her and thank her; I asked if she was up for meeting for a coffee, I wanted to give her a big hug on behalf of all the single mums out there, learn more about her journey as a single mum and just spend time over coffee with this incredible woman. To receive a response so quickly and positively from her was great, and we arranged to hook up in London, on my way to Norway.

I would stop with Rob and his family, before making my way into London to meet Libby; then it was on a plane to Norway for the Ignite Your Inner Game Changer dinner which I was hosting with my friend Tonje[16]. We had already started running the five-day Ignite Your Inner Game Changer Challenge and had our own online community who were taking part. The results many were having were incredible, others were simply just not showing up, as is the case with so many coaching and personal development events (and gym memberships!). You have people that play full out, will do whatever it takes to create the results in their lives, and then you have the others that dip their toe in the water, join the course or the workshop and don't do all that is asked of them (with a large percentage of these people blaming the coach/trainer/the world for their lack of success in life). Being one of the ones that took action, and daily repeated actions at that, I was in a space where sometimes I couldn't believe the breakthroughs I was having. Realising so much about myself and what was holding me back was incredible. The weight upon my shoulders was lifting, and I was having increased amounts of energy. I felt so alive! So limitless, even the negativity of studying the law was taking on a whole new premise for me. The only downside to doing this work was I was able to see so much more of the bullshit and toxicity others had going on within them; and in some ways I was grateful as it showed me more about myself that needed working on. I had learnt about mirroring years ago whilst at a NLP business event, but now mirroring was taking on a whole new meaning. Those issues and things that were showing up in other's lives were an opportunity to dive deeper into my own stuff.

When I had been catching up with an old friend about what we were up to these days, I happened to mention all this work I had been doing on myself. She told me that I had to stop because I was making myself wrong in so many ways. "Other people have the issues Dawn, not you. FFS! I have known you 20 years and you are one of the most successful, honest and loving people I know. Everything you set out to do, you achieve. You have the biggest heart, and I think you have taken this whole Scotland Saga too deep within you. They have made you paranoid. Stop doing this to yourself." I was taken aback. Not just because of the praise, but because I didn't believe I was being paranoid. I honestly believed I was simply clearing stuff that had been held deep in my subconscious and had been limiting me. With her next comment, a truth came out "And if you don't think you are successful enough, or achieving enough, you must think I am a complete waster."

I knew in that moment, her view on the work I was doing was less about me, and all about her; and her own feelings of lack. When I said this to her, she just looked at me as if I'd smacked her in the face, and then something shifted in her, and I saw her sob her heart out. What she said to me next will always remain between the two of us, but just know that her whole life has changed and she is now going after her ultimate dream, something that is such a polar opposite to her office life she had been living. I am so proud of the way she has taken herself on, faced demons of her past and made a lot of changes to the way she was living her life. To see people get what is possible for them is such a buzz for me. To see them go after AND achieve their dreams really does give me the warm fuzzies, and makes me smile from deep within my soul. I want everyone to be happy and living a life they love, and as I said to my mum when I lived in Egypt, "If I want my human rights recognised, I have to help others get theirs recognised." The same goes for my success. Helping myself to become successful is one thing, but helping others do the same, well that is just the best way to do things... surely? It's like all these laws I was studying, they all seemed to be put in place to control and monitor the behaviours of others, just because one person or a small percentage of people have done something stupid or evil, we are all held to account and held back. How about we start lifting each other, educating each other, raising the vibration of the planet instead of holding ourselves and others back?

With my trip to Norway coming up any day, Naasir noticed I had been saying, "I'm going back to Norway".

He'd pull me up saying, "Mummy you have never been to Norway."

"No, I haven't, not in this lifetime," I'd reply with a little wink and a smile. I knew I had Viking in me, I'd grown up in East Anglia where the Vikings had settled centuries before. Being in Norway was incredible. Getting up at 5am to go for a swim, journaling, co-creating, making plans for the future, coaching each other and developing a friendship that I know will last a lifetime with Tonje. She's such a powerful and incredible woman who is transforming the corporate world one client, one university lecture and podcast at a time. If anyone can rid the corporate world of the poor mental health and stress jealousy it's Tonje.

Playing in the snow with her daughters, going for morning walks in the fresh snow, and taking a break from the legal study was just what I needed. I returned home in such a zen space everyone noticed. It lasted about a month, and I can tell you that dropping off my inner Viking back home in Norway, I have been a lot more relaxed and have had less angst residing within me.

I returned to the law study and working on my business with renewed vigour and a new mental space. I also continued working on this book. Reading through what I had already written was interesting. I noticed the different flow, the way in which I had grown and how much had shifted; but I also knew I had a way to go until this journey was over. I still hadn't heard back from the lawyers and so I started looking at how to represent myself. What did I need to focus on? What were the rules of the courtroom? What evidence would I need to gather? I knew I was good at debating, but being new to a game of manipulation, especially with a system that was already showing great incompetence, I had to prepare myself. John was supporting me in so many ways, everyone was, but there was still a distance between us. I kept pushing it to the side, and hoping it would all go away once the court case was over. I wasn't going to allow them to destroy us, and I wasn't going to allow my own insecurities to destroy us. I knew I had to dive deep into it; look at what was really triggering me. Why was I feeling the way I was feeling?

Eleanor Roosevelt once said, "No one can make you feel inferior without your permission," and I know there was a lot of truth in that. I just had look into my mirror and face my own triggers, own them, work through them and release them. Everything started and ended with me. I had the power to do everything I truly desired, have everything I truly wanted, I just had to get out of my head and go with the flow, being in action every day, but the right action. It was time to go deeper within.

---

[13] "The flexibility of words affords a danger to logic as well as an effective aid to explanation" Rt Hon Lord Templeman, MBE, Lord of Appeal in Ordinary

[14] "The lawyer is a manipulator of words" Rt Hon Lord Templeman, MBE, Lord of Appeal in Ordinary

[15] www.tireetrust.org.uk/uploads/2016

[16] *Ignite Your Inner Game Changer* is also the name of Tonje's book and can be found on Amazon.com. Tonje's full name is Tonje Elisabeth Aaroe.

THIRTY

LIFE IN CHAINS

Being sat at the laptop writing, studying and working on my business I was in desperate need of a workout. With the gym a 45-minute walk away, and an hour's bus ride away, I used the time wisely. I would either take the time to just clear my head walking, or use the bus rides to read books and journal. Being able to also observe human behaviour and connect with random people on the bus and at the bus stop provided some very amusing moments and some really delightful conversations.

One of the things I'd noticed in some of the groups I had started to belong to was the ever growing arrogance of, "Oh no! I had to engage with 'normal' people today!" and "Ugh! I had to go on the train and travel economy!" It was something that left a bad taste in my mouth and made me leave a lot of the 'high vibrational' groups I'd joined. Looking down upon people just because they were not 'enlightened', not wanting to make millions, or because they were not badass enough really was ugly in my opinion. We're all in different places in our lives, and yes, I agree the environments we choose to be in, and the people we surround ourselves with are important, but dismissing people who are not yet in the space we are in doesn't give 'spiritual unicorns' an excuse for being arrogant and dismissive.

I have always told my boys, "It isn't how big your wallet or your home is that matters, it is how big your heart is," and even though I wish to make a lot of money, it is what I do with that money that will determine whether I am a good person or not. Money doesn't make you a better person unless you do great things with it, and using it as a weapon to belittle others in an attempt to elevate yourself just feels very dirty to me; especially when we have no idea about how far others have travelled and where they may have fallen from, or the journey they have been given to teach others. One of the things I have taken with me from my life as a Muslim is this, "Always think of seven excuses, and if you can think of seven, think of ten, then another seven if someone does wrong by you, and others." (And no that isn't an excuse for some of the atrocities we see happening in the world, just a way of always trying to see things from another's point of view).

My gym sessions were just what I needed. Pushing through the weights, the reps and then getting in the pool and smashing out a mile, or simply getting into the pool and swimming until I couldn't swim anymore, most of the time smashing through two miles. It cleared my mind, made me realise just how strong I was physically and mentally. I also enjoyed the Hydro Power classes – the swimmers equivalent of bootcamp, just in the water... oh it was the highlight of my week; especially as I really did miss the bootcamp and MMA sessions. Being asked to leave had impacted me in more ways than I had realised, but I wasn't about to dim my light just because other women were intimidated by it. That was stuff they had to work through, not me. I was too busy working out my own stuff; and calling in my clients.

Calling in my clients was proving tough as I was dealing with so much of my own emotional stuff surrounding the court case, and the distraction of not hearing from John as much, believing that he was losing interest in me, that the universe was simply telling me to heal myself first before attempting to coach others. With the debt from the first court case expenses hanging over my head, and the payments due to my own coaches and mentors, agreements I had entered into before this secondary case came up, I was eager to make some money. I knew I had it within me to make a vast amount of money, had the skills, knowledge and experience to elevate myself and others. I just had to keep persevering and believing in myself.

I'd received the date for the court case, and had started looking up travel costs and accommodation costs. The entire two day trip would cost me approximately £380, including basic food, just to Oban. I had travelled to Norway and back and stayed a week for only £45 plus the costs of my meals. It was absurd. I called David at Beltrami and had told him that David at McCusker, McEllroy & Co was still not returning my calls and did he know of anyone else who would be able to represent me. I informed him of the ridiculously high cost to get to Scotland and how having looked into representing myself wasn't really an option. Would he be able to get the date changed for me? When he said no, he couldn't help me any further, that I should try and speak with the other David again, and that I really didn't have any option, I had to go to court on that date otherwise I would face a warrant being issued for my arrest, I told him I just couldn't go. It wasn't right for them to simply demand I go on a date that didn't give me enough time to generate the costs to pay for the expense of getting to Scotland, and to go without having time to build a case with a solicitor. So I called David at McCusker's again, and this time David was available. He informed me that as I hadn't filled in the legal aid forms yet, this is why he had not been returning my calls. When I informed him I hadn't received them, he reiterated that unless I filled them in, he wouldn't represent me. And that I had to go to court otherwise risk a warrant for my arrest being issued.

Now bear in mind, I have been working in the private sector for 20 years. If someone cannot make a meeting, it is quite easy for the meeting to be re-arranged. All I wanted was for one of these lawyers to arrange an alternative date, whilst forms were filled in and I had been able to generate the additional cash to cover this two day trip, and arrange childcare and someone to look after Kelt. I knew I could do it, but just wasn't confident in representing myself. Who would be when a 13 year-old child was making false allegations of assault against them? Especially when the same Police Force and Justice system had already tried to screw me over the year before, and had done zero investigation into this case thus far. How could I trust them? I couldn't. I had zero faith in the Scottish system, from the Police, to the lawyers and the Courts. I phoned the court myself and told them the situation and spoke with one of the ladies in the court admin office. She advised me that she would speak with someone and that someone would call me back. So yet again I waited, and waited, and waited. I didn't hear anything further, not by letter, phone or email. So I just carried on with my work, I called in a new client and put the money aside for the new court date. Then I got another client in, and put that money aside for the court date. Whilst I was doing this, I was also paying off some of the bills that were outstanding and making headway. It was the boost I needed, and it gave me enough cash to finally treat the boys and I to another meal out, so we headed to Gigi's for Italian.

One night I was having a bath and the boys had gone to ramO's for the night. I had been in the bath for about 20 minutes, was singing away when Kelt and my new dog Chewy, a rescue dog who was going to be abandoned, started barking. I told them to be quiet when I saw someone moving around by the front door in a high vis jacket. I got out of the bath and asked who it was. When they replied it was South Yorkshire Police and they had a warrant for my arrest, I told them to give me a couple of minutes whilst I got dressed. I also messaged John and told him the police had arrived with a warrant for my arrest and put a status update on Facebook to a select few friends who knew what was happening, just in case things went south and I needed the boys and the dogs taking care of.

I answered the door and let them in and made them a cup of tea. They explained why they were there, and then asked me to explain why I had not turned up in court. When I explained to them what had happened, and that I was still waiting for the lady in the court and someone else to call me back with a new date, and then explained the full situation to them, they were confused as to why this was even being dealt with by the courts. I then went on to ask them if they were really going to take me all the way up to Scotland on a Friday night, in the back of their car – in handcuffs, to put me in a police cell until Tuesday as Monday was a bank holiday; and that was if I would be seen in court on the Tuesday! Tuesday would have been the earliest so that would mean at least three and a half days in a police cell in Scotland awaiting a trial date. The senior officer immediately got on his radio and explained the situation to his superior at the station. He then returned to me and said they were walking away from this case. It was ridiculous what was happening and they were returning the warrant to Scotland. During this time I had received a call from a friend at Nick Clegg's office, and she had asked me how things were going. I gave her a full update in front of the police officer who was still sat at my dining room table. She wished me well with my book and told me to ensure I called her if there was anything I needed, and to make sure Nick got a copy of my book. How opportune that that call should come in whilst the police were there!

My friend Leanne arrived at the back door having seen the status update, bottle of wine in hand and my friend Amity had called from France. I let Leanne in through the back door and the police officers looked at each other, told me to take care and hoped I would get all of this nasty mess sorted out. Thank goodness for South Yorkshire Police having some humanity about them and being able to see the bigger picture. I felt blessed to have had such a positive interaction with them and for them to realise the ridiculousness about it all.

As soon as they were gone Leanne handed me a glass of wine and told me that she was relieved to see me still there. She told me the police car was parked right up against the front door as if to stop me making a run for it. I understood that, because I am sure the police have had many runners when they have gone to someone's home with an arrest warrant. One of the things I have always maintained throughout all of this ugly Scotland Saga is the fact that I understand the police are doing their job, and that they must come across some really nasty, really violence people, and parents who neglect and abuse their children. I understand them wanting to press charges against people who have done wrong, but as they have failed to do any police investigation, even on the most basic of levels, they have completely messed up in both cases. In the first case they changed their story four times to get a conviction, and then went even further to say my children were too articulate and well spoken. They have done their utmost to cover their own mistakes, instead of just owning them and apologising. In this case, PC Steph Tanner knew of the hassles John's ex-partner has caused him, knows it is a closed racist community, and failed to come and talk with John and I whilst we were on the island. Had he of done this, then he would have realised the lies and the pack mentality of the close knit community – but then again he has to live on the island and drink in the same pub as the locals so why would he upset his life on the island when he can easily create false charges with them to get one over on someone who has made something of himself and left the island? Self-preservation if ever there was a case for it.

I hadn't realised how much I was shaking until Leanne pointed it out, and I realised that my legs had gone to jelly. I was really shaken up about the fact the police had come over to arrest me, and even though I was being brave about it, I was still badly shaken up. If the date could not have been changed, then why did the lady in the Oban Sheriff's office call or write back to me to explain this, instead of issuing the warrant? She had seemed very understanding on the phone, and had said someone would get back to me, either her or the duty solicitor. Neither had, and had obviously not checked with each other to make sure one or the other had done what was needed. I actually began to wonder if people actually cared about the impact their work has on others, apparently not. So long as they get their pay check at the end of the month, and get to pay their bills and live their life, then why would they? Until they themselves, or someone they love and care about ends up being on the receiving end of the work they do; but then again people go around thinking this kind of thing would never happen to them. A very naïve mentality if ever there was one. No one is immune... well the McCann's obviously are, they've made millions from their daughter's death, and got away with murder some would say.

And here's the thing, I would never have left my boys for longer than it would take me to have a shower when we were camping, I would never have left them in a place I considered to be dangerous, I certainly would never have left three children under the age of five years old alone together in a hotel room to go and have dinner for several hours, AND there would be no way I would have hit John's daughter. The fact that I physically threw up at the thought of doing to a child what I was being accused of, and with over 30 character references from colleagues and friends, many who worked in child protection in one way or another, or had trusted me to take care of their children on a regular basis, the police should have had the common sense to drop the cases. They should have realised I was not the person I was being made out to be by incompetence police officers and judges as well as a group of racist, ignorant and bitter members of a family who couldn't move on from the past. The mother of John's child should have realised that carrying on with her anger towards John, and making him out to be a bad father, was doing her daughter more harm than good; but there are a lot of things in the world that 'should' be different, and we can't live our lives with the 'shoulda, woulda, coulda' mentality. We just have to deal with what is thrown at us, learn to dodge it or grow from it. I was choosing to grow, but that didn't stop me from being shaken up by the visit from South Yorkshire Police. It didn't stop me from being afraid of the outcome; it also didn't stop me from going public with what was happening to me on my list of Facebook friends. I had to make it public. I had to rally more support for what I was going through and ultimately raise awareness so others didn't fall foul of the law in the same way I had done.

The support I received from across the world from friends and business colleagues was at first surprising. I was slightly worried that I would come up against some of the nasty trolls that hide behind their computers screens for bravery, as Libby had experienced. I was also worried that the bubble wrap brigade of parents would rise up and condemn me, but I needn't have worried. The support I received was incredible. Each and every parent I knew, across the world informed me they too had left their children for similar amounts of times either in the park, or the car when nipping to get some shopping, or running back into the house, school or office to grab something they had forgotten. And as for me being charged with assaulting a child, and defending myself from the guys who had attacked me, men and women couldn't believe it. Many men were shocked that the men had attacked me in the first place, and then worried about what message that would be giving out to other men who were violent, and to the younger generations of males. Did this mean that any man could go ahead and attack a woman and if she fought back they could have her charged with assault? What if they raped her and she fought back? What then? Women were equally concerned, if not more so. I had some friends provide me with cash to help pay for the legal fees, some as donations and some as loans. Friends were sharing with me links to press organisations who would be interested in the book as soon as it was ready and others who worked in the legal industry referred colleagues to me and sent me a whole heap of legal cases that had helped in similar cases from around the world. Two very dear friends told me to share the email address of the Sheriff courts so friends from around the world could send character references and emails to the court in support of me.

I never heard back from John the night the police came, and although I could tell he had seen the message I had sent him on Facebook Messenger, he never called. I was hurting badly, dealing with the toxicity of his ex, the stuff he had left behind, which was now interrupting my life, and he was nowhere to be seen or heard, unless of course you could see the photos and interactions he was having with everyone but me on his Facebook profile.

He called the afternoon after the police had arrived and I told him I wasn't happy with him ignoring me, and putting me so far down his list of priorities. I was his partner and in my book that meant I came second to him, not his friends, not his job, and certainly not random people who he chose to go and get drunk with in the pub on his nights off from working on the boat. He had a choice, start putting me first and responding to messages and calls or we were over. His silence was unbearable. I said nothing, and then after a few moments he came back and said he didn't have a list of priorities, but of course he loved me and was there for me. I told him his actions said otherwise, and that he had hurt me badly. Things had to change, and then he said he was going to see if he could get a weekend off soon to come and see me. Part of me didn't believe him, especially as I could see he had been having so much fun with all the other crew members. I knew my insecurities of being cheated on again were high, and seeing the women who were on board with him, I felt as though I was losing him. As I had before he left. He'd spent so much time down the allotment with Chris that I had started to resent the fact I had introduced them. The first thing he would do in the morning was check Facebook, and when Chris messaged him to say he was on his way, he'd jump out of bed and be out the door without so much as a morning kiss. He'd return home and get straight in the bath, then spent time in my room alone watching movies. I knew he was processing what was happening; but as the weeks ticked by, contact with John became few and far between.

The weekend before I headed to Glastonbury with my friend EJ we were supposed to meet up, but he'd arrived at the harbour in London and gone to the pub with the crew without calling me to let me know he was back on land, lost his phone and yet again I was so far down the list of his priorities I broke down in tears at my mum's. How could I be with someone who preferred drinking to being with me? How could I trust him? I couldn't. I knew I had to end it, but I couldn't. I knew too much about him, I knew he was in a lot of pain. I knew how much he loved his daughter, and I knew how much his friends meant to him; I just wanted to mean as much to him as they did, more so in fact.

As the weeks went by I sent fewer messages, which also went unanswered, as did phone calls. He blanked me in so many ways I just assumed he had met someone else and didn't have the courage to tell me. I ploughed on by myself. Did what I needed to do and stopped messaging him altogether. I wasn't prepared to chase him anymore. I'd sent him messages asking him to call, and he didn't, and as they say, actions speak louder than words. His silence was all I needed to know he didn't want to be in my life. I was to fight the court case by myself and not count on him for support. I also realised that if I couldn't count on him to have my back through this, I couldn't count on him to have my back at sea. I still loved him deeply, but I loved myself more. I just didn't want to end it by text message, email or a voicemail, so I just resigned myself to the fact I was moving on without him. I stopped following him on Facebook; I just couldn't bear to see him so happy and having fun without me, especially with one particular woman on the boat who was always beside him or opposite him in the photos. I had to listen to my gut instinct. I had to protect myself; and my boys.

Then one day, he called me when I was down in London at a business event. He asked me where I was and when I would be home. I asked him why. He said he was coming home to see me. I knew this would be my opportunity to end it, but I was excited to see him, really excited to see him. I couldn't wait to get home to him.

I arrived late due to bus connection issues and when I arrived, there his was asleep in our bed. He looked so peaceful, and as I climbed into bed, I gave him a kiss goodnight and rolled over to go to sleep. He pulled me close, wrapping his arms around me and told me he had missed me, and that he loved me. Tears silently rolled down my face; I knew I wasn't going to end it. I knew we both had so much to deal with, and he was dealing with something much bigger than me. He was dealing with his relationship with his daughter. I couldn't imagine what he must have been going through. I had wanted to know if there was still that connection between us, and there was; a very powerful connection. The next day we went to the allotment together, he met up with Chris and Rob, and I saw something between them I hadn't seen before. I saw a brotherly love between them; and I understood for the first time why he had spent so much time with them. I understood their friendship in a whole new way. Knowing what I knew about John, I knew instantly why he had behaved in the way he had before he had left. Any jealousy I'd had, slipped away in a moment and I was just incredibly happy for John, because I knew what this friendship meant to him. I started to journal around all the other feelings I had had with regards to our relationship. I explored them further with my friend EJ, the one I had been to Glastonbury with. She had given me some incredible insights into relationships and healing. We had enjoyed energy healing and meditations, we discussed out businesses and how we wanted to grow them. EJ is a relationship coach and works on a deep soul level with sexual healing[17] and spending time with her just as friends was such a powerful experience. I knew that once I had got my finances sorted with regards to this court case, I would be going on one of her retreats; and one of the soul remembrance retreats with Regan and her partner Juan Pa. I just had to clear off other payments and investments first.

John coming home for a week was just what we needed. I understood his silence, I understood to a certain degree what he had been learning and dealing with, and how being distracted with my stuff would have been too much for him. I understood his man cave behaviour. Yes it hurt when he told me, "You deal with things your way, and I'll deal with things my way," but I also knew we were dealing with very different elements of the same situation. I wanted us to both support each other; I mean what is the point of being in a relationship with each other if you do not have each other's back during the bad times. I knew I needed to be strong for myself, not rely on him for his strength. This was my fight. This was my calling, and this was happening FOR me. With him being there and being the one to rescue me and prop me up, I would have never become strong by myself. I would never have been able to resolve the issues that were going on deep inside me. Although I hated the way he had done it, I also loved him for it. It didn't stop it from hurting deeply, and feeling as though he was just using me as a place to stay when he wasn't on the ship. But when he said, "It was great to be home," I was torn into pieces... was he just saying it? Did he feel like it was home? If so, then why didn't he do the jobs around the home when he came back? Why had he stepped back from me and the boys? I kept thinking back to the book *The Queen's Code*, a book recommended by EJ... there was a good reason he was doing this. I had to believe this... I had to believe there was a good reason for his behaviour, otherwise he was a massive asshole and I was better off without him; but every time I journaled, and thought about what he was going through, I found peace. But then I would think about how our relationship had changed since he had stayed with Sam in London ... then how he had supported me with writing my second book *Walaahi*... and how I had neglected him in so many ways when he had chosen to come back to see me, instead of going back to Tiree... the insecure part of me thought it was a cost saving exercise, that maybe he was just using me; but then I knew when he looked at me, he loved me. You couldn't fake that look in his eye, I just wished he would let me in. Drop some of those barriers he had built up... but I knew it would take much longer than the time we'd had together.

In August 2016 I finally received the court summons for the arrest for not showing up in court; four months after South Yorkshire Police had come by to arrest me and take me to Scotland. Would I have been sat in a police cell all this time had they have taken me up there that night? Who knows? As I had been putting money aside to make my way up to Scotland, I booked all transport and accommodation for the three days I would need to be away. It took me over 12 hours on the train to get to Oban from Sheffield, and another 12 hours back again. The train connections meant I would need to catch the 12:11 train from Oban to Glasgow, and I couldn't guarantee I would be out of court in time, so I had to book two night's accommodation and arrange for the boys to be with ramO for three days, and have the dogs. During the train journeys I did my best to focus on my business development and marketing; I even tried to write this book, but I just could not focus. This was ridiculous. Why could they just not change the date to one that had given me more time to sort out a lawyer? Were they setting me (and many others) up to fail? Or was it just another way of asserting their authority (and bully boy tactics) over us all?

I was also very apprehensive about the group of people who had attacked John and I in Tiree attacking me again in Oban. Apparently it wasn't unusual for people from the islands to go over to Oban for the day. I wouldn't even recognise them even if saw them; so how would I be able to defend myself? With the worry of what was to happen in the courtroom, and the worry of another attack, I could feel myself getting really anxious. I practiced some breathing techniques that John had taught me, but with the level of stress rising in my body I couldn't relax. I started shaking and my chest started hurting. I then started feeling a cold sweat coming over me. I needed to get to the accommodation and quickly. I wanted to get off the streets of Oban, but first I needed to meet with the lady I was staying with and get something to eat. I had remembered a place John, the boys and I had eaten when we had left Tiree the year before the attack happened, the first year we had got together, so I had arranged to meet her there. I headed into Cuan Mor and ordered my dinner and a glass of wine. We were sat at the back of the restaurant looking out into the open space, just so no one could approach me from behind. I realised I was fighting tears falling from my eyes because I realised how afraid I was, I couldn't let on. I hadn't even been this afraid living in Egypt during the Uprising! My mental state was not a good one, and it wasn't about to get any better either. I had to leave the restaurant and walk to the place I was staying. I didn't want to waste money on a taxi, but equally I didn't want to walk, so my host and I headed straight to the taxi rank by the ferry terminal.

The memories of what had happened just over a year ago came flooding back, and that's when I realised this case had been going on a year. There was an older guy stood waiting at the taxi rank and he saw that I was anxious and offered me a cigarette. I hadn't smoked for a very long time, but that night I accepted the cigarette and thanked him. He asked me if I was okay and if he could do anything to help. He could see that I was looking around me at every young man's face and asked if someone had hurt me. When I released a nervous giggle he said, "Right okay, well you get into the first taxi that comes, I can wait a little longer."

I looked at him and he reminded me of the really lovely people that had helped the boys and I on our first trip to Scotland before the whole Scotland Saga had started. If only the officers involved in this whole ugly mess, the judges and the lawyers were as nice as the people on the streets and trains I had met.

I thanked him and just as I put the cigarette out, a taxi pulled up, we got in and headed back to her home. My host had told me she had taken the day off work the following day to come with me, and I was so surprised, as well as really grateful.

I settled in for the night and fell asleep. It had been a long day, and I was absolutely shattered. Little did I know just how tired I was going to be once this whole Scotland Saga was over.

---

17 EJ Love – www.ejlove.com Sexual Healing and Relationship Coach, Author and International Speaker

THIRTY-ONE

MEETING MR TOM

I arrived at the courtroom the following day with my host, and after about 20 minutes realised there was no one there to represent me... as I had been told there was going to be by David at McCusker, McEllory & Co. I had spoken with him maybe a week before the court date and he told me that he would be there, informing me that although I still had not received the paperwork for legal aid, he would meet me in the foyer of the court and we would go through it and fill it in there. My host told me to ring the lawyer's office. There was no answer. So I asked the lady in the admin office. She said she would ask the duty solicitor to speak with me, at which point I remembered the last time a lady from the courts had told me the same thing. I didn't feel hopeful. Whilst I was waiting for the duty solicitor to speak with me, I called the offices of McCusker McEllory and Co again and got through to one of the ladies who worked there. When I explained who I was, and where I was, she told me that they were not representing me and so no one was going to attend. I was shocked; and frightened.

When I asked her what she meant by they were not sending anyone, and that I had arranged to meet David to sort out the legal aid paperwork, she told me that she would ask him to call me. I told her that I found this whole situation unprofessional and that they had left me in a vulnerable position. I informed her David knew I was travelling up to Scotland, from Sheffield in England, to deal with this, and leaving me in a position of believing I was going to be represented, was really not acceptable. I asked her how they could do that to someone. She told me that I was being aggressive and said she was hanging up. I asked her how am I being aggressive?

The lady who was hosting me and the court clerk looked at me with confusion on their faces. When I realised the woman at the lawyers had hung up on me, my legs went to jelly and tears burnt my eyes. I had travelled all this way, and had no legal representation. That was not just rubbish on so many levels, it was incredibly disrespectful and dismissive of human ethics and morals. The court clerk took me into the witness room to the left of the stairway and said she would be right back with a cup of tea, and not to worry. Everything would be alright, and not to listen to that woman as I had not been in the slightest bit aggressive. My host and I were seated in the witness room in total disbelief. How could they have done this? It was so unprofessional! Did lawyers lose their humanity for the sake of money? Had they lost touch with their human side? How could David have allowed me to travel up to Scotland knowing I wouldn't have any representation, especially after the last court date and me being fearful of not being represented?

After a few moments the court clerk came in and with her was the duty solicitor. I explained to him what had happened and he didn't look in the least bit surprised. He then told me what would happen and how I would more than likely just be given another trial date and everything would be fine. Fine! How could everything be fine? Such a relative word. How was anything that had happened in the last two years fine? Talk about lawyers being manipulators of words!

During the court session I was told that I was wasting the courts time, money and resources by refusing to come the last time; I nearly laughed out loud. Me wasting courts time, money and resources? Surely the judge should be looking at the men in their black gowns in front of him and the ones wearing the police uniforms before casting aspersions on me! I wasn't given the opportunity to explain myself, nor was I given a choice of dates to return for the next stage of the trial. I was just ordered to return, and given a warning that if I didn't return on the next date I would be arrested without warning and charged with obstruction of justice and wasting court time. I was shocked (again!) and in total disbelief. Again I nearly laughed at the absurdity of it all. Someone really should hold up a mirror to those within the system, instead of them throwing around ill-informed judgements on members of the public who they knew nothing about. I was told to leave the courtroom. My host asked me what I wanted to do for the rest of the day. I felt too sick in the stomach to eat, but I needed to eat. I wanted to walk along the beach, but again I didn't want to be alone in case the 'Tiree Thugs' were in town. We headed back to her home and spent the afternoon going through what had happened, and then I journaled. I journaled like my life depended on it, because I realised after what had happened today, it did. I journaled about the kind of lawyer I wanted to represent me just like the only female lawyer I had seen in the courtroom. She was REALLY on the ball. She didn't falter, stumble and she knew her cases inside and out, unlike the male lawyers who didn't even seem to be able to string a sentence together, let alone represent someone with belief and conviction. I wanted her to represent me. I also liked her boots, and the way she styled herself, even under the black lawyer's gown; shallow things to notice for some people, but it showed me that she had not yet conformed to the system. She was decisive, assertive and confident in everything she said. She instilled faith in me and I wasn't even her client. She also had more positive outcomes for those she represented than any other lawyer that I witnessed during the time I was in the courtroom. She spoke with her clients kindly, as humans, regardless of what they were on trial for, and other than being a lawyer, she seemed like my kind of woman.

For the rest of the evening, I went through the business ideas of my host, and the ideas she had for her books; staying with her was done in exchange for a coaching session, something I didn't mind doing. If she was kind enough to open her home to me and invite me to stay, then I would be kind enough to repay the favour; even though this is not something I do any more, at the time it was a good exchange.

The next day I headed into town to catch the train back to Sheffield. I was still very nervous walking through Oban town centre, but I held my head high and knew that it didn't matter what happened in this whole stupid Scotland Saga, that I had done nothing wrong, and the way I was being treated by the police, Scottish Judges and layers, said more about them than it did about me.

Whilst on board the train, I stared out of the window, replaying everything over and over in my mind 'wasting courts time', 'lack of police investigation', 'guilty before even being questioned', and 'lack of professionalism by all three sectors of the police and so-called justice system'. There was no way I was going to give up without a fight. I had lived my entire life as someone who had always been there to support and encourage others. I had always been on the right side of the law. I had support, motivated and encouraged so many people to always do the right thing... and here I was met with a section of society that just seemed to feast off causing other people problems and hardship without even giving a second thought to the repercussions of their actions. I had met some unsavoury characters during my life, but these people in Scotland that I was having to deal with, they didn't just take the biscuit... they took the whole bloody packet!

Whilst sat on the train from Glasgow to Manchester, I called my mum to let her know what had happened. I didn't call John. If he wanted to know what had happened, he would call me. I had to focus on myself and the boys. I had to keep rising in my own power. My mum was not impressed with everything that had been said to me, nor was my dad, and for my dad to say something, you know he was not impressed. I then called my friend Rob, Tina and then a few other friends. Arriving back in Sheffield at almost midnight, I fell into bed completely exhausted. It wasn't just the emotional or the mental drain, it was the physical drain. Now some people may not understand that, especially as I had been sat on trains for the last 12 hours, but bear in mind I am an active person. I swim, I do weights, I run and I hike. I also walk at least 10 kilometres every day with my dogs, so to be sat still for 12 hours on trains, not good. Not good at all.. This court case was having a massive drain on me in so many ways; and the following day when I booked all the trains back to Oban for the next court date, I had to tap into some of the limited savings I had put aside to do something fun with the boys. I was gutted. Little did I know that with each and every trip up to Scotland, I would be £350 on average, down each month – just to prove I was innocent.

Having booked the train tickets over breakfast, I knew I needed to clear my mind, so I walked the dogs and then got my swim gear ready and walked to the gym. I needed the three mile walk there; it was a great warm up. I swam my two miles and as I was getting out of the pool, there was a gentleman who was getting into the pool as I was getting out. We made small talk and I found out his name was Tom, and he was from Liverpool. When he learnt I was an author, he asked me what I wrote about. I gave him a brief synopsis but didn't tell him the next book would involve this court case or the one before it.... until he looked at me and asked, "And what do you know about all that?"

He had one of those looks on his face that said he knew more about what I was writing about then I could possibly ever know; so I replied honestly. Within a moment of hearing the words come out of my mouth, he told me to meet him in the café as soon as I was done in the sauna. He was going to do his water workout and then he was going to give me insights I needed. He had a steely determination on his face and a look in his eye that told me he meant business; so I went for my sauna, closed my eyes and just lay there. I was so tired I nearly fell asleep and if I hadn't felt myself drifting off, I would have probably slept there for hours, or at least until someone had found me. I realised the eye timer had done it's 15 minutes and so I got up, headed for the showers and just allowed the water to run over me. Man I loved the water. I knew time was ticking by and I had to meet Tom, but the water was so good. I had to drag myself from the water, and as I walked into the café area, there was Tom with a cappuccino waiting for me, "I didn't know what to get you so I went with the most middle class author drink I could think of." He was a cheeky one!

We sat over coffee and he asked me question after question, getting angrier with every answer I gave him. I had to stop the questions to ask, "Why are you asking me all these questions, and why are you getting to angry?" It turned out that Tom had been a social worker for the past 40 years, and worked in the department liaising directly with the emergency services and foster care, handing out Emergency Protection Orders to those children who were at great risk of harm. I repeated my question, "Why are you getting so angry?"

"Because I have seen what has happened to you to too many people and I am fed up with the police and the way in which they go after the wrong people. You do realise they kidnapped your children don't you, Dawn? You do realise that them failing to give you the relevant paperwork for your boys going into that foster home for those few days when you were in custody, anything could have been happening to your boys, and now there is no trace of it. You have no proof of where your boys were. That is effectively kidnapping your children whilst putting you under duress, putting you under pressure, frightening you, and NOW THIS? THIS assault charge? Assaulting a child? Look I have only met you for the last 30 minutes and I can tell there is no way you would hurt a child. When you have worked in the game as long as I have, you learn a lot about people. You haven't got a malicious bone in your body have you? You need to fight this and fight it smart. What are you doing now?"

Over the next few weeks Tom and I met up and went through so much paperwork together. He had so much knowledge and experience, contacts, as well case law in his head, it was overwhelming. He would collect me in the morning and we would go to the gym together. He took me out into the Peak District for a long walk, and then took me to lunch. Whilst all this was happening we were building my case, looking for a lawyer to represent me and I was getting present to just how much danger I was in. We had written my Statement of Account, and I had asked all my friends to send character references into the Oban Court on my behalf. I was in action and I was moving forward. Tom was like an angel sent from above to help me through this, and during this month, I managed to secure a new lawyer, the woman I had seen in the previous court visit. I felt a huge relief lift off my shoulders when she agreed to represent me and go after the legal aid on my behalf. I had to prepare so much paperwork for her and get that sent off. The day of the next court case was only a few days away and I was in turmoil. This time I would have to go to court and appear for what would be only 10-15 minutes, before leaving the courtroom to travel home again. A complete waste of my time. I had booked into accommodation along the seafront so I could go for a run before arriving in the courtroom, as I had started doing a 30 minute run every day, and had restarted my T25 exercises. I couldn't allow this to affect every area of my life. I had to take care of my health and set a great example for my boys.

The boys had been brilliant throughout all of this and had really stepped up. They were very aware of the consequences of what may happen if I was found guilty and so would make dinner for us all, Naasir would walk the dogs after school and Khaalid would walk them just before his bed time… knowing I would be up until about midnight to walk them and then again at 6am. Some mornings, after having been working on the case and studying the law until really late in the morning, the boys would find me slumped over books, asleep on the couch with the books and notepad on my knee or I would have left them a note to tell them to walk the dogs as soon as they woke up and that their lunches were prepared in the fridge ready for school because I needed to sleep. I would sense them coming into my bedroom and getting the dogs, and then leaning over to give me a kiss goodbye before school. Naasir would head off to his tennis lessons and youth club by himself and Khaalid would return home after his basketball and climbing sessions. We were working as a team and it was the three of us, no John. He was nowhere to be seen or heard of.

I was also getting present to just how much I wanted my partner by my side whilst dealing with this. I hadn't heard from him since he had been back on board the ship, which had been almost two months. Several of my friends were really angry with him, and I was starting to get angry with him too. How could he leave me to deal with all this bullshit alone, when I wouldn't have even been the target for the racist and physical abuse if I wasn't on the island with him? I knew I was blaming him in part for what had happened, and that wasn't fair on him; but I also wasn't being fair to myself. I didn't even know if he was going to be by my side in the courtroom; and I needed his testimony. I had to work on the premise that he wasn't going to be there, and I had to just move on. I knew I wanted a partner who would be there for me, a partner who would alleviate my doubts, because there should be no doubts in my mind. I wasn't needy, I wasn't paranoid and I was done crying over him not being there. I chose to move on. I chose to end it; and I chose to deal with it in the only way I could… by email. If he wasn't going to answer my phone calls, or messages and he wasn't interested in how I was getting on, then why should I be with him. He was having such a great time with everyone on the ship, I could tell from the photos that would occasionally pop up in my news feed on Facebook; so I chose to unfollow him, and then make him an 'acquaintance'. I couldn't deal with the hurt that pierced my heart when I saw his laughing face with others on board the ship, and seeing him always next to one of the women on board. If he was happier with them, and not interested in calling me, even for five minutes, then it was game over. I deserved better. I wanted better and I was going after it. I wanted to be honoured, respected and supported, not just loved. I wanted a partner, not just someone who turned up when it was convenient, or called when they had no one else to speak with, or nowhere else to go. He'd blown it. It was game over. If he chose to come back for the court case, then so be it, but if he didn't, then at least I was prepared either way.

I had given my lawyer his email address and she had contacted him on my behalf for his testimony. She would be the one communicating with him from now on, not me. I had to protect myself and my boys. It hurt like hell to walk away, but I wanted the old John, the one who was attentive, the one who showed me I mattered to him, the one who complimented me, and the one who had shown me he had my back. I didn't want this new version of John, the one who showed no interest in me, or my boys. The one who ignored me, the one who made me feel invisible. I wanted a partner in ALL senses of the word, one that would support, encourage and protect me. I wanted a gentleman, and the gentleman I had once had in John was gone. I wasn't a time filler, nor was I an option. I was a choice, and he either chose me, or he didn't.

I carried on with my business, I went out with friends, I exercised, I studied and I attended more legal seminars both online and offline. I spoke with a Professor of Criminology again at Sheffield University, Sheffield Hallam University, as well as Edinburgh and Glasgow universities and obtained more information from them, as well as titles of other books that I should perhaps be reading. I spoke with one of the local professors and a PhD supervisor, who also happened to be a dear friend, who told me to write this book as an Auto Ethnography so once it was finished I could then submit it as part of my PhD thesis submission. I was also told that I should apply for a fully funded PhD when all of this was over as the amount of research I have done on law, but also the work I have done on leadership, human behaviour and organisational structure, not to mention my cultural diversity work, I really should be getting recognised for all my knowledge. She told me that she would be more than happy to support my PhD application when the time came. She also told me, "You have the equivalent of at least four PhDs in that head of yours, you know more about your chosen subjects than most people I know who have PhDs."

I was touched by what she had said and I replied, "I have always said that one day I will be Dr Dawn... one day I will go for my PhD, but right now... I have to win this court case."

Whilst all this Scotland Saga was going on, my desire to live at sea, or at the very least by the sea was becoming stronger. The more I thought about my business model and the way I wanted to live my life, the more I kept seeing a boat, a really nice wooden sailing yacht. I wanted one that would enable me to live at sea and host my clients on board. I knew the space I wanted on board, and I started to look for both homes by the sea and for boats. I started working out the figures; it made sense to simply buy a boat. It would be a business asset, enabling me to travel in the most environmentally friendly way possible, as well as give me time away from the hustle and bustle of life on land to clear my mind and write my books. It also meant that I could hold my coaching retreats on board, travel wherever I wanted and fulfil my dream of living at sea.

I told my mum what I wanted to do, and she reminded me of the night I sat on the beach with her drinking a cup of tea whilst dad was stood by his beach fishing rods, and my brother and sister were sleeping in the beach bivvy. She told me that I had been staring out to sea and then said, "I'm going to live out there." I had always been a great swimmer, been called a mermaid many times, a water baby also. I had always yearned for the ocean, but with the boys in school, moving wasn't an option. I started playing around with ideas of how I could make it all work.

I looked at homes down in Falmouth, homes in Barmouth where we had all really enjoyed our first road trip holiday together, before the Scotland Saga reared its ugly head. I considered moving back to near where my parents were, and dismissed it even before the idea had time to finish... there was no way I could move back there. I couldn't get away quick enough when I was home, not because of my parents, but because of the lack of cultural diversity and all the racism in the local area. The energy of the people didn't suit my energy either, and I just couldn't settle, unless I was heading to the beach, my favourite beach being Holkham. If I could move there, then that would be perfect. So I started looking for apartments near there. My friend Jane had moved out to Burnham Market many years earlier, but since Prince William and Kate Middleton had got married and moved there, prices had skyrocketed... well done Jane! In all of the madness that had gone on with Scotland the only place I could clear my mind was being by the ocean, and the pull of returning to the ocean was getting stronger and stronger. The boys picked up on it and told me to do what I coached others to do, "Go live your dream Mummy, we'll be fine." When I asked them what they meant, they both replied, "Go live at sea Mummy."

"I'll go to boarding school Mummy," was Naasir's solution and Khaalid said he would get his own place.

When I told him he wasn't old enough, he said "Well I'll go and stay with Aunty Laura or Aunty Uzzie, I don't know, like you say, something will come up." I finally had a light at the end of a very dark tunnel. Something the boys and I could start planning for after the Scotland Saga was over. I felt deeply excited for the first time in a long time, and I just knew that whatever happened, the Universe had my back and I would win this case, then go live at sea.

THIRTY-TWO

"TRUST IS LIKE A BREADSTICK...

... once it is broken, it is broken." A quote I have taught my boys ever since they were young enough to understand the implications of it, even if on a very basic scale.

"We can always make other things with the breadcrumbs, we can still use the breadsticks, but they will never be the same again." And this is how I felt with so many of the relationships within my life. My relationships with my biological father, my brother, ramO, my parents, John, Sensei, certain friends and most importantly myself; the relationship with myself being the most important one.

The relationships with many people I have known for decades were growing weaker by the day. It seemed the more in tune with who I wanted to be, and the more I went after my dreams, the more people slipped by the way side. The relationships I had begun having with people online from my mentoring and coaching groups were becoming stronger. We were all facing up to our own demons, the things holding us back and going after what we wanted, and it was a shared experience. The people disappearing from my life were either just far too negative or they were energetically draining. Some were just no longer my kind of people, our evolutions taking us in completely different direction. Some of the comments and interactions were simply misfiring, and of the friendships formed over my lifetime I could count on both hands the ones I wished to keep in my close circle. I had become very protective over my space now and only they would be the ones I would allow in, which as an online coach and author of the kind of books I write, seems a complete contradiction, but there is sharing stuff to help others grown and there is sharing stuff.

There was of course my relationship with my friend Jaime. That was just as strong, if not stronger. Rob and Alan were still my rocks and it didn't matter how much was going on, I always knew they would have my back, and they did, in ways that I could never have imagined. Like they say, it is not until you are in the deep trouble that you realise who your friends are, and who is there for you. My friend of 22 years Ciaran was helping me with my business, as well as giving some words of wisdom and some strong words in his deep Irish voice; he helped me keep my head together. Tina always had supporting words and so many giggles up her sleeve that I would end up crying of laughter, a much needed change from crying of the fear, anger, pain, loss and complete disbelief I had been crying from over the last two years. I realised that the amount of people I had lost, and was losing, in my life was a good thing, it was helping me realise who was truly important and enabling me to grow into the person I was born to be and achieve the things I was destined to achieve. My faith was still very strong, and although I no longer had a religion to follow, I was still very much in tune with a higher entity and force that manifested itself within us and around us. I mean come on, when we look at nature in all her beauty there is no way we can argue that there is a much greater energetic force creating and holding everything in perfect balance; something even the animals get. As humans, we could learn a lot from the animal world if only we paid more attention; and we would all get along a lot better if we started to believe in each other (and ourselves) rather than listening to the media paranoia and hatred spewed out on a moment by moment basis. The boys were being raised to think, and to not follow stupid rules, instead challenging them, to challenge themselves, and this was becoming obvious with the way they were encouraging me to go and live my dream of living at sea, writing books. Yes they were young in years, but their maturity far outweighed that of many adults around.

Keeping the balance of the boys' emotional and mental development was something I was very aware of. They had witnessed many things in their lives that many adults never got to see, and more accurately, DIDN'T want to see. They were mature beyond their years, but they were still young boys in many ways. I spent days, weeks wondering how this whole Scotland Saga would be affecting them, not just now, but in the long term. How would this 'life at sea' dream going to work? How would they cope with me being away? I realised that 'the how' would work itself out. Children are more resilient than us adults give them credit for, and with modern technology, I would never be more than eight days away from having a conversation with them, and something would manifest to enable the long promised trip to New Zealand to happen; and sure enough it did.

Kelt, my canine soul mate was a horny little bugger and as soon as Chewy came into her first season, well the hormones racing between the two of them was intense! Keeping one of them in one room and the other in the other room was a challenge in itself. I spoke with the vet and asked him if it was safe for Chewy to get pregnant at such a young age, and he asked me one simple question... "Do you believe in the natural order of things?"

When I responded, "Yes..." I giggled... because how daft was it to think we could control nature? How daft was it to think that a young female bitch wasn't able to cope with getting pregnant and produce puppies when they do it all the time in nature? It is just us humans who domesticated the animals and pamper them beyond belief (we do it to our pets, our kids and ourselves... what is the world coming to?).

We did our best to keep them both apart, but then one night as I went to the toilet, and as I closed the bathroom door, the wind travelling through the apartment; due to me always having my windows open, pushed open the kitchen door, and by the time I had gone for a wee, washed my hands and come out of the bathroom, they were tied. I couldn't help but giggle when I saw the look of pure joy on both their faces, which then turned into a look of, *Uh oh! We got caught out!* and then when they heard me say, "I get it, it's a great thing sex isn't it!" the look of joy returned to their faces. Bless them, and blessed we all were, because a few weeks later we noticed that Chewy was indeed pregnant!

He shoots, he scores!

It was a wonderful thing to watch unfold to be honest, because the more the pregnancy unfolded, the more Kelt took care of Chewy. He would bark at another dog going near her, He would wait for her more when we went for walks, he would snuggle up to her more when they slept and when we were cuddling up on the couch watching a movie. He even allowed her to eat her food first, and if she took food from his bowl as well as her own, he never minded. Seeing the behaviour between them change was eye opening and heart-warming. It gave a very pleasant experience as the trial date was coming up.

I knew John had been emailed by my lawyer when he called and spoke with me about his statement. He told me that he wasn't going to court to defend me; he was going to court to tell the truth. This was the first time I had truly believed he was going to go to court since he had distanced himself. He had said he would months earlier, but with his lack of communication and distance, I had started to lose faith in not just our relationship, but also his word. To hear him say he was simply going to tell the truth meant so much to me. I didn't want him to defend me; I wanted him to tell the truth because I believe the truth will set you free. I also knew that if the judge decided to punish me for telling the truth, and for John telling the truth, then so be it. I would rather be punished for telling the truth, than lie and get off with an innocent verdict. When I received John's statement, I sent it to my lawyer. John also told me when he would be 'home'. That sent me into turmoil all over again. How could he believe that it was okay to disappear for so long without contact and still expect everything to be okay? Especially when my two love languages were communication and touch? He asked me what was wrong and so I told him, to which he replied, "Dawn, you've got to stop putting yourself in this place. I have been busy working and sorting my own head out; and why are people questioning our relationship?"

"Because I am John!" was all I said, before reminding him of how I wouldn't be in any of this mess if it wasn't for his past, and yet he thought it was okay for him to be within reach of a good mobile signal, going out all the time with the crew members, responding to other people over social media and acting as if I was invisible. I deserved better, and I wanted better, so he had a choice to make. I was a choice, I wasn't an

option, and I didn't like being ignored. At that moment, he told me again
to stop putting myself in places where I didn't need to be and that he
would see me in a couple of weeks. We then hung up and I re-read his
statement. As I read it again, I saw his pain. I saw his turmoil. I saw such
a loving father who had been put in an awful situation, an impossible
situation. I saw the reasons he had to take time out for himself. I saw the
love he had for me. I saw his commitment to us and our future; and I
realised he had been in his man cave all this time. I realised that my own
insecurities were the thing that was getting to me. I saw him as my mirror.
I saw the choice he was making, and I knew it was time to do some more
deep internal work on how I saw myself, the insecurities I had that were
being brought up by the feelings I had for this man, and what I wanted
from my future relationship with him; and what I had to let go of. I either
loved him for all of him, or I didn't.

Whilst doing this work, I was reminded of the time when wives were
left home for months, years on end whilst their loved one was away in the
war, or at sea, and didn't have any way of being in contact, other than a
letter; but I still couldn't get passed why he would be in contact with
others and not me. Was he blaming me? Was he just too confronted by
the whole situation and how his past was now threatening to ruin our
relationship? Why was it easier for him to be with others and not me?
Answers only he could answer and they had nothing to do with me. I had
to figure out what I wanted, what was important to ME. These were the
only answers I had to seek, and of course a 'not guilty' verdict when the
trial date came.

I was due to travel up to Oban again for the intermediate trial and
have the trial date set. This would now be the third time I had travelled
to Scotland, with only ten minutes of actually being spoken to by the
judge himself. It would take almost three days out of my week for just a
ten minute session, and cause me no end of hardship in the realms of
emotional, mental, physical and financial. Why they could not do a video
link up from the magistrate's courts of Sheffield was beyond me, but then
it wouldn't appeal to the power and ego trip that thrived within this space
of dark energy; and dark energy it was.

Having arrived in Glasgow, awaiting my train to Oban, I had a call
from my lawyer. The legal aid had been refused. I was gutted. When I

asked her why, she told me it was because I received too much money from my child benefit and working family tax credits. I asked her how is that even a realistic reason for them to give! I was a single mum, rebuilding my life after a divorce, my business wasn't even 18 months old and during the first year it had been delayed due to the incompetent, over-zealous policing in Inverarary. I was only just able to keep my head above water with these benefits coming in. How did they expect me to afford legal fees of £167 per hour, knowing there would be at least ten hours of legal representation and work to be done? She was, herself, dumfounded. She told me she had no words, but due to the massive cuts in legal aid assistance there was nothing we could do. She did tell me she would appeal on my behalf, and I told her thank you. I also said that if the police didn't go around arresting people for no reason other than proving their jobs were needed and their own job security (at the expense of other people's security), and actually did proper police investigation work, then there would be less claims going into Legal Aid departments, meaning there would be more money to go to those who needed it. She said she agreed with me, but unfortunately that was the way the system was. My response was, "Well Mubarak had a system in Egypt and look where that has led!" I was shocked at the absurdity of the situation. We said our goodbyes, agreed to meet up 15 minutes earlier than previously arranged the following morning.

I sat there in Queen Street Station, Glasgow feeling as though the bottom of my world had fallen out. Not only did I not get told about the fact I could have had legal aid during the first case, I was now not allowed it because I was a working mum in receipt of working family tax credits and child benefit. A lady walked up to me and asked if I was okay. I didn't realise I was in a daze. She told me I had gone really pale, and asked if I wanted a fresh coffee. I looked at her and it seemed as though everything was in slow motion. I had to ask her to repeat herself, even though I had heard what she had said, it didn't quite register what she was asking me. She sat down next to me and asked me again if everything was okay. I replied, "The system is screwed, how can they do this to people? What is wrong with people? Are they just so numb to humanity they just push paper around, hitting keys on their keyboard and don't actually think about the consequences to their actions? It's like the Nazi officers who 'just did what they were told to do'."

She put her hand on my shoulder, and said, "I don't know what's happened love, but I agree with you whole heartedly. There are some really heartless people working in these government departments. Can I get you another coffee?" I nodded and a few moments later she came back with a GF chocolate brownie too, telling me to eat it as I was too pale, I needed some sugar. She then asked me where I was going and I told her, and she told me I had enough time to drink and eat up before it arrived, and that she too was going to Oban. We then started chatting and she reminded me there were some really beautiful people in Scotland, it was just a shame that their policing, justice department and the government systems were not as lovely.

Before court that morning, I got up and went for a run. I only had time to do five kilometres before getting back to the YHA Hostel on the seafront. It was the only place left available with a sea view that was in my price range, and Mr Tom had helped me find it. It was great to be running along the seafront and filling my lungs up with sea air. I had visions of being in a marina and running along the shoreline when I finally got to live on a boat. One day that dream would come true. One day. After my run, I showered, packed and checked out, heading towards the courtroom. Whilst waiting for the court to start, I sat journaling, and then as the Judge walked in and we were all told 'All rise' I couldn't help but release a cheeky smile. I had just finished reading 'Rise, Sister Rise' by Rebecca Campbell, a book all about women rising in their power and shining their light on the darkness in the world. I was going to rise, but not in honour of the judge, I was going to rise in my power. I was going to observe, make as many notes as I possibly could and I was going to win this case if it was the last thing I did. But today, it was about getting a trial date, and then I could head home to my boys and my dogs, which had now increased by five little boys; all of which were sold and due to be collected.

Whilst I was waiting for my trial date to be set, I saw a man who was obviously mentally ill sent to prison, two young men get sent to prison – with one of them being told there was 'nothing good about you' – my heart sank. How could this judge sit there and say that to someone he doesn't even know? These young lads had been done for driving without insurance and apparently it wasn't their first motoring offence, but REALLY? 'There is nothing good about you?' What right does the judge have to say that to anyone? This young lad looked broken, and all I could see was pain within him. He was crying out for attention and as the saying goes, 'Sometimes the most loving of kids ask for love in the most unloving of ways' and I was reminded of Judge Ward in the court the year before condemning a woman to being 'insane' just because she was having therapy to deal with a traumatic loss in her life.

Does this make Rio Ferdinand insane because he had therapy to help deal with the death of his wife through cancer? Does this make Will Smith and his wife insane because they have therapy for their marriage on a regular basis? Does having therapy make everyone insane? The way these judges were allowed to speak with people they did not know, based on biased and corrupt police and prosecutor fiscal reports astounded me. Seeing these people get sentenced really shook me up. This was the very same judge who would be residing over my case, and I didn't feel hopeful. I pulled my journal out and started journaling about the positive outcome that I wanted, and how my innocence and telling the truth would prevail in the end.

I was then called to the stand, asked to confirm my name and date of birth and then told the charges I was on trial for. I was then asked how I pleaded and I replied, "Not guilty." My lawyer went on to ask for the court date to be extended as she had not had time to go over the details thoroughly, we were denied an extension and I was once again told I was wasting the courts time. I simply raised my right eyebrow and couldn't take this man seriously. I understood he was faced with people every day who probably did waste their time, but I wasn't one of them. I knew he was only acting on the lies and fabricated stories that the Prosecutor fiscal had fed him. I guess it wasn't his fault but I had always believed that we were all innocent until proven guilty, obviously not the case in Scotland. In Scotland it seems you are guilty until you have proven your innocence, very backward indeed.

After ten minutes of standing in the dock, I was given my next court date, the date of the actual trial and told if I did not attend I would be found guilty in my absence. I was then asked if I understood what had just been said, I said yes, and was then dismissed from the courtroom. I couldn't have got out of there quick enough. I had enough time to go and get a cup of tea before heading to the train station, and making the 12 hour trip back to Sheffield. I would be home just before midnight. I had four weeks until I had to make this trip again, and I was going to go over everything that had happened thus far and send thoughts, ideas, and my learning and questions to my new lawyer. I was going to win this case, and nothing, absolutely nothing was going to stop me from winning it.

With just four weeks to go until the trial date and an end to the nightmare, I booked my accommodation. A new friend Bea offered to lend me her car so I could save on costs, and I couldn't have been more grateful, it would mean that I would get appear on a podcast that I was already booked to speak on. It was broadcast from the States on the Sunday and I would still get to do my author presentation at the Central Library in Sheffield on the Tuesday. It would mean driving back to Sheffield after being in the courtroom all day on the Monday, but I was not going to allow this court case to negatively impact my business any more. I would make it work, even if I had to have a tonne of sugar and coffee just to keep me awake and alert enough to drive home. The friendship had come at a really crazy time and completely out of nowhere. But I had just finished reading *The Universe Has Your Back* by Gabriella Bernstein and I knew before reading it the universe had my back, but hearing so much about this book by others who had read it, I just knew I wanted to read it. I wanted to hear another person's take on it, someone who had believed it so much they had written an international bestselling book about it. I read it within a couple of days, and with so much resonating with how I felt, I had a sense of calmness. Many of my friends had thought I had been experiencing the first signs of a breakdown 'talking all this universe crap' or that I had 'lost my mind', I was allowing myself to be 'led easily' into some 'new age hippy shit'. If they knew me, paid attention to me, they would already know that I have been a hippie at heart all my life – especially if that meant being in love with the natural world and wanting to protect it, being humble enough to believe in a force or energy greater than myself. Even those who had read my first two books and never met me in person would know I've always been a hippy. I remember speaking with my friend Tina and she told me, "It is so lovely to see you being yourself, beautiful. You have been hiding yourself for a while."

My closest friend Jaime, who's known me since I was eleven, had commented a few times it was so nice to see 'Dawn' emerging again. It seemed the more faith I had in the universe having my back, the more faith I had in myself and the brighter my light was shining... even with the darkness of the court case and a conflict in my heart. I could deal with the court case that was something that I could study, attempt to make sense of; but seeing the man I had fallen so deeply in love with going through what he was going through, and the distance it had created between us was harsh. It was like the man I had fallen in love with had disappeared and only a man that looked like him remained. Where had my attentive, loving John gone? Why was he allowing this court case, and his ex, drive this wedge between us? But more importantly why was I? Was I really going to allow my own insecurities and fears destroy us? No, I wasn't. So I left it to the universe to deal with. I knew what I wanted, and I wanted him. But I also knew if he was supposed to be in my life, then he would be. I wasn't going to beg him to stay; I just wanted to discuss how I felt with him, without him telling me to 'stop putting my head in these places'. If he was in communication and didn't ignore me then my head wouldn't be in these places. He had to take some of the responsibility, whether he would see that or not was another matter. I did need him in the courtroom if I was going to a higher percentage of winning, but I had faith I would win anyway. I had to believe I would win. I had to. I had no choice. In my mind, a victory was the only outcome. I was innocent. I hadn't done what they were accusing me of, and it really was as simple as that.

Leading up to the trial, I kept wondering how I was going to pay for the lawyer's legal fees, especially now legal aid had been denied. I did a live stream on my Facebook page to give friends an update on what had happened in the courtroom, and that I had been refused legal aid. I also gave them updates on the new things I was learning about the law in Scotland, like how if you are attacked in Scotland and you defend yourself, it is only seen as self-defence provided three conditions were met:

1)if you have nowhere to go to escape

2)your life is in imminent danger

3)you use a reasonable amount of force

So in terms of a rape case where does that leave a woman? What is reasonable force? How would she know he was 'only going to rape her?' What if the man could out run her? Or had a car/van nearby?

Looking at the area where the attack had happened, where would I have run to, had I been able to get away? The homes of the other people who lived locally? Friends and family of those who were attacking me? Running out of the pan and into the fire? Maybe I could make a swim for the mainland, some four hours by ferry away? Such a stupid piece of legislation. And ALL three elements of this legislation had to be met, not just one, but ALL three! I told my friends and followers about the situation with the legal aid too, and was told to set up a crowdfunding page, and what happened next was overwhelming. I received a message privately from a friend of only a couple of years, who offered to pay the legal fees and I could pay her back whenever I could. No time limit, no conditions, just one sister helping out another; one mother to another. Someone who also opposed the stupidity and injustice that was happening stood by my side and said, "Here, let me help you. Here's the money for the legal fees." I was overwhelmed with emotion. Here was someone I had only known for a couple of years, a fellow author making her way in the world as a single mum, with a similar soul, stepping up to help a fellow sister, both of us shining our lights together to fight, and expose the darkness. It was a wonderful gift, and one I shall treasure always. Honouring the gift would mean I would also never reveal who it was who gave me the air to breathe, but she knows who she is; and she knows the depth of my gratitude. A bond sealed for all of time; not just for me, but for all those I will be able to help who have been, are and will be at the hands of the darkness and need the air to breathe, the light to see and the strength to rise.

THIRTY-THREE

HOW DO YOU PLEA?

Throughout the whole process I kept being asked, "How do you want to plea?" I didn't quite understand why the two male lawyers would ask me this question, especially as I had already told them I hadn't done anything wrong. I had defended myself from being punched in the face, and then spat in the face by this vulgar man (if he warrants that title behaving in the way he did).

When my new lawyer asked me, I asked her, "Why do you ask me this when I have told you I didn't do what I am being accused and charged for?" She told me that if I admitted to the charges being brought against me, then the punished would be less community service, less of a fine or less of jail time. When I told her I was not guilty and not prepared to take a bribe, which incidentally I found highly unprofessional and immoral, she told me that it wasn't a bribe and she wouldn't be able to represent me if I thought the plea bargain was a bribe. I asked, "How can it not be a bribe when the prosecutor is asking me to admit to something I have not done in exchange for what *could* be a lesser sentence? It's a bribe, or blackmail, either way it's not right."

Being told that Scottish Lawyers did not offer bribes, blackmail people and they were a bound by a professional code of ethics underpinned by the Scottish Law Society didn't make a difference in my book, what I was being offered in my mind was a bribe. They were blackmailing me, and I wasn't going to entertain the idea of being blackmailed. I declined the 'offer of reduced sentencing' because like I had said before, I would rather be punished for telling the truth, than lie and 'get a lesser sentence'. Part of me couldn't understand why my new lawyer couldn't see what I was saying and how what was being offered to me was a bribe. She was a very intelligent woman, and yet could not see what I thought was a blindingly obvious piece of corruption within the Scottish 'justice' system.

We continued to discuss how I was going to plea and I told her I wanted her to push for self-defence, and if she didn't then she was not representing me in the way wanted her to. She said it would be very hard to get a self-defence plea, but if that is what I wanted then she would look into it further. I reiterated that if we did not push for self-defence, then we, as women, would both be confirming that it was okay for a woman to be charged with assault when defending herself from an assault, but also if we were not able to push for a self-defence counter claim, then that would mean that Police Scotland and Scottish 'Justice' believe that verbal, physical and racial abuse is fine in the eyes of the law. You can imagine the headlines: "Welcome to Scotland Ladies! The land where you can relax knowing our men are free to abuse you!" and even "Welcome to all you non-white Scottish folk! Our country men and women are free to verbally and physically assault you. Please let us know upon arrival where and when you would like this to happen and we'll make all the arrangements for the police to come and arrest you, making sure there is a cell ready for you, and a courtroom drama laid on just for you!" I am sure the Scottish Tourist Board and the people of Scotland would love to read these headlines!

My live streams about the case were now becoming a regular thing as more and more people were shocked at what was happening. I was also using the lives streams to request help from lawyer friends, fellow researcher friends and as a way of creating an audience for this book. When I informed my friends and followers about this 'plea bargain/bribe/blackmail' friends in law from around the world came back and told me that it was either illegal in their country for the very same reasons I had pointed it out it was immoral and corrupt, or that plea bargains had been 'a thing' in the past but had not been used in recent years, some as long ago as 50 years. Interesting how the Scottish (and American) court systems still blackmail people into admitting guilt for something they did not do as a weapon of fear against those who do not know any better, are fearful or 'have too much to lose'. I was disgusted even more about what I was finding out, and the more I studied, the more I discussed case law with criminal lawyer friends, some of whom are barristers, the more I realised I HAD to fight this and go for self-defence; and do my very best to get this archaic and antiquated, immoral and corrupt piece of legislation removed from Scottish law, because it represented itself as UK law. I as a woman couldn't stand by and allow another woman to go through this, as a mother of boys I couldn't allow this, and more importantly as a human being I couldn't allow this. I had to fight it; and listening to the response from all those on my social media, they were also in agreement with me that this 'plea bargain' business was something that needed to be removed from the legal system.

One of my friends met with me on several occasions, not just as a legal mind, but also as a dear friend. We had only known each other briefly before this whole ugly scenario raised its head, but now, well let's just say the love I have for Marnie is very deep. A wonderful mother, a kind and gentle soul, with a very generous heart; a role model for so many, and she chose to give up hours of her time to support me in the last few months of this trial. She gave me ideas on what to ask, on how to channel the process into the outcome I wanted, didn't ideas on how to deal with the whole scenario and more importantly encouraged me to be kind to myself. I know that if ever Marnie ever needed anything, I would do whatever I could to be there to help her; and I know she gave all she could give me because she saw the injustice, she could see beyond the obvious. She helped because she knew it was the right thing to do for a friend; and because she saw the incompetence of the Scottish Police and the Prosecutor Fiscal. She helped because she had the knowledge to help; and to me, all these reasons to help, and her other own private reasons, showed her to be a truly wonderful soul.

Reading legal text book after text books, with case law after case law,

I was astounded at how this whole Scotland Saga had even got this far. I spoke with a friend who was a social worker and magistrate who was absolutely dumbfounded at what was happening. She urged me to take civil action once the verdicts were in. She warned me that if I didn't, then they would keep getting away with it, destroying lives and communities, spending precious public funding that was needed in other areas and wasting the resources that were dwindling due to so many government cuts. She gave me a list of people who needed to see this manuscript when it was done, told me that what I had experienced needed to be exposed; and she wasn't the only one. I had a friend whose father was in CID, another friend who studied Criminology, friends in social care work, friends who worked in the media and in the prison service; mothers, women, men, all of the people finding out what I was going though said this needed exposing. I knew it did, but I also knew that it was very easy for those to say it needed exposing but how many of them would be prepared to stand by me when I did expose it? How many people were willing to put their own neck on the line; their own head above the parapet and stand with me when the time came? Only time would tell; but regardless, I had already made the choice to expose it all. I couldn't allow this to happen to anyone else. I wouldn't be able to live with myself knowing I had gained all this knowledge and experienced all of this and then not used it to help others who didn't have the strength, courage, resources or support to fight their own cases. I asked my current lawyer what my next step would be, and she said I would need to take civil action against the police for gross incompetence, and if I believed I had been targeted due to my children being of a non-white British heritage, and me speaking Arabic to them in the first instance, as well as being an independent, educated single mother, then I should look into discrimination on the grounds of racism and gender inequality. Something I had already considered doing, so it was great to hear it from her as well.

My next task was to call Imran Khan and Partners, the law firm headed up by the lawyer who had dealt with the Steven Lawrence case. They said they would consider my case, but came back and said they couldn't represent me as they did not specialise in Scottish Law, as well as a few other considerations, which they would not divulge to me. They recommended I called Scottish law firms and ones that would work on a 'no win, no fee' basis before wishing me the very best of luck. So I called law firm after law firm in Scotland to see if they took on cases dealing with professional incompetence, racism and sexism. Every single law firm I spoke with said yes they would be able to help, but they couldn't as taking on my case would be 'a conflict of interest' as Police Scotland were already a client.

Great. So due to the fact that Police Scotland had used every law firm that specialised in the areas of law I needed to help me, meant they had secured their position to ensure no one could ever take them to court on the grounds of incompetence, racism, sexism or any other professional misconduct. Whether it was done with this intention or not, didn't really matter in the grand scheme of things at this present time, but it took the wind out of my sails that was for sure.

One of my friends in the media, told me, "Just get the bloody book written and then send a copy to all those places on your list of influencers and I guarantee you, not only will you get compensation, but you'll gain the support of a lawyer who has everything to gain and nothing to lose. DO NOT LET THEM BEAT YOU DAWN!" And when these last seven words were said in such a tone, I knew I had to keep fighting regardless.

John arrived home and although my heart skipped a beat and I was so pleased to see him, I was still hurting. He looked good in so many ways, but there was a sadness in his eyes that I didn't like to see. His eyes were always so sparkly and playful, loving and kind; and I didn't like seeing this shadow hanging over him. I wanted to reach out and hold him as much as I wanted to be held by him. There was so much pain and anger in both of us about what had happened and I just knew that once all this was over, we could get back to being Dawn and John. I was on edge, I just couldn't relax. I hardly slept the night before we had to go up to Oban. I snapped at John, and it wasn't the first time. I knew I hadn't been easy to be with, and that this whole scenario had taken over my life so much that he just wanted to forget about it and move on. He had his own way of dealing with it all, and being a man was able to departmentalise everything; unlike us women where everything is connected to everything else, once twice and a third time over. He had put up with a lot from me, even though he was dealing with his own stuff.

I'd had to keep reminding myself the situation he was in himself. His daughter was going to be one of the ones lying in the courtroom. His daughter was the one who had been raised to be vindictive by her mother and all the other haters; unbeknown to her how much her dad loved her and how it broke his heart to not have her in his life any longer. She was too young to understand the complexities of the bigger picture, but I wasn't. I had the knowledge of the man I loved, knowledge of what he had gone through and the knowledge of it was sometimes difficult to get my head around, without first-hand experience of it. I knew I loved this man more than any amount of words could say, even the words I love you which were used by so many for so many things, the words had almost lost their power these days. I knew he was the love of my life, next to the ocean and me of course. I knew we would get through this and I was not prepared to let his ex, or his past come between us. We were both too smart and too strong to let that happen; we just had to get through the next few days.

Driving up to Oban was tough. We were both in our own head spaces and he was catching up with friends on his phone whilst I was driving. I wanted his attention. I wanted to go over the court case. I wanted us to catch up on all the stuff that had happened outside of the court case, but he was only interested in his friends and his phone. He didn't even want to look at me, or that's how I felt. I didn't realise it was enough for him to just to be in my company, being at peace in all this madness. I couldn't be at peace, because I was more worried about being charged with assaulting his daughter when I hadn't. Again the thought of it as it passed through my head made me feel sick. I was not in a good place, and it didn't seem to matter how hard I tried to put on a smile and be happy just to be with him, the closer the trial came, the more I realised I was resenting him and his communication with his friends and I just wanted to throw his phone out of the car window. I got cross with him. I didn't like the way he was being, his dismissive attitude towards me hurt me and he came across as if he just didn't care. In those moments I hated him and wished I had never met him. My life had taken on a whole new level of crazy since meeting him and I just wanted it to be over; but then when I looked at how much greatness had also happened with him, I was just couldn't see a future without him. I wanted a future with him, but things had to change, and change soon, otherwise it would be over for good, regardless of how much I loved him. I'd gotten over ramO and I could get over John, it may take time, but if there was one thing I had learnt it was that regardless of how much I loved someone else, I always had to love myself more.

THIRTY-FOUR

THE TIREE TRIAL

Arriving in Oban I had to make my way to meet with my lawyer. John went for a walk around Oban whilst I was in the meeting going over the case details and it was good news. We were going for self- defence because the video footage had clearly been edited to remove the part where the guy had hit me. You could see him stepping back out of the punch and dropping his arm. We went through the rest of the details with a fine tooth comb and I felt positive. My lawyer was confident that there was not enough evidence on any of the charges and it all came down to what they said on the stand.

Waking up the morning of the trial, I wanted to roll over into John's arms and stay there. I wanted him to reassure me that everything was going to be okay. I knew he couldn't do that. I knew that neither one of us knew what was going to happen; we just had to have faith that truth and common sense would prevail. I wanted him to tell me he had my back, but the fact that he was here with me already told me that. Why did I need everything saying, instead of just seeing the blatantly obvious right here in front of me? My head was all over the place. I was hungry, but couldn't even eat the breakfast I made for myself. I didn't even make John his breakfast because I was still hurting from the way he had focused on his friends and the news going on in his phone the day before. I needed him. I wanted him to be with me, to talk with me but he was still choosing the world inside his phone. He didn't want to talk about the court case; he didn't want to talk about the impact on my life, on our relationship; and the more he avoided talking with me about it, the more it was killing it from the inside; even though I knew he was so secure in our relationship he didn't have to doubt it, but then I had never given him reason to.

He had been really nasty to me on the drive up from Sheffield and then told me to go and relax in the bath. I said I wanted some wine. So we went for a walk. For the first time in a long time, he held my hand. I was so jumpy as we walked to McColls to get a bottle of wine. Every skin-headed man I saw, every group of guys in the distance made me jumpy. I held onto John's arm even tighter. He told me to get a grip on myself, and I told him I was scared and just wanted to get back to the AirBnB we were staying at. I needed the walk, and wanted the wine, but I just didn't feel safe in Oban. As we walked passed a house at the bottom of one of the hills, he saw the van of one of the guys who lived opposite him; I felt his body tighten and I followed his gaze, and then I saw it, recognised it and started panicking. I held onto him so tightly and he told me they wouldn't hurt me again, and that I had to be strong. I kept holding my breath and realised I was starting to have an anxiety attack. I started breathing slower and deeper, reminded myself I had this. The Universe, my boys, my Mum and Dad, my friends and John all had my back. I had just got myself back into a good space when we arrived back at the AirBnB and I headed straight into the bathroom and started to run a bath.

I poured myself and John a glass of wine. He didn't drink his, but he did eat the sweets that had been very kindly left for us by the hosts, all Scottish made. I stayed in the bath for quite a while and then went into the room, poured myself another glass and tried to snuggle up to John but he was more interested in the TV. My heart felt like it was breaking. How could he be more interested in the TV than me? We hadn't seen each other in months. I had achieved so much, and done so much more than this court case, and so had he; but he wasn't interested in sharing.

He wasn't interested in even talking about what was on the TV. Here I was lying here in bed next to him and all he wanted to do was watch TV. I sat up, finished my wine and then rolled over and was about to go to sleep. Inside I was crying to myself, feeling so alone, feeling unloved and unwanted, and then he started to watch *Dragon's Den*, a programme I enjoyed watching. So I thought I'd watch it with him, or at least watch it, even if I felt more alone than I had ever felt. It's true what they say 'being around people and feeling alone is the loneliest feeling in the world'. As I watched it, he started to talk about the programme, inviting me into a conversation with him. I resisted but chose to join him in the conversation. Within moments we were chatting away as if everything was good in the world again; and for the rest of the programme it was. I was tired though, it had been a long and emotional drive and tomorrow was going to be a big day. As I rolled over and went to sleep, I hoped he would cuddle into me, but he didn't. Again tears rolled down my face. I wondered once again where my John had gone. I missed him. I wanted him back. I didn't like this new lookalike version.

In the morning I woke up and I felt sick from the get go. My stomach was in knots. I kept flitting between my future with John and the trial. Thoughts of: *If I am found guilty today, then the last night we had spent together I might have well been alone, with feelings of meaning nothing to the man I had spent the last couple of years with, and invested so much into.* I looked over at him and he was already on his phone. There was no, 'Good morning, how did you sleep? How are you feeling?' Nothing. I felt as though I didn't matter to him. There were thoughts of him just using me to see his daughter, even under these awful circumstances. Thoughts of him using me to just make his way back up to Scotland. He had always told me he didn't want to be a distraction, and he had always been a distraction. In the beginning he was the best kind of distraction, a welcome one, but now, he was the worst kind.

When I should have been thinking about my boys, myself and my future success, all I had were negative thoughts of him, as well as the thoughts of me going to prison, of having my children taken off me and never being allowed to see them again without supervision, because that was one of the possible outcomes, along with in a worst case scenario of not being allowed to see my children again. There were thoughts of my career as a career coach for teenagers being over. Thoughts of my family name Bates being dragged through the mud, when all I had ever wanted to do for my Dad and Grandfather was to honour them both by using their family name to do great things in the world, to build a positive and powerful legacy that would provide for my boys, their children and their children long after I was gone. Everything I had been working towards ever since I had become a mother, a single mother and ever since I had sat around the dining room table in Dore shortly after the split from ramO with all my A1 flip chart sheets on the table and stuck to the wall; all the work I had done on myself and all the growth I had done, all the belief I had gained in myself and all the time, effort and money I had invested in myself, my boys and this God-awful situation all came down to this one day, and all John could do was hide in his bloody phone!

I was angry at him. I was angry at Scotland and I was on the verge of tears. I had a shower, got dressed and went into the kitchen to make breakfast, but I couldn't bring myself to eat it. I could only just manage to drink my coffee. Then he walked in the kitchen, made his own breakfast and sat there and ate it. I left him to it and went back into the bedroom. On the morning we should be strong together, we were more distant than ever. I felt broken. As I put my makeup on, he came back into the room and called a taxi. Then he looked at me, stepped towards me and put his arms around me. He told me to keep strong and I nearly laughed. I had been strong, all the way through it all. I'd had to be. For my boys. For my own sanity. I just nodded fighting back the tears, and then he looked me in the eyes and wiped away the first tear before it even had time to fall. Then he kissed me on the forehead and I saw a flicker of my John again, somewhere under all the distance between us, I saw him and my stomach flipped, my heart fluttered.

As we left the property together we 'sucked it all up' and put on a united front. The taxi driver arrived and it was the guy I'd used before. He remembered me and was shocked to see me again. He was even more shocked to find out the updates and went into a full on rant about how rubbish the police were and how stupid and wrong this all was. He told me that the female judge that used to be in Oban wouldn't have entertained it all in her courtroom, and maybe the Prosecutor Fiscal was trying a fast one on this new judge, but I all honesty, it didn't really matter what this chap said, I had seen this judge in action and had been on the receiving end of his attitude and judgements already, so I knew what to expect really.

Walking up the steps into the courthouse, John was holding my hand, and for the first time talking softly to me, words of encouragement. I was met by my lawyer. She wanted to have a word with me away from John as he was my key witness and couldn't be privy to what she needed to say. As I walked away I saw a red headed woman walk past me, I didn't recognise her at first but I knew I had seen her somewhere before. Whether it had been here in the courthouse on a previous visit or somewhere else I wasn't sure, but I heard her say, "Oh my God, it's him." I don't know who she was talking about or too as there was no one with her, but I just followed on behind my lawyer and up the stairs to the witness room. We went over a few more details of the case and reiterated what we had gone over the night before.

As we came out of the witness room, I saw John and we all went back in together, went over the running order and then my lawyer and I had to leave to go in the courtroom. John was standing a distance away from me and he was looking at me with love in his eyes. I asked him for a hug, and he came over to me and put his arms around me so tightly, I nearly melted in his arms. Tears pricked my eyes and he kissed me on the side of the head a couple of times. He told me to just tell them what had happened and to know that I never did anything wrong, and that we would get through this. I nodded, and did my best to smile but I just couldn't. I told him I would see him in a bit, as I had to go into the courtroom.

I had my journal and notebook with me and as I sat there, I started journaling. I journalled and started manifesting the outcome I wanted. I noticed the red headed woman sat to the other side of the courtroom and she just kept turning around to face me and smirking. I could see her out of the corner of my eye and I could tell she was trying to intimidate me. It was then the penny dropped who it was. It was John's ex, the mother of his daughter, and she was sat next to an older lady. Just as I was about to send a text to my boys to let them know I loved them before switching off the phone, I saw a message from John, he had asked me to go into the witness room. So I did. That was when he told me who the woman was with his ex. He looked gutted. Betrayed and knowing who this woman was, I was gutted for him. He was facing the ultimate betrayal from another member of his family. My lawyer then came in and told me that I shouldn't be in the room with John as he was my key witness and so I left and told him not to worry, like he had said, we would get through this.

Court started and as the morning progressed I saw two seventeen-year-olds sent to prison, a woman and another guy who was also not well mentally. He was rocking back and forth and his face was so vacant. He didn't need prison, he needed medical help, and lots of it by the looks of him, and that was exactly what his lawyer said. Seeing all those people get sent to prison on the morning of my case was not what I needed to see, at any time in fact. This was not my world. I should not have been there in the first place, and I couldn't wait to get out of there. Court stopped and as John was outside the courtroom, I was not allowed to leave the room. I was told by my lawyer they were going to do the court dates next and then my trial would start. After lots of re-arrangements and trial dates set it was time for another break, then it would be my turn. I'd had to move from where I was sitting as the red head had been getting up to go outside several times and had to make sure she walked passed me every time she did so. So I moved to the last row and sat in the corner so no one could walk passed me and it was difficult for her to get away with trying to intimidate me as he would have had to turn around.

After the break I was called into the witness box and once again confirmed all my details and reiterated my plea of 'not guilty' to the three charges of assault being brought against me; one against the thug who had punched me and spat in my face, as well as directing racist abuse at me including calling me a "Paki lover" and telling me to "F*** off, you and your Paki sons are not welcome here" along with a whole lot of other ugly comments; with another charge against the younger lad who had hurled racist insults and comments one after the other, who I had not touched, and then the final charge of assault on John's daughter, again who I had not touched.

I sat in the dock with my notebook making notes as the first thug came on to the stand. Some of the things he said and the way he spoke with my lawyer was shocking. He admitted to knowing my full name, and that I was John's partner, but didn't know John's full name. He said I had punched him constantly for five to ten minutes and I had to smile as I don't think even the UFC fighters could managed to go that long, and apparently I had broken a new world record of throwing ten punches in about four seconds! He was coming out with so much rubbish and digging himself a hole. The more he dug, the more notes I made. The more aggressive he was towards my lawyer, the more he showed his contempt for educated, strong women. He admitted he jumped over the fence to come and confront John and I even though he didn't have a problem with us... so why jump over a fence to come and verbally and physically assault us? He admitted he wanted to come and 'have words'. He admitted to not actually knowing what was supposed to have been said by me, and couldn't actually tell whether it was a man's voice or a female voice. He said he thought he heard the word 'whore' and believed I was referring to his partner, John's ex. I couldn't help giggling to myself at that, because if I hadn't mentioned anyone's name, why would he think I meant her, unless he (or others) thought that of her; a strange comment to make in my opinion, but also amusing for a few of us in the courtroom who had understood the inference of what he had said; even the judge looked up and raised his eyebrow, with the press officer to the right of the courtroom sitting there trying to hide the smile that was creeping onto his face. This guy made so many stupid comments that even the judge raised an eyebrow or two.

When both my lawyer and the Prosecutor Fiscal were done with him, I felt a surge of confidence. He had made himself look like the aggressor several times and he hadn't even realised it. I didn't like the video footage of me at all, and I could hear the fear in my voice and see the fear on my face; and not being too vain here, but the camera angle wasn't very flattering at all, but hey, that was the least of my worries. What was interesting was the Prosecutor Fiscal had tried to make out I had caused a cut on this first thug's face. There was absolutely no way I could have made that cut with it being the shape it was, unless I had something like a square angled ring on my hand, which I didn't. Apparently one of the reasons it had taken PC Steph Tanner three days to interview him was because I had damaged his face so badly that he couldn't speak for three days; when asked by my lawyer why photos of his injuries had not been submitted to the court, it turned out there were no photos of his injuries at all. So why, if I had caused so many injuries to his face that the police officer couldn't interview him for three days, had there not been photographic evidence of his injuries? That would have been the first thing to have been done, and a full medical assessment done on his facial injuries, especially with the kind of injuries he was on about, there would be been a possibility of internal head injuries. The more he spoke the more it was becoming obvious he had been gunning for John, and I was just collateral damage. It was also obvious that he was making so much of it up with the amount of contradictions he was making. His testimony took so long and with the Prosecutor Fiscal clutching at straws, and what I believed to be leading the witness, I sensed desperation in the Prosecutor. During the whole time this thug had been speaking, I had been making notes. Not looking at him, just making notes on everything he was saying. As he stepped down for a break, my lawyer and I went over a few points he had raised and then when he came back in and as my lawyer cross examined him, he faltered even more. There was definitely something going on with the police officer on the island, I just couldn't put my finger on it, but the thug was too close to him; far too friendly and close.

We stopped for lunch after this thug had been on the stand and I was told I could go into town for lunch. I told my lawyer I didn't feel safe going out there alone and going to get lunch by myself, so we went and got lunch together and then went to her offices to go over everything we had just heard and the notes we had both been making. I told her I could feel John's ex burning her eyes into the back of me, and she told me to just forget she was there. Easier said than done!

When we went back into the courtroom it was the turn of the younger lad, who was being treated as a minor and had a support worker there with him. How ridiculous! Especially when he has the confidence to be abusive and threatening, racist and vile in the street but when it is in a courtroom he needs a support worker! That was messed up, but what was even more messed up was what he said. He admitted he had been told by one of the guys that attacked John that he 'had to go film it'. This is whilst they were all still in the garden, of John's friend Sam. I knew I didn't trust Sam, and I really didn't like the fact that John was friends with him. There was just something about him I didn't like and knowing these thugs had permission to be in his garden just raised more and more questions about him. This younger guy also admitted inadvertently that on the night in question, it wasn't the 'first time' the thug had referred to my boys as Paki's and to me as a Paki lover. Hmmm interesting don't you think Mrs Lawyer! When asked about the comments I was supposed to have made, he said he hadn't heard anything, he had just seen us from Sam's garden. He also kept looking over into the public gallery so much so he had to be asked by my lawyer to stop seeking approval for his questions and answers from the public gallery i.e. the thug and John's ex... who incidentally were now both sat behind me with this older woman. I could feel their eyes burning into the back of my head. It was awful, but not as bad as the testimony this younger lad was giving was confirming a lot of what I had said happened, as well as confirming what and why I believe what had happened, had happened. He had gone against the grain with his friend and was strengthening my case with every word that came out of his mouth. He got confused at so many of the questions, even though they were really straightforward questions.

Next up was John's daughter. Again she had to be supported, but this time there was a screen between her and I so she couldn't see me. So once more, she was confident enough to not only charge forward to scream, shout and swear at me in the street, lashing out like a wild animal, but to also stand in a court of law and lie about what happened, but she needs a screen to protect her from me looking at her; which I didn't do to any of them. I focused on writing notes about everything they were saying, and shared thoughts, comments and ideas about what was being said. She couldn't even decide between what I was supposed to have done and where I was supposed to have done it. She had also admitted that she came at me screaming and shouting at me. She admitted she had never met me before and admitted that she never saw me hit anyone else. She confirmed that she had not been examined by the doctor, which as a mother shocks me on quite a few levels because I know that if an adult had of hit my child in the way I was supposedly hit her, my boys would have been taken to the doctor straight away for an assessment. Why had her mother not had her assessed? Other than the fact they knew I hadn't hit her. I was sat there in the dock listening to this fourteen year old girl lie, call the local police officer by his first name and say that after just four months of the thug that had hit me being in her mum's life, she saw him as her dad. I felt a pain in my heart. She had a dad who loved her so deeply and would give her the world if he could, and yet due to the spiteful, vindictive nature of her mother, she just didn't want to see her dad, and called this violent, aggressive and foul mouthed man 'Dad'.

After these three had given their evidence, I was in total disbelief that this case had not been thrown out. How could they continue with this farce? How could the judge sit there and continue to waste everyone's time? So far we have had the three people I am supposed to have assaulted, all proving more about my case than each other's. It was obvious, even to a blind man, that the police and Prosecutor Fiscal were doing their best to stitch me up, but again, for what reason? I still couldn't shake the feeling that something much bigger was at play here. There was just too much determination to see me convicted. But why? Was it my relationship with John? Or the fact that I was an intelligent, independent woman who was fighting the stupidity and over-zealous policing? Because I wasn't prepared to just take the racist and sexist abuse from the police officer in the first instance in the first case? Was this a retaliation agenda?

We took a break after John's daughter has given her false testimony and when we came back, it was time for PC Hogg to take the stand. He was there for less than five minutes and lied through his teeth from start to finish. He said he cautioned and charged me, and all I had said was, "I didn't do it." He denied I had shown him my injuries. He denied I had told him we were the victims of the attack, and that arresting me was akin to arresting a rape victim.

He denied I had requested to make a statement and he denied he had obtained our details by deception telling us, "You are not in any trouble; everything is fine; we just need to confirm your details." He also denied the fact the female officer with him had told us that if we were not happy with what was happening we could go over to the Oban police station and make a statement.

I was so appalled at the lies coming out of his mouth I heard myself say, "Are you for real? You're lying you know you are!" When I saw the Judge, my lawyer, the clerk and the press officer look at me, I realised I had said it out loud. The judge told me to be silent, and then went on to write something down. PC Hogg had lied so much I felt disgusted by his arrogance and audacity. When he stepped down, we broke for another break.

My lawyer came over and we discussed points on what I had just said out loud in the courtroom. I told her, "He doesn't deserve to wear that uniform. The police wonder why people do not respect them and it is police officers like him that make it difficult for all the good coppers out there! He lied, he knows he lied!"

My lawyer told me to join her in the witness room, which was a good idea as I needed to go to the loo anyway. We went over everything that had happened throughout the day and where we were at in terms of the evidence. We went over what was to be used in summing up the evidence heard thus far and that we were running out of time for today that my evidence was not going to get heard. I would have to come back again. I had wanted it all to be over, but I had to come back and face this all again. She told me that we could either wait to hear John's evidence on the same day as my evidence or he could be called now. She also said that the Prosecutor may want to hear John's evidence straightaway, calling John as his witness so he could close his evidence, which would mean it would weaken our position slightly. I told her she would need to speak with John.

So she went and explained the situation to John. I went back into the courtroom and sat in the dock waiting. My lawyer came back into the courtroom and told me that John wasn't prepared to come back on another date so would be giving his evidence that afternoon. All I heard in that statement was John had decided to become a witness for the Prosecutor and wouldn't be there to support me on the final day of the trial. Tears pricked my eyes and I felt betrayal. How could he support the Prosecutor by going as his witness? How could he not stand by my side on the final day of the trial? I turned to look at him, saw him shake his head, and then the tears fell. He looked confused, but I didn't care. I didn't want to look at him anymore. I turned away from him and sat down with my head in my hands and just cried. My lawyer did her best to console me, but it was too late. He had made his choice and his choice was to become a witness for the prosecution, and not come back and be by my side in the courtroom on the day I would give my evidence; the final day of the trial.

So if I got a guilty verdict, I would be alone; with no one to be there for me, to hold me or to support me. My lawyer told me she was so sorry. I looked up at her and said, "Don't be, I've got used to doing this by myself, what's another day?" She looked at me with such sadness in her eyes, and in those last few moments I knew I didn't want to be with John any more. I wanted to be with a partner who would be there by my side in the good times and the bad, not desert me because it wasn't convenient for him. But then again, where were my family? My friends? Why was I sat in a courtroom with no one there with me, to support me? Why was I doing this alone? I would never have allowed any of my friends to go through what I had gone through alone. I would have been by their side, to either support them or celebrate with them. My head was in a mess. I wiped my face, took a deep breath and composed myself. Sucked it all up and realised this was my life, a lone wolf in many ways. I was supported from afar by many, some complete strangers, but many of my friends lived in different countries, and those who lived in the UK worked for other people or had small children. These visits to Scotland took three days out of my week, how could my friends give up three days of their week?

John was called into the courtroom and I couldn't look at him; didn't want to look at him. We were all told to 'rise' again as the Judge walked in, and again I chose to rise in my own power again. I felt like the angels were lifting me up when I stood up; I felt protected. I felt so light and as if I had floated up. We then had to sit back down and the Prosecutor started questioning John. I still couldn't look at him, and I could see him out of the corner of my eye looking at me. I made notes on what he was saying and he confirmed for the court he wouldn't be with me if he knew, or thought, I had hit his daughter, or any child for that matter. He also told the court he had not seen the first thug hit me, as he was protecting himself from the beating the second thug was inflicting on him, the one who had told the young lad to film everything. John confirmed he had heard all the racist abuse coming in my direction, and the insults on me as "dumb f****** blonde" and how he had heard his daughter shout and swear at me; which he'd never heard language like that come from her mouth before. He said he was very disappointed in the negative behaviour she was exhibiting after him only having been away from the Island for a year. He also confirmed that there were several incidences of the mother of his daughter causing problems for him, which PC Steph Tanner and the local doctor were aware of. She was known to have caused many problems not just for him, but a few of her ex's; and that this was a pattern of behaviour of hers that needed to be taken into consideration because it wasn't just him it was affecting, it was me and my boys, and my family.

After he had given his evidence he walked to the back of the courtroom, looking at me. I still couldn't bring myself to look at him. He had hurt me, again; and this time I knew I had to end it. He was hurting me because I was allowing him to hurt me, and I had to draw the line in the sand and set my own boundaries. He was then asked to leave the courtroom whilst we set another date for me to return to give evidence. I was asked to return the following week but I knew I had school governor training and I didn't have the funds to return. I was then given a date for the January, and I knew I was off on holiday with the boys and would be starting a world book tour, taking my business to a whole new level. I also knew I wanted the court case over in 2017. I wanted to start 2018 with a clean slate. When I refused both of those dates giving the reasons of school governor training and a global book tour, it took everyone in the courtroom by surprise. I had just spent the day in a courtroom being made out to be some crazy, violent woman who assaulted two males and a young girl and here I was telling them I was a school governor and an author. Looks of confusion spread around the courtroom, and left the reporter looking a lot more interested. The only date the court had left was the 6th December, my 40th birthday. I shook my head with a sad grin on my face. Bloody typical! Well it had been a lucky day for me before, being born, so hey, why not. So it was set, I would be returning to Scotland the day before my 40th birthday to appear in court on my birthday, alone. Great.

John was waiting for me outside of the courthouse and I told him I was hungry and wanted some food. I knew I wanted some fish and so we headed to Eesk, the place we had eaten on our first date together. How ironic. As we sat there he asked about how things had gone and what had been said and so I told him. I was just going through the motions. I felt so detached from him, almost like I was still floating with the angels protecting me. I was tired, but I knew I had to drive back to Sheffield so I could be at the Central Library to give my talk the next day.

After I had given John the update on what had happened, he told me about what had happened during the day for him. I was sad for him, really sad, what he had experienced that day was toxic in many ways, but I just couldn't connect to it. I was hurting too much; not just from what he had done and said that day, but also by what had been said about me, and what I had seen in the courtroom. It had been a long day. I had seen four people sent to prison, three of which obviously needed a different kind of help. Prison wasn't the answer for them, nor was it going to be an answer for me. John told me he wanted to visit his brother's graves on the way back and was disappointed when I told him, "No, it's too much of a detour and staying overnight wasn't an issue due to costs and timings for my event." He accepted it but I could tell he wasn't happy about it; but hey I wasn't happy about the fact he had chosen to go over to the Prosecution's side, which he told me he hadn't been aware of the implications. I found that hard to believe as my lawyer was so thorough, and I also knew that John wanted to get his part of the court case over and done with. Maybe he hadn't understood the implications clearly enough, but it still didn't excuse the fact that he didn't want to return again with me, the woman he was supposed to love, to stand with me on the day I would receive the verdict of this awful trauma I had been through, my boys had been through, my family, and the thing that had destroyed so much of what we'd had. The bill was paid and we walked back to the car, with me still worried that the Tiree thugs would still be in Oban. I just wanted to leave.

The journey home was just as horrible as the journey up to Scotland. John was still being unsupportive of me, choosing to go to sleep instead of helping to keep me awake, which we'd had a disagreement about. We arrived back in Sheffield and as he woke up, he had changed. It was as if he had slept off all the negativity and nastiness. He did everything to make me comfortable and when I got up the next morning to go to the library for my event, he got up, made me coffee, wished me luck and said, "You've got this." I knew I had, I was going to do what I knew I was great at; inspiring others to go after their dreams, this time as an author, but also to inspire others with my author story.

When I arrived back home John had left me a message to say he had gone to the allotment and would be back later; also adding to call him to let him know how my talk had gone. I went home, cuddled my dogs, took them for a walk and then let him know all had gone well and that I would be going to sleep for a few hours. When he came home, I was just stirring from my sleep, not quite awake but awake enough to hear him come around to my side of the bed and kiss me softly on the forehead, making sure I was covered up properly by the duvet. I had never known him to do that before. As he walked away, tears rolled down my face. I was going to end our relationship and it was almost as if I was being given a sign not to. I covered my head with the duvet and cried. When I woke up, John and the boys had been talking and cooking dinner. John then told the boys he was going to take me over the road for a drink. Whist we were on our way over to the pub his phone rang, it was his new friend from the boat he had been on. I expected him to answer it but he dismissed the call, telling me he was with me and it was our time. Again, I was surprised but it felt like it was a little too late for these gestures.

Sitting in the pub with a glass of wine and him with his pint, we were talking and things just got too much for me. I walked out of the pub telling him he had been really nasty to me over the last few days and months, and I'd had enough. I got back home and told the boys I was taking the dogs for a walk. On the walk, I cried my eyes out, I was tired, I was exhausted and I was hurting, and when I got back home with the dogs, I gave my boys a huge hug and told them I was sorry for everything that had happened over the last year, how much time I had been away from them and how upset they had seen me be. They both told me it was okay, and they didn't blame me. We spoke some more and I held back more tears until Naasir went to bed.

I sent John a text message telling him it was over, to never contact me again and that his stuff was in the backyard. He came back to the apartment after an hour had passed and was banging on the door to be allowed back in. I ignored him. I heard him call Chris to come and collect him. I watched him walk with all his stuff over to the garage. He looked lost. My heart broke. Chris collected him and as they drove past, John didn't even look up at our bedroom window. And then he was gone. We were over. If he didn't want to stand by my side in the courtroom on the final date, he wouldn't stand by my side at all.

THIRTY-FIVE

HITTING 40

Growing up I never envisioned being 40 and alone, especially after having gotten married and had children. I had done a lot of work on myself learning to like myself and I knew I was a lovely person. I knew I was a great wife and mother, and I knew I wanted to get married again, to spend the rest of my life with that one person, living at sea, having adventures, creating memories and taking care of each other as we grew old together. I had hoped that would have been ramO, but that wasn't meant to be.

I went through a lot of growth and healing to even begin to consider having another relationship, made a list of the kind of characteristics, values, morals and interests I wanted in my future partner, and John had shown up. He had blown my mind, and I had resisted being in a relationship with him for a long time. He had been patient. He had been on the receiving end of my insecurities and upset for the past two years. He had supported Khaalid during so much, even though it should have been ramO, his father, by his side. I had known John a long time and now not only had I lost a partner who had rocked my world to my very core, I had lost a friend. He had supported me through so much, but when it came down to it, he was unwilling to be the man I wanted. Instead of promoting my business which would benefit us both, he chose to promote a mutual friend's business. Instead of acknowledging me, he would acknowledge other women, telling everyone how they had the biggest heart he had ever known, how this woman was an incredible mother and choosing to interact with others rather than me and my boys. I was jealous of the attention he showered on others; and I missed him terribly. I missed who we had been. I missed his energy, his breathing, his giggle, I missed our conversation, I missed cooking with him and I knew I had to get some coaching.

I had to know whether I was just afraid of being alone or if I really truly wanted to be with him. I re-read *The Queen's Code*. I went over the coaching videos EJ had put out in her relationship coaching groups, I went deep and then deeper again into what had been coming up for me. I got present to the story I had been telling myself. I got present to how I had wanted him to do things the way I would have done them, but how could he? First of all, he is not me. Secondly, he is not a woman. And thirdly, I either choose him as he is, or I don't. I couldn't expect him to be perfect, because no one is, and I also couldn't expect him to change the way he did things just to suit me. What I could expect from him though was to be present to me and listen to my concerns like he used to; but I had to step up for him and be present to him and his wants – which I hadn't done because I was so focused on building the business, fighting the court case and creating a balancing act between him and my boys. I had neglected him on many levels. I hadn't *heard* him or *seen* him. I also got really *present* to the depths of what he must have been going through and how that had more than likely been the reason behind his actions. Even after everything that had happened, I still loved John, there was no doubt about that at all. He had confronted me on so many levels that I had been forced to grow. I may not have liked the way in which he had gone about things, but the end result was still the same. He had told me countless times not to put my head in places it didn't need to be; but with his actions and lack of attention, my head had gone places that had raised the demons within me and forced me to face them.

After going deep with my coaching and journaling, I knew I had to see him. I knew he was still in Sheffield, so I sent him a message asking him if he would meet me. He replied almost immediately saying he would. My heart didn't just skip a beat, it skipped several. We arranged to meet up a few days later, and we had a lovely evening together.

What happened after that changed things dramatically between us. We started to rebuild, and we both knew we were committed to a future together. How it would work with my upcoming global book tour after my holiday with the boys was going to be interesting, but I needed to do it.

I needed the time away from Sheffield, from my boys, from John, from everything I knew, to heal. I hadn't given myself chance to heal since Egypt. It had been one thing after another for so long. One of my friends Debbie reminded me that I had been fire fighting ever since she had known me. Everything from being given 24 hours to live six weeks before I was due to give birth to Naasir; recovering from that; packing the house up to move to Egypt; living through the Uprising, writing my first book *Friday Bridge* and dealing with a really bad publisher; fighting to get my book back from them. Then returning to the UK and dealing with everything you have read about in this book. I needed to recharge. I needed to step back so my boys could step up; for the boys to build a stronger relationship with ramO. I needed to do me for a change, and going to do my global book tour would be the perfect opportunity. I just had to head up to Scotland win the case and then five days later fly off to New Zealand with my boys to take a much needed holiday together, before taking my business location free and promoting my books; all whilst living at sea and writing more.

I was in regular contact with my lawyer and having gone over our notes from the previous trial date, we were confident we would win. We had to. There was no other option if there was any justice at all in Scotland; and no other option for me and my future. John had stayed over a few nights and it was lovely to have him home again. The boys enjoyed him being there as well, so did the dogs. Whilst he was down the allotment during the day, I was preparing everything for the trip. I started sorting the finances out with Jorja, my accountant, so all bank statements went to her, cancelling everything my business no longer needed. The boys and I had sat down together on many occasions over the last few months discussing how they would feel about ramO moving into our home whilst I was away on the book tour. They were both cool with it as it meant they got to stay in our home and be close to all the things we loved about the apartment. I had a lot of internal dialogue to sort out with regards to my ex-husband moving into my home and being in my space again. I wanted him to be very clear that this was not a way of him moving back into my life as a partner, it was just a temporary arrangement whilst I was away on business and healing all at the same time. He understood that and so did the boys. It was also a really great example for us both to set the boys; parents working together for the sake of the children, even when they were not together in a relationship other than a parental one. Like I had said to the boys when ramO and I first split up, we will always be the Aysha family even if ramO and I were not together anymore. Many people thought I was crazy letting him stay in my apartment, but to me it just made absolute sense. I loved that apartment. I loved the area and it was home for the boys and the dogs. There was no point unsettling the boys or the dogs any more than was needed. ramO and I set about organising the change of bank details on all of the utility companies whilst I was away. I finalised certain projects and sorted out outstanding issues that needed to be dealt with.

With all the puppies sold and the flights booked, everything in place to take my business to the next level, everything sorted with ramO and the boys, John being more attentive than he had been for well over a year and things going really well between us, all I had to do was win the court case. I booked my accommodation for the 5th Dec until 7th December, because my mum had told me that regardless of whether I won the case or not, I was not to travel back to Sheffield on my birthday. I was to go out for a meal to celebrate my 40th, even if I was alone. I booked into the same place John and I had stayed at the month before and then booked all the trains; I had got so good at knowing how and when to book the trains I ended up saving more money to travel each and every time I went. The boys stayed with ramO and gave me big hugs telling me I was going to win; they were so positive I would win bless them, even if it was just an external positivity. John gave me a big hug and a kiss, reaffirmed so many things about me and told me to keep strong; I knew I was innocent, he knew I was innocent and told me to keep focused on a positive result. Those words meant so much to me, and I set off to Scotland with a happy heart. I had six days before the boys and I flew off on holiday and I had a lot to look forward to. Arriving in Oban was emotional; I knew this would be the end a very traumatic time in my life and my boy's lives. We had all been through a heck of a lot at the hands of an incompetent system, one so broken police corruption and inadequacies were damaging families and societies, and the really sad thing is, no one really gave a damn about the ones on trial. We were all just another face, another case and blight on society; even if we hadn't done the things we were in court for. The lies I had heard spoken, the intimidation I had seen over the last two years from one police officer to another was unbelievable, and here I was someone who knew about it prior to seeing it; and seeing it took things to a whole new level.

Relaxing in a hot bath with a Neal's Yard face mask on, just one of the many product lines I had added to my business, with a glass of wine and UB40 playing in the background, I relaxed for the first time in a long time. I had been learning some new breathing techniques to help combat the stress I had been under. John had been teaching me to breathe deeper and slower too, ever since I was rushed to hospital a week before with a suspected heart attack or clots on my lungs and heart. I had woken up at 3am in the morning unable to breathe and in a lot of pain. I could hardly move. I thought it was a trapped nerve so I booked an emergency appointment at my chiropractor. My usual chiropractor wasn't there that day and so I had to be seen by someone else, and he pretty much refused to treat me because of the chest pains and told me to go directly to the hospital. I was supposed to be collecting Naasir, so we could have dinner with his friend from school and his mum Jane who I was also friends with. Whilst on the tram on my way to collect Naasir I called the hospital and explained what had happened, as directed to by the chiropractor. A lady sat opposite me and she told me that I had to go to the hospital; it turned out she was a nurse and everything she had heard me describe to the man on the phone was pointing to a heart attack or clots on my heart and lungs. I was told to get off the tram immediately and wait where I was for the ambulance. I couldn't believe it. On the way to the hospital, with the blue lights and sirens going I was worried I wouldn't be able to fly to New Zealand, but nothing was going to stop me. I locked in a positive outcome and knew I would be flying.

I called John and he was just leaving R1se, our friend Jenny's new hot yoga studio he had been helping to get ready for launch. I told him I was on my way to the hospital and really wanted him there. But traffic was so bad I told him not to come as I wouldn't be long, I was just going to be checked over, and by the time he would get through the traffic I would be home anyway. But oh how I wanted him there, to have him say he was coming to be by my side regardless, to be by my side, the woman he said he loves, rather than spending more time with the twins.

Whilst at the hospital I was seen immediately and then hooked up to machines and monitored very closely. I kept giving John updates and had informed him about getting to Naasir, who had made his way to the pizzeria where we were meeting his friend. Jane was also on her way to get Naasir, and the restaurant had a close eye on him as well, keeping him entertained. John and I were texting back and forth to keep updated of how close he was getting to Naasir and eventually I told him it was okay as Jane had arrived and so he could go back to Chris and Rob's house. He told me to contact him as soon as I knew what was happening. I was later released from hospital with strict instructions to relax and take some time out. The chest pains were due to stress and nothing physical. Thank goodness for that, I could still fly on the 11th December. I arrived home and reassured Khaalid I was okay. Naasir was fast asleep and I would reassure him in the morning. I woke up the next morning and ended up collapsing on the floor again with Khaalid calling the ambulance as I was unable to breathe and had really bad chest pains. The paramedics were there in moments and ran tests on me again, which resulted in me producing the same results. I was told to rest and take things easy. This court case had really taken its toll on me and this was the end result. The police in Scotland had a lot to answer for; but what did they care? They had managed to get an arrest, a court case and their jobs were being proven worthwhile, even if they were lying through their teeth and concocting stories to do it.

Laying in the bath at my AirBnB in Scotland, knowing I was going to be 40 the next day and celebrating by myself, was a strange feeling. I didn't feel 40, even though I had no idea what 40 was supposed to feel like. I lay in the bath for over an hour before realising I hadn't said goodnight to my boys, so I got out and dried myself off and went to call my boys. I noticed I had received so many messages of encouragement and support for the court case the next day, as well as many birthday greetings. I had people all around the world rooting for me to win this court case, hundreds in fact; and it felt great. I spoke with the boys briefly before wishing them a good night's sleep and then started to read a really great book called *Pussy: A Reclamation* and ladies... I recommend you read this book even if it is the only book you ever read again! Oh and *The Queen's Code*, powerful stuff both of them. Just as I was reading and relating the book to different areas of my life, John called. He wanted to wish me a good night's sleep and told me he would call me again in the morning. I fell asleep shortly after and woke up to my 40th birthday, in a luxury King size bed, as toasty as you like knowing that whatever happened, it was my birthday and I cry if I wanted to; but I chose to smile. Today I was going to win.

I walked to the court house and met with my lawyer, who was smiling away. She told me she was pretty sure they were going to be dropping the charges against the young lad, the one who had been really racist against me and my boys, calling me a stupid blonde bitch and telling me to f*** off I wasn't welcome on the island; but I still had to give my testimony. We went through everything again and then it was time to go inside. She also wished me happy birthday. Sitting in the courtroom I watched the medieval marketplace unfold itself again with sentencing and court dates being set for future trials. At around about 11am I was called to the witness stand to give my evidence. I had previously explained to my lawyer about the hospital visits and she had advised the clerk who made sure I had enough water with me.

My lawyer asked me to confirm my name and all the basics and then asked me what work I did. When I informed the court I was an author, a business mentor, an accountability coach for individuals and businesses, a qualified police assessor, a school governor and online entrepreneur the judge just looked at me as if he was seeing me for the first time. I looked up to the press gallery and realised that there was no one sitting there, something I found quite strange, especially as there had always been a press representative there. The judge looked at me different, and then when my lawyer asked me to tell the court about the kind of books I wrote about and I said, "My first book was about social stereotypes and rural racism, with the second book, which is an international bestseller on three continents, being about the systemic failure of governance, policing and the education system in Egypt, and the third book being about the passive aggressive dictatorship and police corruption in the UK," the judge looked at me again with his eyebrow raised. The Prosecutor Fiscal went bright red and looked rather uncomfortable and quite bloody right he should too! I heard a few sniggers from the public gallery and the word 'cool!' being said, at which point my lawyer went on to ask me about different aspects of my work. She was helping me to show who I really was and the kind of woman I was, the kind of parent I was and the kind of community worker I was, bringing to the forefront all the charity work I did and how I had achieved it with events that I had organised, the sporting events I had entered and the roles I had played as Master of Ceremonies at charity events, as well as the regional regeneration projects I had been involved in. I liked what she was doing, and I liked watching the Prosecutor Fiscal squirm in his seat. The back of his neck would start to go red and then so would his whole face.

Whilst we were going through the evidence I was asked to say what the Tiree thugs had said to me, and although I beeped out what they had said, I was asked to repeat what they had said word for word. It felt uncomfortable using their vocabulary, but if that is what I had to do, then I had to do it, remembering they were the words these thugs had chosen, not me. We went through why the boys and I were on Tiree, what had happened leading up to the attack and what had happened right up to the point where we left the island and were met with the police officers in Oban, going on further to mention police Sergeant Brown, who had recently retired (how convenient!) had refused to take my statement when we had attended Oban police station. When my lawyer sat down and handed over the questioning to the Prosecutor, he did his best to tear me apart saying I only wanted to go to the police station to make a statement when I realised I was being charged; to which I replied, "Of course I did! I wanted to make sure the police had a balanced view of the situation to avoid wasting hundreds of thousands of pounds of precious resources; as well as getting them to see that we were the ones who had been attacked."

He then went on to say my injuries were "not obvious and so were not serious".

I replied to him, "So you don't agree that cancer, brain tumours, heart disease and epilepsy are serious then, using your own logic in that question?"

Again his face flushed red and he realised what a stupid question and statement he had made insinuating just because my injuries were not serious; although also admitting I did have injuries which by default meant his client's witnesses had in fact assaulted me; his client being the police by the way. He continued to grasp at straws using opening statements such as "I put it to you" and "I suggest you" with me coming back at him saying "You can suggest and put whatever you like to me, it doesn't make it true".

When he mentioned the police officer PC Hogg's statement and I responded with, "He is a discredit to the uniform with the lies he told, he doesn't deserve to wear it," he didn't like that either. He tried to state that I had been the aggressor and I told him that I could not have been the aggressor as I had not known the individuals were there and certainly didn't know any of them as I wouldn't mix with people like them, had never socialised on the island and never been introduced to them. When he told me my posture in the video was one of a fighting posture, I informed him I did mixed martial arts and I was in what they called a 'guard stance' ready to defend; and if I had really wanted to cause an injury to any of them I could have done, but I am not in the habit of wasting my time and money invested over the years by assaulting someone as I would lose my license to train. He tried to get me to state why the nurse who had examined me had written down 'left side' instead of 'right side' on my medical records, and when I told him "You would need to ask her, I cannot answer for anyone else; I can only surmise that she is human like everyone else and occasionally gets her left and right mixed up; but if you looked at the notes, you will clearly see she has corrected her notes to reflect the injuries were on my right side." He soon gave up on his questions and sat down rather flustered, before my lawyer went on to clarify a few other issues.

The summing up was interesting, with the prosecutor telling the judge the witnesses had been clear and precise in their delivery of their statements, when in fact they hadn't at all, more like a group of bumbling idiots; which was confirmed by my lawyer (but in a more professional manner than the way I have just described). The prosecutor struggled to make a fluid summing up and his sentences were broken, spoken without any confidence at all, whereas my lawyer was as fluid as water, clear concise and confident; just as I had seen her to be in the courtroom for her other clients. I felt very confident. After the summing up was done, I was asked to stand in the dock and await the verdict. It felt like it took forever, but it was only a few moments. The judge came back with the verdict of 'not proven' on all charges, and I let out a breath I didn't even know I was holding. My lawyer looked at me with a big smile on her face, I thanked the judge and he simply nodded at me and left the courtroom. My lawyer came over to me straightaway and congratulated me. I thanked her for all her help and told her I knew she was an excellent choice even before she represented me. She told me I had handled the questions well and performed very professionally, even if I had confronted the prosecutor a little bit. She smiled, I smiled and we walked out of the courtroom together.

She asked me what I was doing for my birthday and I said, "Celebrating my win, my niece Karlie's birthday and of course my own, by going out to dinner to Eesk." I had saved some money for some champagne and a really nice seafood dish. I was 40 and I was going to celebrate. I was finally free of the toxic world of Scotland Policing and the Scottish Judiciary system, and I was finally smiling. It felt good. I knew I was innocent and now it was on record that I was innocent. I knew the truth would set me free. I knew the universe had my back, my family and friends had my back, but most importantly, I believed in myself; and that belief got me through it.

Now it was time for me to relax, celebrate and focus on the future.

And that is exactly what I did.

EPILOGUE

Throughout this whole Scotland Saga I have believed in myself. I knew I had done nothing wrong. I knew I had not broken any laws. I knew what I had done, I had done with the very best of intentions and knowledge that I was doing the right thing. After all the research and study of the law I have done over the last two years, I KNOW I didn't break any laws, so why were the police and so-called justice system so eager and willing to drag me through the courts, take my children off me and then convict me, before admonishing the conviction, meaning it never has to be declared? Why would they do that? What was their reasons? Racial hatred? Anti English? Anti empowered women? Anti single mums? Realised they made a mistake and couldn't back track? Something more sinister involving my children being in a foster home for a few days?

I may not think the same way as those involved in these two cases, but as you have read throughout this book, I am a very dedicated mother, a person who likes to raise others up and encourage self-belief and belief in each other. I am a fighter. I am someone who loves deeply and passionately. I am determined and I will stop at nothing to protect my boys, and my family. I am determined to live my life purpose and answer my soul calling, taking my life and business to new heights all the time; enabling others to do the same as I rise up.

In the first case against me, I saw nothing wrong with leaving my two boys alone in the car for 15 minutes in what appeared to me to be a safe and quiet area. Parents do it every day in parks, campsites and in their local area, sending their children to the shops, or going in shops themselves, leaving children in the car listening to music, watching DVDs, or reading books. As I mentioned in the main body of this text, had I have been in a busy area, a lower socio economic area of Glasgow, known for drug and gun crime, or a busy city centre, there would have been no way I would have left my boys for the 10-15 minutes it took me to walk up the hill, check the opening times and cost of a ticket, let alone leave them for the amount of time the police came up with in what was their fifth accusation, knowing the first four would not be able to be proven. Not only am I an intelligent woman, able to make my own risk assessment of an area due to the community regeneration work that I have done, but due to the people we had met, combined with the amount of travel around the world I have done to remote parts of countries visited, I trusted it would be safe. Knowing it was good enough for the Dowager, Lord Grantham and Lady Mary to stay in Inveraray (due to the research ITV would have done prior to commencing filming), then I knew it was good enough for me and my boys to park up and watch the sun rise over the loch, having slept in the car overnight. I trusted they would be okay for the amount of time it would take me to walk up the driveway of the castle. At no point did I feel it was unsafe to trust my boys and the local community. The racism directed at me, by PS Wilson, for speaking to my boys in Arabic was disgusting and reminded me of the copious amounts of racism we are seeing in police forces around the world; especially the United States, and more so in the UK since the Conservative government have been in power in the UK.

With the second case, I had no way of knowing these thugs and small-minded islanders would set upon John and I, and had no way of knowing that the police would be willing to corrupt themselves in such a way as to make up the three charges against me, charge the others involved and then drop the charges of the three thugs who assaulted me.

I am the only woman, the only outsider in all of this, and the only one to have been charged. The rest have all got away with a racist hate crime, an assault crime (two men against one woman) with the help of

Police Scotland. The fact the Prosecutor Fiscal was keen to see me in court, and was keen to get me convicted of these crimes is questionable, very questionable indeed. By their actions alone they are stating that racial hatred is acceptable in the west coast of Scotland, and they stating that violence against women is acceptable. Not only this, but they are also stating that it is okay for gross misconduct and poor policing to bring a trial to court, wasting hundreds of thousands of pounds of public spending, which could be put to better use such as actual child abuse and paedophilia, better salaries and facilities for our healthcare and schooling. With the actions of the Police Officers, Judges and Lawyers involved in both cases, we are seeing how ego, job preservation, corruption and an abusive form of control is in existence within the very organisations that are supposed to 'protect and serve' the state; the state being the family unit.

What the police, judges and lawyers have done is violated my family in ways which has caused irreparable damage and they have also done the exact opposite of what they were set up to do. They have made me lose copious amounts of work hours, resulting in two years' worth of lost business, put me in thousands of pounds worth of debt, taken time away from my children which I will never get back, and they have affected my mental, emotional and physical health in such negative ways. I have suffered from anxiety attacks, currently dealing with PTSD, have found myself withdrawing from society, choosing to connect with only those I know in the real world, and via social media for my business. As a result of these court cases I now have zero faith in the system, not that I had much before, but now, none is present. I now choose to spend time by myself, away from others, unless I have to.

I have also chosen to take some time away from my children, leaving them with their dad, as the trauma, anxiety, immense pressure and exhaustion I have experienced due to this Scotland Saga has impacted me in such a negative way that I am unable to be the mother I wish to. I needed to step back and heal, as far away from others as possible; as far away from land as possible, so I chose to go and heal at sea, on my beloved ocean; fulfilling a dream of living at sea that I have had since I was eight years old. Making this choice was not easy, especially with the judgements and social pressures on mothers to stay and focus purely on their children and their husband/partner, supporting them rather than going after what lights her up. With the knowledge that I had fought against a charge of wilful neglect and abandonment of my children, I struggled with leaving them with their dad. I knew I was not abandoning them, I knew I was not neglecting them; I was leaving them to have much needed quality time with their dad, and I know if I was a man, no one would bat an eyelid, but me being a mum… WOAH! Bad Mother! Social guilt and mother guilt in abundance. But I had to go. I had to take a time out. I had to regroup and I had to nourish my own soul, fill my own love cup up and love my boys from the overflow. I had to step back so the boys and their dad could step up, because whilst I was around, they relied on me to0 heavily, a cultural and social norm in both the Western and Eastern world. I couldn't give them what they needed, because I had forgotten who I was, I had forgotten how to be the fun mum, how to give myself what I needed. I also needed time to focus on my business, time to write my books and time to heal from the hurt caused during the last year of my relationship with John. We were on very thin ice. The court cases had changed us and driven a massive wedge between us. All areas of my life needed healing and I couldn't do that in a place where so many memories haunted me.

I have not written this book for a sympathy vote. I have written it to give you the information I have learnt, taking my understanding of the world we live in, to a much deeper level; a world which many will not understand as they are white, English speaking citizens, with no diversity in their lives whatsoever. Many will not know what it is like to see someone exhibit racism towards a child, *your* child; or be the subject of racism simply because you happened to marry someone who is not white, or at least European; unless you are of course Polish, Lithuanian, Romanian or Yugoslavian.

Many of you will not know what it is to be a single mum, the courage, the relentlessness it takes to get through each day, the level of exhaustion you feel; or understand the judgements and in some cases pity that married couples send your way. Those of you who are single parents may not have the strength, the knowledge or the support that I have had to do the equivalent of a five year law degree in two years across the fields of Human Rights, Family Law and Criminal Law; all whilst working your weekly job, let alone building an international business. Many of you are simply just too tired of it all to bother with the fight and just take what gets thrown at you *because it is easier.*

Many of the police officers today are simply bullies in uniforms, and they make it harder for those within the police force who have joined the force to make a positive difference. Sadly though, we are the sum total of the five people we associate with, and sooner or later, these individuals who joined for good intentions will either become corrupted or they will leave, after having trained for years to get in, and for many, giving up on a childhood dream.

Becoming a Police Assessor for West Humberside Police all those years earlier had paid their dividends, even if I hadn't worked for them since I had left for Egypt. The concept of policing hasn't changed. In fact, with all the new Human Rights and cultural laws, it *should have* evolved; but it hasn't. In the west coast of Scotland it is still archaic and antiquated. It is still tribal, and has racist and religious prejudices exist on a very deep level.

The gender issues are still very much in existence, being very much male dominated, with women being forced, or rather 'managed out' if they have, or choose to have children. The attitude on the west coast, in the more rural areas of Scotland (and other areas within the UK) towards women is still very much one of 'we should do as we are told' resulting in not standing up for ourselves as humans, even though we are 50% of the population, mothers of men, sisters to brothers, daughters to fathers. This was very evident to me as I sat and watched the attitudes towards the women on trial, the female staff within the courtrooms and the lack of female lawyers; David from Beltrami & Co confirming to me that going to Dunoon was like going back in time twenty years. We as women are matriarchs, we are intelligent, can be incredibly empowered, we build bridges with different cultures, we are raising families alone, we are well educated. But we dumb ourselves down; we feel guilt when we shouldn't.

With the outcomes of both trials it became very clear to me that those of us who are raising culturally diverse families are not welcome in the west coast of Scotland. With the attitudes of the police, lawyers and judges it was a warning to me that women do not fit into the male dominated, male controlling world and we must remain in the traditional little housewife ways of old.

Did the police go full out because I dared to stand up to them? How dare I stand up for our rights? How dare I challenge a small-minded police officer who doesn't know the difference between speaking a different language and being aggressive? How dare I travel alone with my children, trusting them to behave and listen to me, obeying my instructions, and how dare I stand up for my right to be heard! How dare any of us women do that? Who do we think we are? We are mothers. We are women and we are not going to be silenced just because men who need to prove their worth, the ones who are stuck in the dark ages, need to put out our light to make their own shine brighter.

I have used my skills as a business woman, a coach, a mentor, a human being, and as a self-confessed bookworm and geek to discover all the information I could on the laws that governed us as citizens. I downloaded the new and updated behavioural frameworks, The Code of Ethics, the Leadership Review from the different website and policing organisations; I spent hours upon hours studying the law books that were given to students studying law from PACE, the lawyer's role in the courtroom. I spent hours trawling through Scottish law on websites such as The Law Society Scotland, Police Scotland, NSPCC Scotland, International Human Rights websites and I had sacrificed so much to win this case, and now, due to my drive and determination I am a winner in many ways.

These two court cases have held me back, stopped me from growing my business as quickly as I needed it to grow to provide for my boys. The actions of the police and justice system in Scotland forced me onto benefits, something I never ever wanted. I have gone without food so my children could eat, sold my car to keep a roof over their head, and borrowed money from friends to pay legal fees; and I am one of the lucky ones. I nearly lost my partner because of the pressure and choices we both had to make to survive the second court case. My parents, my mother especially, have been put under unnecessary stress. My boys have had distractions and absences from school, had to go without just so I can pay for transport and accommodation up and back to Scotland. They have lost precious time with me at a time when they needed it the most, just because of the amount of time these court cases have taken up. That is not right; and yet the police and law courts don't care.

They have to prove their worth, prove their jobs are worthwhile, when in fact, if we look at the whole situation realistically, the more crime drops, the less people get arrested, the more valuable and better job the police are doing, not the other way around! The more arrests you make, the worse the police are! Or is that just too simple for the powers that be are to actually comprehend?

My boys have seen me, their mother, work every hour they are awake just to make ends meet and study so late into the night they have woken up to find me fast asleep with a book on my knee. This is not a healthy situation for my boys to witness because it shows them that mummy has to work hard just to survive against the system. It may show them a strong work ethic, but it teaches them no respect for the systems that are supposed to be there to support the citizens who pay he wages of the politicians. We are the ones who pay their wages with our taxes and yet they screw us over time and time again... is there any wonder the youth of today have zero respect for the police when they see this all happening? My boys have been through their own incredible journey, and whilst it is character building, the damage it has done to all of us has far reaching effects we are not going to see for some time. They do not trust the police. They do not respect the police and they do not respect the justice system. Not only have they seen the police and justice system punish their mother for being an incredible mother, but they repeatedly punish and criminalise Arabs, Pakistani's, Muslims and anyone who is not white. They punish the youth from lower socio economic backgrounds and reward only those who can pay their own way, or who are the rich white folks, as per the McCanns, in society.

As I said, I didn't write this book for a sympathy vote, more of a wake-up call. Just as I wrote my first two books as insights into the Egyptian Uprising and the world of rural racism and social stereotypes; ironic how both books have led me to be able to utilise all my professional experiences and personal experiences to culminate into this book. I also wrote this book because I know that whatever happens in the four countries of the UK, the motherland of the Commonwealth, it will spread across to other Commonwealth countries such as Australia, New Zealand, and Canada. It already is.

I also wrote this book to expose the corruption within Police Scotland as I experienced it, to expose those involved in these two cases; because you can pretty much guarantee, it runs throughout the rest of the cases they have worked on too. I know when the content of this book gets looked into properly, by those within a position to make a positive difference to the way in which policing and the justice system is run in Scotland, there is a risk that other cases, high profile ones at that, will also get looked into. I also know there will be some who will see no problem with the way the cases were handled and these will be the people who are also part of the problem. They see no harm in not investigating or interviewing someone being wrongly accused of such serious crimes against children, violent crimes against women, and racial hate crimes. These are the people who also need investigating, and removing from the policing and justice profession. The world is getting smaller, social media is exposing so much, and people are able to access more information to protect themselves from the corrupt governments and police forces that run our countries. Leaders have to start becoming leaders; otherwise the people will rise, like we did in Egypt.

I am calling in a law firm who is willing to help me take civil action against Police Scotland, regaining my expenses, legal fees, the lost income, as well as compensation for the trauma my boys and I have been through the last couple of years. Those involved need to be held accountable; all of them, including those who were involved, such as the dark, overweight slimy man from social services who no one bothered to look into. Who was he? Why was he so threatening? Why did he arrange for my children to be taken off me just because I couldn't give names and addresses of family and friends who may have been able to help? Why was I never given the paperwork of who had my children? The thoughts of what may have happened to my children, without even their knowledge – were they filmed whilst taking a shower? Were they drugged and photographed? I know none of this and yet I am supposed to trust a system that behaved in such an aggressive, corrupt manner.

I have suffered from such a high level of stress, so much so I was rushed to hospital with the medical professionals thinking it was a heart attack or possibly even clots on my lungs and heart, but it was stress; and I am one of the stronger ones. What does that say for those weaker than myself? What does their life look like? Hmmm I wonder!

I can put this first phase of the Scotland Saga behind me. I say first phase, because this book is the next phase, a phase of awareness, and a phase where I am calling in proper justice.

I am calling upon each and every one of us to rise up against the system and its corruption. I intend to take action to reclaim my losses, to win compensation, but with the legal firms spoken to already they are either unable, or unwilling to help me take action. That stinks in my book that they are willing to allow the police and justice system get away with penalising a single mum, who is do her best to rebuild her life, a woman who was falsely accused and had the police change their story multiple times, a woman who was the only one charged out of five people, simply because she didn't 'belong' in the small minded racist community, and because she fell in love with 'the wrong guy'. It stinks that these police officers, lawyers and judges are allowed to get away with destroying, or at least attempting to destroy someone's life, just because they do not choose the lifestyle for themselves.

Some of the choices I have made may not be the choices others would have made; but I don't eat the same as others, I don't dress the same as others and those people who know me and my two boys will tell you we are all very loving, polite and respectful people. They will tell you my boys are a credit to me, and that does not come without a certain amount of self-sacrifice and tough love. My boys are highly educated, not just academically but socially and emotionally. They are not followers of the crowds, or 'sheeple' that do what others want them to do, they think for themselves and they make wiser choices at 15 and 11 than a lot of adults twice, three times their ages. They chose to take the coaching and they made it their own. They are the ones who deserve the credit, because like my brother, sister and I prove, you can be raised in the same family, get given the same rules and lessons, but it is what we ultimately do with that information and guidance that makes the difference.

I know that when people read this book, there will be haters out there criticising me for something they do not agree with, but hey, the haters are going to hate, and many are going to do it hiding behind their keyboards. They have not walked a day in my shoes, they have not lived my life and they have not studied and experienced all that I have studied and experienced, but I am hoping that by reading this book, and the first two in this trilogy, they will at least get an insight into who I am and know that hurting a child in anyway is not something I would ever do.

The majority of people who will read this book will be firm supporters of what I am doing, calling the police and the justices system to task. Calling for parental rights to raise our children in the best way we know how, making informed choices on what we know about our lives, values and beliefs, knowledge bases and experiences. We all have the right to raise our children in any way we see fit so long as we are raising children to be happy, contented, healthy, respectful educated individuals. Some may choose to home educate, removing their children from the school system that dumbs down our children in a way that discourages thinking, and creates sheep who simply follow the history and the cultures that the Education Ministers in our respective countries deem fit. Take the film *Captain America* for example, and if you haven't seen it, I highly recommend you do, or the film *I, David Blake*. I also know that many parents who read this book will totally get how difficult it is to raise children single handedly. I know there are many people out there who will resonate with many aspects of this book, whether it is police corruption, whether it is parenting or whether it is learning to love and trust yourself to allow another person in your life as a life partner.

I have written this book to expose the corruption, the lies, the miscarriages of justice, the vile attitudes that exist in the courtrooms, the differences between Scottish and English law, which is referred to as UK law.

There is NO SUCH THING as UK Law.

It is Scottish Law and English Law, and THEY ARE VERY DIFFERENT.

I have written this book to be used as a tool to give you all the confidence to be YOU.

To live your life WITHOUT FEAR of the system.

To give you the COURAGE TO FIGHT back against the system.

To CHOOSE YOU!

I have written this book in the hope that it creates a movement of parents and individuals that are fed up with the arrogance and ego of the government, the police and the so-called justice systems in the world, who think they can tell us what to think, what to belief and what to do.

Dictatorships, aggressive ones or passive aggressive, are not healthy. They create mental health issues which we are seeing all over the world, and they are on the increase. What has happened to me could very easily happen to you. You may think you are safe to make your choices to live your life because you are a good person and a good parent, but with the laws changing at an astounding rate, which ALL lawyers cannot keep up with the legal changes, what hope do we have when we haven't chosen the law as a career choice? As the saying goes 'You are free to do as we tell you' but how and when do we get told? The moment we do something that is outside someone else's comfort zone and reports us to the police, or when someone has their ego bruised, or we choose a different path in life and they feel offended. We are all criminals waiting to be discovered according to the laws and their numerous amendments.

We live in a world where parents are policed by other parents, where single parents are blamed for the break down in society, when we are the ones doing the job of two parents, being forced into poverty because of the bureaucratic, antiquated, disjointed systems used in central and local government.

Single mums are seen as predators for married men, feared by the wives who are insecure in their own marriages.

Single dads are seen as predators, perverts and even paedophiles if seen shopping with his young daughter for her first bra in department stores.

Teachers are not allowed to comfort a pupil these days for fear of being accused of sexual assault.

We live in a culture these days, regardless of which country we live in, where mistakes are not allowed to happen. Failing forward is becoming a thing of the past. Poor performance is punished instead of supported with insights and education. If one person makes a mistake we are all penalised for it, dumbing down nations rather than raising each other up.

We live in a culture where a difference of opinion becomes an offense in many different ways; resulting in a lack of freedom of speech and law suits in abundance.

We cannot take responsibility for falling over in the street or slipping on water in a work or public place, we have to sue the company, when in fact it was walking along with our heads stuck in our smartphones that led to the fall.

We live in a world where we are over governed, over policed and we are not allowed to make our own choices, based on our own risk assessments. Comfort zones vary, and if we are governed by those in a pampered world, then those of us who are risk takers, entrepreneurs, innovators, climbers, sailors etc will be suffocated beyond belief.

We live in a world where we have become paranoid of everyone is out to hurt or kill us; steal from us and cheat on us.

We have become so risk averse our children are not even allowed to climb trees or eat without washing their hands.

We are distracted by celebrity, fed sugar and additives that numb down our brains, which create diseases such as cancer and heart failure, even in young children. Our health is suffering in so many ways.

We are told we are no good if we do not have this qualification or that certificate, and yet our countries are run by highly educated idiots who are so institutionalised they have no idea about the real world people are living, and the implications of their actions.

I encourage you all to fight for what you believe in, to fight back against the system that is killing us softly and slowly; the system that is taking away our rights to live life abundantly, to parent the way we wish to parent, just because of the actions of a few; and most of all, I encourage you to believe in yourself, speak up and reach out to others to support you. You are not alone. Your time is now, choose you, choose joy and go live a life you love! It's the only one you've got!

As for me? I'm taking my business location free, going to heal my soul on the ocean, enabling my 32 year-old dream of living at sea to come true. I will be writing *The Mermaid's Guide*, a series of books about sailing, travel, food, the environment and cultures; and of course empowering women to live their dreams. The boys will spend much needed time with their dad, and we will meet up in different countries around the world having incredible adventures together. I will lead my boys in the very best way that I can, by example. I will teach them that their dreams, and goals, in life are important. The goals and dreams of the woman they love are important, and both must be respected. We must love ourselves first, so we can love others from the overflow. We must lead by example, and me telling my boys there is a big wide world out there for them to explore and enjoy, when I haven't done the same, would be hypocritical. For me to not follow my dreams but tell them to, would also be hypocritical, and I may be a lot of things, but a hypocrite I am not.

Writing this book had brought up many painful memories, many heart breaking moments. Writing this book has been a challenge, not just because of the content, but because this book is the ending of three books. It is the accumulation of the last five years work, of 40 years of growth and experience. I know it is a big book compared to today's standards. I know many people hate reading, but for those who have got to this page, I thank you. I thank you for reading my story, the story of many unable to tell their story. I thank you for supporting my journey, and for being compassionate. I truly hope this book helps you, or at least someone you know. Together we are stronger, and the only way we are going to beat the corruption and lies within the police and the government is when we rise up and say, "No! I am not that person, and you are NOT going to make me that person!"

And as Winston Churchill said, "Success is not final. Failure is not fatal. It is the courage to continue that counts." So you have two choices, you either become a victim of your circumstances, or you choose to rise above them and elevate yourself and your vibration.

If you need a coach to get you there, then let me know. If you need to go to the police, or trust in someone to expose something, then DO IT! If you need to make your voice heard, then make it heard, because like I say to my boys, "You have a voice and a mind that needs to be heard. You have a heart to be loved and a life to be lived. Go do your very best and live life to the fullest!"

With love,
Dawn xx

P.S. It was suggested I set up a GoFundMe page to receive donations to cover the costs of the court fees and legal expenses towards taking further action against Police Scotland and the Justice system. I know this is a big project, but one I am willing to undertake to prevent others from going through similar situations as me and my family.

Unfortunately GoFundMe will not allow any fundraising for legal fees, so I will be using my PayPal account instead to collect donations for the legal action and to cover the costs of coaching others going through a similar process. Your donation can be made using www.paypal.me/dawneebe – please use the reference ScotlandSaga when making your donation so I know how to use the money donated and make sure all financial records are correct and above board.

Thank you in advance for your support and kind donation. Let's go make the world a better place! To keep up with my journey subscribe to www.dawnbates.com/blog or follow me on social media using the tag @DawneeBe

ACKNOWLEDGMENTS

Writing this acknowledgment is loaded, because of the enormity of what my sons and I have been through in the last four years.

The boys and I have been blessed with so many wonderful people, who have helped us get through the toughest times we have ever faced. There are so many to mention for so many different reasons, but a very special mention goes to Rob Staff, Alan Richardson, Tina Rodgers, Julie Wells, Jorja Gill and Debbie Miller. The ones who have held space for me in so many ways, without them the journey would have been a hell of a lot harder and lonelier.

Thank you to the wonderful Jerry Lampson, who has been more than a graphic designer and the developer of my website, but also for being the voice of reason and perspective. For 'getting me', and interpreting my crazy briefs into beautiful designs. You're a very lovely man, Mr Lampson.

To Linda Diggle, my publishing consultant, who has supported me with this book, and my last book *Walaahi*, and been there for me when things got tough and emotional; for helping me see a bigger vision with this book.

I also have to thank Libby Liburd for making such a powerful video for *The Guardian* and agreeing to meet with me; enabling us to join forces and tackle issues that are close to our hearts, and our truths. Thank you for agreeing to write the foreword for this book, it is an honour and a privilege to be a co-creator with you.

Omar, this dedication wouldn't be complete without mentioning you. We may not be married anymore, but you continue to support me and you are always there when I need you. Our friendship is deep, and I thank you for parenting our two beautiful boys with me. Here's to the Aysha Family, may we grow stronger together always.

Before I go on to thank my mum and dad – and, of course, my boys and my partner John – this acknowledgement would not be complete without honouring two very special people: Daring Donna and Darren Hunter. Two strangers out walking, who came into my life, my boys' lives, and stood by us, for us and for justice. We honour you, love you and value you more than you could ever know. You have seen me at my absolute worst, in my darkest times, and at my absolute best. You have given me courage, belief in myself and a huge amount of fun along the way. When I say the world is a much better place simply because you are both in it, I do not say this lightly. I cannot imagine my world without you both in it; so here is to many more decades of travel, manifesting greatness, love, peace and acceptance on a global scale. And so it is, and so it is done.

John, what can I say? It's been one hell of a ride for us both, and we have been through more in our short time together than many couples who spend decades together. You have seen me at my absolute worst, and my absolute best, as I have you. The experiences of the last couple of years have tested us, nearly broken us, but like they say 'What doesn't kill you makes you stronger'.

Now to my Mum and Dad, I honour you both. You taught me so much growing up, and still do to this day. I am the woman I am today, because of the things you taught me, knowingly or unknowingly. Mum, your strength, courage and resilience is outstanding. You have always been an inspiration to me, even when I have not wanted to admit it, or see it. When you became a single mum, it wasn't the 'done thing'; but you were, and still are a most wonderful mum, a wise woman who doesn't own her own power – yet! Dad, you are the strong silent type, a fierce protector of my mum, loving and accepting all of who she is and who she is not, and I am so proud to call you my dad. The tough love you have shown me over the years has enabled me to be a strong, responsible and courageous woman. Since becoming a single mum myself, I have understood things I would never have understood. Dad, you chose to be my dad, when you chose to love my mum. You taught me what it means to be a dad. You taught me to respect my mum, and myself. You may be a stubborn arse, but I love you regardless. You are a very special kind of man, of very few words, so I won't go on much longer, but just know this… I love you. I love you. I love you… and your slippers… and your hoodies… and your garden. The journey I am writing about in this book has brought us all closer, and helped me to understand just how tough you really are mum. You have both taught me to use my voice, to stand up for myself and to stand up to bullies. A few years ago, I would have written I hope I have made you proud of me, but now, I know I do. I love you both more than I have ever done.

Khaalid and Naasir, what can I say? You both know I love you, you see it, you feel it and you hear it daily. You know the truth, you stand in the truth, and I honour you both for the courage and maturity you have shown throughout the last four years. You have had your world turned upside down on many occasions, had to start over many times, and you both do it with positivity and self-assurance. You have been patient, loving, and supportive of each other and of me. You have a deep confidence that I admire, because I never had that level of confidence until much later in life. Your level of understanding of what has happened over the last few years would put most adults to shame, your courage even more so. You make me so proud to be your Mummy. Without you I would have probably given up many times, but I knew you were watching. I knew I could never give up and let you down. I live and breathe for you both. Thank you for your smiles, your hugs, your love and for your support. You are incredible young men and I know you are both born to be leaders in this world. Always, always stand up for yourselves, always speak the truth, let your ideas, feelings and opinions be heard in a respectful and confident ways, because what you think and feel is important. Never let anyone silence you, not even me, or your dad. I love you and I honour you.

ABOUT THE AUTHOR

As well as being an international bestselling author and author coach, Dawn Bates is an online entrepreneur and life coach.

Using her life as a catalyst to highlight important subjects in today's society, Dawn's first trilogy, *The Trilogy of Life Itself*, is powerful. It brings together the multi-faceted aspects of the world we live in and takes you on a rollercoaster ride that will leave you wanting more from life.

Incorporating *Friday Bridge*, *Walaahi* and *Crossing the Line* – a body of work that captures life around the world from the last 30 years – it is a time capsule that inspires, motivates and empowers all who read it.

Dawn's power lies in enabling you to create exceptional results by igniting the passion and fire within. She is an authority on enabling others to live an inspired and joyful life.

Discover more about Dawn's work by visiting:
www.dawnbates.com

www.ingramcontent.com/pod-product-compliance
Lightning Source LLC
Chambersburg PA
CBHW030449210326
41597CB00013B/600